From Generation to Generation:
A Family Story

by
Ruth Rahn Budd

Published 2012

To contact author, e-mail: ruthbudd@post.harvard.edu

TABLE OF CONTENTS

Photos

Visits to Germany

The Past Leads to the Future

Acknowledgements

As I think back on the long time it has taken me to complete this family history memoir there are many people who had been of invaluable help and support throughout this process.

I begin with Gisela Naomi Blume, whom I discussed in the memoir and whose enthusiasm for reconstructing the history of our family was so important in getting me started on this venture. Our numerous visits with Gisela, both in Germany and in the United States, were extraordinarily helpful in providing me with information and encouragement.

Next I want to acknowledge the availability of the documents themselves. For them I am indebted to my deceased parents who carefully kept them, packed them before leaving Germany, and stored them in Denver after they emigrated. I brought these many boxes to my home after they died in 1970, not knowing what they contained, and they remained in the back of my attic until we renovated our third floor just before I retired in 1990. I then realized what they contained and that this merited a story for the next generations. It was access to these resources that provided me with the possibility and the opportunity to tell so much of our family's story. I only wish I could have the opportunity to speak to my parents now — I have so many unanswered questions.

Since so many of the documents and letters were in German, I acknowledge those who helped translate many of them. Gerda Breit, of blessed memory, translated mother's Bechmann Family History and also Daddy's prison letters. When she was a graduate student at Harvard, Anjeana Hans, translated many documents, and then my dear friend Eva Gordon, of blessed memory, translated many more, including all kinds of letters and documents, and her friendship and assistance continued to provide encouragement. Tomas Nolden translated Lilli's poetry. More recently, Sally Huebscher read and reread rhe entire manuscript and provided innumerable editing suggestions, not only about the content, but especially about style and format which she formulated for me.

My children, Karen and Rachel, have often asked me how this project was coming along, and seeing how eager they were to read this memoir also kept me going. I couldn't have done this memoir without the work of my sister, Evy. In 1972 Evy brought mother's Bechmann Family History up to date. Evy has enthusiastically supported me throughout this process, and meticulously read the entire memoir. Her comments and suggestions have made this a much richer document. I truly appreciate her collaboration and support.

And finally, I cannot express enough my appreciation for the support John has given me. As my computer facility was, and still is, limited, John willingly stopped whatever he was doing and came to my assistance whenever I called to him as he sat in the adjacent office. Even when I asked the same computer question numerous times, John's patience was unflagging. I have truly been blessed by having such a loving and supportive husband. I am also so fortunate to have my children and grandchildren live relatively close by. It is for these next generations, who live in a time and place so different from where I was born, that this family history memoir has truly been written.

1
INTRODUCTION

The purpose of this story of my family, at least as I write it at this point, is to tell our family's story to my children and grandchildren. It may develop into something else with a wider audience, but that is not my immediate intention. For my children, Karen and Rachel, and particularly their children, Addison, Gabriel, Emily and Nathaniel, currently living in Massachusetts and Maine, the impetus to write this story becomes even more important because their lives, and the environment in which they live and will grow up, is so different and far from that into which I was born.

The writing of our family history has been incubating in my mind for a few years, and even now, as I sit down to write these first words, I have no idea how it will develop or even how to proceed in this endeavor. For almost all of my life, until very recently, I wasn't very interested in the family history or my German background. I did not grow up feeling that I was a German refugee or "survivor" in any sense of the term. Of course I knew I was born in Germany, that my family was German, and I grew up thinking Germany was a hated place. My parents avoided buying any products from Germany and my mother would not ride in a Volkswagen. Despite all this, I always felt 100% American. My parents never talked at home about Germany or their experiences, and I never asked any questions. But this all changed a few years ago.

In the spring of 1996, my husband, John Ehrenfeld, was invited to teach and do research in Lausanne, Switzerland. I took a mini-sabbatical of three months from my law firm and was very excited about spending a few months in Switzerland, a country I loved, having spent a summer there as a Girl Scout in 1953 and having studied for a year in Geneva during my Junior Year Abroad from Smith College (1956-7). It was my daughter Karen who originally suggested that it might be a good idea for my sister, Evy Megerman, to visit us while we were there, and we could go to Germany together on a "roots" trip. Although I had been to Fürth, the town where I was born, in 1973, it was a brief and not very satisfying trip and Evy had never been there. So Evy and I made plans for her to come to Europe and we would go to Germany. We planned to meet at the Park Hotel in Fürth, Germany, rent a car and visit sites and houses we already knew about in Fürth and then we would wend our way back to Lausanne, visiting Rottach on the way and seeing some of the sights of Switzerland. Rottach was where my mother and her family spent each summer, and although they never talked about their life in Germany, Rottach was

*Evy Rahn Megerman
and Ruth Rahn Budd
daughters of Lilli
Bechmann Rahn and
Alfred Rahn*

the exception. We had heard about this beautiful place. A few weeks before Evy's departure, we each received a letter from a man in Israel, Mr. Ernest Rosenbluth, whom we didn't know. He was going through some family documents, found some papers and photos of our grandparents and wrote to us. His parents had been close friends of our grandfather, Sydney Rahn. I spoke to Evy, and she agreed to call him and find out more about this, and mentioned in the conversation that she would be going to Germany in a couple of weeks with her sister. Mr. Rosenbluth said that if we were going to Fürth, we must stay at the Park Hotel (where I had stayed in 1973) and look up Gisela Blume, who knew a great deal about the Jews of Fürth. I offered to call her from Lausanne, thinking we would have our obligatory meeting with her and be on our way. I wrote her name down as Gise La Blume. In the course of that telephone call, she asked me to give her some of my family names, which I did. I told her where we were staying and when we would arrive, and said we would call when we got there. I didn't think much more about it, and made my plans to take the train from Lausanne to Fürth and meet Evy, who was flying in from Boston, at the Park Hotel after I rented a car.

I arrived at the hotel several hours after Evy's arrival, and found Evy and Gisela ensconced in a room in the hotel, each sitting in front of their laptops. Evy and I had agreed that she would bring hers so we could record our thoughts and impressions as we traveled. Gisela had arrived with our entire family genealogy! Now we already had this genealogy, but to have a total stranger come up with it, all printed out, was a total surprise and shock to us. Gisela proved to be an invaluable help, guide and a dear friend. We ended up spending all our vacation time in Fürth, and had to leave only because we had to rush back to Lausanne so Evy could catch her flight back to Boston from Geneva.

I digress here for a moment to say a few words about Gisela Naomi Blume. How did Gisela get so interested in Jewish history and particularly in the Jews of Fürth? Gisela, a widow, was not Jewish at the time we first met her. About six years before our meeting she had been on a trip where a member of the trip from another city in Germany began speaking about the Jewish history of his town. She realized that although she grew up in Fürth and had some sense that there had been a number of Jews there prior to World War II, she really knew nothing about Fürth's Jewish history. She began by going through the Old Cemetery, i.e. the cemetery for Jews

Gisela Naomi Blume

who died prior to 1906. As she went through this cemetery, much of which was destroyed, she felt it should be reconstructed. She learned that if she wanted to have this done, she would have to do it herself, and she did! She not only put the family graves back together and personally cleaned the tombstones but she also catalogued where they were located, making it very easy for visitors like ourselves to locate the gravesites of our ancestors. In 2007 Gisela published her book entitled "Der Alte Jüdische Friedhof in Fürth" (the Old Jewish Cemetery in Fürth) - 1607-2007. She became passionately interested in the history of the Jews of Fürth, and in Judaism itself and some years later she converted to Judaism. After conversion, Gisela added Naomi to her name, but I will refer to her simply as Gisela Blume in this memoir.

It was this trip that got each of us so interested in our background and history, and we remembered that we each had numerous boxes of documents, photographs and materials stashed away in our homes. Neither of us really knew what we had, and when we returned we had occasion to look again at the trunks and boxes of memorabilia which had been brought by our parents from Germany. This turned out to be a rich storehouse of material, extraordinarily interesting and moving, and we agreed that it needed to be written up in a story for our family and for posterity.

Since this trip in 1996, Evy and I have each been back to Fürth several more times. Evy and her husband, Joe, went to the Memorial Service in the summer of 1997, a ceremony commemorating the last transport of Jews out of Fürth on June 18, 1943. John, Karen and I went to Fürth and Erlangen in February 1999, to be present at the first award of the Lilli Bechmann Rahn Prize at the Friedrich-Alexander University in Erlangen. And then Evy and I went back in July 1999 as guests of the city, which gave us an opportunity again to visit the family homes and other sites. John and I also returned to Nuremberg and Fürth in September 2003 to view an exhibit on notable women from Franconia, the region of Germany where Fürth is located, and which featured Lilli. These visits will be described in more detail later in this memoir.

All of these trips, plus our aging, and wanting to share this history with children and grandchildren, has made the writing of this story an imperative for me. So it is with this background that I begin, as an amateur in the writing of a family memoir, but I will let the story speak for itself.

I add here just a few words about the scope of this memoir. After my parents died, in 1970, we discovered among the many boxes of documents we had, copies of a family history my mother, Lilli, had written during 1935-36, ending before I was born in 1936. As she wrote in the Introduction to that work:

> *At a time when so many Jewish families are being scattered all over the world, the family history gains great importance as the last uniting link. And so it is with great pleasure that I am presenting just at this time the history and genealogical table of the Bechmann family.*

This family history consists of 18 pages of text, and 22 pages of family genealogies of various branches of the Bechmann family, which was Lilli's father's family line. I have appended this family history to my memoir, and have made no attempt to repeat it or even to update it. When we first found these copies in 1970, all were in German, and we had this family history translated into English. Like so much of my parents' lives, we never knew this history existed until after their death. In 1972, Evy made contact with whichever relatives she could find, and brought this family history up-to-date. I have not attempted to update it to the present time.

In terms of content, my primary focus is therefore on the more immediate family, particularly my parents, their immediate ancestors, their lives, and the whole amazing story about how we finally got out of Germany in 1939 and how our lives were recreated in the United States.

I have gone through the many boxes of documents that my parents brought out of Germany, and have struggled with wanting to write a story, on the one hand, and wanting to preserve the contents of these documents, on the other hand. I have had the most significant documents translated from German into English. It is my intent, when this family history has been completed, to give the original documents to a museum or library, such as the Leo Baeck Institute in New York, or the Holocaust Museum in Washington, DC, or some similar institution. As a result, some of this history will consist of quoting from the original documents and letters, so that they can be preserved in this fashion. I have therefore erred on the side of inclusion rather than exclusion so as to preserve the richness of the material, retain factual accuracy, preserve the contents of the material herein, and most importantly, tell the story.

2
FÜRTH

Where does the family come from? In our case, unlike many others who research their family backgrounds, the answer is easy. We are from Fürth, which is located in southern Germany. Specifically, it became part of Bavaria in 1806 and is more specifically in Franconia, and even more specifically, in Middle Franconia. It is close to the much larger city of Nuremberg, and also to Erlangen, where the Friedrich-Alexander University is located. I have throughout this memoir spelled the name of my home town as Fürth, with the umlaut above the "u". In quoting some documents, however, I have retained the alternate spelling which is Fuerth.

*Map of
Germany*

History of the Jewish Community Growth in Fürth

When I, Ruth Marion Rahn, was born in 1936, Fürth was really a separate city from the larger city of Nuremberg. Today, it is considered a suburb of Nuremberg.

Fürth Logo

The first Jews in Fürth can be found in the 14th century; by the 16th and 17th century more and more settled there. According to the family history that my mother wrote, our ancestor, Rabbi Salomo, was in Fürth by 1711. The Jews soon built synagogues, cemeteries, a hospital for the Jewish community and founded a Talmud School as well as Hebrew printing companies. At the beginning of the 19th century, one out of six Fürth citizens was Jewish. Fürth in 1800 claimed a larger proportion of Jews than any other city in the Holy Roman Empire — Fürth's 2400 Jews made up 15 percent of the population. Its Jewish population rose to 3000 in 1848 or 17.6 percent of the general population. Even as late as 1935, 50% of the wholesalers, 14.5 % of the retailers and 23.1 % of the manufacturers in Fürth were Jewish. In 1933 there were 1,990 members of the Jewish congregation in Fürth.

A little history. Nuremberg drove the Jews out of their city in 1499 and again in 1548. In order to understand this, one has to know that for centuries there had been territorial and political quarrels about Fürth between the rulers of Bamberg, of Brandenburg-Ansbach and of the imperial town of Nuremberg — they all "owned" part of Fürth. You could say Fürth was a town with three different sovereigns. The disagreements between these rival rulers often kept the courts busy, but also had distinct advantages for the development of Fürth; what you couldn't get from one you could get from the other. While the Jews were persecuted in Nuremberg, they could settle in Fürth, receiving the status of a Jew with special protection from Bamberg or Brandenburg-Ansbach. Fürth was within easy traveling distance of Nuremberg where Jews could do business but lacked residence rights. As a result, in the 17th and 18th centuries, Jews from Poland, Vienna, Czechoslovakia and elsewhere found refuge in Fürth. In 1835 the first railroad built in Germany ran from Nuremberg to Fürth. I have a silver napkin ring and a pewter stein (dated 1840) commemorating this event.

The Jewish experience in Fürth was special, perhaps unique in Germany. From the 16th century onward, Fürth had no ghetto. Thanks to the rivalry of the three magistrates governing the town, the Jews won special legal rights and were able to integrate easily. By the 18th century Fürth Jews enjoyed privileges unique for a German city: no restrictions on building synagogues, Jewish could move to Fürth without needing permission, and two Jews sat on the City Council.

Fürth not only had distinguished rabbis, but also a Hebrew printing industry dating back to 1690 and in continuous operation until 1868. Fürth became known as a center of printing, especially for religious books. In 1607 the Jews were able to establish their own cemetery. In existence for four centuries, this cemetery has been enlarged at least 30 times to accommodate over 20,000 graves. Jews founded Fürth's first hospital in 1653, Germany's first Jewish orphanage in 1763, and the Stadt-Theater (City Theater — on Konigstrasse, almost directly across the street from my birthplace) was started by Jews.

The first synagogue in Fürth, known as the "Altshul" (old synagogue), was built in 1617, almost 90 years after the beginning of consistent settlement of Jews in the market village of Fürth. In Yiddish, a synagogue is often called a "Shul", showing that it is not only a place of worship but also of learning where the Torah (the first five books of the Old Testament) and the Talmud (interpretations of the Torah) are studied. Since the end of the 17th century a Talmud University was housed in the main synagogue, established by a family that had been expelled from Vienna. This university made Fürth one of the major centers of Jewish learning in Germany in the 18th century. The Talmud University was closed in 1830. In the 19th century the main synagogue was redesigned as the place of worship for the more liberal members of the community, and the orthodox Jews used the three small synagogues around this square. All but one were completely burned down on Kristallnacht (November 9, 1938 - the Night of Broken Glass). Fürth's beautifully restored Synagogue (one of seven Fürth synagogues to survive Hitler) is at the site of Germany's first Jewish orphanage.

One of the most famous nineteenth-century Fürth émigrés was Julius Ochs, whose son, Adolph, would transform the foundering New York Times into the greatest newspaper in America. One of the most prominent Fürth natives of the 20th century is Henry Kissinger.

Our family had been in Fürth since at least 1711. Our earliest known ancestor, Rabbi Salomo (1666-1767) came to Franconia, at least by 1711 from Kolin, Czechoslokia, apparently at the request of Rabbi Baruch Rappaport of Fürth. One of Rabbi Salomo's children, Jona, who became a mohel (did circumcisions) was born in Fürth. We searched without avail for Jona's gravestone in the cemetery in Bechhofen. Rabbi Salomo, who you can see had a very long life and lived to be 101, married Edel, his second wife after his first wife died. Edel, who came from Fürth, died in 1748 and was buried in the Bechhofen cemetery. When John and I went to Germany in 2003, we went with Gisela Blume to the Bechhofen cemetery and found Edel's gravestone. This was quite exciting because it is so old. We have seen and photographed many of our ancestors' tombstones, in both the Old and New Jewish Cemeteries of Fürth, but this is by far the oldest. Some photos of the cemetery and of Edel's gravestone are shown in the section entitled Visits to Germany. In the late 18th and early 19th centuries, laws were passed requiring Jews to adopt surnames for taxation and conscription purposes. Ashkenazic Jews, which our ancestors were, often chose surnames from localities. Since my ancestors came via Bechhofen to Fürth, they chose the name Bechmann as their family surname.

Kristallnacht

For many centuries the center of the Jewish community was in the street today called Geleitsgasse. During the night of Kristallnacht on November 9, 1938, the entire square with its four synagogues and many community institutions, especially the chancellery, the living quarters of the rabbi, Mikvah (ritual bath), and place for kosher butchering were burned and destroyed. In 1933 Fürth's population was about 77,000 of which 1,990 were Jewish. The town had seven synagogues altogether. Five of them were burned on Kristallnacht, November 9, 1938. The only reason the other two were not burned was because they were situated very close to non-Jewish establishments and there was fear that if they were set on fire, the non-Jewish establishments

Monument to the seven synagogues of Fürth that were burned on Kristallnacht, November 9, 1938. Above: flames around eternal light, Bottom: flames of destruction surrounded by Psalm 79.

would be harmed. The first deportation of Jews from Fürth took place on November 29, 1941. Their destination along with others from Franconia was the death camps of Latvia. According to Gisela Blume, who is truly an authority on this, 1060 Jews or about half of all the Jews living in Fürth were murdered by the Germans, and the remainder managed to emigrate. Today the population of Fürth is about 116,000 and there are only about 300 Jews living there, almost all of them from the former Soviet Union. In the summer of 1997 there was an extremely moving memorial ceremony commemorating the last transport of Jews out of Fürth, which Evy and her husband Joe attended. This is more fully described in the chapter entitled Visits to Germany. On a large plaque on the wall in the new Jewish cemetery are the names of all those murdered, including our uncle, James Rahn, Alfred's older brother.

In the square, which had been surrounded by four synagogues, a very simple and moving monument by the Japanese sculptor Kunihiko Kato, who lives in Fürth, was erected in 1986. The top of the monument symbolizes the flames to represent the eternal light. There are seven bumps representing the seven candles of the menorah and the concept of new life, as well as seven destroyed synagogues. On the bottom are more flames representing the flames of destruction. At the very bottom, carved in Hebrew and in German, is Psalm 79. In relevant stanzas, this psalm contains the following:

> *O God, heathens have entered Your domain, defiled Your holy temple, and turned Jerusalem into ruins.... Let the nations not say, "Where is their God?" Before our eyes let it be known among nations that You avenge the spilled blood of Your servants... We, your people, the flock You shepherd, shall glorify You forever...*

In contrast, Nuremberg has quite a different history. Before the World War II, as one of the guidebooks says,

> *Nuremberg was one of the most beautiful medieval cities in Germany. Whole blocks of half-timbered burgher's houses with embellished gables made a setting so typically "Germanic" that the city was chosen by the Nazi party for its huge annual rallies each September. It was in this "ideological capital" of the Reich that the notorious anti-Semitic laws were promulgated in 1935; and it was here that the Allies held the war crimes trials when the fighting was over.*

In contrast to Fürth, which remained relatively intact during World War II, most of the city of Nuremberg was destroyed during the war, so it now has a fairly new look. The huge stadium where the Nazi rallies were held and the podium from which Hitler spoke at this huge park are still there. On the main road between Fürth and Nuremberg is the Palace of Justice where the Nazi war crimes trials were held. Behind the Palace of Justice is the prison where my father, Alfred Rahn, was imprisoned for 14 months.

Konigstrasse, the main street in Fürth, marks the course of the old east-west road in the Middle Ages. If you wanted to travel from Frankfurt to Nuremberg and Regensburg, you had to pass through Fürth on this street, and it is therefore still one of the major thoroughfares of the city. The facades of the houses, including the Rahn family home at 129 Konigstrasse, where I was born, are part of the historic district.

Konigstrasse/Hornschuchpromenade

The most elegant street in Fürth is Hornschuchpromenade with its palace-like buildings and trees characteristic of a Parisian boulevard. The first German railway was built here, connecting the towns of Nuremberg and Fürth in 1835 for a length of 6 kilometers (about 3 1/2 miles). It ran until 1922 and the tracks were pulled out shortly thereafter. On each side of the tracks was a promenade with pedestrian walks and gardens. Toward the end of the 1800's, rich merchants, including Louis Bechmann, my great grandfather, and his brother, Maier Bechmann, built mansions on Hornschuchpromenade. The homes on Hornschuchpromenade, and specifically the Bechmann homes, are often included in books with pictures of notable buildings in Fürth. Just across the street is Konigswarterstrasse, also a beautiful street, where the Bierer house was located and where I lived with my mother, Lilli, while my father, Alfred, was in prison. Ernest Bierer married Emma Metzger, sister of Ida Metzer Bechmann, Lilli's mother. Thus, Ernst and Emma Bierer were Lilli's uncle and aunt. Konigswarterstrasse was renamed Adolph Hitlerstrasse during war, but reverted to its original name after the war.

The history of the city of Fürth is inconceivable without the Jews, who were among its wealthiest citizens. With their innumerable charitable foundations and philanthropic donations they provided the vital incentives for the town's economic development and enhanced its prosperity. Jews were major contributors to secular activities in Fürth, such as the theatre, museums, orphanages and even the Catholic Church. Amongst our documents we have receipts from several charitable organizations, evidencing that wealthy Jews, such as the Bechmann family, contributed to the civic life of the town. Jews encountered exceptionally positive living conditions and financial equality in Fürth. However, here as well as elsewhere, Hitler's National Socialism put a cruel end to the tolerant coexistence practiced in Fürth, and to their way of life, as well as to their lives themselves.

Kolin Torah Scroll

I mentioned previously that my earliest known ancestor came from Kolin, Czechoslovakia. I need to say another word here about another connection to Kolin, Czechoslovakia. In 1972 my synagogue, Temple Isaiah in Lexington, received a Torah Scroll from Kolin, Czechoslovakia. This was one of 1564 scrolls taken by the Nazis from synagogues throughout the areas they conquered. Hitler decided there should be a visual reminder of the Jewish people he was determined to destroy and murder. He therefore ordered a museum for Jewish artifacts, so that future generations could see for themselves how justified the Nazis were in exterminating the Jews. His concept was that people would come from all countries of the Judenrein (Jewish free) world to inspect the memorabilia of a dead people. Preparations were made in 1940 to create this ghastly museum in the old Jewish section of Prague. Here, from synagogues throughout Czechoslovakia and other countries, were brought 1564 Torahs and other ceremonial objects seized from the Jews and their synagogues. The task of arranging and cataloging this so-called "exhibition of an exterminated ethnic group" was assigned to talented Jews, who received a reprieve for their labor before being shipped off to their death. When Hitler and the Germans were finally defeated in 1945, the objects belonged to the Czeckoslovakian State which felt it was important to maintain this Museum as a silent witness to what the Jews endured and as an enduring appeal to the conscience of humanity. But a question remained. What should they do with the most precious of all these Jewish possessions, the Torah scrolls? Somewhere in this mass of Torah Scrolls was the one from Kolin. In 1964 these scrolls were sent to Westminister Synagogue in London where they were examined and classified. Some were in good condition; others were beyond repair. It was decided to distribute these scrolls throughout the world. Our rabbi at the time, Rabbi Cary Yales,(of blessed memory) had written to the rabbi of Westminster Synagogue, requesting a scroll beyond repair because Temple Isaiah already had three beautiful scrolls. In 1972 Rabbi Yales and his wife drove to the airport to pick up this scroll. Rabbi Yales' Dedication Sermon for this scroll on September 17, 1972 is so beautiful that I have attached it in the Appendix.

But what does all this have to do with me? The Kolin Torah is only removed from the Ark once a year, on Yom Kippur, when the Rabbi reads from it and it is paraded around the synagogue so all can touch and kiss it. It always is, for me, one of the most moving moments of the High Holiday services. It never occurred to me that I had any personal connection to this Torah. In the early 1990's a committee of the Temple wanted those members of the congregation who had been affected by the Holocaust to write their stories and this would be published in a book. They anticipated about a dozen people would respond. Amazingly, 42 people responded and wrote a chapter. Announcement of this request was made at a Yom Kippur service, just after reading from the Kolin Torah. I decided that I too would write a chapter and after I came home, I pulled out the family history my mother had written. I had not looked at it for years, and it was at that moment that I first made the connection between the earliest known ancestor of the Bechmann family, Rabbi Salomo, with Kolin. Our Kolin Torah was written in 1720, perhaps after my rabbi ancestor had left Kolin. But I want to believe that my ancestor read from this Torah, and if not this one, its immediate predecessor. *We Shall Not Forget! Memories of the Holocaust* was published by Temple Isaiah in 1994 with 42 chapters by Temple members, including one by me.

More will be said later of the visits I took to Fürth with Evy and with John, including our visits to the Old and New Cemeteries where a number of our ancestors are buried. The New Jewish Cemetery, opened in 1906, holds those who died after 1906 unless a place had been reserved for them in the Old Cemetery, such as those in a double grave. We found the graves of our ancestors in both cemeteries.

At this point, however, as I want to describe the relationship of our ancestors with Fürth, it is significant to note that both the Rahn and Bechmann families were successful and well integrated members of the Fürth community, and the Rahn family home on Konigstrasse, and the Bechmann family home on Hornschuchpromenade were situated on two of the most historic and pre-eminent streets in Fürth.

3
LILLI

Lilli Bechmann Rahn

My mother, Lilli Bechmann, was born in Fürth on February 10, 1911. Her ancestors on both sides had been long-time Fürth residents and were well established in the community. Her father's side of the family had been in Fürth for about 200 years. Her mother, born Ida Metzger, was the oldest of three children and came from a socially prominent family. Lilli's father, Hugo Bechmann, had continued in the footsteps of his father and was a successful businessman dealing in Bavarian glass. At the time of her birth her parents were already living at 7 Hornschuchpromenade, one of the finest and most magnificent houses in Fürth. Lilli often joked that she was the child of a funeral because her parents had married in May 1910 and went to England on their honeymoon. They arrived just as

King Edward VII died. The country was in mourning and everything was closed in honor of his death. Lilli was born 9 months later. Ida and Hugo had no other children.

Forebears
Without going into the entire genealogy of the Bechmann family history in this memoir (The Bechmann Family History, which

Hugo, Ida, and Lilli Bechmann — Rottach, Summer 1915

Lilli

Lilli wrote in 1935, where she traced the family back to 1666 is found in the Appendix), let me begin with just a couple of generations back to give the proper background to this successful and well established Fürth family. In brief, Lilli's father was Hugo Bechmann,(1878–1942); his father was Louis Bechmann (1848–1921), and his father was Wolf (known as Wilhelm) Bechmann (1820–1908). Parenthetically, the two portraits I have hanging in our front hall are of yet another generation back — they are of Nathan Hirsch Bechmann (1780–1859) and his wife Esther Neustettel-Neuhaus (1780–1859). As Lilli writes in The Bechmann Family History, Nathan Hirsch Bechmann was a writing teacher and occupied with the Holy Scriptures. I urge anyone who is interested at this point in the family history to read Lilli's history of the family in the Appendix (the text is only 18 pages) as it gives a wonderful synopsis of the ancestors and their occupations. She writes that with Nathan Hirsch Bechmann and Esther's children, the Bechmann family began to enter the great emancipation movement of Judaism which took place in the middle to late 19th century. Whereas up to this time interests were directed primarily to the events and contents of Jewish life, the following generation began to turn its main attention to the world at large. This is shown outwardly both in the changes of first names and choice of professions. Work was no longer principally of Jewish content, but more secular. So by the time we come to Wilhelm Bechmann, Lilli's great grandfather, we find a very enterprising and hard-working man who began the fabrication of mirror and mirror glass in Fürth, which was one of the first in Fürth producing these products. Through his success the family gained great respect from the last third of the 19th century until they were forced to sell the business and leave Germany in the 1930's.

Wilhelm's son, Louis Bechmann (1848–1921) was the one who originally bought the home on Hornschuchpromenade, and was the father of my grandfather, Hugo Bechmann (1878–1942).

History of the Mirror Glass Business

I will digress here to give a little more history of the mirror/glass business based on the original documents we have concerning the firm and its principals.

The firm W. Bechmann had its beginning in the Mirror Glass establishment founded by Wolf (Wilhelm) Bechmann, born on June 25, 1820, the son of the writing teacher Nathan Hirsch Bechmann. After having completed his mandatory schooling, including a 7-year attendance at the Israelite Religious School, Wolf Bechmann (known as Wilhelm) (1820–1908) began his business apprenticeship in 1836, at age 16, with Fürth businessman Baer Juda Rindskopf. Following that he worked for 9 years as a merchant assistant in the Mirror Glass and Manufacturing business of A. K. Weinschenk in Fürth. Beginning in 1846 he wanted to become independent and marry. The request was denied because of overcrowding in the field; the number of Jewish marriages was limited by the government. If there were already too many Jews, one wanting to marry had to wait until a married man died or gave up this coveted spot. Fortunately, Wilhelm's future father-in-law, the 82 year old merchant of the Meyer Offenbacher-Oppenheimer Mirror Glass firm, renounced his concession so that his daughter could marry Wilhelm. Wilhelm thus entered the firm of his father-in-law which focused on the retail trade in mirror glass. With his own assets and the dowry of his wife, he was able to buy the house at 16 Blumenstrasse on September 9, 1859 and carry on his business from there for the time being.

Some time prior to October 1, 1847 the firm changed its name to W. Bechmann and, according to our records, was located at Alexanderstra #328 in Fürth. On January 1, 1879 Wilhelm brought into the business, as his associates, his two sons, Louis (1848–1921), Lilli's grandfather, and Louis' brother Maier (1856–1947), Lilli's great uncle.

By the end of the 1860's Wilhelm had obtained a permit for the manufacture of mirror glass, and in 1885, together with his two sons, Louis and Maier, he opened a tin foil and mirror glass factory in lower Floestrasse 33 and integrated it with the former mirror glass installation in Blumenstrasse. The second most important element besides glass, the tin foil, could now be produced in his own establishment. The only thing missing now was his own glass factory in order to carry on production and sales independently. Six years after bringing his sons into the firm, on January 1, 1885, Wilhelm retired and turned over the business to his two sons so that they became the sole owners of the firm and the name was changed from W. Bechmann to Louis and Maier Bechmann, Mirror-Glass Fabrications and Commerce. We have all the original documents and contracts for these transactions.

From the report of an exhibition of the Bavarian State in 1896 in Nuremberg, the enterprise in Fürth employed 110 workers and owned five glass works driven with water power. The firm had extensive connections in Europe as well as close contacts to important import firms in the United States, such as that owned by W. H. Bechmann in Cincinnati, Ohio. The firm then fused with E. Kupfer and Sons and the Bavarian Mirror and Mirror-Glass Factory AG was formed by Hugo Bechmann, a son of Louis Bechmann and Lilli's father, and Moris Kupfer, a son of Eduard Kupfer. Emanuel Loewi functioned as representative, a partner of Fürth Mirror Glass

Commissioner Carl Loewi. This Board was chaired by Louis Bechman; Maier Bechman was vice-chairman and there were 8 other distinguished members. The purpose of the enterprise was the "Production and Distribution of Mirror and Mirror Glass".

This company continued to develop until the start of the World War I. Soon after its founding the enterprise opened branches in Berlin and Hamburg and owned properties in a number of places for grinding, polishing, producing window glass, and after the war, plate glass. It was the only Bavarian enterprise in this field and was able to maintain independence from the German Mirror Glass Producers (VDS) after the latter acquired, in 1934, shares in the company. In 1942 it was taken over by the Nazis and became known as Mirror-Glass Union, and ten years later, simply Unionglass AG.

The obituary of Louis Bechmann, who died on May 23, 1921, reads as follows:

At age 73, Councilor of Commerce Louis Bechmann passed away on May 23, 1921 after a brief illness, softly and quietly, as a result of bronchitis, in Bad Kissingen, where he had sought recuperation. With him, the city of our fathers, Fürth, loses one of its most valuable citizens and a most eminent important industrialist. Since the age of 14 he was employed in the parental firm of W. Bechmann, which changed in 1905 to the Bavarian Mirror and Mirrorglass Factory, A.G. Before that, it was called W. Bechmann, and before that, Ed. Kupfer and Sons. Since the formation of the association he served uninterrupted as Chairman of the Board, and until his last days he took a lively interest involving his energy, his excellent intellectual abilities and indefatigable work in the advancement of the enterprise. He was a senior member of the Fürth glass industry, and with his loss the industry loses a knowledgeable advisor. A year ago his wife, with whom he had lived a most happy marriage, preceded him in death. As a born citizen of Fürth he was devoted to the city of his fathers and supported all its efforts for improvement and advancement. For many years he was a member of the Board of the Art Association and as its first Chairman led the business activities in a most selfless manner. He likewise devoted himself selflessly to all social enterprises: he always had an open hand for fellow citizens in need. In 1919 he founded the Louis and Mathilda Bechmann Foundation to fight against childhood diseases with RM. 50,000 ($20,000). This foundation focused on the use of installations to fight lung tuberculosis. He was a simple man whose favorable life circumstances did not deter him from following his strong ethical principles to lead a modest life. Fürth is losing in the deceased one of its best sons.

The obituary put in the newspaper by his firm reads:

We hereby fulfill our sad duty to announce the demise of the Chairman of the Board of our association, Councilor of Commerce Louis Bechmann. His entire life, his entire energy was devoted, as co-owner of the family business, to the enterprise. He served with tireless striving and restless activity in the development of the association. His rare abilities and rich experiences are lost to us with the loss of this outstanding personality. His memory stays with us forever.

After his father Louis' death in 1921, Hugo, Lilli's father, headed the firm along with Lilli's uncle Maier. In 1925 Hugo was given the very prestigious title of Councilor of Commerce. A letter to him by the Chamber of Commerce of Regensburg reads: To his Most Honorable Council of Commerce, Hugo Bechmann, Factory Director, Fürth.

Esteemed Mr. Councilor! We have noted with exceeding pleasure that the Bavarian State Government has bestowed upon you the title of Councilor of Commerce. We do not want to fail to express our most heartfelt and cordial congratulations to this well-deserved high honor.

Also, upon receipt of this award, he received a letter from the Association of Bavarian Mirrorglass Factories reading:

Esteemed Councilor of Commerce!
We permit ourselves to congratulate you on the receipt of the high honor of Councilor of Commerce most cordially. We see in this honor an expression of the recognition and evaluation of the great merit which you have deserved through years of successful work as Chairman of our Association in the cause of our industry. That applies especially to the difficult representation in customs and trade negotiations. We don't want to fail to express our sincere gratitude to your co-workers.

In July 1926, Hugo, who was already a Councilor of Commerce, was nominated to become a member of the Justice of Commerce at the Chamber for Commerce at the State Court in Fürth. Although I am not exactly sure what this position entailed, I quote these letters to show how prestigious these awards were and how very integrated into the city the Bechman family was. They were highly respected businessmen and appointed to the most prestigious business associations in the city.

On October 9, 1926 Hugo received a letter from the Mayor of Fürth thanking him for the receipt of the final 5000 RM (approximately $1200: in 1925, 4.20 RM = $1.00)) which "will be used, as have been formerly transmitted donations given to me, to use at my discretion for the generally useful and social purposes. Your generous and highly laudable contributions, which testify to a noble citizenship and willingness for sacrifice, will, like before, be a real blessing in the future. I am looking forward to your announced visit. Most respectfully and best regards (signed) Chief Mayor."

Hugo was recognized and honored as an esteemed and respected businessman, a generous contributor to the city and to other charities in Fürth — who could imagine that just 7 years later with the election of Hitler as Chancellor in 1933, all would change so drastically.

Ida Metzger Bechmann   *Hugo Bechmann*

Ida Metzger Bechmann and Hugo Bechmann

Hugo and Ida Metzger (July 29, 1888 — January 2, 1978) married on May 16, 1910. Ida's large wedding portrait, painted that year, and which hangs in my front hall, shows her to be a beautiful stately woman. She was tall, had an erect bearing, and had been quite a good tennis player in her day. I have some of the tennis trophies she won — silver bowls engraved with her prize. She was the oldest child of Max and Caroline (sometimes spelled as Karoline) Metzger who lived in Nuremberg. Max and Caroline had two other children, Ida's sister Emma, (1890-1990) who was 15 months younger, and her brother Ernest, (1905-1984) who was 17 years younger. Emma married Ernest Bierer (1883-1967) and had three children — Walter, Fred and Dora. Just for the record, Walter, and his wife Regine had two children: Peggy and Joan; Fred and his wife Sally had three children: Linda, Barbara and Michael, and Dora, who married Herbert Weiner, had three children: Tim, Richard and Tony. Ernest Metzger married Doris and they had one child, Eva Metzger Brown. It is this generation of children with whom we are friendly today and who constitute our extended family. A genealogical chart of these family members is found in the Appendix. Lilli was close to her grandmother, Caroline, and there are pictures of Ruth sitting on Caroline's lap when Caroline was sitting in a wheelchair. Caroline was taken in 1942 from her home in Nuremberg and murdered by the Germans in the Theresienstadt concentration camp. A copy of her death certificate (in the Appendix) which Ida obtained from the International Red Cross Tracing Service shows the number of her transport and date of death, September 11, 1942. The reason for incarceration: "Judin" (Jewish). Ida had written the Red Cross for this information about her mother on March 7, 1957, and received her reply on July 28, 1975, eighteen years later.

In 1930 Hugo and Ida moved to Berlin. Lilli did not move with them because she began her studies at the University in Freiburg that year in May, 1930. The headline of the newspaper clipping which we have, dated June 16, 1930, is headed: "Nuremberg-Fürth Leading Industrialists Move to Berlin."

Again, as we just learned, two big leading industrialists will move their domicile to Berlin, to wit, Mr. Max O. Dukas, owner of one of the largest Nuremberg-Fürth printing establishments, and Councilor of Commerce Hugo Bechmann, Fürth, one of the leading personalities of the Fürth Mirror-Glass industry who will take over the leadership of the Berlin marketing organization of the Rhenish Glass and Mirrorglass enterprises.

Ruth in Caroline Metzger's lap (1938)

Lilli's parents lived in Berlin throughout the 1930's — and thus they were not living in Fürth when Lilli returned to Fürth to pursue her studies at the University in Erlangen or at any time until we emigrated. I learned for the first time, from the Fürth archives, that Lilli and Alfred went to Berlin to get married. They were married by a Justice of the Peace, with two signing witnesses: Lilli's father Hugo and Dr. Julius Koburger, Hospital Director. Alfred's address was listed as his home, 129 Koenigstrasse in Fürth while Lilli's was listed as that of her parents, Berlin-Wilmersdorf, Darmstädter Strasse 7. One of the things Evy and I found most curious is that there are absolutely no photos or memorabilia of Lilli's wedding to Alfred on July 3, 1933. We can only speculate — I think Hugo, Lilli's father, never approved of Alfred and Lilli's marriage for a number of reasons. We had heard from our cousin Walter Bierer. Lilli's first cousin, that Hugo was a very proud and vain man, and I suspect he thought Alfred wasn't of the same "class" as Lilli and that her marriage to him was a step down. There was also the issue of Alfred's schizophrenic brother James, which is discussed elsewhere in this memoir. In any case, we found it most curious that Lilli, who created albums of photos of her many travels and many photos of herself and Alfred skiing and hiking in the mountains, never had any photos taken of her wedding day. Why did they travel to Berlin to get married, instead of getting married in Fürth which had been the city where both prominent families had long roots? Although Lilli studied at the University of Berlin from October, 1930 to April, 1932, there is no evidence that Alfred ever spent any time there. His family and friends were not present; nor were there family and friends on Lilli's side at the ceremony. It's one of those questions to which we will never have an answer.

While in Berlin, and particularly after the Nazis gained increasing power, we have evidence that Hugo obtained trading licenses from such places as Norway and Sweden which allowed him to take orders for goods from abroad. Hugo emigrated by himself to Sweden in 1938 and Ida followed him in 1939. It is my understanding she didn't want to leave Germany until she was sure Lilli and her family had gotten out safely.

Hugo died in Stockholm on July 19, 1942 from complications of a routine gall bladder operation. Lilli authorized Ida to represent her in the administration and distribution of his estate and, as Hugo's only child, surrendered to Ida all of her rights of inheritance. Ida then came to the U.S. via a very circuitous route, arriving in Denver, where we were living, in 1945. This journey was recounted by Ida in her charming autobiography, which is included in the Appendix.

I will never forget seeing my mother upon receipt of the telegram informing her of her father's death. She stood at the front door of our house in Denver at 1195 Holly Street, and the sun streamed in through the door. She wept, openly, and this was the first and only time that I, who was then 6 years old, ever saw her cry.

I do not recall ever meeting my grandfather Hugo but it was clear that Lilli was very close to him even though he left Fürth in 1930 and Germany in 1938. I don't recall seeing any photos of him and me

Ida and Lilli

when I was a baby, and I have the feeling that he lived somewhat apart from family concerns. After they moved to Berlin, which is a considerable distance from Fürth, I don't know how often Lilli saw her parents. While Alfred was in prison, she did go to Berlin from time to time, but the period from 1930-1938 were incredibly busy and stressful years for Lilli — first to complete her doctorate in 1934; then, becoming aware of the dangers of Nazism, she wrote the family history; gave birth to Ruth in 1936 and then dealt with Alfred's imprisonment from February 1938-March 1939, and, at the same time, undertook the unbelievable efforts to obtain the visas so we could leave. Lilli did take a trip with Hugo to Copenhagen in 1935, according to our records. This might have been while Alfred and his mother came to the United States to "look around" and reconnect with Alfred's brother Max, who had emigrated from Germany in 1928. The sense Evy and I got of Hugo was of an arrogant and somewhat self-centered man. We also heard that in Stockholm he had a mistress who obviously left when Ida arrived in 1939. As a businessman he was inclined to take more risks than Alfred, and Lilli also was much more of a risk-taker than Alfred. Lilli stated that if she had gone with Alfred to America in 1935, they would have made the decision at that time to emigrate, never returning to Germany!

Lilli's mother, Ida, was born in Nuremberg on July 29, 1888. About 5 years before she died on January 2, 1978, we asked her to write (dictate) her autobiography since her life was so fascinating and full of such enormous changes. Because it was written with her usual and charming sense of humor, I will append it to this memoir and just give some other information here.

She was the first child of her parents, Max and Caroline (nee Salberg) Metzger. Her sister Emma (later Emma Bierer) was born a year later, and her brother, Ernest, was born 17 years later in 1905. Her father, Max Metzger, died in 1908. Ida married Hugo Bechmann on May 16, 1910 and moved into the Bechmann house at 7 Hornschuchpromenade. She led the life of a typical and privileged society woman of her time — played bridge, excelled at tennis where she won a number of tournaments, embroidered tablecloths and other needlework, and had servants, cooks and a chauffer at her disposal. She also was a talented artist, and just before we left Germany she wrote a creative poem about Ruth and a dog and illustrated it with her drawings. She spent from May to September with Lilli, her only child, in Rottach am Tegernsee, (now called Rottach-Egern) an elegant summer resort south of Munich in the Bavarian Alps, where Hugo rented large home adjacent to this magnificent lake. Evy and I visited Rottach in 1996.

Ida playing tennis

To make a longer story short, which Ida so interestingly describes in her autobiography, she and Hugo moved from Fürth to Berlin in 1930. Because, as a Jew, he had lost his job with his family business in April 1938, he moved permanently to Stockholm because it was too risky to return to Germany. Hugo already had business dealings with Sweden, culminating in his establishment of a glass firm, Hultberg, in Stockholm in 1936. After we all left Germany in the March 1939, Ida left for Sweden. After Hugo died in July 1942, Ida decided to move to Denver where we were living. In 1944, during the war, she arrived, via Scotland; London; Ireland; Lisbon, Portugal; Dakar, French Morocco; Natal, Brazil; Trinidad; Puerto Rico; Bermuda; New York and finally, Denver. It was quite a trip — read her description of it appended to this memoir. As had Lilli and Alfred, she went to the Opportunity School in Denver to learn American history and prepare for the citizenship exam. She was determined to be financially independent — an amazing fact and feat for this 56-year-old woman who had never worked a day in her life; had never cooked or even boiled water for herself. Maids, cooks, and other servants had always taken care of these chores. She

Ida's drawings for Ruth's book

had also lost everything and came to the United States almost penniless. She first got a job at The May Company, as a sales lady in the stockings department. Her description of that job in her autobiography is both humorous and touching. Later, from 1947-1966, she worked in the dietary department of the National Jewish Hospital in Denver. She prepared the diet trays for the patients. She lived in a small room in the nurses' quarters, and was able to have her meals in the hospital cafeteria, much to the relief of Lilli and Alfred. She never wanted to live with us, and thus her bed and board were available without her having to cook. In 1965, when she was 77 years old, The Canteen Company took over the hospital kitchen and soon let all the older employees go. She was incensed that she had been "fired", so Lilli and Alfred sent her on a cruise to the Mediterranean, her first return to Europe since she had emigrated. I remember her tales of the cruise — she made good friends wherever she went because she was an excellent bridge player, and enjoyed a drink or two before dinner. As a result, people invited her to play bridge, and to join them on the daily excursions. On her return, she moved into Kentucky Circle, a home for healthy seniors in Denver. There she took up painting and we have a number of her paintings around our house and in Maine. Soon after Lilli and Alfred died in 1970, she heard that the larger unit she had applied for was available and moved into it so she could have a separate room for her painting and a place for Evy and me to stay should we visit. In 1972 she had a stroke which paralyzed her on her left side. Evy and Bill had moved to Denver in 1972 and when they returned to live in Boston in 1975, Ida came with them. She moved into a nursing home until her peaceful death, at age 89, on January 2, 1978. She was absolutely lucid and a delight to be with right up to the last day.

There are a number of memories I have of her. Before she arrived, my governess, Helen Lorz, who had come over from Germany with us, had been trying very hard to make me right-handed. She believed it was a distinct disadvantage to be left-handed in America. She made me do various exercises and promised she would give me a watch if I became right-handed. When Ida arrived in 1945, she brought me a watch, and I stopped my efforts right there and then.

Ida used to walk from the National Jewish Hospital to our home on Holly Street, which was a distance of several miles. Somehow, she almost always (or at least often) would find a four-leaf clover and bring it to me. She and I were convinced this brought us good luck. I had put these 4-leaf clovers into a book, and when I found them years later I had them embossed in plastic.

I have many of her table linens and the sets of Meissen china and Limoges china also came from her household. The silverware set in Evy's home has Ida and Hugo's initials on it. When she was living in one room in the nursing home, she once said, in a joking manner with a smile on her face, that she once had a tablecloth and china to serve 60 people, and now lived in this small single room. This was said without rancor or regret. I have her tablecloth on which 60 people could be served, and once took it to a seamstress to cut it down so I could use it on my table. She returned it uncut — saying she couldn't possibly cut such beautiful linen. I also have a number of her tennis trophies — silver bowls and dishes. Ida and her sister Emma were evidently excellent tennis players, often competing in the finals of their club tournament. Ida told me once she thought she was a better player than Emma, and sometimes picked out the prize she wanted ahead of time.

Shortly after 1963, when my parents' correspondence with lawyers in Fürth for restitution payments had run its course, Ida told my parents she thought she would be entitled to restitution payments from Hugo's Social Security. By that time Lilli and Alfred were so happy to be through with this painful correspondence that they told her just to forget about it, as they were unwilling to open that door again. Lilli had, however, requested Ida's siblings to sign off on any rights they might have to the Metzger/Bechman claims so that Ida, who arrived in the U.S. with nothing and had no current source of income, could pursue those claims. Ida's sister, Emma, did so immediately, but her brother, Ernest Metzger, who was then living in New York, declined to do so. According to Lilli, this led to a life-long estrangement between my parents and Ernest Metzger. It appears, however, that the origins of this rift were many and varied and went back many years. So, with her usual charm and determination, Ida found someone at the National Jewish Hospital to help her, filed the claims and began receiving payments of several hundred dollars each month. These were deposited directly into her bank account. Each year, in November, she received a green document from the German authorities requiring her to return it during the month of January, notarized, verifying that she was still living. While in Denver she made friends with the woman who worked at the German consulate and went each January by herself to submit the document and have it notarized. After she moved to the Boston area, she was most worried about how to fulfill this obligation. I told her it could be done by mail, and I would notarize it, which I did each year. I visited her on January 1, 1978, and she insisted on signing and having me notarize the green document that day. She died quietly and peacefully in her sleep that night, and Evy and I debated about whether we should submit that document for another year of payments from the Germans. In the end we didn't, but it was tempting, particularly since they had taken so much from her.

What amazes me most, as I think back on her, is her omnipresent good cheer and positive outlook on life. I don't remember one moment of her feeling sorry for herself for what had happened to her. Given her background and life, there wasn't one iota of bitterness or regret. She made friends easily and truly enjoyed other people. She was always so grateful for anything you did for her, or anything you gave her, however small it might be.

Lilli's Home

Lilli's Home on Hornschuchpromenade

Before returning to Lilli's history after this digression into the business and family background of the Bechmann family, I need to describe the house in which she lived because it was, and actually still is, undoubtedly one of the finest, if not the finest, house in Fürth.

Lilli's Home

The house at 7 Hornschuchpromenade, where first Louis Bechmann (1848-1921), Lilli's grandfather lived, then his son Hugo and where Lilli grew up, is an extraordinarily large and beautiful mansion by any standards. Next door, at 8 Hornschuchpromenade, lived Louis' brother, Maier (1856-1947). Louis and Meier were two of the ten children of Wilhelm and Getta Bechmann (1824-1901) and they were both in the glass business. Louis married Mathilde Gutherz (1854-1920) and they are my great grandparents on Lilli's side of the family. Meier married Mathilde's younger sister, Emma Gutherz (1871-1938). Louis and Mathilde died within a year of each other and both were cremated. Their urns rest in the Jewish cemetery in Nuremberg. Louis and Mathilde had two children, Hugo Bechmann, my grandfather (1878-1942) and Karola Bechmann Loeffler (1881-1960), my great-aunt. Karola, Lilli's aunt, married Julius Loeffler (1873-1946), a judge in civil court and later a Councilor of the Superior Provincial Court in Nuremberg. Both of them emigrated to the United States and resided and died in Los Angeles. My memories of Julius are dim though he and Karola came to Denver and we have photos of all of us in the mountains together. Although Julius died when I was 10, I remember "Tante" Karola's annual visits to Denver very well. She brought with her this special thinly sliced brown bread, which my mother used to serve with goose fat and salt. As she usually came around Christmas time, my mother usually made a goose (the only time it was available in the grocery store, as I recall) and saved the goose fat for Karola's visit and her brown bread.

Maier Bechmann (1856-1947), as previously mentioned, became a manager of the Bavarian Glass Factory along with his brother, Louis. After his wife, Emma Gutherz (1871-1938) died in Fürth, Maier and his two children moved to England and both children became members of the Church of England. When I went to London in 1953 as part of my Girl Scout trip to Switzerland, I met Maier's granddaughter, Anna Sahlman (born in 1906) and her daughter, Monica Sahlman, (born in 1934). My diary of that summer reminds me of the visit; I knew only these were relatives but had no idea of their relation to me. Lilli's Bechmann Family History tells us that Monica married Peter Rosenbaum and had two children, Susan Ruth Rosenbaum, born in 1962 and Anthony Henry Rosenbaum, born in 1965. We have totally lost contact with these relatives, but I found it interesting that the children are about the same ages as Karen and Rachel.

On his father's death, Hugo continued to live at 7 Hornschuchpromenade and when he married Ida Metzger, this became the family home for the two of them and Lilli, their only child. This was Lilli's home from the time of her birth until she married, when she moved into Alfred's family home at 129 Konigstrasse. Although the Konigstrasse home was also very large, and on a main street of Fürth, it was clearly not of the same size or class as the one on Hornschuchpromenade.

The stately homes on Hornschuchpromenade are magnificent and the two Bechmann homes are truly mansions. In many books and articles about Fürth which I have seen, the Bechmann houses are pictured. Hornschuchpromenade is a rather short, lovely tree-lined street that is divided by a grassy and tree-filled esplanade. It is remarkable to me that she, as an only child, lived there with her parents and no other relatives. Of course there was also the help that lived there, which must have consisted of at least a governess, a cook, perhaps a chauffeur, cleaning personnel, and others. The offices of the glass works were also in the home. I have now been there several times.

In 1995 one of the banks in Fürth put out a calendar, as banks are wont to do, entitled "Facades of Fürth" Each month had a beautiful large photograph of a unique building façade in the city. Of the 12 beautiful facades, 8 Hornschuchpromenade was the only single family home shown. Although this was Meier's home, the architectural description is accurate and identical for the adjacent mansion owned by Louis. The other photos were of churches, a restaurant, marketplace, City Hall, commercial buildings, a casino, row houses and an apartment building. On the back of each photo was a description of the exterior façade chosen. It was described as follows:

> *The Residence at Honrschuchpromenade 8 (1897)*
> *In the same year as the Exporthaus, 1897, the other important Fürth architect of this time, Fritz Walter, was building the beautiful house at Hornschuchpromenade 8.*
>
> *Let us follow with our eyes the façade from bottom to top. The basement floor is situated rather high. This is where the janitor lived, while the offices were located on the ground floor. It is built with roughly hewn sandstone squares. The rich façade ornamentation, the balcony, the bay and the window decorations begin only on the first story. This was the "belle etage", the most beautiful residence where the homeowner himself lived. Often he had his own staircase. The inhabitants of the upper stories reached their rooms by a simpler, second staircase. Under the roof were the lodging quarters of the servants, who were absolutely necessary for the upkeep of such a large residence of more than 200 square meters.*
>
> *Especially beautiful on this house are the wrought iron balcony rails with the vase motifs, the bay, and the splendid richly ornamental portal. The four-cornered bay is decorated on the first floor with a three-cornered gable, on the second floor with a half-round one, on the third floor it is fashioned with many corners and finally*

finishes in a gable on the roof. On Hornschuchpromenade, as well as on the other side of Konigswarterstrasse, to the left and right of the Old Ludwig Railroad, the Fürth upper class of the end of the 19th century built and lived — the factory owners, big businessmen, and bankers. Many of them were Jews. Number 8 belonged to the Jewish commercial businessman Bechmann. The architectural style of the groundbreaking years is called Historismus because one worked with the building forms of the old, historical styles. The architect used many baroque forms in order to build an exceptionally extravagant house. The splendor of these house reflect the need for status and the desire for prestige of the newly rich citizens.

The above description was evidently written by someone the bank commissioned when they put together the calendar. The size mentioned, 200 square meters, seems to me much too small for the dimensions of this mansion.

After this diversion into the history of the Bechmann family business and the house in which Lilli grew up, let me continue this story of Lilli by describing her mother, Ida, and then discussing her artwork, poetry, summers in Rottach, and education and other aspects of Lilli's life.

Artwork

Lilli's interests and achievements during her early life were not restricted to purely intellectual endeavors. We have among our papers a portfolio of her artwork, some of it dated 1924, when she was just 13, and then a number of very sophisticated drawings from the period 1927-1930, when she was 16-19. It is clear that she took drawing lessons, either individually or in a class, and there are a number of drawings dealing with perspective, as well as drawings and sketches of heads, busts, feet, inanimate objects and still life. This part of her life, like so many of her early passions, was never evident in the mother we knew.

Poetry

Another major activity during Lilli's early life was her vast and extensive output as a poet. She began writing poetry at an early age, and among our papers we have literally hundreds of poems she wrote. From her youngest days, we have several bound notebooks in which these poems were written by hand. Volume I covers the period, as she notes on the title page, from November 26, 1923 to November 6, 1926. Lilli was 12-15 years old as she wrote the numbered 61 poems in this book. A title index to all poems is at the end of her book. We don't have Volume II, which must have contained poems numbered 62 to 123, since Volume III, which begins on September 4, 1927 to October 20, 1929 starts with poem #124 and ends with poem #155. Her age during this time was 15-18. At the top of each poem she wrote where it was written and the date. All poems in Volume I were written in Fürth. The first few poems in Volume III were written in Fürth, then during her time in Geneva, and then back at Fürth and a few other places where she was during this period. The last ones in these bound volumes, in 1929, are clearly love poems, as she had met Alfred by this time. And then we have, among our papers, a sheath of papers which contains over 200 poems and other writings covering the period from 1923 to 1937. Most are poems, and then there are outpourings of feelings, written as if in a diary, on trains, on vacations, and so on.

She also had some of her poems published in three separate anthologies of young leading German poets. Each of these books of poetry is inscribed to her "dearest Alfred." One book, published in 1931, when she was 20, is entitled "Sontag der Seele", meaning "Sunday of the Soul". It is inscribed "To my dear Alfred on his thirtieth birthday from his Lilli." Berlin, January 28, 1931. There are a total 133 poems in this book — each is given a page on which is written one or two poems by different young poets. The authors are organized alphabetically. The note of the editor at the beginning of this volume is as follows:

The collection does not follow any identical pattern, does not serve any particular trend. The versatility of lyrical expression is to be given space in any case. Still, I have tried to give the whole something resembling a theme by choosing poems in which the "Sunday Expression" appears most clearly. This is not always joyous: Sunday of the soul is also present where sorrow tears it from the commonplace.

The Editor

The two poems in this volume written by Lilli are entitled "Silence" and "Understanding" and have been translated as follows:

SILENCE

The leaves move quietly ---
A footstep dies away in the distance ---
An eternal calm
Lies on the broad fields ...

But I stand amid this.
Alone — abandoned by everyone –
And indeterminable longing
Takes hold of my heart. ---
It pulls me and urges me –
And I don't know to where,
It lures me and calls me –
And I don't know from where –

And regardless where I turn,
I cannot find the calm,
For unsatisfied longing
Devours my soul.

UNDERSTANDING

We understood each other,
Your eyes said so.
We understood each other
Yet we did not ask.

We only smiled quietly;
The others hardly noticed,
How our souls united
In the broad universe.

Another anthology entitled Neue Lyric, (New Lyrics, with its subtitle of "Anthology of 29 Young Authors") appears to be an annual publication and Lilli's poems appear in the Anthologies of 1930 and 1931. In the 1930 edition, she has two poems, entitled Schneegestöber (translated as Snow Flurry) and Hauch (translated as Breath).

SNOW FLURRY

White Flakes are drifting in the sky,
Millions upon millions in colorful swarm,
Not knowing, how they will get to lie down.
Not knowing to whose end and to whose gain, -
Falling from a wise hand
Onto the land.

Many people are drifting on earth,
Eternal fate, vanishing and becoming!
Created, like flakes, out of nothing,
Not knowing how to find their way to earth
And awaiting, in trouble,
Death.

The 1931 edition was subtitled "Light in the Fog". Lilli inscribed it "To my dear Alfred, the spiritus rector (inspiring power) of these little lines, from his Lilli." Her poem in this anthology is entitled "Death".

DEATH

A shadow lowers itself onto the land,
Darkness empty of light surrounds your being,
The limbs stiffen in dread full of presentiment,
And numb knowledge envelopes your thoughts.

A dark guest has walked through the bedroom,
He is not stopped by lock nor prayer
A poor wanderer has finished his suffering,
A new ray goes from here to the hereafter.

And you, the living, start to shudder,
You feel that death is not the last thing,
And even if one were separated by a thousand walls,
One being never forgets the other.

And you recognize, relieved, that death and life
Form a great unity in this world,
For without death there can be no becoming,
And becoming is what holds together being.

Thus death cannot be the end,
He is only the bridge to another being,
And there, so far from the spirit of this world,
Death and life enter into the unity.

To me this is a rather somber poem for a 20 year old. I wonder whether this theme of death was precipitated and inspired by the death of Alfred's father, Sidney Rahn, and his uncle, James Rahn, who both died the year before on the same day, September 13, 1930. Neither knew of the death of the other.

I quote these few poems to give an idea of the depth of her sentiments and emotional being, as well as her ability to express these feelings in poetry that was considered worthy of being included in anthologies of young poets. These books of poems were also stored away among the family papers, and were never alluded to or mentioned during her lifetime. We never knew they existed and we only discovered them after her death. If I had to sum up these poems, all I can say is "this is not the mother we knew". I believe that the experience of living through what happened to the Jews in Germany radically changed her.

Rottach — Summer Resort

Throughout her childhood, the family spent each summer in Rottach, a fashionable resort on the Tegernsee. Rottach-Egern as it is now called, is south of Munich in the Bavarian Alps. The guidebook describes Tegernsee as "an Alpine lake dotted with sails in summer and ice-skaters in winter. Its wooded shores are lined with flowers in late spring; in fall its trees provide a colorful contrast to the dark, snowcapped mountains." When Evy and I visited Rottach in 1996, the beauty and elegance of this

Ernst Metzger, Ida and Hugo Bechmann
and Lilli in Rottach

magnificent spot were evident, even on the cloudy, rainy day that we were there. We visited the finest hotel in town, the Bachmair, which existed at the time she was there and still is a beautiful operative hotel right on the lake. Today Rottach is filled with the finest upscale shops of clothes, shoes, accessories, and leather goods, with absolutely no t-shirt or souvenir shops. The guidebook said that shopping here was better than Munich. According to our cousin Walter Bierer, (Lilli's first cousin who was just a year younger than she — Walter's mother, Emma, was Ida's sister) whose family also often summered in Rottach, Hugo rented the most fashionable house in town. They arrived each year with all the baggage needed to spend the summer there, and my grandmother Ida told me they (meaning their chauffer) drove the first car that was driven into Rottach. Ida also told me that Lilli was a real tomboy, and always carried worms around in her pockets because she loved to fish in the lake. Although Lilli never talked about her experiences of growing up in Fürth, her education, and all her other activities and accomplishments as a child and young adult, she did talk on occasion about Rottach so that I grew up knowing she had spent her summers in a resort community on a lake, loving the out of doors, and nature. Memories of Rottach, which were just a part of her happy and privileged childhood, were evidently something that could be talked about, whereas what came later was repressed along with the horrors of the Nazi regime and the trauma of getting out of Germany.

Early Education

Lilli's educational experience, for a young woman of that time and social standing, was quite remarkable. Her pre-university education can be summarized as follows:

September 1917 — February 1, 1921 — Staedtische Volksschule (Elementary School)

April 1921 — April 7, 1927 — Staedtisches Maedchenlyzeum (High School)

September 1927 — June 1928 — School for Modern Languages, Geneva, Switzerland

April 1929 — April 1930 — Oberrealschule (High School) and Arbiturium (University Entrance Examination).

Sometime at the end of or shortly after World War I Lilli had typhoid fever and was home-schooled for two years. After attending elementary school and the German equivalent of our high school in Fürth, she wanted to attend university. Her parents were not very supportive of this desire because young women of their social milieu didn't do that sort of thing, so she spent a year, 1927-28, from age 16-17, at the School for Modern Languages in Geneva, Switzerland where she received specialized training in the French language, literature and history. Since her mother, Ida, had only a high school education, she hoped that a year in Geneva, at what was then called a "finishing school", would satisfy her intellectually ambitious daughter. In fact, it did just the opposite and when she returned to Fürth she completed another year of study at the Oberrealschule to pass the required exams and obtain the necessary degree, the Arbiturium, to enter the university. She passed this exam in April 1930 and began her university studies immediately, in May 1930, when she was 19 years old.

University Education, Including Erlangen and Lilli's Thesis

Unlike the American college or university experience, it was quite common in those days to move from one university to another, often because the particular professor in your field of

THE PHILOSOPHIC FACULTY OF THE

FRIEDRICH-ALEXANDERS-UNIVERSITY

grants in the Rectorate

of o.oe.Professor Dr.med. et med.dent.h.c.

Johannes Reinmoeller

through its Dean,o.oe.Professor Dr.phil.Alfred Klotz

MRS.LILLY RAHN,born BECHMANN from FUERTH

on the strength of her treatise

"The Darmstadt Circle of Friends.A contribution

to the comprehension of the sentimental

Conception of Soul of the Eighteenth Century

by virtue of very well passed examination

THE DEGREE AND DIGNITY
of

DOCTOR OF PHILISOPHY

Erlangen,May 2nd 1934

The Rector: The Dean:

sig.Dr.med.Johannes Reinmoeller   sig.Dr.phil.Alfred Klotz

Seal

Translated by:

Munich,Sept.25th 1937   Justizrat

GERMAN REICH
STATE OF BAVARIA
CONSULATE GENERAL
  OF THE UNITED STATES
  OF AMERICA AT MUNICH   Sworn and official translator and
                           interpreter of the English langu
                           at the courts of Munich.
     I,   James M. Bowcock , a Vice - Consul of the United
States of America at Munich, Germany, duly commissioned and qualified, do hereby certify that
Dr.A.Veit
whose true signature and official seal are, respectively, affixed to the foregoing document,
was at the time of signing the same sworn & official translator & interpreter of
the English language of the courts of Munich, Germany,
to whose official acts faith and credit are due.

    In witness whereof I have hereunto set my hand and the seal of this
Consulate General this 27th day of September, A.D. 1937

James M. Bowcock

FEE NO. 58
SERVICE NO. 4218
$ 2 . U.S. CURRENCY

Lilli's Ph.D. Certificate

study was there. Over the next four years, from May 1930 until April 1934, Lilli attended four universities. She began at the University of Freiberg, (May 30 — July 30, 1930) where, among other courses, she studied philosophy and history of philosophy with Martin Heidegger. She then spent about a year and a half at the University of Berlin, (October 10, 1930 — April 7, 1932) where she specialized in History of the Theatre. While there, in 1932, she was honored with the degree of Member of the Berlin Institute For Theatre Science at the University of Berlin on the strength of a long treatise she wrote entitled "The National Stage of Nuremberg". This extensive research work discussed historical theatrical problems, especially on the German National Stage of Nuremberg. Due to political developments, this book was never published. She also published various articles on the History of the Theatre and on modern stage in several periodicals. Her parents, Ida and Hugo, were living in Berlin at this time, but Lilli had her separate apartment. After this experience she spent several months at the University of Vienna (May 14, 1932 — July 1932) and in October 1932 began the last two years of her higher education at the Friedrich-Alexander University in Erlangen, (October 25, 1932 — April 1934) where she obtained her Doctor of Philosophy degree (Ph.D.) in April 1934. Her dissertation for the Ph.D. degree was published in book form and was entitled: *The Darmstadt Circle of Friends. A Contribution to the Comprehension of the Sentimental Conception of Soul during the 18th Century.* At Erlangen, she took a number of courses from Professor Von Wiese, who was also her thesis advisor. Her major was the German language and literature; her minors were Modern and Medieval European History, History of the Theatre and History of Art and Philosophy.

Unlike Freiberg, Berlin or Vienna, Erlangen was very close to Fürth. No doubt one of the reasons she transferred so close to home is that she and Alfred were planning to marry and did so on July 3, 1933 while she was still completing her doctoral studies. This meant that in the middle of her studies and doctoral dissertation, she moved from her family home to Alfred's home at 129 Konigstrasse, which was not far from her former home. In April of 1934, at the age of 23, she received her Doctorate of Philosophy (Ph.D.) from the Friedrich-Alexander University of Erlangen. She was the last Jew to receive her doctorate from this University, as well as one of the youngest. By this time she had published various articles on the History of the Theatre and on modern stage in several periodicals. One of these was a long thesis entitled Theatre and Film in Soviet Russia — 1932. Lilli traveled to Russia in order to do the research for this paper. I have a copy of this document, but have not had it translated into English. It did, however, receive acclaim, as there were articles about it in both Erlangen and Fürth newspapers, as well as in a film review.

Her dissertation for the Ph.D. degree was published in book form entitled *The Darmstadt Circle of Friends. A Contribution to the Comprehension of the Sentimental Conception of Soul during the 18th Century.* We found about 25 copies of her dissertation (in German, of course) among her papers after her death. This doctoral thesis, 68 single spaced typed pages in length, was written under the tutelage of her advisor, Prof. Dr. Benno von Wiese and is dedicated to "My Parents". Parenthetically, von Wiese was evidently an extremely well known philosopher and historian. When I had Lilli's thesis translated by a graduate student studying German at Harvard, she immediately recognized his name. Additionally, the fact that she worked under von Wiese is one of the reasons that her thesis was selected, many years later in 1999, for a prestigious award which was then named the Lilli Bechmann Rahn Award.

A word about the content of the thesis is required here, though anyone who is not particularly interested can skip this part. The Darmstadt Circle functioned roughly from 1771-1773 and was made up of members of the Sentimental Movement. Meeting in the city of Darmstadt, near Frankfurt, the group included major German authors, Goethe, Herder and Merck, as well as lesser-known figures and a number of women. Lilli's dissertation examines the mentality of members of the Sentimental Movement, which was one of the main influences on German literature during 1740-1755, and persisted until roughly 1780. The Darmstadt Circle falls relatively late in the period, existing at the beginning of the 70's. Sentimentality was a movement that focused on a psychological approach to life. The Enlightenment overemphasized the rational view, thus leading to a reactionary development: the irrational world of Sentimentality. The thesis focused not on the history of the ideas of Sentimentality, but rather on the specific emotional and psychological points of view of its adherents, i.e. not on the concepts and motifs the members of the group dealt with, but rather on how they dealt with them. The structure of her work comprises, firstly, a historical overview of the members of the circle; secondly, a specific examination of selected works; and thirdly, an elucidation of their overall positions. The Darmstadt Circle was strongly influenced by its ties to the Hessian-Darmstadtian court and most members had ties to the court, whether through birth or career. For the women in the Darmstadt Circle, Sentimentality, in placing all worthwhile experiences into the internal psyche of the individual, gave them the only possibility of independence. The specific nature of the Darmstadt Circle, that aspect that makes it distinct, is the lack of any actual aim, any 'useful' goal. Rather, the emphasis lies on feelings themselves. One main aspect of Sentimentality, then, was its basis in a desire to escape material circumstance through the creation of an illusionary, internal world. For the Sentimentalists, the imaginary sphere was the only sphere of freedom. They sought community not for its own sake, but for the sake of finding an environment in which they could best develop themselves. The group is based, then, on extreme individualism among its members, who look for others in whom they can "mirror" themselves. Their friendships were not based on a connection between specific individuals, but rather on the concept of a 'universal' or 'abstract' form of friendship. One key focus was the subject of death, and the afterlife, thus retreating from reality. Melancholy, a driving emotional state, was no longer associated with genius, but denoted an uncreative sadness that was paralyzing, even fatal, to emotional life. The crisis of weakness culminated in an illness that climaxed in suicide. Thus, Goethe's *The Sorrows of Young Werther* (1774), a work that depicts suicide of a young man, was followed by a rash of suicides. Goethe (1749-1823) wrote this as a young man of 25 and it became the prototype of the romantic hero. Lilli's thesis concludes that three movements dominated the German culture of the eighteenth century: The Enlightenment, Sentimentality, and Sturm and Drang. The members of the Darmstadt Circle functioned as a cross-section of these movements; the discrepancy between nature and individual, which would become a driving theme in German Classicism, was already evident in Sentimentality, particularly the figure of the 'beautiful soul', which constituted the desired synthesis of nature, and soul. The close ties between the

Enlightenment and Sentimentality demonstrate the duality of the 'German nature': a desire for scientific knowledge and discovery coupled with a desire to overcome earthly constraints through creativity. Later, members of the Sturm and Drang movement emphasized the need to actually 'live' emotion whereas the members of the Sentimental movement did not experience the intensity of emotion because of their constant observation thereof. Their tendency to place their own sphere of influence entirely into the internal life, points ahead to German Idealism and the dangers therein.

I realize that this was a rather long interlude into the content of the thesis, but I saw so much of Lilli's younger days in these romantic individuals. She too had immersed herself in romantic and emotional poetry, writing hundreds of poems. What is so interesting for me, and indeed sad for me, is that few of these qualities or passions appeared in her later life, at least not to me. I never knew she was a poet, and to me she seemed the epitome of the rational human being, and was certainly not overly emotional or sentimental in any way. I believe that her experience with the German Nazi brutality and murder truly killed that side of her. Being "goal-less", emotional or sentimental was no way to survive, and survive she did — not only herself but also her family.

After she came to Denver and was applying for a teaching position at the University of Denver, she listed all of the undergraduate and graduate subjects she had studied and the semester hours she had spent in each area. A semester hour is 16 weeks of instruction. I thought this gave the best idea of the breadth and depth of her education:

German Language — 16 semester hours

German Literature — 65 semester hours

Modern and Medieval European History — 24 semester hours

History of Art — 18 semester hours

Philosophy and History of Philosophy — 7 semester hours

Language — general — 3 semester hours

World Literature — 5 semester hours

English Language and Literature — 6 semester hours

French Language and Literature — 7 semester hours

History of the Theatre — 9 semester hours

Political Science — 3 semester hours

Social Science — 1 semester hour

From the curriculum vitae we have, which Lilli used to apply for various positions at the University of Denver, we have the chronology of her studies, which she describes as follows:

1917-21 — Elementary School, Fürth, Bavaria

1921-27 — High School.

1927-28 — School for Modern Languages, Geneva, Switzerland

1929-30 — High School (Arbiturium)

1930-34 — Universities of Freiburg, (Germany), Berlin (Germany), Vienna (Austria), Erlangen (Germany)

Major: German Languages and Literature; minors: Modern and Medieval European

History, History of the Theatre, History of Art, Philosophy

Under Degrees and Honors she lists: "In January 1932 I was honored with the degree of Member of the Berlin Institute for Theatre Science (Theaterwissenschaftliches Institut) at the University of Berlin on the strength of my treatise "Die Nuremberger Nationalschaubuehne" (The National Stage of Nuremberg). 1934 Ph.D., University of Erlangen."

Travel
Before she graduated with her doctorate from the University in Erlangen, at age 23, she had done an amazing amount of traveling, as evidenced by her travel diaries, photo albums and her curriculum vitae, which we have. She had traveled extensively in Germany, Austria, Italy, Switzerland, and Czechoslovakia. She also visited and spent several weeks in: Denmark, England, France, Alsace-Lorraine, North Africa (Tripoli), Hungary, Poland, and Russia (Leningrad, Moscow, Krakow, Kiev). Some of these travels were sponsored by the University of Munich for research and study purposes.

Reorganized Fürth Library
From 1934 to 1936, now married and having completed her education, she reorganized the entire library of the Jewish Community in Fürth, Bavaria. She wrote that it was in great disorder because the Community had never had a specialist librarian for it before. The library consisted of about 20,000 books, covering all sorts of subjects, e.g.: novels, biographies, European and Jewish history, philosophy, psychology, history of art, music, law, modern and ancient languages, sociology, politics, geography, geology, physical sciences, medicine, children's literature, etc. The Community also owned a fine collection of old newspapers, manuscripts and historical documents that she classified so they could be used for scientific and historical research. It was interesting to learn this fact about her, which I never knew, because the first job she had in Denver was in a book store, which she also helped to re-organize.

Wrote Bechmann Family History

It was also during this period, 1934-36, that she researched and wrote the history of her own family, the Bechmann family, and was able to trace the family back to 1666. It became increasingly evident to her, as the spread of the Nazi party increased to many areas of life, that documents, manuscripts, official records, gravestones and other archival material might be destroyed, so she did the research and photographed as many graves of her ancestors as she could find. She wrote this history in German, and included photos of the gravestones in the manuscript. Evy and I later used those photos to find those graves ourselves. Like almost all other aspects of her life in Germany, she never told us about this history and we first learned of it after she died, when we discovered about 20 copies of this family history among the family papers which had been stored away. In 1971 our close family friend, Gerda Breit, translated it into English. Evy then took Lilli's current address book and contacted as many remaining relatives as she could identify in an attempt to update the history. Amazingly many of them had copies of the family history and responded, and Evy then updated this history to 1972. I have not, in this memoir, brought it up to a more current date. A copy of this family history, as revised by Evy, is in the Appendix to this memoir.

Meeting Alfred

It is not clear when or how Lilli met Alfred, who was ten years older than she was, just as her father, Hugo, was ten years older than her mother, Ida. They lived in the same town, not far from each other, and the families must have known each other. From her intense educational and intellectual commitments and activities, as well as her travels, and from her basic personality which I can assess as her child, she wasn't much "interested in boys" while she was growing up. Although she came from a socially prominent family, her interests were intellectual rather than social. I believe, however, that she had good male friends with whom she shared her intellectual pursuits and skiing as we have numerous such photographs of her with both male and female friends. They met in about 1929 and it does seem that it was "love at first sight". In that year Lilli was 18, and Alfred 28. They enjoyed skiing and hiking together, and there are hundreds, literally hundreds, of poems she wrote to him on an almost daily basis from the time they began to go out with each other, until after they married.

Lilli's Wedding Portrait?

Alfred, on the other hand, resisted marriage because he feared having children. He had a schizophrenic brother (to be discussed more in detail below), and he believed a child of his might inherit these traits. He was the owner and active participant in his family's metal and ironworks business, which he took seriously. On the other hand, he was an extremely handsome man, well established in his family's business, and was probably sought after by many young ladies. I think when he turned his attentions to Lilli she was flattered and felt loved and wanted by a man for the first time. They shared their interests in the out-of-doors, and there are albums of photos of them hiking and skiing in the Alps.

The other very curious fact that we discovered in going through all the family documents, photos and memorabilia, is that there is absolutely no record and no photos of their wedding on July 3, 1933. Perhaps the photo on this page is a wedding portrait, but it is the only photo like it we have. The wedding took place in Berlin, where Hugo and Ida Bechmann, Lilli's parents were living at the time. We have a copy of the Marriage Certificate, numbered 167 from the

Lilli

Fürth archives, but it is dated October 16, 1937, indicating that it was a copy and one of the many documents needed to emigrate. The marriage was solemnized before a Justice of the Peace. Lilli's address was listed as Berlin-Wilmersdorf, Darmstadter Str. 7, which was the address of her parents at that time. The witnesses were Hospital Director Dr. Julius Koburger and Lilli's father, identified as Director, Commercial Councilor Hugo Bechmann. The certificate states that, "The Justice of the Peace asked the couple singly and in sequence if they intended to enter the marriage with each other. The couple affirmed this, and the Justice of the Peace announced hereon that they were now, according to the Civil Law, legally united marriage partners." There is no evidence that more than a few people attended this wedding ceremony. We have a printed card which most likely was afterwards sent to family and friends which reads:

Councilor of Commerce Hugo Bechmann, Ida Bechmann, express their most cordial gratitude for the kind attentions shown on the occasion of the betrothal of their daughter, Lilli, to Mr. Alfred Rahn.
Berlin W15 Darmstadter Strasse 7

Given the many photo albums we have of Alfred and Lilli's experiences together before their marriage, especially skiing and hiking, and Lilli's many albums containing photos of her childhood, her prodigious travels, and their propensity for taking many photographs all their lives, it is curious that we have no wedding portrait and no wedding photos. We can only surmise that since Hugo appears to have been against this wedding (probably because of Alfred's schizophrenic brother or perhaps also because of a class distinction), no formal ceremony was celebrated.

Contributions to the Fürth Community

Lilli and Alfred each made a number of contributions to the Fürth community. Given their social and economic status in the community, and the fact that both families had for generations been involved in the affairs of the community, this is not unusual. I add this short paragraph because we have documents among our papers in which thanks and appreciation to Lilli and Alfred are expressed.

Lilli had made a contribution, and also some suggestions regarding the defraying of costs of a convalescent home for children in the Israeli Orphanage for boys and girls. On February 5, 1935 she received a letter from the Israeli Orphanage, signed by D. Hallemann, thanking her for her interest and suggestions. I mention this because the fate of Dr. Halleman and the children of the orphanage was so tragic. He had an opportunity to flee Germany but chose to remain with the orphans he cared for. Though at least one of his own children left for Israel, his other children and those in the orphanage, as well as himself, were taken by the Nazis to Auschwitz and murdered there.

On March 29, 1935 Alfred was notified that he had been elected to the Administrative Board of the Israeli Culture Community of Fürth.

Ruth's Birth and Early Years

When Lilli was 25 years old, I, Ruth Marion, was born on June 15, 1936 in the Jewish Hospital in Fürth. Among the documents we found in our possession, is a book entitled Ruth Marion's Tagebuch (Day Book). It consists of 52 handwritten pages, written in ink into a book with plain pages and gold edges. It covers the period from June 15, 1936 until March 31, 1938. It begins with a dedication, as follows:

Lilli and Ruth

> *To you, my dear daughter, Ruth Marion, this book is dedicated. It shall show you one day, when you are grown up, how you have become and grown, and help you to know yourself and to understand the ever same and ever new development of the generations. Fürth, June 15, 1936.*

This dedication page is followed by a genealogy chart, showing my ancestors on both sides of the family going back four generations, i.e. to my great-great grandparents. (A copy of this genealogy chart from the front of the Tagebuch is included in the Appendix)

The first entry, on June 20, 1936 says that the incomprehensible start of my existence took place the same night as my great grandmother, Caroline, suffered a stroke and thereby practically withdrew from an active life, though spiritually she remained entirely unbroken. "There you appeared, new little person, to continue the eternal chain of the generations."

"Those months, before you saw the light of the world, when you still belonged entirely to me, were a good time, because you made it easy for me and never before had I felt so good." I was born at 2:00 p.m. with the umbilical cord wrapped around my shoulder, which the physician had to help along with forceps. I was a strong little girl, weighing 8 lbs. 6 oz. at birth and measuring 21 1/2 inches.

> *With long black hair and a little snub nose, according to the judgment of objective viewers, a pretty baby, besides, in the opinion of the doctor, Dr. Mosbacher, and the midwife, Therese Mannlein, entirely the papa. That there was entirely no resemblance to me was confirmed by the question of the Catholic night nurse who asked me if the child had such a beautiful father, because it was so pretty! Your father is of course totally enthusiastic, and while he had previously hardly noticed small children, he developed in your case an astonishing power of observation.*

The next entry, on June 22, when I was a week old, said I "began drinking well and we got a taste of the uncomfortable sides of life, because both of us suffered with the great heat. On June 24, accompanied by the best wishes of all, we left the hospital". It is amazing to think that in those days, a routine birth with no complications required a hospital stay of nine days. By June 25, when I was only 10 days old, Lilli wrote that "she was brought outdoors for a long stretch and was in the garden in the early afternoon. This "airing" agreed with her splendidly".

On July 3, Lilli wrote that in honor of their wedding anniversary, Sister Edith (who evidently was one of the nurse-maids at that time) "surprised us by putting the first panties on the little one, in which she looked indeed quite charming, when she brought her down to us at 6 a.m. for the first meal, with a little basket of roses on her arm." I had been receiving some additional milk from the bottle because Lilli's milk production had slowed down a bit, but it seemed to agree with me. Then, amazingly on July 5 Lilli writes that "besides the panties, which

Ruth 1937

we are wearing during the day instead of diapers, Ruth, as of today, is wearing little dresses and looks like a real little girl". I simply can't believe that it was the custom to put a 3 week-old baby in panties!

Then there is a break in the diary until December 1, when she summarizes the small progressions I had made. When I was exactly 5 1/3 months minus 3 days I got my first tooth. Because some of the early child rearing practices are so different from what I did, or what my children did with their children, I thought it interesting to quote some of this part of the diary.

During the day you are usually good and know how to entertain yourself alone with my ring and a few celluloid animals which are hanging from my basket on little strings. In the afternoon, after the meal, you are allowed to kick a bit and exercise to your heart's content. Like a frog you push yourself forward with your legs and in a few strokes you have moved on your back from one end to the other. Yesterday you propelled yourself with great élan from your back to your belly and you were indeed somewhat surprised at your own accomplishment. In the opinion of all who know you, you are a particularly lively child, especially for a girl. For a few weeks now you have also become one of the thumb suckers, but only when you are tired or hungry. You do your business still quite punctually in the morning after the milk and at noon between vegetables and fruit. Lately, however, I arrived with the potty into which you deposited your business since your 6th week, a bit too late, but I shall attribute that to your teething. You are a very friendly child, always grateful and happy when one attends to you, but never weepy or angry if one goes away and leaves you alone, but always right away busy with something. For weeks now you have been making great efforts to sit, when one leaves the room you raise you head and shoulders quite high and follow one with your eyes. You are also very talkative, as well when you are alone as when one talks with you. For weeks now you have been developing a very definite time schedule, actually exactly since September 27 you have been put on a 12 hour night schedule, to which you keep exactly: you wake up in the morning between 5 and 6 and talk to yourself rather loudly until I come at 7 with the milk bottle (150 gr. Milk, 50 gr. Water, some Soxlesugar (I don't know exactly what this is, but it was apparently added to the milk), 1/2 piece of cube sugar. After drinking, whereby you now frequently hold your own bottle, you do your business into the potty. Then you get your toys hung up, play about 1 hour and from 8:30 — 9:30 you have a nap. Meanwhile I have fixed your bottle, including next day's breakfast milk. Now you are bathed entirely with lukewarm water, before that we exercise, which is always a special fun for both of us and especially for Papa when he is there. When you are finished you get the breakfast bottle (120 gr. of which is 80 gr. Milk, 40 gr. Water, some sugar and Soxlezucker) and then back to bed. Now you usually play for an hour and nap from 12-1. Now comes the noon meal, 250 gr. Vegetable, after which you punctually do your second big business into the potty. Then there is fruit juice (tomato, orange, apple, banana, whatever is available). After the meal we usually go for a drive. When the weather is fairly nice, also in the morning from 11 — 12:30 your grandmother Johanna takes over this task. At 4 o'clock there is some fruit and biscuit or the morning bottle, when there was fruit in the morning. Then comes playtime. At quarter to 7 you have a bath, again after preliminary exercises. Lately during the bath you engage in prodigious splashing so that every night the room is awash, but it is probably great fun for you to splash around with hands, feet and the entire body. Sometime I am actually afraid you might slip out of my grasp — that's how wild you sometimes get. After the bath your get 259 gr. Gruel, farina, or zwieback and then some fruit juice, apple or orange mostly. Now the day is over for you; you are really good and do not stir until the next morning. You are, as people say, a pretty child and advanced for your age. It goes without saying that we and the grandparents think so! But you are indeed an especially good kid. You have kept your deep-dark blue eyes, your hair has become lighter; it is dark blond and very fine and not yet very long, so that you often look like a little boy. You are now about 70 cm. long. During the 23d week, that is to say at 5 months, your original weight has doubled; now you weigh 15 1/2 pounds. But you are not at all fat, more filled out, but your flesh is firm, which I value greatly. You have particularly taken your father to heart, when he arrives you beam all over your face. But he really is too funny and plays all kinds of games with you. Grandmother Johanna, too, is always trying to cheer you up and Mutti, on the other hand, is there for the necessary but less pleasant tasks: washing of face, nose and ears, etc. You are less pleased with that than to do one-two exercises with you.

By December, I was holding the milk bottle in the morning and afternoon all by myself, which, as Lilli said, saved her a lot of time to pick up, prepare diapers and many other things. "You are indeed a competent child", she says.

On December 14, when I was 1/2 year old, I already had two teeth, the second since yesterday. And now Lilli becomes philosophical again:

When I was a little girl, I always secretly dreamed of having a little doll's town filled with little living people, a real Lilliput! Now my wish has come true because you are there. A small but very lively person. I never liked to play with dolls, you too will prefer to play with other things because I have the feeling that you are very much like me. Grow strong, my child, because then everything will be easy for you. Grow strong and remain true to yourself, even if you follow different paths than the crowd. Not everything that "is done" is right, but most people lack the courage to admit that to themselves and even more the courage to act accordingly. Grow strong and do always what you think is right even if others do not do it or turn away from you. Remain true to yourself, then you will not be disappointed, not confused about yourself. Be strong and honest and brave. That is my wish for you, my child.

Ruth and Helen Lorz "Tante"

On January 5, 1937, Lilli writes that they had left me alone, in good care, for 10 days with the Sister. I now eat porridge and vegetables with a spoon and drink alone juice from a cup. "You hold your afternoon coffee bottle, you drink generally coffee rather than milk and sleep in the big bed. In short, you are beginning to act like a grown-up person. And often you are already quite reasonable, you dear little creature."

The next entry, March 12, 1937, tells us that from the end of January until the middle of February I was left alone with the nanny. Lilli returned after an absence of almost 4 weeks and was pleasantly surprised at how much I had changed. On February 10 (Lilli's birthday) the nanny had written her that I was able to sit and play with everything that came into my hands. If I stood up at the edge of the playpen or bed, I remain standing there, holding on tightly.

A favorite game is "Bunny"; that is you kneel, and support yourself on the mattress with your hands and you swing your body forward and back. When you get put to bed at night and one thinks you would have to fall asleep immediately, you are so tired, one might find you five minutes later, when one enters the room in the dark, playing "bunny" instead of sleeping. A few days ago I woke up at night because I heard you squealing with delight; when I checked I found you playing "bunny" in a pitch dark room, and the bed looked like a battle field. It was 3 AM! In general your bed always looks unbelievable. Everything is contorted and trampled; sheets and undercovers removed, top sheet and cover pushed away, and you somewhere crosswise or at the other end of the bed in high spirits and if one starts talking with you, that is the climax, you are convulsed with giggles. Your hearing and your eyesight are very keen. When, while you are eating, the door behind you opens or somebody moves, you turn around immediately and stop eating; also when you hear or see the birds outside the window. You miss no sound, no motion, in your environment. That's why I have to ask energetically for quiet when you are eating or sitting potty.

Then follows a lengthy discussion about what a good eater I am — "eating everything that we eat — vegetables, mashed potatoes, noodles, spaghetti, rice pudding, brain, Bries, veal, chicken, sauerkraut, codfish, cherries — nothing pureed, only finely cut or squashed with a fork. Thus we have gotten over the most difficult time — now you must be trained in cleanliness. It will take a little time before we are there." Mrs. Lorz (the former nurse of Lilli's grandmother Caroline) now takes care of me four times a week in the afternoon from 2-7. Helen Lorz, being 1/8 Jewish and a Mischling (the word for Jews who were only partly Jewish) , eventually emigrated to the United States with us and lived with us for a while, then moved out to be a nanny in another household and returned to our house when Evy was born. By March I weighed 20 pounds and got a 3rd tooth, with the 4th ready to appear any day.

The other day I discovered, by the way, on your left hip a small but clearly visible birth mark! Your Papi has one in the same spot! Even in that you seem to resemble him, because in looks you are a regular Rahnle. Only the blue eyes seem to come from my side. And for personality — above all in temperament — you seem to have a great deal from me. Most important is that you turn into a complete human being; where you get it makes no difference then.

By April I was already walking gradually and often let go of one hand. On March 18th, the 4th tooth had come in, and I had been getting colds, maybe due to teething. Since the start of April I was, after all, not yet reliably toilet trained.

In any case you absolve everything punctually and quickly into the potty, which is a great convenience for all concerned. Daily you are getting more cheerful and more fresh and come up with new ideas every day. In the pram you neither want to sit or lie but only to stand and from this position, like a gladiator, you address all passers-by or look after them. The vocabulary is increasing and the volume of your voice is often astounding and would do credit to any adult. For the past two weeks you have been sleeping more; in the morning from 1-11/2 hours from 9:30 — 11. At noon after the meal (you are now eating at 12), 1 hour and usually in the afternoon after the walk from 4:30 — 6, when one has to wake you up frequently. (Note the strict regimen — eating, sleeping, taking a walk, and especially sitting on the potty — all are done by the clock.) But you are awake at 5 in the morning as before. You seem to develop into an early riser. So much the better! Now you little person are already 10 months old! How much longer and the first year has gone by and went so fast. Stay healthy and happy, we shall take care of the rest.

On April 16, 1937 I was vaccinated by Dr. Mailander, but without success, so it had to be repeated in the fall. By mid-April I weighed over 20 lbs. I slept less but ate with doubled pleasure and immense portions.

But you are not getting fat because, first of all, you have an excellent and punctual digestion and secondly you are much too lively to put on much fat, with all that, thank

God, not nervous. Below the freckle on your left hip (where your father has one also)
there appear two small dark spots. Unfortunately you are not yet clean. On some days
we have no diapers; on others you wet more frequently. I am trying now to keep you
dry during the night — make you go at 11 at night and get up at 5:30 for the same
purpose. You are not very wet then, but only once were you completely dry. I would
like to have you clean soon; that would be a great relief for both of us.

Almost a year elapsed before Lilli made another entry into the diary on March 13, 1938. It is certainly easy to see why the events during this period kept her from writing. The decision had been made to emigrate and the Rahn home at 129 Konigstrasse had been "sold". Reservations had been made to sail to the United States and the visa and ship tickets had been obtained. And then the Gestapo came and discovered some money in the home, leading to Alfred's arrest, trial and sentence of 14 months imprisonment, which began in February, 1938. Because the new owners of 129 Konigstrasse wanted to move in, Lilli and I, along with Helen Lorz, the governess, prepared to move to the Bierer home on Adolf Hitler Strasse (formerly Konigswasserstrasse) since the Bierer's were about to leave for Paris. This large home was very close to Hornschuchpromenade, where Lilli had grown up, and also within walking distance of the Rahn house on Konigstrasse. It is in this house that many photos of me were taken on the small porch with iron grillwork. When we first went to Germany I looked for this porch in the Rahn house, but there was no such porch. It was only when I went back to Germany a second time, with photos of myself on the porch that I was able to undeniably identify the grillwork. The street has also been regiven its former name, Konigswasserstrasse. Lilli and I lived there during the entire time Alfred was in prison until our emigration out of Germany to the U.S. in March, 1939.

There are six entries during the month of March 1938, and then the diary ends. Undoubtedly the whole effort of obtaining the visa for emigration and all the heartache, correspondence and travel to the American Consulate in Stuttgart more than occupied her time and energies during this period. At the same time life was becoming increasingly difficult and dangerous for Jews. New restrictive laws were being promulgated frequently and the urgency to leave was increasing. Lilli was in the midst of the voluminous correspondence with the consulate, Uncle Max (Alfred's brother), and others to obtain new visas, since theirs had expired during Alfred's prison term. But Lilli writes nothing in the diary of what is going on around her or in her personal life. She re-began entries in the diary by stating:

"For almost a year I have not touched this book. It is inexcusable, and only the special
circumstances and events and especially all the hardship which we had to experience
since the start of the year can explain this neglect, although they do not excuse it. I shall
try, little Ruth Marion, to fill in the most important events of this long time, whereby
much has to remain unsaid, because this past year meant for your development
immense progress.

Ruth with "Charlie Chaplin" wind-up toy

I got two more teeth last May and was;

...turning into a little lady, because for the first time you are dressed in a Dirndl dress, white with green and red flowers and a little white apron, and in it you looked entirely adorable. A great attraction is an old, gigantic zinc bowl with a diameter of at least 1 meter which Papi found somewhere in the cellar and which has now become, filled with water, an excellent wading pool. All summer long you spent most of the day, sometimes naked, sometimes very lightly dressed, in the playpen in the garden and your soft skin acquires such a brown tone that even now, in winter, people ask how I do that. They ask if I put you under a sun lamp? These vernal open air baths have probably hardened you, because you are thank God not affected by changes in the weather.

Lilli continues to recount my development over the past year.

Besides a small cold two or three times you never had anything. In the middle of June I went to Marienbad for four weeks, left you with Helen Lorz, and when I returned in the middle of July you came running toward me all on your own across the room. And now that you can climb and run you are discovering the world! Many things will soon be no longer safe from you and your already lively temperament is coming really into its own. You are plucky and reckless without being confused. Very soon now you are climbing the steep steps which lead to the garden pavilion. Wherever you can climb and exercise, you go. With other children, whom you always greet with joy and affection, you are always the initiator, but when the others, which happens most of the time, do not respond, you are not angry but you change to another toy. Lacking still is an understanding of the feelings of the other child. But you have great pleasure with animals. The Bow-wow, the Meow, which you can already name, always arouse great enthusiasm in you With great pleasure you stand at the house door, watch the people, sometimes even follow someone and when you are supposed to get away from the door

there is always a big scene. Starting in
the late fall, when running and jumping
is no longer difficult, talking begins to
make great progress. At first there are, to
be sure, single words which you notice,
imitate and use correctly. Already before
Xmas, when you were 1 1/2 you already
had a nice vocabulary, and after Xmas,
in January you started with sentences.
Now, in mid-March, you are already
clearly speaking in complicated sentences
or words. (here she gives examples of
seeing myself in the mirror or my thumb,
which is bound up so I don't suck). Into
the telephone, which you call "a Hallo"
you say "hallo" in tones which neither

Ruth

Papa nor I had ever heard before. The other day I used a hand shower on you. When
you saw that you said "a Hallo?" I said "no, this is a douche". (shower). Thereupon
you said "a tasche? (pocket) and put your hand into the pocket of your apron. So, quite
logical connections are being formed in your little head. In general, you usually know
quite well what it is you want, but you are easily guided and not stubborn. You are
friendly toward anybody and laugh and are never shy. But there is no reason for that,
as you have not had any bad experiences with strangers. Since mid-November, when
Mr. Held showed you pencil and paper, these play an important role. With those you
can keep yourself busy longer than with any other toy. Of course you draw with your
left hand, as you do other things, because you are now a little southpaw. With the
right you are more clumsy in everything and always try to take everything into your
left hand. If one says "draw a ball", you draw a nice, big, round circle — right handed
the result is always a small, cramped, dot-like something. You are happy when you
are allowed to use a blunt needle with some string in it and a piece of cloth and poke
around in it, but everything with the left.

For the past four weeks now you have been distinguishing between "one" and "two"
and "many" and you are very exact with that (examples given). Not only intellectually
have you grown prodigiously during the last four months but also physically. Size 3
shoe is going to be too small for you soon and your legs are long and firm. In general
you are not fat but strong and sturdy. You eat as much as an adult and quickly and
well. You never gave us any trouble about eating . We are continually surprised what
you can put in this little belly. Your behavior, your looks (especially because of the
slowly growing hair) are rather boyish. You are immensely mobile, lively, and agile.
Yet, at times, you can be thoughtful and girlish, but the liveliness predominates.

Often you talk about Pappi, whom you have not seen in almost 3 months and whom you will not see in almost a year. Every night and every morning you ask for his picture, which hangs in every room, and you give him a long "russie" (kiss). This love for your Pappi is all the more touching because in the case of others, no matter how much you loved them when they were around, like "Mami Anna", you never asked for them when they were gone.

In the March 14, 1938 entry there is a long discussion about thumb sucking.

"Because lately you suck your thumb (of the left hand and especially since you fall asleep that way) —

Mrs. Lorz puts cotton batten around your thumb every night and the entire hand was wrapped in a little cloth. The thumb goes beddy-by and you are quite agreeable about that, think it is entirely in order, so much in order than when the cloth came loose recently a couple of times you cried and called loudly "thumb, thumb" until somebody came to put the thumb back into its bed. Since I then started with the thumb of the right hand, it is made "pfui" (distasteful) by being painted with Vermouth, which is not to my liking.

She explains the thumb-sucking is due to toothache and it usually coincides with increased uncleanliness, restlessness and reduced need for sleep.

The entry on March 26, 1938 indicates that is the day we moved to the Bierer house. For me it was evidently a festive day since there was a lot of confusion and men around. I got used to the new home very quickly — racing up and down the stairs. Evidently the Bierers were still there, although they were about to leave for Paris, because Uncle Ernest, Emma's husband, is referred to as the landlord and becomes the "hauserr" (house husband) for me. Occasionally I call out the window for Meier, Lilli's great uncle, who lived across the grassy divide on Horschuchpromenade. From the window I can see the street car and cars go by, shouting out to all. Orderliness is inherited from Ami Johanna (Alfred's mother). I have a repertoire of songs and the newest word is "schmeiss" (throwing smash) accompanied by purposely throwing a pillow from the pram, or a beer bottle (yes, that's the word used), after looking at one of them searchingly, and then throwing it with élan and laughter. "To blame for this delightful game" is Ami Ida, who probably laughed the first time it happened. The only game that is not tolerated is "a Gucku", which means you take a comb or any other sharp instrument and with it comb the hair of your victim. That quickly degenerates into a wild hair-plucking and head-hitting. Since Ami Ida experienced it once, tolerant as she usually is, she does not tolerate this game any longer. She fears, in light of your energy, for her sparse hair growth. But, she says, you obviously enjoy this game.

Lilli is amazed at how well I articulate words at 1 year, 9 1/2 months.

And here the diary ends. The events of 1938 undoubtedly consumed her energies, and perhaps even diminished her maternal instincts.

What do we make of all this? I am amazed at the regimen which was imposed for eating, sleeping and toilet training. I now know why there are so many photos of me sitting on the potty. Lilli was never, in my recollection, an emotional, cuddly mother — maybe during my first year of life she was more that way than in later years. She clearly loved having a child, and took great pleasure in dressing me in a dirndl and in my learning capabilities. I was also put outside a great deal — the thought being that the fresh air, from the first week of life, was wholesome and healthy. There is little introspection about how she felt about things, and except for the move and the mention that I hadn't seen Papi for three months and wouldn't see him again for a year, there is nothing about what is going on in her life or outside the home. But maybe a baby diary wasn't the place for these kinds of thoughts, concerns and musings.

RUTH

4
ALFRED

My father, Alfred Hermann Rahn, was born on January 28, 1901 into a prominent, relatively wealthy family in Fürth as the second of three boys. It must have been a great joy to his parents to give birth to this healthy, handsome and normal baby boy as four years earlier James, their eldest child, had been born hydrocephalic and was already not developing normally. As a result, Alfred became the "golden boy" of the family and all efforts and hopes were poured into him from a very young age. His brother, Max, five years his junior, was also a healthy baby boy, but he was spared the pressure of the aspirations and expectations that were put onto Alfred.

Alfred Hermann Rahn

Parents

Alfred's father, Sidney Rahn, (1866-1930) was actually born in England, the eldest son of Karoline Farrnbacher Rahn (1837-1908) and James Rahn (1829-1867). As a young couple, Sidney's parents had emigrated to England for business reasons, and on settling into a life of a Brit

Sidney Rahn

his father changed his name from Johan Kahn (too German and too Jewish!) to James Rahn. When she was pregnant with her second son, Karoline's husband, James, died. Alone in England after the birth of her second son, whom she named James after his deceased father, Karoline moved back to Fürth to be near her family and there she and her children, Sidney and James, were cared for by her family, the Farrnbacher family. Sidney ultimately became the president of M.S. Farrnbacher, his mother's family's metalworks firm, and his brother James became a physician. Sidney and Johanna Goldmann, my

Karoline Farrnbacher Rahn and grandsons
James, Alfred and Max, sons of Sidney and
Johanna Rahn

129 Konigstrasse

grandmother who was from Mannheim, wed on April 12, 1896 and lived upstairs from the business, located at 129 Konigstrasse in Fürth. It is there that Alfred and his brothers were born and it is also there that I was born.

The house at 129 Konigstrasse, situated on a main thoroughfare of Fürth, is now in a historical landmark district. It consists of four stories and a lower level. The street floor and the lower level was where the family metal business was located. The family business dealt in all kinds of metal products used by contractors, architects and the like.

When Alfred and Lilli married on July 3, 1933, his mother (my grandmother), Johanna, moved to the third floor while Alfred and Lilli, and then I, lived on the second floor. The maids lived on the top floor. I have been back to this house now several times, and will describe it more fully in the section entitled "Visits to Germany".

Both Sidney and his brother James died on the same day, September 13, 1930, neither being aware of the death of the other. September 13 was thus always an ominous day in our family. I never knew either of my grandfathers.

My grandmother Johanna was an only child and her father also died when she was very young. It is interesting to note that both she and her husband, Sidney Rahn, were raised by single mothers. After Sidney died in 1930 she shared ownership of the family business with Alfred, her son. She left Germany in January 1938, living for a while in the Excelsior Hotel in Milan, Italy, before emigrating to New York, where she came before we did. After we arrived, she moved from New York to Denver with our family, living first with us and then in an apartment in a family home near other German refugees. She was small, always immaculately coiffed, and kept everything, including my clothes and our silverware drawers, in perfect order. She also loved to bake, and always made those wonderful crescent-shaped pecan cookies, rolled in powdered sugar, for various occasions and especially when I came home from college. I always think of her when I make or eat those cookies. She also had what we now know as osteoporosis. She experienced the joy of knowing my daughter Karen, but unfortunately died peacefully in 1965, before Rachel was born. Rachel's middle name, Joanna, was given in her memory. She had been a widow for 35 years. Only at the very end of her life was she living in a nursing home and I recall how difficult and painful it was for Alfred to visit his mother there.

Let me first discuss a bit about Alfred's two brothers, James and Max, and then diverge into a brief history of the family firm, M.S. Farrnbacher before going on about Alfred's life.

James

My great uncle, James, was the oldest child of Johanna and Sidney, and Alfred's older brother. He was born on January 5, 1897 and was clearly "not right" from the beginning. He was diagnosed as hydrocephalic, and ultimately with schizophrenia. The social milieu of the day created an enormous stigma to have such a child, and I suspect this was felt by the entire family. Additionally, physicians of that time recommended institutionalization for such children. It must have taken much courage for Johanna, despite the views of the community, to keep him at home and also to have another child 4 years later (Alfred), and then another one 6 years after that

James Rahn

(Max). Sidney made efforts to include James in the family business, but James' limitations made his usefulness negligible and his condition worsened. However, he did live at home until February 3, 1927, when he was 30 years old. By then it appears from his medical records that it was impossible to control him, and Johanna had him institutionalized nearby in the town of Erlangen. Alfred was extremely fond of his older brother, and I believe never really forgave his mother for institutionalizing him.

The existence of James Rahn was one of the family secrets. We (Evy and I) didn't even know he had existed until we were going off to college. In a "whispered" tone and behind closed doors our mother told us that "daddy had an older brother". Until that moment each of us had thought there were only two Rahn "boys" — our father and his younger brother Max. Mother told us about James' medical problems and about her family's concerns about her marriage to our father, fearing they would produce defective children. She told us James had died (been murdered) during the war and that no one in the family ever talked about him. And most importantly, she insisted that James remain a family secret. We were never to discuss his existence with anyone, and particularly not with our father. Evy, who went to social work graduate school in 1966 and learned more about the human mind and emotions, felt compelled to discuss James with daddy. As she described it:

> *Gingerly, when home on a school break, I carefully closed the door to our den, asking him if we could talk about a most sensitive subject. Cautiously and bravely, I told him I knew about James and that I had loads of questions. He was open, non-defensive, and very willing to discuss him. The spell had been broken and, for me, that was a great relief. Three years later when my first husband had passed his boards for his Ph.D., to congratulate him, my father sent him a gold watch — each of the Rahn's had received an engraved gold watch for their respective Bar Mitzvot — and daddy had*

sent Bill the one with JR on it for James Rahn. James, after 50 years, had come out of the closet.

Lilli (and apparently also Alfred) thought it was extremely important to keep the existence of James a secret until Evy and I were "old enough" to absorb this piece of family history. I was first married in December, 1957, and although I perhaps had some knowledge of James at this time, I do not recall having any serious discussions about him, and never saw the folder of his medical treatment. This also was among the many boxes of documents we had. His medical history was kept in a manila envelopes entitled, in large capital letters written by Lilli, "CONFIDENTIAL PERSONAL". At this time, in March 1958, I was married and a senior in college.

Below, again in large capital letters was written: MEDICAL HISTORY RAHN', and below that:

May only be opened and read by the following persons:

Alfred H. Rahn
Johanna Rahn
Ida Beckman
Max Rahn
Maria Rahn
Ruth Marion Rahn — Budd
Matthew Budd
Evelyn Rahn (if over 18 years of age)
Signed: Lilli Rahn, Denver, Colorado 3/14/58

James was treated by his uncle, Dr. James Rahn (his father Sydney's brother) who kept a detailed medical diary of his case history, beginning from the date of his birth and ending with the last entry on March 24, 1929, when James was 32. This history consists of 5 single-spaced typewritten pages. In the early years Dr. James Rahn saw him and made entries into his diary monthly, and then bi-monthly. The following comments are taken from this diary.

From the earliest moment, James's eyes didn't seem to focus; he had an enlarged head, no appetite, retarded mental development, poor physical development, etc. There is a big gap from 1905-1918, where Dr. Rahn describes that he developed well physically, and passed 8 years of elementary school. After school he entered his father's business and did mechanical work. At age 19-20 he was called up several times by the military, but as Dr. Rahn attested, he had "congenital intellectual retardation", and was deferred. By 1926, according to the family, he became very mean and wasn't able to do anything constructive in the office. He could be used for clerical work and, as Dr. Rahn writes, he seemed again to be under the influence of some woman. The entry at the end of November 1926 indicates that he had gonorrhea. In November 1926 his behavior became so difficult that it became impossible to leave him at home and he was taken to the hospital in Nuremberg. When Dr. Rahn visited him on December 1, 1926 he hardly took notice and said "I am in love", "Who is it?" Dr. Rahn asked. "A Miss Hoffman", he responded; then also "I am insane". In February 1927 he was institutionalized and had to be taken to the supervised ward and fed by tube. Over the next couple of years he became increasingly aggressive, unclean and had to be placed in a special cell. Dr. Rahn noted he was "unapproachable, no mental activity."

James's condition was of enormous concern to the Bechmann family when Lilli's relationship with Alfred in the late 1920's became serious and she contemplated marriage. It was also of great concern to Alfred and he feared having children. What is amazing to me is that they all, independently of one another, sought advice from professionals, as evidenced by the following letters.

On September 26, 1931 Lilli received a letter from Prof. Friedlaender from Freiberg who wrote to "Miss Lilli Bechmann, Nuremberg". It appears she wrote him about her two basic concerns; namely, their intellectual differences and the possibility of hereditary consequences of James' condition. It is curious that he writes to Lilli in Nuremberg c/o Herrn Rat Loeffler. Lilli's aunt, Carola, (her father's sister) married a man by the name of Loeffler, who was an attorney and "Rat" stands for attorney. It appears Lilli directed a response to her inquiry to go to Carola rather than to her so her parents couldn't see it. Prof. Friedlaender refers to the position of Lilli's father, who, from all evidence we have, was strongly against this marriage. The letter was as follows:

Dear Miss Bechmann,

Many years ago I took place in a prize contest about the question: "Who should one marry?" Among more than 10 entries I received first prize. Thus I was supposed to be among the first experts in this field; but, in my work I pointed out that the best advice had only theoretical value because it was asked for too late, that is, at the time when the decision has practically been made.

You will counter: just because I have not made a decision, I ask for advice.

But may a psychologically oriented and perhaps experienced man dare play fate? You have known the man in question for three years, at times you wrote him daily, you attribute shining qualities to him and offer only two reservations. One concerns the differing intellectual orientation, the other hereditary events in his family.

Concerning the former, entering a marriage would most probably mean the end of your studies. The question whether you could tolerate a certain descent from your "intellectual heights" in the long run depends entirely on your judgment. I should assume that he understands your intellectual requirements even if he does not have them to the same degree, and that he will give you the freedom in the marriage to satisfy these needs, just as it would be your task to participate in his business matters in a spirit of partnership, even if you do not have the same understanding for it that he does.

The second reservation, the health question, has to be taken more seriously perhaps. In the so-called cultured countries there are practically no untainted families and especially not in Jewish families. Our knowledge of eugenics and hereditary consequences are by no means so solidly founded that we should have the right to say in a case like yours that marriage is advised or is definitely ill-advised. In no case would I, generally speaking, advise a marriage if from the start children are renounced, who in the truest sense of the word are the blessing and the glue of the marriage.

The last lines of your letter betray such a strong bond with this man that even this circumstance of giving a responsible advice does not seem indicated. Not to be ignored is the position of your father. To be sure, I know him too little to permit myself a judgment about his attitude. In similar cases one advises a one-year period of separation and cessation of any written communication. In your case, it is probably useless to propose that, since you have apparently weathered a sufficiently long trial period.

Thus, in conclusion, I can only recommend: consider with your dear friend if upon entering marriage the important intellectual freedom will be maintained, which is so important to you, and if he can overcome his anxiety concerning the question of progeny. A union which renounces this should be advised against by the physician for health reasons which concern first of all the woman. Should you have the opportunity to come to Freiburg for a consultation, some things might perhaps be clarified which is impossible in writing.

I really regret not to be able to show you a definite path and hope that your goal-directed personality and womanly instinct, which I value higher than much often imagined knowledge, will be able to shine light into the still existing darkness.

I remain with cordial greetings your S.S./Friedlaender, called "Vaeterlein".

The term "Vaeterlein" may have been some kind of term of close friendship, indicating that Mr. Friedlaender was close to Lilli. She may have known him during her studies in Freiburg.

Alfred too expressed his concerns, and wrote to the Director of the Middle-Franconia Nursing Home in Erlangen, where James was institutionalized. On March 24, 1932 he received the following reply:

Esteemed Mr. Rahn!

Your brother is suffering from schizophrenia on the basis of a hereditary defect condition. The probable prognosis is that there will be a gradual weakening of the intellectual abilities which might advance to the highest degree of imbecility, but which might also stop at any step. The danger for you to suffer from schizophrenia can be estimated to be 4-5%, that is, of 100 siblings of a schizophrenic, experience shows about 4-5 become sick.

Presuming that there are no Fürther cases of schizophrenia in ascending lines of your relatives I believe that you need not necessarily avoid a marriage with a healthy woman.

Sincerely, Dr. Kolb

Included — one bill

Lilli's father, Hugo, was obviously very concerned and contacted Dr. Med. Steckelmacher, a neurologist in Nuremberg. On October 13, 1932, Dr. Steckelmacher wrote to Hugo as follows and also enclosed a letter he had requested from a colleague of his in Munich:

Most Esteemed Kommerzienrat!

I permit myself to send you the medical opinion of Professor Rudin of the Research Institute concerning your question. You see from it that one has to count on an increased risk in the case of Mr. R. for his children, a risk that is almost twice that in the average population. About your daughter, Prof. Rudin wrote, like about your relatives, that they are completely healthy; he did not know that I too had researched into the side lines; but we can add that ourselves. According to your information there are only mentally healthy people in your own family as well as that in that of your wife. Mr. R. is, according to the description by Dr. Bluth, quite inconspicuous and worldly. I am of course ready to get to know Mr. R. in this connection. Your daughter gave the impression of a healthy person who knows what she wants.

Whatever Fürther research into the families may produce, the statement of Dr. Rudin remains, that one cannot clearly approve a marriage into a tainted family. On the one side there exists a definitely tainted family, on the other side one knows, to be sure that in one's own family clearly mental disturbances did not exist; but who knows his forebears so well that he can exclude with certainty the existence of difficult and odd characters especially in the less known side lines.

The last decision will remain, under such circumstances, with your daughter who will be able, with the help of the risk numbers to form a picture about what is involved. Parents, after all, can only make clear what their life experiences have taught them. I shall gladly be at your disposal in the future, and remain, with best regards, your humble Dr. Steckelmacher.

Professor Rudin of the Geneological Department of the German Research Institution for Psychiatry (Kaiser Wilhelm-Institute) in Munich wrote to Dr. med. Steckelmacher in Nuremberg on April 11, 1932 as follows:

Esteemed Colleague,

I am answering your friendly letter of the 8th of this month as follows; According to our researches, the incidence probability for schizophrenia in the average population is approximately 0.85%. The corresponding disease probability among children is approximately ten times as much, that is approximately 9%. Fürther it is to be assumed that even healthy children are schizophrenic carriers, that is they all can pass on the trait to their progeny. And by adding this trait to the one which this progeny has inherited from his other parent, this can lead to an overt disease in this progeny. I am therefore of the opinion that schizophrenics must not propagate under any circumstances.

According to your description, schizophrenia occurred at home in the family of the presumptive couple. He himself is healthy but is a sibling of a schizophrenic. The disease possibility for siblings of schizophrenics is in general 5%, which is about six times that of the general population. To be sure, the gentleman in question has already passed the dangerous period to a large extent. According to your description he seems to have a character which (insofar one can draw such conclusions based on personality alone) does not lead to the supposition that he himself might become schizophrenic. The chances in his case would be considerably under 5%. But should he get ill nevertheless the chances of disease for his possible children would be as indicated above.

If he stays healthy, the probabilities for his children are the same as those for the nephews and nieces of the schizophrenics. It is generally 1.4%, which is not quite twice the number as for the average population. Therefore, I would not necessarily dissuade every sibling of a schizophrenic from propagating. However, we have found that the constitution of the children of siblings of schizophrenics depends to a large degree on the constitution of these siblings, as well as the marital partner of such a sibling. If such marital partners both are apparently quite inconspicuous, cheerful, open people, then the possibility of disease for the children is considerably smaller than 1.4%, but if they are, even if not mentally ill, but in their character conspicuous, then the disease possibilities are higher. It is highest if both parents show "Schizoid" characteristic, odd behavior.

According to your description such characteristics don't seem to be present in the marriage candidates. To be sure, the description is so short that you have to determine yourself to what degree I am right in my suppositions. You did not write to me about the personality of the young lady; she would have to be counted as an important factor in the equation. It would also be significant what is known about the uncles and aunts and other indirect relatives of the young lady. You only mention her direct forebears. Should there be no taint on the part of the young lady and should both candidates, in your opinion, have the above-mentioned psychic characteristics a marriage should not necessarily be discouraged. On the other hand such a marriage can also not be encouraged. There is, no doubt, an increased risk, and the striving of any healthy person should be to marry a healthy person from a healthy family.

I hope these brief clues are of some value. A regular medical judgment cannot be given based on the brief descriptions. I also do not expect a fee.

With collegiate esteem, Prof. Rudin

Also in our materials is a handwritten note, in Lilli's handwriting, referring to an article in the May, 1934 issue of "Volk Und Rasse" (which can be loosely translated as "People and Breeding") and she copied the following chart:

Children of Schizophrenics 10 times more endangered
Nephews and Nieces: 1.7%
Cousins: 1.8%
Grandchildren: 2.4%
Siblings: 7.5%

Lilli and Alfred married on July 3, 1933. These inquiries, from Lilli, Alfred and Hugo certainly evidence the anxiety that surrounded Lilli and Alfred's relationship and their upcoming marriage. When I was born healthy, it must have been an enormous relief for all concerned.

James continued to reside in the Sanatorium and Nursing Home in Erlangen from February 3, 1927 until September 16, 1940 when he was physically removed from the sanitarium, deported and murdered by the German Nazis the following year. There is a note in the year 1929 in the papers left by the last Erlangen religious teacher, prayer reciter and Shochet, Justin Fraenkel, about the patients of this institution who were under his spiritual care, including James Thomas Rahn. On September 16, 1940 he, along with 20 other Jewish patients were "removed" from the Sanatorium. James is listed in the Fürth Gedenkbook entitled In Memory of Those who the Nazis Murdered — Jews of Fürth, 1933-45. The entry in this book really says it all, particularly the cause of death:

In this book, on page 327, James' photo appears along with the following information:

Family name: Rahn

First name: James Thomas

Birthdate: January 5, 1897

Birthplace: Fürth

Father: Sidney, NF

Mother: Johanna "Hannchen" Goldmann

Familienname:	**Rahn**	ראן
Vornamen:	**James Thomas**	ז'מס תומס
Geburtsdatum:	05.01.1897	
Geburtsort:	Fürth	
Vater:	Sidney, NF	סידני
Mutter:	Johanna "Hannchen" Goldmann	יוהנה
Ehepartner:	ledig	
Wohnung:	Königstr.129; Hupfla ER '27	
Deport. datum:	16.09.1940	
Deport. ort:	Eglfing Haar	
gestorben:	1941	
Sterbeort:	Chelm II	
Todesursache:	"Euthanasie"	

Lebenslauf: James Rahn wurde am 3.2.1927 in die Heil- und Pflegeanstalt Erlangen aufgenommen. "My father had an older brother who was born hydrocephalic, institutionalized, and killed by the Nazis after they came to power" schreibt Ruth Budd, Tochter von Alfred Rahn. James' Geburts-Eintrag ist beigeschrieben "#4233/41 Chelm II". Der Mutter und den beiden Brüdern Max (geb.1.8.1906) und Alfred mit Familie gelang die Emigration in die Vereinigten Staaten.

Quellen: JK+Hupfla+Geb+Ge+NF.VIII/240; Ruth Budd+Evy Davis

Spouse: unmarried

Address: Königstr. 129; Hupfla ER '27

Date of Deportation: September 16, 1940

Place of Deportation: Eglfing Haar

Date of Death: 1941

Place of Death: Chelm II

Cause of Death: "Euthanasia"

He was taken from the Erlangen Nursing Home and "removed" to another Nursing Home near Munich and then deported to Chelm, near Lublin, Poland, where he was murdered.

James is also listed with the same data in the Erlangen Memory Book for Victims of the Shoah with the same data, including his photograph.

It is somewhat ironic that despite the long and distinguished history of the Bechmann and Rahn families in Fürth, no physical trace remains in that city of the accomplishments and contributions of those families to their community. James' name, however, is memorialized in stone on the interior marble wall of the New Jewish Cemetery where all names of those from Fürth who were murdered by the Nazis are engraved.

In the end, of course, all this information did not prevent Alfred and Lilli from marrying on July 3, 1933. Alfred had been worried about having children and passing James' illness on to his progeny. He was 35 when I was born in 1936, which was somewhat late to become a father in those days.

Let us now turn back to Max, Alfred's younger brother, and his wife, Maria.

Max and Maria

My uncle Max, the youngest son of Johanna and Sidney, was born August 1, 1906. Being the youngest, he wasn't going to inherit the family business. He also attended the Heinrich Schliemann Gymnasium down the street from the family home on Konigstrasse. In 1926, when he was 20 years old, he decided to emigrate to the United States with his friend, Richard Kunreuther. They came to New York, and Richard stayed in New York, while shortly thereafter Max got a job with the General Cigar Company, which sent him to Puerto Rico to become a tobacco examiner and buyer. He met his wife, Maria Pintado, in Puerto Rico; they married and lived there until 1950 when Max got another job in the tobacco business, in Havana, Cuba. Although they had supported the revolt against Batista, the new regime in Cuba run by Fidel Castro turned against

Max Rahn

many people, particularly foreigners, and they left in the fall of 1960 with only their suitcases and the clothes on their backs and moved to New York City. Max had always kept his wealth invested in the United States and so they were stable financially. Initially he thought he might resume work in New York but when he could not find anything at his level in the tobacco industry he decided to retire. In 1971 Max and Maria returned to Puerto Rico where they lived the final years of their lives. Max died in September 1977, and Maria in July 1991. They never had any children, as Maria was unable to have children. They came to Denver every couple of years to visit, not only to see his brother, but mostly Johanna, his mother, who lived in Denver until her death in 1965. I remember Max well. He had a portly frame and always wore a white shirt with a level bottom outside his pants. This was quite a contrast to Alfred who dressed for work each day in a shirt and tie, sporting a pearl stickpin in his tie. Alfred dressed this way even though he worked alone in his office.

Maria was one of six children who grew up in Ponce, Puerto Rico. In High School she had a teacher who had gone to Smith College and recognized Maria's intelligence and abilities. She encouraged Maria to go to Smith, which she did. She graduated in 1928, returned to San Juan briefly to begin a social work career. After a few years of working there (during which time

Maria Pintado Rahn

she met Max), she went to Chicago where she obtained her Masters in Social Work from the University of Chicago after which she returned to Puerto Rico to teach social work at the University of Puerto Rico. She eventually became the Dean of School of Social Work at the University of Puerto Rico and extremely well known in her field. Maria and Max lived a good life in San Juan. They were wealthy and moved in the upper echelons of society. They were good friends with Rex Tugwell, the American governor there. Maria was not happy about moving to Cuba where she could not find meaningful employment. When they moved to New York City, she taught at the New School for Social Work and was "discovered" by New York Mayor Lindsay, who gave her a position of training social workers who would work with Puerto Ricans. She was, however, very happy when they moved back to Puerto Rico in the early 1970's.

Maria's roommate at Smith College was Kay Burrage, who lived in a beautiful home on the water in Manchester-by-the Sea. Whenever Maria and Max came to Boston, she wanted to visit Kay. The last time they were in Boston, in 1977, we were invited for lunch at Kay's, and they left the following day to return to Puerto Rico, stopping in Washington, DC on the way where they had other friends. Max died suddenly in Washington, and per his instructions, his body was given to the hospital there. A curious anecdote just to show how small the world is. My good friend, Marie-Claire Mermod, with whose family I had lived when I studied in Geneva 1956-57, had gotten divorced and remarried Michel Jeannet, a physician. Shortly after her remarriage, Michel, who had done some of his medical training in Boston, came to Boston for a meeting and we invited him to dinner. He said the next day he was going to Manchester to visit the owner of the boathouse where he and several other doctors, all of whom loved to sail, had lived during their training. And yes, you guessed it — the boathouse was owned by Kay Burrage and that's who he was planning to visit. Small world! Maria continued to live in Puerto Rico until she died in 1991.

Education

Alfred attended Elementary School from 1907-1911 and the Heinrich Schliemann Gymnasium from 1911 to 1917. The way we learned, originally, that this was Alfred's gymnasium is really a funny story. When Evy and I were in Fürth in 1996, we were walking down Königstrasse toward #126, my birthplace, and we saw a large school called the Heinrich Schliemann Gymnasium (named after the German archeologist who discovered Troy, Mycenae and Tiryns), still operating as a school. Could it be, we wondered, that this was Alfred's school? It wasn't far away and on the same side of the busy street as his home. We walked inside and upstairs to the office.

Alfred RAHN,

CURRICULUM VITAE.

Personal status:

Name: RAHN, Alfred
Adress: 1565 Franklin Street, c/o Mr.P.W.Rasmussen, Denver,Colo.
Date of birth: January 28th, 1901
Place of birth: Fuerth/Bavaria, Germany
Nationality: German - applied for first papers
Marital status: married
Children: one girl, 3 years old.

Education:

1907-1911: Elementary School, Fuerth, Bavaria.
1911-1917: Gymnasium,   "   "
1917-1919: Apprenticeship, Darmstaedter & Nationalbank, Nuremberg.
1919-1920: Commercial High School, Munich.
           Typewriting, automobile driving.

Experience:

1920-1923: In 1920 I entered the iron and steel business of
           L.J.Ettlinger, Karlsruhe/Baden, where I acquired
           a thorough knowledge of the iron line. After two
           years I left this firm in order to enlarge my
           knowledge and worked in sheet metal department of
           Coutinho, Caro & Co, Hamburg, in 1923.
           (Certificates of these two firms are enclosed).

1924:   In this year I entered my father's wholesale iron
           and metal business M.S.Farrnbacher, Fuerth/Bavaria,
           which has been in the hands of my family for about
           140 years. The business consisted in distributing
           the below mentioned materials, i.e. I bought the
           goods from the mills and sold them to the manufac-
           turers. I had a warehouse from which I supplied my
           customers and besides that I delivered carloads from
           the mills directly.

           I especially sold iron bars, band iron, hot rolled
           sheets, cold rolled sheets, plates, galvanized sheets,
           tin plate, zinc sheets, copper sheets, brass sheets,
           aluminum sheets, wire, nails, screws and all kinds
           of metals as lead, tin, zinc, copper.

           Besides I have been the representative of the most
           important German aluminum concern (Aluminium Walz-
           werke Singen, Singen/Hohentwiel).

1927:   My father retired and I became the sole manager
           of our firm. A good deal of my work consisted in
           visiting my customers and the steadily growing
           tendency of my business during the last years
           in spite of the continually increasing anti-jewish
           propaganda has been due to the good personal
           contacts I had created with my customers.

1937:   It was only because of the anti-jewish laws that
           I had to sell my business to a Christian steel-
           concern.

1939:   I arrived in this country in April 1939.

References:

Mr.B.G.Meyer, President, General Cigar Co, 119 West 40th Street,
                                                      New York, N.Y.
Mr.L.I.Estrin, Vice President, Irving Trust Company, 1 Wall Street,
                                                      New York, N.Y.
Mr.N.Henry Beckman, Alms Hotel, Cincinnati, Ohio.

Alfred Hermann Rahn

It had been raining so we were looking rather bedraggled with our raincoats and umbrellas in hand. Several women were behind the desk in the office. We introduced ourselves, and said that we were just wondering if perhaps this was the school where our father went to school. "When was he here?" we were asked. We really didn't know but said he was born in 1901. We were told to wait a moment while one of the women literally reached over and pulled out a huge tome and began thumbing through it. "I see here a Max Rahn", she said. "Oh", we said gleefully, "that's our uncle". Max was five years younger than Alfred. And then she found the registration sheets for Alfred. We read his records and copied pages of his attendance at this school. We walked through the halls of the school thinking about the little boy who would now be in his 90's, taking his schoolbag and walking down Konigstrasse, not having to cross any busy streets to get to his school where he would study. When we asked why the books of over 80 years ago were so readily accessible and not on some back basement shelf, she told us that on June 22, 1996 they would be celebrating the school's one hundredth anniversary and they were in the process of putting together lots of names of graduates and other people who would be interested in this event.

In 1939, as soon as we arrived in the United States, Alfred prepared a Curriculum Vitae which he used to obtain employment. The address he used was our very first address in Denver, so this document was prepared about August, 1939.

Although Alfred's family was not particularly religious, he had a Bar Mitzvah. We know that because he received a beautiful initialed gold pocket watch, which I still have.

M.S. Farrnbacher

Let me now turn to the history of M.S Farrnbacher, the Rahn family business. This may not be the most interesting reading, but since we have the underlying documents I felt it was necessary to preserve this history in this memoir. It also verifies how well established and respected the Rahn family was in Fürth.

The firm of M.S. Farrnbacher was the one Alfred worked in all his adult life. In general, it was a firm that dealt with iron and metal products. Along with researching the genealogy of various family members, Lilli also researched the history of this firm and was able to trace it, through the documents, back to 1774. In that year, Seligmann Farrnbacher was born, and he was the first member of the Farrnbacher family to devote himself to the iron and metal business.

Seligman's son, Moses, lived from 1804-1889. It is his large portrait which I have hanging on the second floor in my Lexington home. The oldest business letter we have dates from 1818 which is a letter from a Mr. Tscherpel of Kempted in Allgaeu to Seligmann Farrnbacher concerning several sheet metal and metal shipments. In 1828 Moses received his official concession as metal merchant, and in 1829, Moses received his official right to do business with the firm. In 1830 Moses became an associate in the firm of his father. One of the large documents I framed years ago is a passport issued to Moses in 1825 from the "Police of the Kingdom". Down the left side of this document is a column entitled "Passport for Abroad", containing a description of Moses. This clearly would be necessary before we had passport photos. Moses was described as being 21 years old, medium height, black-brown hair, wide forehead, black eyebrows, gray eyes, oval chin and face, healthy complexion and without identifying marks. Then he signed it, and below his signature is written: "In the county seats the passport has to be attested to by the Royal Government and the owner has to present himself there for this purpose". The main body of this passport, headed by the words "Police of the Kingdom", reads as follows:

> *The Royal Commissary of the City of Fürth asks, with the promise of complete reciprocity all military and non-military authorities of foreign states, to permit unhampered passage to the metal dealer's son, Moses Farrnbacher, born and living in Fürth, who travels in business matters of his father's via Augsberg, Munich to Salzberg and farther on, and to grant him also if needed protection and assistance. The present passport is valid for 1 year. Thus written Fürth. The 26th of July, 1825.*

In 1835, when Moses was 31 years old, his father transferred the firm to him pursuant to a written contract. Three years later, in 1838, Moses purchased a house at 68 Old Gruene Markt in Fürth as his living quarters and place of business. We have the original purchase contract. In 1862 Moses was entered into the official Commerce Register of the city.

In 1866 Moses purchased the property at 127-131 Konigstrasse. The genealogy here is that Moses Farrnbacher is the father of Karoline (1837-1906), whose marriage to James Rahn produced James and Sidney Rahn. Sidney was Alfred's father. Moses is thus Alfred's great grandfather. This is the house where Alfred was born in 1901 and where Ruth was born in 1936. The business was on the ground floor and the living quarters were above.

Moses had 6 children, including Hermann and Karoline. Karoline was named after Moses' mother. In 1872 Hermann Farrnbacher, Moses' son, took over as sole owner of the firm and again, we have the official contract for this change of ownership. I hadn't realized, until I looked at this history of the firm, that Alfred's middle name, Hermann, was undoubtedly named after Hermann Farrnbacher, his great-uncle. It appears that Hermann married but had no children. Moses died in 1889. In the meantime, Karoline had married James Rahn, a physician and they moved to England. They had one son, Sidney, who was born in England and shortly thereafter, when Karoline was pregnant with her second child, her husband died. She returned to Germany to give birth to her second son, named James, who also became a physician. In 1895 Sidney

Rahn joined the firm as an associate of his uncle Hermann and in 1908 Sidney became the sole owner. The official printed announcement, dated January 9, 1908, states:

We herewith have the honor to inform you that our Mr. Hermann Farrnbacher leaves our firm after 36 years as active Senior Director of the firm on January 31, 1908 in order to retire to private life. On this day the business transfers all its active and passive activities under the name of the previous firm to the sole ownership of Mr. Sidney Rahn who has been an associate of the firm since July 1, 1895. We recommend ourselves to you, most respectfully, M.S. Farrnbacher.

  Hermann died in 1912.

Among the documents we have are what appears to be periodic letters attesting to the solvency and credit-worthiness of the firm. For example, we have such a document from 1901 which describes that M.S. Farrnbacher dealt in sheet metal wares, raw metals, and mine and foundry products. These periodic reports appear to have been solicited, or perhaps required, to retain the firm's favorable credit status. This report Fürther states that:

The firm is the oldest of its kind in Fürth and exists since the 1840's. In the 1860's the business was taken over by Hermann, son of the founder. Hermann, who was childless, took his nephew Sidney Rahn into the business. He is a very competent and solid businessman who, because of his solid business principles, enjoys high esteem among Fürth factory owners. Rahn too is taking an active part in the business completely. It has prospered for years and has made Farrnbacher, who was already well situated through marriage and family, a wealthy man. He is also the owner of the place of business. Rahn gained about M. 80,000 (approximately $32,000) through marriage in 1896 and is expected to inherit as much some day. The firm is given any credit it asks for. The firm is first in white and zinc metal and works in these articles with the largest metal ware factories in Nuremberg, Fürth and the environs. Sometimes they are said to sell at prices in order to get the business where, according to our informants, they do not make a profit. The business is led almost exclusively by Rahn. He is described as a competent, ambitious, diligent businessman. The financial situation of the firm is considered favorable; there should be no impediment to a credit relationship, even in large sums, in the opinion of our experts.

A supplement (1905) states that "the firm continues to be considered first rank in the correspondent fields in Nuremberg and Fürth. The assets of the firm are estimated at several hundred thousand marks." Questions were apparently asked about Sidney himself, since another letter states "your question concerns Sidney Rahn. He is, as you see, co-owner of the above named firm. You can see from this information all the details about Rahn's circumstances. As we hear, conditions of the firm are unchanged and favorable. Rahn's assets are estimated to be approximately 150,000 marks

($60,000). He and his cousin, Oscar Goldscheider, who is working in the business, are expected to take over the firm alone in the near future."

Another "Special Report" on the firm and Sidney Rahn in particular was done before 1922, when he acquired 129 Koenigstrasse. Although quoting from these reports is somewhat redundant, it does give a first-hand account of the status of the business, as well as its managers. This report reads as follows:

The business is one of the oldest and most significant of the line here. It was founded in the 1840's by the father of the present owner, under whose careful and intelligent leadership it developed quickly. At the start of the 1870's it passed on to Hermann Farrnbacher who is a capable, skillful businessman who managed not only to maintain the reputation of the firm, but also to increase the sales of the business constantly. According to entry in a commercial court on July 12, 1895, Farrnbacher took into the business his nephew, the businessman Sidney Rahn, as rightful partner; he too is described to us as a competent, diligent man. He partially does the business trips and is said to be very popular with the customers.

The financial conditions of the firm are described as very favorable; the business has always prospered and has made Farrnbacher a rich man. He is working with more than adequate means; is in the black with his bank (branch of the Dresden Bank) with large amounts and the credit of the firm is thus considered first class. The business is carried out in the house "Konigstrasse 129" which is valued at 65,000 M. ($26,000) and not mortgaged and owned by Farrnbacher.

Your special inquiry regarding Sidney Rahn is answered by our informants thus: Rahn is about 30 years old, the son of the retired Karoline Rahn, widowed for 24 years, a sister of Farrnbacher's. He grew up in the business of his uncle, is diligent and able and is likely to take over the business later, whose manager he is already mainly. Rahn owns a considerable fortune of his own and through marriage with the daughter of a gentleman of independent means, Mr. Goldmann from Meiningen, he has received allegedly a dowry of M. 50,000 (according to other information, M. 80,000 ($32,000)). After the death of his in-laws as well as that of his mother he can expect Further inheritances. The fortune of Rahn, as we hear, is now working in the firm Farrnbacher.

A brother of Rahn's has settled in Fürth as a physician; the family enjoys general respect.

On November 6, 1922 Sidney purchased 129 Koenigstrasse from Mrs. Eugenie Farrnbacher, referred to in the sales contract as a widow of Hermann's and of independent means. Sidney and his wife, Johanna, my grandparents, were already living there. The property is described as a residential home with storage rooms, storage house with connected building, yard and garden with small cottage. The sales price was 450,000 marks ($180,000). Sidney took over the mortgage to the bankers' children, Siogfried and Edgar Loewe in Fürth of 18,000 marks ($7200). Sidney paid 207,000 RM ($82,800) in cash and the balance through a mortgage to the seller of 225,000 RM ($90,000) at 6% interest. Johanna was listed as co-owner in the Registry of Deeds. The following year (September 25, 1923) they received a notice that the taxes were not raised as a result of the transfer of property.

On January 1, 1928 my father, Alfred Rahn, Sidney's son, joined the firm as an associate. Even then certain documentary evidence was assembled to vouch for the honesty and reputation of Alfred. For example, there is an official document, dated September 17, 1919, when Alfred was only 18, from the Council of the Bavarian City of Fürth which states "that the bank employee, Alfred Rahn, born January 28, 1901, living in Fürth, stands in very good repute." Alfred was expected to get some experience before entering the business. In November 1922, he was hired for a brief period in the accounting department of a firm in the city of Karlsruhe. His salary was to be 30,000 marks per month ($12,000) and the firm would provide state health insurance. By printed announcement in 1928, Alfred became a partner of the firm.

When Sidney died on September 13, 1930. M.S. Farrnbacher sent out the following printed announcement:

> *"With deep sorrow I inform you that my highly esteemed senior principal, Mr. Sidney Rahn, has passed on this month on the 13th. The deceased has dedicated the work of his entire life to the growth of the firm. I shall always highly honor his memory. The firm will continue unchanged under the leadership of the son of the deceased, Mr. Alfred Rahn. I am asking you to continue your good will. Respectfully, M.S. Farrnbacher."*

Sidney died on the same day as his brother James, neither knowing of the death of the other. Many years later, in 1960, Carola (Bechmann) Loeffler, Lilli's aunt, also died on September 13th. It was always a day of anxiety and sadness in the family.

In 1930, after Sidney's death, Johanna Rahn, Sidney's wife and Alfred's mother, took the place of her deceased husband as an associate of the firm, but she was so in name only.

In 1933 another of these periodic credit reports was done reiterating the information previously outlined. This one too stated that the business existed over 100 years, was founded by Moses Salomon Farrnbacher. Beginning 1880 the business was taken over by the son Hermann. He took in his nephew Sidney Rahn in 1897 and from 1908 Rahn was sole owner of the firm. In April 1928 Rahn took in his son Alfred as associate. After Sidney Rahn died, his widow, Hannchen Rahn (Johanna), became a Fürther associate. This report continues:

> *The business is considered the oldest of its kind in this place and is located at the above address, which property is, according to our informants, owned by the owners. The firm is Fürther reported to us as owner of 115,000 sq. ft. of real estate on Karolinenstr. in Fürth. The firm deals in wholesale of iron, metals, sheet metals and*

girders; Fürthermore the firm represents larger works. Buyers are mostly metal toy manufacturers, locksmiths, etc. Personally Alfred Rahn, who represents the business, is considered a diligent and active businessman. Rahn, born 1901, has been married to the daughter of Commercial Counsel Hugo Bechmann since July 3, 1933.

The financial position of the firm is considered well regulated. The property at the above address plus other real estate is valued at the moment at approximately 200,000 marks (about $80,000). Any mortgages are not known to us. Present inventory is valued at present approximately 200,000 RM and the yearly sales are quoted to us as approximately 800,000 RM [about $320,000]. As we heard, payments in larger amounts were also taken care of with settlements. Bank connection: Bayrische Staatsbank and Dresdner Bank.

Alfred Rahn

There is little doubt that the long and distinguished history of this firm was one of the major reasons Alfred decided not to leave Germany after his initial trip to the U.S. in 1935. He came with his mother, Johanna, to "look around", and also to see his brother, Max, who he had not seen for nine years. Alfred was the head of a secure and profitable business, founded 170 years ago at that time, and I think he felt the weighty responsibility to carry it on. Giving up such a business to flee to America, in 1935, must have been emotionally, psychologically and financially extremely difficult, particularly for someone who was somewhat risk-averse. Although hindsight showed that this was a big mistake, it is easy for me to understand why he made the decision he did. He just couldn't believe that what was beginning to happen in Germany would last and have the consequences it had.

Alfred was a complicated child and a complicated adult. All his life he was a mixture of boyish joy, especially when he was skiing or hiking, and brooding worry. His mood swings were difficult, extreme, and unpredictable and they complicated and compromised his family relationships, yet he had a heart of gold and a good will that was winning. His attention to detail was both his strength and his nemesis and as one can see from his bookkeeping and his letters, he was meticulous to the last penny in all his dealings, both business and personal. He liked his days to be carefully planned and had difficulty with changes, particularly sudden ones. For example, when already living in Denver when a ski day was planned but due to inclement weather and hazardous driving conditions we decided to cancel, Alfred spend the day brooding and sulking — it was difficult for him to switch gears and just enjoy the moment. Planning and executing plans as they were intended were a long life pattern. Spontaneity was difficult for him. And yet, there was an emotional and warm side to him that I didn't often feel from our mother. I felt particularly loved and cherished by him, and in addition to his personality, given his family history and the circumstances surrounding my birth, I can understand why.

5
BACKGROUND OF POLITICAL SITUATION

It is not the object of this memoir to give a history of the rise of Nazism and anti-Semitism in Germany, and its effect on the Jews living there, but I thought a little background history would be important, especially for you, my children and grandchildren, niece, nephew, and grand-nephews, and those who come thereafter, since these events are truly "history" for you. Much of the information below is taken from Nazi Germany and the Jews, (Volume 1) by Saul Friedlander.

As you can see, from reading about our family's background– both the Bechmann and Rahn sides — they were truly integrated into German life and society. They were able to prosper and contributed enormously, both financially and in social service, to Fürth, their hometown. Lilli's family had been in Fürth since the late 1600's and Lilli was able to trace Alfred's family in Fürth back to 1774. Fürth seems to have been somewhat protected from whatever anti-Semitism existed elsewhere. Neither side of the family was particularly observant as Jews, although their identity to themselves as Jews was clear. Both Lilli and Alfred received some Jewish education, and we know that Alfred and his two brothers all had a Bar Mitzvah because they each received gold watches for this event. Alfred gave his to Ruth's first husband, (now back in Ruth's possession), Matt, and Evy's son Adam inherited the gold watch Max received for his Bar Mitzvah. James' watch went to Bill, Evy's first husband.

Educational and professional opportunities were open to them, and they certainly never expected to have any interruption to the rather privileged life they saw before themselves. It is into this context and way of life that Hitler and Nazism came, and destroyed it all.

Many factors shaped the overall historical context in which the Nazi mass murder ultimately took place. There was a long history of anti-Semitism in Germany, which has been more fully described in a number of books on this topic, including *The Pity of It All*, by Amos Alon, and *Constantine's Sword*, by James Carroll. As Alon put it: "The Third Reich was, of course, also a product of the past: the failed revolution of 1848, authoritarianism, militarism, racism, the lost war of 1914-18, hyperinflation, and the 1929 depression. Any one of these factors would not have been enough to bring Hitler to power." Alon says, "In short order, every unresolved problem and all the world's evils from the crucifixion of Christ to capitalism, Communism, syphilis, and the lost war were projected onto a tiny minority representing 0.9 percent of the population." In 1870,when more than thirty independent German states consolidated to establish a united Germany, called the Reich, Jews were still an insignificant minority of slightly more than 1 percent. Sixty years later, in 1933, on the eve of the Nazi takeover, when the total German population had risen to sixty-five million, the relative number of Jews had dropped to 0.8 percent, and numbered approximately 525,000. One wonders how so small a presence could have triggered, even indirectly, such vast enmity.

Hitler, who had written the anti-Semitic *Mein Kampf* (My Battle) in 1925, brought these factors together, and was driven by ideological obsessions of racial anti-Semitism, which led to his ultimate decision to exterminate the Jews. In the 1930 elections, Nazi party representatives in the Reichstag (Parliament) increased and they became the second largest party. Hitler was appointed Chancellor by President Hindenburg on January 30, 1933.

Developments after Hitler's appointment as Chancellor followed so rapidly upon one another that within a few months the Nazis had managed to set aside the entire Weimar constitution — the Basic Rights of the Citizens, as it was called — and launch the process that would lead to total dictatorship. For the first time since the emancipation of German Jews in 1871, a government, by law, reintroduced discrimination against the Jews. The event the Nazis turned to their advantage was the Reichstag fire of February 27, 1933. The cause of the conflagration is still debated, but the Nazis swiftly exploited it as an excuse to arrest Communists as well as Jews and others. Initially, Communists rather than Jews were imprisoned in newly created concentration camps. Dachau, near Munich, was established on March 20, 1933.

After the mass arrests that followed the Reichstag fire, it was clear the "Communist threat" no longer existed, but the new regime's frenzy of repression and innovation did not slacken, but turned instead against the Jews.

What German Jews then experienced was the steady building of pressure against segment after segment of their community. It began with robbing people of their livelihoods. The came the introduction of racial laws, exclusion of Jews from civic life, and finally even from the streets and parks of the cities, isolating them from the gentile community. It divided families, separated friends, and turned those years into a time of desperation.

Two months after the Nazis took over, they scheduled a boycott of Jewish business for April 1, 1933. The parliamentary SA (Storm Troopers) force — called the Brown Shirts — which had previously devoted itself to marching, singing, aggressively collecting funds for the party and beating up opponents, now sprang up everywhere in full brown uniform to jeer at those who dared to enter Jewish stores. More drastic were decrees that followed rapidly in April and May, forbidding 'non Ayrans" (the new laws defined "non-Aryans" as anyone descended from a non-Aryan, particularly Jewish parents or grandparents) to hold positions as government employees, which meant teachers in secondary schools and universities as well as administrators, elimination of "non-Aryan" doctors from health insurance programs and on April 25, 1933, the Law Against the Overcrowding of German Schools and Universities as passed. It was aimed exclusively against the Jews and limited matriculation of Jewish students in any German school or university to 1.5 percent of the total new applications, with the overall number of Jewish students in any institution not to exceed five percent. Universities became infested with militant anti-Semitic student fraternities, and this was especially true of the Friedrich-Alexander University in Erlangen.

I mention this particular law against university students because in April 1933 Lilli was beginning her last year of Ph.D. studies at Friedrich-Alexander University. She was a student there from October 25, 1932-April, 1934 when she received her Doctor of Philosophy degree. I cannot resist commenting here that for some months in 1930 Lilli attended the University of Freiberg where she took a course from Martin Heidegger. After Heidegger became Rector of Freiberg University in April 1933 his anti-Semitism came to the fore and he announced that economic support would be denied Jewish students or anyone else defined as "non-Aryan" according to the new laws. He also refused to continue supervision of doctoral dissertations by Jewish students. Hannah Arendt had been one of Heidegger's students (as well as his lover) and after she left the country, she said the main reason was the behavior of her Aryan friends, including Benno von Weise who, subject to no outside pressure whatsoever, adhered enthusiastically to the new system's ideals and norms. I only mention this here because von Weise became Lilli's thesis advisor at the Alexander-Friedrich University in Erlangen. By May 1933 student organizations throughout Germany that had been taken over by Nazi students organized the burning of books by Jews. Students in boots and brown S.A. uniforms threw books by Jews into the fire, and formed honor guards. In Berlin, the Nazi propaganda chief, Joseph Goebbels, led the proceedings, proclaiming "the end of the age of Jewish Intellectualism". Bonfires occurred in most of the university cities and towns of Germany, and as will be mentioned later, when I was in the courtyard of the Freidrich-Alexander University in Erlangen, there was an engraved stone amidst the brick cobblestones of the courtyard which read "Here they Burned the Books".

In September, 1933 Jews were forbidden to own farms or engage in agriculture. In July, the Law for the Prevention of Genetically Diseased Offspring was adopted. This law allowed sterilization of those suffering from supposedly hereditary diseases, such as schizophrenia, among others, and ultimately ended in euthanasia as part of the "Final Solution". A Jewish schizophrenic, as was James, Alfred's brother and my uncle, had no chance to survive.

As Saul Friedlander puts it in his book, *Nazi Germany and Jews*:

In Nazi racial thinking, the German national community drew its strength from the purity of its blood and from its rootedness in the sacred German earth. Such racial purity was a condition of superior cultural reaction and of the construction of a powerful state, the guarantor of victory in the struggle for racial survival and domination. From the outset, therefore, the 1933 laws pointed to the exclusion of the Jews from all key areas of this utopian vision: the state structure itself, (the Civil Service Law), the biological health of the national community (the physicians' law), the social fabric of the community (the disbarring of Jewish lawyers,) culture (the schools, universities, the press, the cultural professions), and finally, the sacred earth (the farm law). The Civil Service Law was the only one of these to be fully implemented at this early stage, but the symbolic statements they expressed and the ideological message they carried were unmistakable.

Nazi Rally, Nuremberg, 1935, photo taken by Lilli

Very few German Jews, Friedlander continues, sensed the implications of the Nazi laws in terms of sheer long-range terror. As was true in many towns, smaller businessmen and their families were well assimilated and for several generations had been an integral part of the community. This certainly was the case with the Rahn and Bechmann families. As will be discussed later, Alfred and his mother came to the United States in 1935 to "look around", and decided not to emigrate. They believed what was happening was temporary and would pass.

In September 1935 the annual Nazi Party Congress was held in Nuremberg, which is adjacent to Fürth. It was the first and last time that the Reichstag was convened outside Berlin. Nuremberg had been the site of a German Reichstag (then the assembly of the German Empire's estates) in 1543 and was considered to be a prime example of a German city, architecturally and otherwise. The escalation that had begun in the economic area moved into a new sphere in 1935 with the promulgation of the Nuremberg laws. Three laws were introduced: 1) The Reich Flag Law which proclaimed that henceforth black, red and white were the national colors and that the swastika flag was the national flag; 2) The Citizenship Law which established the fundamental distinction between "citizens of the Reich" who were entitled to full political and civil rights and "subjects", who were now deprived of those rights. Only those of German or related blood could be citizens. Thus, from that moment on, in terms of their civic rights, the Jews had in fact a status similar to that of foreigners; and 3) The Law for the Defense of German Blood and Honor, which forbad marriages and extramarital relations between Jews and citizens of German blood. The preamble to the third law revealed all its implications. "Fully aware that the purity of German blood is the condition for the survival of the German Volk (People), and animated by the unwavering will to secure the German nation forever, the Reichstag has unanimously decided upon the following..." These edicts attacked not only the functions of Jews in society but their very being. By creating elaborate distinctions among Jew, "Aryan" and Mischling- a person of "mixed blood"— and by requiring detailed research into ancestry for several generations, the Nazis created an atmosphere that successfully divided the nation into two parts, Aryans and Jews: accomplishment, virtue, and wealth all became irrelevant in a world where only race counted. My governess, Helen Lorz, was a Mischling, and thus needed to leave Germany also, and therefore came to the United States with us. When the Nazis took power in 1933, eleven of the forty German winners of a Nobel Prize in the sciences had been Jews. But they, too, were no longer regarded as anything but members of an "inferior race".

Thirty-seven thousand of the approximately 525,000 Jews in Germany left the country in 1933; during the four following years, the annual number of emigrants remained much lower than that (23,000 in 1934, 21,000 in 1935, 25,000 in 1936 and 23,000 in 1937). The rest remained, at least for a while, unwilling or unable to leave. As will be discussed later, Lilli and Alfred decided in 1937 to leave but were unable to until 1939. Friedlander also points out that the material difficulty of emigrating was considerable, especially in a period of economic uncertainty; it entailed an immediate and heavy material loss. Jewish-owned property was sold at ever lower prices, and the emigration "tax on capital flight", which was originally levied on assets of two hundred thousand Reichsmarks ($80,000) and up, was raised by the Nazis to a levy on assets of only fifty thousand Reichsmarks ($20,000) and was, therefore, almost prohibitive. The Reichsbank's purely arbitrary exchange rate for the purchase of foreign currency by emigrants Fürther depleted the steadily shrinking assets. Thus, until 1935, Jewish immigrants exchanged their marks at 50% of their value, then at 30%, and finally, on the eve of the war, at 4%. Although the Nazis wanted to get rid of the Jews of Germany, they were intent on dispossessing them first by increasingly harsh methods. These facts also bear directly on what happened to the Rahn residence and business, which were "sold" for far below their value. Fortunately, Lilli and Alfred had the funds to pay these inordinate taxes. In fact, keeping liquid funds available for just such taxes was what led to Alfred's arrest and detention.

As Alon stated, "That so many Jews stayed in the country of their birth reflected not so much lethargy but the lingering conviction that the horrors were transitory. Baffled, incredulous, shocked, many refused to believe that the nearly two-thousand-year-old Jewish presence in Germany was coming to an end." Alfred was certainly a risk-averse personality and we often heard that if Lilli had accompanied him in 1935 to the United States, she would have definitely decided to leave then. Also, being ten years younger than he was, and being in the student milieu, she perhaps had more first-hand experience of the expressions of anti-Semitism that were occurring than Alfred, who had stepped into the family business. Also, as Friedlander points out, Hitler was very concerned about international reactions to his policies and his Minister of the Economy of the Reich, Hjalmar Schacht, appointed in 1934, insisted that no major interference with Jewish business would be allowed. In general terms Hitler backed Schacht's position until the new transition period of 1936-37. It may be that things eased a bit, and the thought that these policies were just an aberration was believed by many.

Why didn't Lilli and Alfred leave earlier? It is a question I have often asked myself, and I had answered it for myself by saying that it must have been very difficult to uproot oneself from a community where both families had lived for hundreds of years, and were truly established and integrated. But I think what I quote below, gives a much better and more truthful answer.

One of the things I discovered in going through the many boxes of documents we have is a large binder of speeches and letters that both Lilli and Alfred wrote and presented to groups during their very early years in the United States. Lilli in particular began speaking to various organizations as early as the fall of 1939, just months after we arrived in Denver. One speech in particular, undated, but written and presented to an unnamed group in 1940, or at the latest 1941, warrants inclusion here. It may have been part of a fund raising effort to help Jews leave Germany. I have the original document which consists of four typed pages, single-spaced. Once again I am so impressed with her command of the English language, but that is not the reason I am including it here. It is titled "Jewish Life in Germany 1933-39" and explains to me more than anything else what was going on, and why they waited as long as they did to leave Germany. Although it is long, I think it creates an important and relevant context for this memoir. The speech she gave was the following:

To understand the persecution of Jews in Germany during the last years it is not enough to know the details of this persecution, to listen to the description of individual experiences, but it is necessary to understand and to realize what lies behind all this, why all these things happened, what the real reasons were. There are certain facts, certain phases which seem to be especially unbelievable, unconceivable for Americans and I therefore will try to answer these questions, believing that this may be the best way to make things clear to you.

One of these questions is: Why didn't most of the Jews leave Germany immediately after Hitler took over the government? There was no Jew in Germany who didn't realize on January 30, 1933 that he had to face an extremely serious situation. But on the other hand, nobody, Jews or Gentiles, except the 100% convinced followers of the new government believed that Hitler would carry out all he had said in his book, "My Battle" (Mein Kampf) or all that was written in the program of the NSDAP (National Socialist Party). Every sensible, every reasonable person believed that the most radical ideas in these programs weren't but a means of propaganda and that he certainly would modify his program once being the Chancellor of the German Reich. This speculation was a fundamental mistake. Many articles of the National Socialist program have not been carried out, but all the articles concerning the Jews have been carried out. But who could have known that in 1933? Most of those Jews who left Germany in 1933 didn't leave it because they were so much more intelligent than all the rest of us, but because they had a special reason to leave the country as quickly as possible. Maybe they had played a prominent part in the former government, maybe they had some quarrel with a party member, maybe they had been prominent members of masonry lodges, peace leagues, etc. or maybe that they belonged to those who lost their job almost immediately after Hitler had taken over the government, the young lawyers, the young physicians who had been the first who were forced out of their jobs by the new government.

On April 1, 1933 there was the first great anti-Jewish boycott. There were pickets on every store, people who went in the stores were photographed and their pictures afterwards published. Especially the Jewish department stores were the goal for numerous attacks. But in spite of this boycott and the anti-Jewish propaganda, Jewish business in Germany continued to go well. Not even that, but many businesses prospered. That may sound unbelievable, but I think that it is the best proof against the N.S. accusations of Jewish businessmen. These businesses were old established enterprises and the gentile customers had been satisfied with their purchases for many years. They stuck to these Jewish firms. Take for example my husband's business. He owned a sheet metal and iron business, which had been for more than 140 years in the hands of his family. It was the oldest business of that kind in town. The business didn't only remain on the same level it had had in 1933 but it steadily became better and better and the best year he ever had was in 1937, in the same year in which he was forced out of it, in the same year in which it was taken away from him without a single cent of payment.

Changes came very gradually and slowly. My husband was in this country in 1935 to see his brother who lives here already for more than 12 years. But at that time, in 1935, he couldn't yet make up his mind to remain here, because business was so good. You may say now: how could he have preferred money to the life in freedom and liberty here in this country? The answer is that things over there changed so slowly that we didn't realize all that was going on and we were too near to all these things to be able to have a clear head. At that time there haven't been any direct laws intended against Jewish businesses. There have been laws against Jewish lawyers and physicians. The young lawyers and physicians lost their licenses, but there were quite a lot of exceptions made for the older people, for those who already had a license before 1914, for those who had been in the war or decorated during the war, etc. And the official reason they gave was that the percentage of lawyers and physicians was too big and that they wanted to make it agree with the percentage of Jews in the entire population. Of course it was rigid for those who were affected but it was by far not yet so cruel or inhuman as many of the measures taken years later.

The first regulations that affected the Jewish businesses were the regulations that said that no government order should be given, directly or indirectly, to a Jew. That meant that institutions such as railways, mail, public service, etc. were not allowed to buy from Jews any more. This should be such an important measure in normal times, but at that time the German government had already started to take over one business after the other and therefore the percentage of government orders was already much bigger than in former times, and it steadily increased. But also in spite of this fact most of the Jewish businesses still flourished.

Only after 1936 when things went politically worse and worse and when the government needed somebody to blame for the failure, the anti-Jewish campaign was intensified. Hitler didn't start the anti-Jewish movement in Germany. Germany always has been an anti-Semitic country. But he was the first one in Germany to make it a leading state principle. As all other dictators he had immediately realized that the fate of a nation depends on the young generation. He therefore had, soon after he had taken over the government, replaced the older teachers by young party members whose duty it was to make most loyal National Socialists of these youngsters. One of the things they were taught was that all Jews are evil, that they are the worst people in the world and that they haven't but one desire and that is to dominate the world and to destroy Germany. So they were brought up as real anti-Semites. Most of them didn't know Jews any more, because the isolation of Jews had already become very great. Jewish children weren't allowed any more to go to the public schools, universities, etc. Jews weren't allowed to enter a general hospital. they weren't allowed to go to a restaurant, public swimming pools, places of entertainment as movies, theaters, parks, etc. The government promised to let them have their own cultural life. So they started Jewish theaters with Jewish actors for Jewish audiences. In Berlin they had a movie theatre where only Jews were allowed to go. They had concerts and lectures for Jewish public only. But as a matter of course all these things couldn't be carried out except in a few big and rich communities. The smaller communities had not money or people for it. And as in Germany a very great percentage of the Jewish population lived and lives in villages and small towns, especially in southern Germany, those people very soon were completely isolated. Many of them couldn't even do their purchases in the stores of the village any more; they had to do it through children of their Gentile neighbors and these children asked for a regular tribute for this work. Of course they got the worst merchandise too. But at that time all these things were not yet a law, it was pure chicanery of single individuals. It was not until 1938 until all this became law.

In 1937 the situation had become so bad that whoever had a relative or somebody to rely on wished to emigrate. Till 1937 emigration was comparatively easy. Quite a lot of foreign countries were willing to take in the refugees and the German government let them go after they had paid the 25% Reichsfluchsteuer (Reich Flight Tax). At that time they were still able to transfer about 30% of their money to another country.

But things were going worse and worse in 1937 and 1938 and more and more people were seeking a haven in other countries. Most of these countries closed their frontiers and soon the Jewish people who wanted to emigrate didn't know where to go. The German immigration quota to this country had not been filled until 1937; shortly after it was filled and now there are applications for 6 or 7 years in advance. But these weren't even the worst troubles. It had become so awfully difficult to get out that people willingly went to countries they had never heard the name of and they were willing to endure any hardship if they were able to leave. They didn't even ask themselves what they would do outside without any money, old, tired. They had only one desire — to leave, whatever the price may be. And the price was high enough. In fact they had to give away everything and anything. It was a perfect robbery. But no one of the Germans knew that because all this was perfectly legal, based on the law.

To understand this I must tell you a little bit more of the foreign currency regulations in Germany. Germany doesn't produce enough raw materials and food to supply its needs. So it always has to buy these things from foreign countries and needs foreign currency. It got this foreign currency for its industrial products by its foreign trade. After Hitler took over the government in 1933 confidence in Germany sunk rapidly, the foreign trade became less and less and Germany was soon very short of foreign currency. They started very strict laws and one of the first measures was to not let Jews change their money any more into foreign currency and to prevent them from taking out the money. The real value of the Reichsmark sunk rapidly. In 1933 100 Reichsmark were 40 dollars; in 1939 100 Reichmark were 2 dollars. That is the real value. But inside the borders of the German Reich a Mark is still a Mark and people didn't realize at all that they were fooled. Only the Jews realized it because when they wanted to emigrate they only got 5% for their Mark. But you are mistaken if you think that they got 5% of their whole property. In 1939 before they left they had to pay 55% in taxes of all the property they had owned on January 1, 1935. These taxes were not only based on the money and real estate but also on jewels, works of art, pictures, stamp collections, in short on everything that could represent a value of some kind. Even if these things couldn't be sold at all or only to a much lower price as they were estimated. As the taxes must be paid in cash most of the people haven't got as much any more in 1939, and therefore they had endless troubles and were the objects of endless chicaneries.

I suppose you have read "It Cannot Happen Here" by Sinclair Lewis. Mr. Lewis gives a very good picture of what happens to opponents of a Nazi government - jail, imprisonment, etc. But what he doesn't describe because he cannot know it, because only somebody who has lived over there can know it, is the discrimination and the fear. Jews were absolutely discriminated. They had to stand back, they were treated like slaves, beaten, and if they dared to reply sent to a concentration camp.

And then there was the fear. Everybody could step into your house whenever he pleased, take fathers away from their wives and children, brothers from their sisters, take even women away and send them to jail or into a camp.

My husband was in jail. I was alone in the house with a little child of two and a maid. They came at night at three o'clock. They searched the house for men and as they didn't find any they wanted me and the child to come with them. I resisted. The maid was ill. Finally they let me stay. But they left two men in the house, with guns and revolver. They laid their guns on the table and remained there the whole night. I had no fear. But I spent these hours in a trance. If you have experiences of things like this nothing that happens to you afterwards can frighten you and what hardship whatsoever one should have to go through in another country it will be easy to endure. Now you can realize how glad we are to be here but on the other hand how worried we are about the fate of our friends and relatives who are still in Germany.

They are without money, without law, haunted, frightened. They haven't any possibility to earn money because there is no Jewish business left in Germany, no employer and no employee, no lawyer, no physician. They are condemned to starve as soon as the little money which was left to them is spent. The New York Times a few days ago wrote that the entire Jewish fortune in Germany will last for 18 additional months. Then they will not have a cent to spend any more. But that means that already now there are numerous families who haven't enough to live.

No effort will be great enough, no contribution big enough to help these people. We have to do the utmost to help them to escape this hell because the responsibility will fall on us if we let them starve and perish.

I believe this section of this memoir gives some background as to why we and others had to leave. The more specific description of the difficulties we had follows.

6
GETTING OUT OF GERMANY

As I worked on this family history — reading the many documents, letters, manuscripts and other material we have, my strongest feeling has been the realization of how lucky we were to get out of Germany. It is simply amazing to me how close we were to not getting out and suffering the fate of the 6 million Jews who perished. I had no idea of this as I was growing up, and my parents never talked about their experiences in any way. In the four years from 1935 to 1939 there were so many times that things could have happened differently — and it is hard to explain or even comprehend how some people got out and others didn't. Reading the documents and voluminous correspondence involved in getting the necessary paperwork reads like a mystery — a real cliff-hanger, that looks, until the very last moment, as if there would an outcome different from the one that occurred. The woman I used to translate many of the documents, Eva Gordon, said that working through this material was like an Agatha Christie mystery, and even though she knew the outcome was favorable, she had no idea how it would play out.

Surely luck played a role, but there also was the dogged, persistent and steadfast determination of Lilli who, because of her intelligent dedication, extraordinary hard work and probably also because of financial ability, was able to orchestrate our emigration. It is hard for me to imagine the incredible stress she must have been under. In addition, there was the incredible persistence of Max, Alfred's brother and my uncle, who left Puerto Rico and went to New York and then Washington to advocate for Alfred, and was able to get the case before Homer Cummings, the United States Attorney General. Max was working for the General Cigar Company in Puerto Rico and the story that has been passed down to me is that he talked with the president of the company, Mr. Duys, and told him of Alfred's situation and the visa problem and he said he had to go to New York and Washington. Mr. Duys gave his blessing and responded by saying "there are some things a man simply must do". Max never forgot it. It seems to me that Mr. Duys could be listed in Yad Vashem as a "righteous gentile" Few employers would have given their blessing to Max's request and most would have complained about an employee missing work for months or taking on such a difficult task. Mr. Duys probably never saw himself as "righteous" but he, in fact, helped save our family.

And then there is Homer Cummings, who, for reasons I do not yet understand, chose this as his very last case in the office he served longer than any other United States Attorney General except one. Despite the long and accepted tradition of American law, which was that "full faith and credit" be given to judgments of foreign jurisdictions, Cummings decided, in his 14 page opinion dated December 31, 1938, that this case required one to look behind the judgment of the foreign court to the circumstances existing in Germany at the time. The critical last sentence of his opinion stated, "I advise that you would be warranted in granting him a visa". More about this opinion will be written later. Like Mr. Duys, Homer Cummings exhibited a compassion for Alfred's situation which was exemplary.

We recently watched the movie about the ill-fated ship, the St. Louis, that left Hamburg exactly one year after we did, in April, 1940, and, after being refused docking in Cuba, the U.S. and other ports, was forced to return to Europe and land in Antwerp. Only a small percentage of those passengers survived, having been dumped back into German occupied Europe and sent to concentration camps. At a time when it was so easy to follow the existing rules and so easy to make it someone else's problem, the actions of Mr. Duys and Mr. Cummings are truly extraordinary.

This section of this memoir, which I have entitled "Getting Out" focuses on the efforts of my family members, specifically Lilli, Max, and others, in getting the visa and other documents necessary for us to leave. Also included is a section entitled "Prison Letters", Alfred's correspondence from prison from December, 1937 until March, 1939. Simultaneously with these efforts, which are documented primarily by correspondence, official records were being kept and recorded at the Nuremberg Archives. Evy and I had an opportunity to spend a day in Nuremberg at the Archives, and the chronology of the documents we were able to copy there are found in the section entitled "Documents from Nuremberg Archives". They are the basis of much of this story, and therefore somewhat repetitive of the story, but I wanted to keep a record of the documents from the official archives.

Alfred's Trip to the U.S. — 1935

Let me begin this tale with a trip Alfred took with his mother, Johanna, to the United States in 1935, to "look around". Certainly the idea of emigrating had entered their minds after passage of the Nuremberg Laws in September 1935, but even then there didn't seem to be much urgency, so they decided to take the trip which was from October 31—November 6, 1935. Lilli was pregnant with me at the time. They had the means to travel on one of the premier passenger ships, the Hansa out of Bremen, and spent their time in New York. Alfred was able to meet with his brother Max, who had emigrated to the U.S. in 1926 but lived in Puerto Rico as

Max Rahn

a representative and tobacco buyer of the General Cigar Company. Max was just 19 or barely 20 when he came to the U.S. with his good friend Richard Kunreuther. He apparently was not interested in the family business and emigrated to find his fortune elsewhere. Max came to New York and met Alfred and Johanna at the pier where he hadn't seen his brother or his mother in nine years. There were some relatives and others they contacted, and then they returned to Germany, deciding that they would not

Alfred and Johanna arriving in New York on the Hansa. Max Rahn is in foreground.

move. After all, as Lilli wrote, "Alfred could not decide about his business in Fürth which existed for 5 generations in his family". As for so many others, there was a belief that this insanity couldn't last — not in the country where the Jews had become so assimilated and were truly integrated into the community. Alfred was a cautious man by nature, not a risk-taker — and it is interesting to speculate whether the decision would have been the same if Lilli had made that trip with him. But never did I hear any remonstrance later about having made the decision they did at that time. Lilli, with her usual poetic and artistic bent, gave to Alfred a booklet of drawings, accompanied by a poem of the trip. It was called "Bilberbuch einer Amerikafahrt von Wulle Für Micky oder: Der Eine macht mit Geld die Reis, Der Andre Macht sie Schwarz auf Weiss. Translated — "Picturebook of a trip to America from Wulle for Micky (their nicknames

Johanna Rahn

for each other). One makes a trip with money; the other makes it black and white." In New York the three of them went sightseeing — seeing Rockefeller Center, the Empire State Building, and in the evening, the Rockettes. When they said good-by to Max, they probably didn't know when they would see him again. Neither Alfred nor his mother had met Max's wife, Maria, whom he married in 1933.

Ruth was born in June 1936 and some time in the following year the decision was made to emigrate as the situation for German Jews was becoming increasingly intolerable. They "sold" the business and the house and by October 1937 had obtained American visas. They had planned to travel to the United States in December 1937.

Alfred's Summary of Events

What follows here is a typed, two page summary which Alfred prepared of the events that followed. This was written after we arrived in the United States and is undated. I will reproduce it in its entirety, because it is his version of the events. I don't know why he wrote this or for what purpose it was intended, but because it is in his words, it is most interesting. Afterwards I will expand on this summary of events by quoting more in detail from the documents and letters of this period. Again, my purpose here is both to tell the story in a readable form, and to preserve the contents of the original documents.

During the summer of 1937 my wife and I realized that there was no hope for an early end of the Nazi rule in Germany and we decided to leave for the U.S. My brother Max Rahn and his wife, both U.S. citizens, residing in San Juan, Puerto Rico, furnished us with the necessary affidavits and on October 18, 1937 I applied for U.S. immigration visas at the American Consulate at Stuttgart, Germany for myself, my wife, Lilli Rahn, nee Bechmann, my daughter, Ruth Marion, then 2 years of age and her nurse, Mrs. Helen Lorz, nee Bergen, and furnished all required evidence and documents.

On November 18, 1937 we all appeared before the U.S. Consul at Stuttgart and on the same day received U.S. quota immigration visas (Quota No. Alfred R. 8458; Lilli 8459; Ruth Marion 8460; Helen Lorz 8461).

We purchased tickets for the S.S. Manhattan of the US Line, which was due to sail from Le Havre during the last days of December. During October and November I sold our real estate and wholesale sheet metal business to a non-Jewish firm in Northern Germany which wished to establish a branch in Bavaria. These sales were subject to approval by the Nazi party but after the contracts were submitted, the approval was never given; however, on December 25, 1937 I was arrested. In a fake trail in January 1938 I was sentenced to 14 months imprisonment.

The validity of our immigration visas expired on March 17, 1938. Mrs. Rahn therefore went to see the American Consul at Stuttgart before the expiration date to inquire what procedure had to be followed in order to get them renewed after Mr. Rahn's release. She submitted authorized translation of the sentence to the Consul, Mr. H.J. L'Heureux, and he said later, having read the document, that in his opinion there was nothing in it which would hinder Mr. Rahn from getting his visa renewed, but that he would rather have his opinion confirmed by the Washington authorities and he therefore asked Mrs. Rahn to supply sufficient German and English copies of the sentence which he would send to the proper authorities in Washington.

She was advised that whenever a prospective immigrant was unable to use his U.S. quota immigration visa before its expiration date for reasons beyond his control, the visa would be renewed and that she should not worry and come back as soon as they were able to leave and that their quota would be reserved for them.

During the spring and summer of 1938, however, due to the rapid enactment of anti-Jewish legislation in Germany, the American Consulates were swamped with applications and Mrs. Rahn went again to see the Consul in order to make sure that their quota was still reserved for them. At this occasion she also furnished an authorized translation of the court judgment and Mr. H.J.L'Heureux, the American Consul at Stuttgart, after having read the document, again assured her that in his opinion there was nothing in it which would hinder Mr. Rahn from getting his visa renewed, but Mr. L'Heureux said he would rather have his opinion confirmed by the proper Washington authorities in order to eliminate once and forever any difficulties which he might have in renewing his visa or in entering the U.S. He asked Mrs. Rahn to supply 6 English and 6 German copies of the judgment which he would send to the proper authorities in Washington.

A few days later, however, to her greatest surprise, she received a latter from Mr. L'Heureux in which he flatly refused to send the documents on to Washington and also refused to issue a visa because the case, in his opinion, involved moral turpitude. The favorable opinion expressed by the solicitor of the Department of Labor, to which he referred in his letter was given to Mr. Max Rahn, who, on his own account, had inquired in Washington and had informed his sister-in-law that the general opinion he had received was a favorable one.

Upon receipt of this unfavorable opinion from Mr. L'Heureux, Mrs. Rahn immediately went to see him and asked him for his advice because Mr. Rahn's very life was at stake. If he was not in possession of a valid U.S. visa the moment he was to be released, the Nazis would keep him locked up indefinitely. During this visit Mr. L'Heureux advised Mrs. Rahn to ask her brother-in-law, Mr. Max Rahn, to contact the Washington authorities directly. He personally could not do anything, but he would, of course, issue the visas, if so advised by Washington. He declared that Mr. Max Rahn in the U.S. has the right to inquire directly and that it was entirely possible that the Washington authorities would judge the matter quite differently, but he had strict regulations and it was not his duty, as an administrative officer, to go behind the judgment in order to determine the real nature of the judgment.

Mrs. Rahn immediately contacted her brother-in-law, Mr. Max Rahn, in Puerto Rico and advised him to take up the case in Washington. Mr. Max Rahn did so, and on December 31, 1938 an opinion was given by the Attorney General, Mr. Homer Cummings, which decided the question in favor of Mr. Rahn and once and forever established his innocence. (Official Opinions of the Attorneys General, Volume 39, pages 215-227). The State Department then immediately advised the U.S. Consul at Stuttgart by cable to issue the visa. Upon the Consul's request (Letter of January 18, 1939) new affidavits and up-to-date evidence were submitted to him, and new visas were issued for the entire family on March 7, 1939, two days after Mr. Rahn's release.

On April 15, 1939, all four of us entered the US at New York harbor on the S.S. Washington, U.S. Line. (green card issued at port of entry was submitted to the Naturalization Bureau with the application for the final papers). German Passport with original immigration visa, quota No. 12758 (Alfred Rahn), and 12759 (Ruth Marion).

Before getting into the details of the correspondence, I want to say a word about Consul L'Heureux. Consul L'Heureux, whose full name was Herve L'Heureux (1899-1957) was an American consul in a number of locations throughout his career, namely: Vice consul, then Consul, in Windsor 1927-35; Stuttgart (1936-39); Antwerp (1939-41); Lisbon (1941-42); Algiers (1943-44), Marseille (1944-48). He was married, had three children and is buried in Arlington National Cemetery. I sensed, in reading through the correspondence he had with Lilli, that initially he took the over-riding State Department position which was to limit emigration to the U.S. He operated within the long and sometimes bitter struggle between the State Department and the Labor Department over immigration policy. Throughout the 1930's State Department officials sought to retain their mandate to regulate the level of immigration through tight control over distribution of visas. Although influential American Jews and American Jewish organizations were the most visible critics of State Department policy, Secretary of Labor Frances Perkins and her subordinates waged bureaucratic war behind the scenes, seeking special consideration for refugees within immigration regulations and an increase in immigration from Germany. Although Perkins won several victories, she ultimately lost the war. By 1940 the State Department emerged with near complete jurisdiction over visa policy. Then, while the Nazis slaughtered millions of European Jews, the State Department maintained and tightened regulations designed to keep foreigners from entering the United States.

Much has been written about the role of the State Department during this period, and the anti-Semitism prevalent in the Department and in the country as a whole. What struck me, however, was the Consul L'Heureux not only increasingly liked and admired Lilli, but truly tried to help her within the constrictions in which he operated. It is important to note that Stuttgart, where the American consulate was located, is almost 100 miles from Fürth. I don't know by what means Lilli made her many trips there — whether by car, train or bus.

Correspondence During the Pre-Imprisonment Period — October 18, 1937 — February 2, 1938

What now follows is a review and narrative based on the actual documents which will expand in detail the summary written above by Alfred. As stated earlier, I want to preserve the original language and sequence of events in all its details. I have therefore organized the documents in chronological order, with the date first. In this part of the memoir, I have placed my personal comments in parenthesis to distinguish them from the contents of the documents. This section can be divided into four chronological periods. First, the period from October 18, 1937 until February 2, 1938, the date of the Judgment, which I call the pre-imprisonment period. In fact, Alfred was in detention beginning December 29, 1937, but the Judgment of February 2, 1938 which sentenced him to one year and two months gave him credit for this prior period of detention. Second, the period from February 2, 1938 to December 31, 1938, the date of Homer Cummings' opinion. Third, correspondence from December 31, 1938 to March 5, 1939, the date of Alfred's release from prison, and finally, the period after March 5, 1939.

The pre-imprisonment period: October 18, 1937 until February 2, 1938.

October 18, 1937 — Letter from Alfred to the American Consulate in Stuttgart. He wrote that "I am intending to emigrate to the United States with my family, which consists of my wife, Lilli, my daughter, Ruth-Marion, the nursemaid, Mrs. Helen Lorz and myself. I politely request herewith the necessary immigration visa and include for this purpose the following documents." Included were duplicates of birth certificates of the four individuals, 4 passport photos of each, duplicate marriage certificates for Alfred and Lilli, and duplicate divorce certificates for Helen Bergen Lorz, who had been married to both Karl Lorz and to Fr. Rossner. Also included were duplicates of the Affidavit consisting of the sworn declaration of Max and Maria Pintado Rahn, letter of the President of the Insular Police Commission of San Juan, Puerto Rico, letter of the banking house of Sartorius and Smith, Members of the NY Stock Exchange, 61 Broadway, New York and letter of the Manufacturer's Trust Company, 513 Fifth Avenue, NY, NY.

Then he wrote, "the still missing good-conduct reports from the police will follow as soon as I receive them. I ask you however politely to schedule me for a summons for personal appearance at the consulate at the earliest possible time. It is signed simply "Alfred Rahn." (I note this here because later correspondence required the addition of the name Israel by all Jewish men, and Sara by all Jewish women.)

On **October 27, 1937**, having decided to emigrate, Lilli and Alfred gave a Power of Attorney to their attorney, Otto Rosenberg. Mr. Rosenberg, whose office was on Konigstrasse 3 in Nürnberg, was "authorized to represent me in all matters of law and property, as far as such representation is lawful".

Undated: A document from the American Consulate, Konigstrasse 19A, Stuttgart, titled: Re: Immigration to the United States. This was apparently a standard form.

This document, from the American Consulate, described all the necessary documents that must be submitted to apply for immigration to the United States.

1. Two birth certificates

2. Four loose passport photos for each person, on thin paper with light background, without head cover. No group or photo-mat pictures.

3. Police record of good conduct, in duplicate, for the past 5 years. The records from the last place of residence must not be older than 4 weeks at the time of presentation.

4. If prior convictions exist, excerpts from the criminal records with exact information.

5. Two marriage certificates or two death certificates if one of the spouses is deceased.

6. If divorced, two divorce documents with facts.

7. Minors who want to travel alone need the notarized permission of the father or guardian. Married persons who want to travel alone need the permission of the partner who stays behind.

8. *Affidavits in duplicate by the relatives who live in the U.S.A. as well as proof of their incomes and property.*

Affidavits are not bound by a specific form; they should be adjusted according to each individual case and should indicate the provisions the sponsor has made in order to provide for the immigrant's livelihood in the U.S. When sending these documents the visa applicant should also report that he has a passport, alien pass, children's pass or similar document. The passport or passport substitute should be valid for the U.S. and may not expire before 6 months. The visa fee for $10.00 or its value in German marks has to be paid upon presentation.

Children of whatever age for whom a visa is requested have to be presented for an examination. Children under 18 should be accompanied by a parent or guardian, unless other arrangements have been made with the consulate. Notarized copies or photocopies of documents in lieu of originals will be accepted.

An immigration visa cannot be issued if there is danger that the immigration could become a burden to the U.S. public. Therefore every applicant had to prove that his subsistence is provided for and that his sponsors are willing and able to provide for him. A specific sum is not required. The rules for the sponsor are set out and requires the sponsor, among other information, to list his debts and other obligations, as well as proof of his income and assets. He had to provide notarized statements of his employer about his income, bank account statements as well as tax receipts. All this must be notarized and presented to the American Consulate. Sponsorship papers should not be older than 4 months upon presentation to the Consulate. The sponsor need not be an American citizen, but he has to be a legal resident. An American citizen can receive preference for his parents, his unmarried minor children and his spouse. In the meantime, the applicant must obtain Form #633 which can only be issued by an American Consulate. The applicant must be in possession of a passport or travel papers valid in the United States and valid for at least 6 months. If the submitted papers are in order the call to appear before the Consulate will be at the earliest available date. The final decision will only be made upon the personal investigation at the consulate.

Max was our family's sponsor, as required above, and had to submit his debts, obligations, income and assets several times during the course of these events.

Undated: Lilli's typed summary of the rules for obtaining a visa for a nurse (for Helen Lorz). The hiring contract had to be made before a Notary Public and had to show:

1. That this is not a limited employment, for instance just for a year, but a permanent job.

2. That the employee receives room and board at the house of the employer.

3. What monthly wages (in numbers) are guaranteed.

The employment contract cannot be made out to a house helper, governess or tutor, but had to be made specifically for a children's nurse, housemaid, cook, housekeeper, etc. The employer had to prove to the Consulate that he is able economically to fulfill the conditions promised in the contract, which can best be done by documentary proof of income or wealth. It is good if the applicant can prove to the Consulate with certificates and documents that she is really a domestic employee, particularly if the passport lists another occupation. Upon request for nurses of children, infants, or patients, it is necessary to bring proof of a state license or diploma. A nursemaid who cannot prove a required education cannot receive a visa if the employment contract is made for a nursemaid. Dress, appearance and behavior when appearing before the Consulate has to be appropriate to the declared profession.

As in other instances, Lilli got the rules and regulations and learned them herself. She truly became an expert in emigration law and regulations. Evidently Helen Lorz met the requirements, but it was another set of procedural hurdles that had to be jumped. Helen Lorz came over with us and lived with us from time to time when I was young. She was older than Alfred and Lilli, having been born on January 16, 1900. She was divorced and had one daughter. I called her Tante (aunt) and have very warm feelings toward her. The fact that I called her Tante signified a relationship stronger than merely a child-care provider. After living with us for a few years after we arrived, I recall that she got a job with a wealthy family who lived near the Denver Country Club. What I remember most about her new family was that their home had an elevator! She returned to live with us again when Evy was born. At some point she moved to New York to be with her daughter. I visited with her once, and then lost track of her. I also remember vividly that she tried very hard to switch me from a left-handed to a right-handed person. She felt it would be very disadvantageous for me to be left-handed. She promised to give me a watch if I would become right-handed, but when my grandmother Ida arrived in Denver and gave me a watch, I stopped this effort.

January 10, 1938 — Letter to Alfred from the American Consulate in Stuttgart which is part of the Foreign Service of the U.S. which is part of the Department of State. They indicate they received the request and inquired if he had corresponded with the consulate. It is signed for the General Consul by H.J. L'Heureux.

January 11, 1938 — Alfred wrote back, notifying them that "the American Consulate in Stuttgart, as you can see from your files, has issued the following visa for my family and my nursemaid on November 18, 1937"

Alfred Rahn — Quota Immigration Visa #8458

Lilli Bechmann-Rahn — Quota Immigration Visa # 8459

Ruth Marion Rahn — Quota Immigration Visa # 8460

Helen Bergen-Lorz — Quota Immigration Visa #8461

And now comes the fateful part of this narrative. I will summarize here what happened. In October 1937, as part of the documents required for emigration, Alfred had to fill out a questionnaire, under oath, required by the Foreign Exchange Office. He had to disclose all property held by himself and his wife, and filled out a similar form for his mother. In this statement he put down RM (Reichsmarks)1500 ($600) in the space that asked for the declaration of "cash on hand". He also listed the property at 129 Konigstrasse as well as the funds held by his business. He had withdrawn money from his bank account to have cash ready as a guaranty towards payments of debts and last minute taxes, and in case his credit balances with the banks were stopped because of his intention to emigrate. He listed this amount, RM 30,000, ($12,000) in that part of the declaration of his business funds. In other words, he listed the funds he had on hand in what the authorities said was the wrong place on the affidavit. This money was in an open strongbox in the house, with no attempt to hide it. A contract for the sale of the home and business had been executed on October 25th, with the sale price of 70,000 RM ($28,000). Of this amount, only 37,100 RM ($14,480) had been paid at the time he prepared the affidavit, and this is the amount he listed. This contract, because it involved the sale by a Jew, needed to be approved by the Nazi Party, and until such approval was obtained, a lien was placed on the property. The buyers, however, took immediate possession. In fact, Alfred never did receive the full amount, and this became one of his grounds for seeking reparations later. The authorities did not believe him, and he was arrested, tried in court, and found guilty of knowingly filing a false affidavit under the German Criminal Code, and also violating the Foreign Exchange Law. The two-parts of the judgment are critical since violation of the Criminal Code results in a prison sentence, whereas violation of the Foreign Exchange Law only results in a monetary judgment. Judgments under these two sections of the law also became critical later, when a determination had to be made as to whether his conduct involved moral turpitude.

Judgement — February 2, 1938

The official translation of the judgment was done by the official translator and interpreter of the English language at the courts in Munich, and notarized by the Vice Counsel of the United States at Munich. The translation is dated March 23, 1938. It was evidently needed by Lilli as she and Max wrote to various people about obtaining a new visa.

The Judgment is headed: JUDGMENT In the Name of the German People! (Exclamation point in original) The trial was held in the Court of Assizes at the District Court of Fuerth with respect to criminal proceedings against Alfred Rahn, Merchant in Fuerth, on account of false affidavit rendered and transgression of the foreign exchange regulations at the public hearing of Tuesday, January 25, 1938. The judgment states that it was attended by 5 individuals, including Fritz Hofmockel, who was the bookkeeper of Alfred's firm. The others were listed as Chairman, Commercial Clerk, Official of the Public Prosecutor's Office and Official of the Records of the Office. It appears that 3 (and perhaps 4) of the 5 attendees were with the Public Prosecutor's office and only Mr. Hofmockel testified on behalf of Alfred.

The Judgment begins with the punishment: Alfred Rahn, born January 28, 1901, in Fuerth, Bavaria, married, merchant in Fuerth, since December 30, 1937 in detention on

Judgment — February 2, 1938
Note end of sentence (Strafende) gives exact date and
time (to the minute) the sentence is to end.

remand in the court's prison at Fuerth, in this matter, is being sentenced to ONE year and two months imprisonment and the costs of the proceedings because of continued transgression of the foreign exchange law according to paragraphs 34, 43, No.5 of the foreign exchange law in connection with the simultaneous misdemeanor of rendering a false affidavit. THREE weeks of detention will be credited. Submitting a false affidavit is a criminal offense, punishable by imprisonment, while violation of the foreign exchange law is simply a misdemeanor, punishable by a fine.

The court's reasons and explanation for the Judgment, covering 7 pages, can be summarized as follows. The court begins by stating:

The accused had since May or June 1937 the intention of emigrating from Germany since, being a Jew, he saw his commercial progress in Germany obstructed (sic). With this object in view he gathered the requisite information from the economic trustee Georg Held in Nuremberg , and was informed of his obligations towards the foreign exchange office. From June 8 through August 23, 1937 some funds were withdrawn from the wholesale ironware business of which he and his mother, Johanna Rahn, were *owners. The balance sheet of the business on December 31, 1936 shows a total of RM 38,217.17 ($15,286) and RM 105,061.58 ($42,024) respectively. He dissolved his and his mother's bank accounts in July, 1937 and the total amount of RM 30,000 ($12,000) he kept in ready cash in a strongbox in the safe of his firm, segregated as to time and place of withdrawals until October 22, 1937 and thereafter in his private residence. About September 1937 he got into contract with the Witness Schulte-Wisserman on account of the sale of his business. On October 22, 1937 the negotiations were concluded with the result that the firm with the house at 129 Konigstrasse in Fuerth was sold for RM 110,000, ($44,000) not including the inventory of goods and the outstanding claims, remaining with Rahn. There were certain liabilities for outstanding salaries and goods. The property at 129 Konigstrasse, being in the name of Mrs. Johanna Rahn, was not sold to the firm of successors but to its partner Terberger as per notarial agreement of October 22, 1937 for RM 70,000, which is contained in the 110,000 above. On October 22, 1937 Terberger paid 75,000 RM ($30,000) into a separate account in the Dresdner Bank in favor of Mrs. Johanna Rahn, with the proviso that the property had to be unencumbered before the amount could be transferred to her. The notarial purchase referred to possible difficulties that might result from certain ordinances.*

(In other words, the court was well aware that the entire purchase price had not been transferred to the seller. Government approval, because the seller was a Jew, was needed, and, in fact, Alfred never did receive the entire amount).

The accused, on October 22, 1937, filled out a questionnaire given to him by the foreign exchange office in Nuremberg on October 19, 1937. He also filled out a like list for his mother, Johanna Rahn, also dated October 22, 1937 and had it signed by his mother. These lists he immediately delivered together with an affidavit as to the complete and true statement of the various amounts of property possessed of by himself, his wife and minor child. In this statement he put down about RM 1500 in the specific space on the form that asked for the declaration of cash on hand. In addition, he included the 30,000 RM which he had at home in cash, on that part of the form asking for business funds. His mother's affidavit had the same amount in response to that question. He also listed the property at 129 Konigstrasse, as well as the debts of the firm. The court stated that the accused had to take care of all the ins and outs of the business without any participation on the part of his mother.

The court stated that he was convicted of having rendered incomplete or incorrect information to a foreign exchange office and by the same action to have rendered knowingly a false affidavit.

Alfred objected that the cash he had on hand was included in the declaration of the business funds, and thus the totals were correct. The court said this didn't hold because he declared only 1500 RM as cash on hand. The court acknowledged that with an open trading company such as the firm through which the accused did business, under the name of M.S. Farrnbacher, the partner is responsible with his private fortune for the debts of the company. Alfred also stated that he wanted to have the cash ready as a guaranty towards payment of debts in case his credit balances with the banks were stopped because of his intention to emigrate. He had previously consulted with the economic trustee about his misgivings as to the closing of accounts. But the court said he was given to understand this was not to be feared if he were not under suspicion. Hence his withdrawal of cash was not to be based on the fear of accounts being closed. Alfred also stated that he always kept ready considerable cash for the prompt payment of his suppliers and thus continued to regard it as business capital. According to the statement of his bookkeeper and witness, Mr. Hofmockel, (a Seventh-Day Adventist) he really often had in readiness larger amounts of cash and paid for consignment of goods upon receipt of the invoice. But the court didn't believe this, stating significantly that this action was inspired "by the known Jewish method, by their financial power to render the furnishers dependent in order to finally dictate to them their terms of selling." The court said that the custom everywhere was that such payments were not effected by cash, but by non-cash transactions. Thereby it is clearly proven that the use of RM 20,000 ($8,000) drawn of the business were taken from the business and thus from the business capital and hence could not be declared as business funds. (This is a kind of circular reasoning that seemed impossible to counter-act).

The court said that he could have, between June 1937 and submission of the affidavit, spent the money and it would have been impossible to trace. It was also true, stated the court, that he immediately admitted to the officials of having a cash amount of RM 30,000 ($12,000)—in the residence and that the strongbox was laying there in open view on a piece of furniture. However, said the court, in anticipation of a searching of the house he could not do anything better than to immediately proclaim possession of the cash, as otherwise he would have the more incriminated himself if he had denied its possession. Hence this isn't proof that his declaration of fortune is correct.

With regard to the house, Alfred stated that it had not yet become the property of the buyer, the transfer having not yet been completed on October 22, 1937 because of the price regulation ordinance and the government housing law. The requisite consent by the bureau of administration had not yet been given. The sale price was included in the declaration of RM 110,000 ($44,000).

The court stated that an affidavit represents a formulated declaration and can only be considered in connection with the prescribed form to which it belonged (how very German!). The prescribed form had to be done completely and truthfully; then only can the complete and truthful answer to every point be verified. That one finally stated amount alone would suffice could not have been considered even upon the most perfunctory reflection. The court seems to be saying that even though Alfred listed the sums he had on the form, they were not in the proper places, and thus the form is inaccurate.

"That the accused has been conscious of the untruthfulness of his declaration is also evidence already by the fact the he, as manager of a larger commercial enterprise, possessed sufficient intelligence to recognize the purpose of the questionnaire which was to render a possibly most exact survey over every part of the would-be emigrant's fortune." (Here we have a kind of guilt by association — you should have known, as an intelligent person, what the exact purpose of every part of this questionnaire was about).

The court continued, in its anti-Semitic tone as follows: "This is Fürthermore being elucidated by the sole possible purpose of a Jewish merchant retaining RM 30,000 — non-interest bearing throughout months - namely with the intention to take this ready cash abroad either in its full equivalent or converted into other easily hidden values, without the control of the foreign exchange office and thereby avoiding the investment in restricted Reichsmark."

He was convicted under two laws — a continued offense against the Foreign Exchange Law and, in addition, of filing a knowingly false affidavit as per par. 156 of the Criminal Code. The punishment had to be proclaimed on the strength of par. 73 of the Criminal Code as per par. 156 of the Criminal Code since such prescribes imprisonment and thereby the heavy penalty in contrast to the foreign exchange law which provides only for monetary punishment.

The court continued in its anti-Semitic decision: "In meting out the measure of punishment there had to be considered at the expense of the accused the considerable public interest prevailing regards truthful information especially in the case of Jewish emigrants, since it must be avoided that non-registered capital is taken abroad and working there in Jewish hands against the German political economy and the German nation."

"The accused having been held in detention on remand in this matter since December 29, 1937 it is only fair to credit him with three weeks and subtract same from the period of imprisonment. Continuation of detention had to be decreed since escape had to be taken into account in view of the good financial circumstances and the already surely instituted foreign connections of the accused as well as the international community of the Jewish race."

As stated earlier, the punishment was exactly one year and two months (14 months altogether) imprisonment from the date of the judgment, February 2, 1938. The three weeks that he had already been in detention were credited. This judgment and another document spelling out the sentence were sent to the Fürth Police Department and recorded there on February 3, 1938 and in the Nuremberg archives (where we obtained our copy). The document containing the sentence is entitled Strafnachricht, which means Notification of Penalty Sentence. Below it lists Alfred's parents, his address and his race — "Rassejude". Below it says Strafort, which means the Place of incarceration: Nuremberg/Zellenstrasse Prison, and Strafende, which means "End of sentence: 5.3.1939 14,45 Uhr. (March 5, 1939 at 2:45 p.m). This prison was where the Nuremberg trials of Nazi war criminals took place after the war. But what I found remarkable is that the end of his sentence is defined not only by date, but specifies the exact minute when his sentence ended. Very Germanic!

I find it absolutely believable that Alfred retained RM 30,000 ($12,000) to pay off any debts of other taxes that might be incurred as a result of the "sale" of the business and the house. Who knew what additional payments, which had not yet been assessed, regarding the sale of the home or business, might yet be imposed? I believe him when he says his credit at the bank might be terminated because of his intention to emigrate. Obstacles of all sorts were being placed in front of Jews who wanted to leave. He fully declared the 110,000 RM ($44,000) which was the sale price of the house and the business. The court couldn't believe that a Jew would immediately pay his suppliers upon receipt of the invoice — but that is 100% Alfred. He hated to be in debt and paid all his debts accurately and promptly all his life. He was a stickler about being totally honest in his business and personal dealings. If a waitress returned too much to him after a meal, even just five cents, he immediately told her and gave it back. The anti-Semitism is not even veiled in this opinion, but the prejudice, suspicion and hatred of Jews is right there in the words of the opinion. The dig that a Jewish merchant would retain 30,000 RM at home, non-interest bearing throughout months, conjures up all the historical prejudices of the Jew as usurer and extorter.

It is impossible to imagine the agony and excruciating pain that Alfred and Lilli must have experienced as this judgment was rendered. In many ways this was a defining moment of his life — his prison letters are replete with references to his stupidity, his shame, his regret, his apologies, and his sorrow at not being with his wife and child. In many ways he spent his life wanting to make it up to Lilli — not only for what he had caused, but also for all she did while he was in prison, which he only found out about later. The hearing was truly a sham, and justice finally prevailed with Homer Cummings' opinion. The "sale" of the house and business at 129 Konigstrasse became the subject of a claim for reparations once they were settled in the United States, and had an interesting conclusion.

Newspaper Articles

We have in our files also two original newspaper articles that appeared reporting on this judgment. I can only imagine the humiliation Alfred and his family must have felt to have this publicly announced, especially for one so impeccably honest in all his dealings.

One such article appeared in the Frånkischer Kurier on Friday, January 28, 1938 on page 8 and reads as follows:

Misdeed of One Eager to Emigrate

The 37 year old, married Jew Alfred Rahn of Fuerth made the decision in the Fall of 1937 to emigrate to the USA. For this he needed from the Foreign Exchange Department a certification of „unobjectionability" by the Nuremberg Foreign Exchange Office. Upon his application he received a questionnaire from this office for emigrants, with the request to fill it out and have it notarized under oath. R filled out this questionnaire on October 22, 1937 and presented it, along with an accompanying letter, on the same day to the Foreign Exchange Department in Nuremberg. Since his mother, Johanna Rahn, also planned to emigrate, he included also a questionnaire filled out by him and signed by his mother. He also included the statement under oath that the declaration of property given by him was the entire property, his, his wife's and his minor child's, including all valuables outside of Germany and any money due to him outside of Germany, and that these statements were compete and truthful. In completing the

Questionnaire, R stated the cash which he and his mother still had as M1500 each. This statement was false, because in reality he still owned M30,000 — which was found in his apartment.

Fürthermore R stated in the questionnaire the value of the real estate at Koenigsstraat 129 in Fuerth as 31,500M and did not mention that he had sold this property and his business on 22 October for M75,000, of which M37,100 had been transferred to the bank account of his mother. He is also responsible for this neglect because he had filled out the questionnaire for his mother.

For these misdeeds Rahn was arrested on December 30, 1937; Tuesday he was brought before a court of jurors in Fuerth. During an interrogation Rahn tried to present himself as not guilty by means of some objections. During the presentation of evidence, however, where five witnesses were questioned under oath, the facts of the accusation were proven. Therefore, the district attorney in his plea demanded a guilty verdict based on false statements under oath, in conjunction with a deliberate crime against the Laws of Foreign Exchange and to convict him to a total penalty of 1 year 6 months of jail, and ordered arrest.

The representative of the Department of Foreign Exchange joined, as additional plaintiff, all the declarations and requests of the district Attorney in their entirety. The defense attorney of the accused tried to prove that Rahn had not been guilty of violation of statement under oath but had simply been negligent in regards to the Laws of Foreign Exchange, a misdemeanor which could be punished with a fine.

The Jury Court in its judgment joined the juristic opinion of the District Attorney and therefore declared Alfred Rahn guilty of false statement under oath combined with a crime against the Laws of Foreign Exchange and convicted him to 1 year 3 months of jail and court costs. The 3 weeks spent in custody already will be counted. Because of danger of flight, continued custody was ordered.

Another newspaper article appeared in the Nordbayrische Zeitung, on January 27, 1938 on page 6 and reads as follows:

Half a year ago the 36 year old Jew, Alfred Rahn had ideas for immigration. First of all, he looked around for a buyer for his business and for the property of his mother. When a serious buyer showed up, Rahn consulted an economic advisor about formalities which had to be completed in view of his planned emigration. Alfred received the desired information. Now he got in touch with the relevant bureaus. He received, among other things, a questionnaire from the Department of Foreign Exchange for him and his mother. The questionnaire was to be filled out to the best of his knowledge and to be given under oath. He filled in a ridiculously small sum, while he owned almost M 100,000. For breaking the Law for Foreign Exchange as well as false statements given under oath Alfred Rahn now stood before the Jury Court in Fürth. Here he tried, however, to present himself as innocent. The Jew acted so harmless, saying he had no intention to keep anything secret. He even made the cheeky comment that if he had to fill out the questionnaire again today he would do it exactly the same way. Based on the evidence the guilt of the Jew Alfred Rahn was clear. He was given 1 year and 2 months in jail, with reduced time spent in prior custody. Thus the emigration of Alfred Rahn will have to wait awhile, because the arrest order was of course not lifted. Alfred might yield to the temptation to emigrate secretly, quietly and noiselessly, without permission.

The anti-semitism in this article is so patent, particularly the snide remark that "emigration will have to wait awhile". In fact, ultimately the United State Attorney General determined that, in fact, there was no intent to defraud and thus no moral turpitude.

Correspondence from February 2, 1938 to December 31, 1938 — The Date of Homer Cummings' Opinion

During this period a number of telegrams, or cables, were sent between Germany and the United States. In quoting these cables as they were written, you will notice the word "stop" in the middle of a sentence or phrase. This is because one could not use punctuation in a telegram, so the word "stop" was used instead of a period or other punctuation.

February 8, 1938 — Letter from Alfred to his mother, Johanna. It is handwritten, from Fürth, on onionskin type paper. Johanna had just emigrated to Milan, Italy where she lived for some months before emigrating to the United States. It's amazing we have this letter — saved by Ami Johanna, and ending up with all the documents we have. He is in custody, in prison, in Fürth, about to be transferred to the prison in Nuremberg behind the Palace of Justice (where the Nuremberg Trials of Nazis were held after the war. Not sure who Alfred L. is, or who the aunts are.)

My dear mother!

Thank you so much for your dear lines and your good wishes of January 26, which got into my hands exactly on time. So far, I am doing quite well and I am content and calm, when I know that you are too. I ask you therefore not to worry at all and to enjoy life as it presents itself to you. If you are always calm and don't worry you give me the greatest pleasure. I expect to get to Nuremberg within this week and will probably not be able to write to you from then on. But I asked Lilli to keep you informed. I ask you to also keep in touch with Max constantly. Tell him that he should please write to you in German, and you can get Alfred L. to translate Maria's letters any time. I heard that Alfred is so nice to you. Tell him, when you see him again, that I am mentally shaking his hand in gratitude for that. Also, that the aunts look after you in such a nice way gave me great pleasure. Please tell them that I thank them cordially for that.

They have immortalized their name with me anyhow because of the marvelous home-baked cookies with which they provided me years ago on the ski trip. Don't worry and stay well! Enjoy beautiful nature, which now, that it is getting warmer, must be magnificent. So promise that you will not worry, then I am content. Hugs and kisses, lovingly, your Alfred.

(Alfred L. referred to herein is probably Alfred Loewi, Carola Loeffler's son-in-law. The aunts are probably Carola Loeffler, Hugo's sister and Lilli's aunt, and perhaps her daughter, who I believe committed suicide before we all emigrated to the U.S.)

February 14, 1938 — This is the first letter we have which Max wrote. He was "put on the case" immediately, as is evident from this letter. This letter was written to the American Consul General in Stuttgart stating that he had "received word from my brother that he cannot leave Germany during the period the visas were issued to him and his family on November 18, 1937. It is my understanding that they cannot leave Germany before the spring of 1939." The purpose of the letter was to ask that the American Consul General do everything possible he can for Alfred and his family when they are able to leave Germany. He sought assurance that the case of his brother and his family would be handled promptly, and offered whatever assistance he could.

February 28, 1938 — Max received a reply, written to General Cigar Company in Puerto Rico, from Samuel W. Honaker, American Consul General. He acknowledged receipt of Max's letter, and stated "The Consulate is, of course, unable to give definite assurances that the Rahn family will be able to quality for immigration visas when they again make their applications, but you are assured that prompt and sympathetic attention will be accorded to their application." He suggested that if they are unable to emigrate before spring of 1939, that Max forward to this office, shortly before January 1, 1939, new evidence of his willingness and ability to provide for them in the U.S.

This letter is a typed (COPY) — not on the letterhead of the consulate. Looks like Max typed it so he could send it to Lilli.

March 1938 — This is another document which summarizes the law, which Lilli wrote, apparently after her numerous visits with the American Consul in Stuttgart. She has really become quite an expert on the American laws regarding immigration and issuance of visas, and she summarized this information in memos she wrote (in German). She actually foresaw immediately the course of action which would ultimately occur, i.e. that the matter would have to be decided in Washington. This memo outlines the plan of action, and I'll reproduce it here.

If people who have a criminal record want to immigrate the United States, there is no obstacle in their way if the violations of which they have been convicted in Germany are not punishable by American law. However, for violations which are also punishable according to U.S. law, immigration is more difficult or impossible. Perjury is a violation which is also punishable by U.S. law. Decisive for the judgment by the American authorities or the local consulate here is exclusively the judgment of the German court and the paragraphs which it cites. Of course the seriousness of the case, the motives which led to the false statement under oath, will also be considered, but only secondly. Should it then appear that the false statement under oath is not considered such under American law, then there is no obstacle to immigration. It is also important that by giving this false statement there was no intent of obtaining by trickery a permit or tax evasion, that is, damage to the national finances. The consul advises, therefore, if the case should be attacked from here, to take the following course: he wants to give six copies in German and six copies in English, notarized translations. He will then take the matter up with the legal advisor of the Consulate. If he does not feel competent to decide the matter (and this will probably be the case), then the 12 copies of the verdict will be sent to Washington and submitted for a decision by the highest Immigration Services. If these authorities give a negative judgment, then immigration for this particular immigrant has been made impossible forever. If, however, the decision is positive, then immigration is guaranteed once and for all. A positive judgment from Washington would, in any case, be preferable to a positive judgment by the local Consulate because, if the consulate here makes the decision, there could still arise difficulties with the immigration which, if there is a positive judgment from Washington, would be out of the question. If the relatives of the immigrant enter the U.S. before the person in question, that would be, in the opinion of the Consul, no relief for the immigrant in question, but that also would have to be ascertained in Washington. In short, the final decision in all questions lies in Washington and can best be authentically decided there.

Although written in a matter-of-fact style, as if it were some event in history, the writing of this memo to herself, and the life and death decision in the balance, must have been excruciatingly difficult. It also appears to put to rest the thought that perhaps Lilli, Ruth and Helen Lorz might leave earlier, giving Alfred some kind of advantage later. All hope now rested with Max, and what he could do in Washington.

August 5, 1938 — Letter from Attorney Otto Rosenberg to General Consul Samuel W. Honaker in Stuttgart. (but stamped on the letter is the name of Mr. J. L'Heureux)

RE: Dr. Lilli Rahn, Fuerth

In my letter of the 5th of this month, I have advised you of the visit of Mrs. Lilli Rahn, Fuerth, and ask you again to make it possible for Mrs. Rahn to have an interview with the pertinent gentleman at your consulate who is already informed by the conversation we have had. Most respectfully yours, Dr. Rosenberg

August 8, 1938 — attached to this letter from Dr. Rosenberg, in our file, is a memo written by Lilli, once again summarizing the state of affairs. Here she writes: The quota number of the visa that expired in March of this year will continue to be reserved for the applicant.

Fürthermore, the Consul will back-date the petitions for new issues of immigration visas given to him on 8/8/38 to March 10 of this year, the day Mrs. Rahn spoke to him for the first time about this matter. A personal appearance again by Mr. Rahn is unavoidable, however, because of this early reservation it can be guaranteed that Mr. Rahn will be called as soon as it is possible for him to appear in person in Stuttgart, so that from this end no delay will take place. If it is at all necessary to get a new affidavit this will be decided at a later date; it is not pertinent today. The feared difficulties on the part of the Stuttgart Consulate may therefore be considered lifted."

August 6, 1938 — Letter from Max, written from Puerto Rico (in English). He and Lilli had begun numbering their respective letters to one another — this one is numbered 17. He thanked Lilli for the snapshots of Ruth "which show that my niece is a d... cute little girl"(in original). In it he wrote about contacting a friend in the State Department with respect to Johanna's visa. This friend was a woman, who informed him that if Johanna couldn't get a certificate of good behavior from the German government, the consul would go ahead and issue the visa. Johanna was in Milan at this point, having gone there in February, 1938.

"As far as your own immigration problem is concerned you will have received in the meantime the news that everything is all right. The decision of the chief lawyer in the Department of Labor under whose authority such cases are decided, was favorable. Walter will give you Fürther details." (Walter is Walter Bierer, Lilli's first cousin. He is the son of Emma Bierer, Lilli's aunt.)

He also wrote that he received a letter from two women requesting an affidavit for one of their sons, which he is not inclined to send. He said to Lilli that unless she asked him to write one for him, he must regretfully refuse as long as "my own family is not admitted to the US, I don't want any Fürther responsibilities". On the back of this letter, handwritten by Lilli, is the name of the Consul of Panama. (She was already beginning to think of other possibilities).

August 9, 1938 — Letter marked No. 2 from Lilli to Max, written about half in German and half in English. Alfred had been imprisoned at this point over 7 months, since December 30, 1937. His sentence was to end on March 5, 1939 at 2:45 p.m. and Lilli is fully aware of the dangers he, or they, would face if they did not have a visa at that point. She wrote to Max the following:

> *I was in Stuttgart yesterday and on the basis of the information you sent me I had a long talk with Consul H. J. L'Heureux, who had already received me some time ago in March and who deals with our matter. He was extremely approachable and very friendly — told me he would do everything he could but could not give me any blind promises. So far his statements are identical with the ones he made in March. He Fürther explained to me that the line of authority for him is not the Department of Labor but the Department of State. The final authority for immigration question is of course the Department of Labor, but the consulates are under the Department of State and have to turn there first. He repeated that he would like to bring about a decision from Washington in order to avoid any later difficulties once and for all. Gerard R. is therefore not directly involved. The course of the matter is now as follows:*

Mr. L'Heureux shall send the documents to Washington to the Secretary of State in the State Department. He said he himself would try to examine the matter to see if it is, as Gerard R. thought, from the American point of view, meaningless, and if he reaches that opinion he would transmit that accordingly. In any case he will do what he can. He is of the opinion that it would be best if Gerard R. could get in touch with the party in the State Department who is responsible for these matters, immediately, before the documents arrive, and to discuss the matter accordingly. He cannot send the documents directly to R. because is not directly in the line of authority, but it is of course possible and desirable if R. could get immediately in touch with the gentleman, whom L'Heureux does not know, but whose identity R. could easily establish. LH promised me to go to work on this during this week and to tell me when he is sending the documents. I shall cable you when they leave here so that you can let R. know when approximately they will arrive in Washington, so that something can be done immediately, before anyone, who may not be familiar with the case works on it independently. R will likely, because of the impression he has already formed, take a positive attitude. Maybe he can also achieve that everything is done as quickly as possible, because I shall understandably be very glad when everything is finally cleared. As soon as the answer from Washington to Stuttgart has arrived, L'Heureux shall notify me. He kept reassuring me that he would do everything possible within his power.(at this point the letter shifts from being written in German to English). I told him "to be or not to be is here the question" and he understood perfectly well that I must have the Washington permission.

He promised me to do anything he is able to and the rest has to be done over there. What concerns a new Affidavit and the other papers we need, Mr. L'H told me that we would talk this over when the Washington answer has arrived. We will have plenty of time then. At any rate he dated my new application for immigration visas which I gave him yesterday with March 10th which is the date when I first came to him and told him about the whole affair. So it is absolutely guaranteed that we will get the visas in time. Once the answer from Washington is here all the rest will be done by Mr. L'H who told me that all correspondence, also from you, if that would be once necessary, should go to his personal address. So I guess I arranged things here as well as possible.

Besides that he gave me a very important hint concerning mother's (she is referring here to Johanna, who had left Germany in February,1938 and was currently in Milan, Italy and making preparations to emigrate to the U.S.) immigration. He told me that in the American Immigration Law (page 25 if I am not mistaken) there is a special law that the Consul has the right, yes even the duty, to grant a visa without certain papers if it is impossible for the immigrant to get these papers or if that would cause him too much trouble. In mother's case, it is quite clear, he told me that the Consul in Naples must give her the visa also without a German police record. He told me to inform you, that you may write to Washington, Department of State, and there not complain, but tell them the facts, that mother tries since the 22nd of February to get the police record and that she did not get it till today and it is absolutely unknown when she will get it. Then you ought to ask them to tell the Consul in Naples that he has to grant Mother the visa without this record. Mr. L'H is absolutely sure that they will do that because it is a law on which this claim is founded. Please write at once and tell them in Washington to write to Naples as soon as possible, because Mother wishes to come to America as soon as possible. You may tell them, that she does not feel herself very at ease in M. (Milan) because she is rather alone, and so on. As I told you in my last letter, Mother has made an application in Naples a few days ago. If she should get a favorable answer within a few days I'll send you a cable, so that you needn't write to W. Otherwise do write immediately after the arrival of this letter. I guess that her affair will come at any rate to a solution now and that she will be able to immigrate before her passport expires.

What concerns our affairs please do whatever you are able to and do inform Mr. R. or whom it may concern as soon as you got this letter. I am so glad, dear Max that you are over there and am so thankful to you for all the interest you take in our affairs. I guess I needn't tell you that. Besides, the same law on which this application for mother is founded may be useful for us later on.

This letter definitely has an upbeat quality to it — despite the consequences if things don't work out as planned. Mr. L'Heureux sounds like he was truly compassionate and trying to be helpful — his offer to have correspondence sent to his home certainly went beyond the call of duty. As in all of Lilli's letters, there is no sense of feeling sorry for herself, what she personally is going through, her anguish, fears, etc. — but that was her character. It had become clear to both Lilli and Max by this time that the State Department, rather than the Department of Labor, would have final authority in this matter.

August 15, 1938 — Letter No. 18 from Max to Lilli. He acknowledged her cable in which she advised him that the documents at Naples were sufficient for the issuance of a visa to Mother. He cited a conversation between a friend of his and an employee of the State Department in Washington regarding his mother's (Johanna) case but is pleased that it is now settled.

He acknowledged her letter of July 31 and stated that he hoped the consul in Stuttgart had written to Gerard Reilly, the Solicitor of Labor in the Dept. of Labor, requesting his official decision on the case. Mr. Reilly can't issue such a decision without a formal request received by him through the proper channels; in this case, the Consul in Stuttgart. Lilli had asked Max to write to the Consul in Stuttgart, but he stated he would prefer not to do so. " I trust you agree with me that one should not ask his friends for favors unless their assistance is necessary and for the time being I think that the possibility of difficulties for your immigration into the United States has been smoothed out".

August 18, 1938 — Letter from Max to Lilli (No. 19). "Thanks for the many pictures of Ruth Marion. Walter also sent us a couple and we are always happy to get them. We also show them to our friends very proudly and they always say, "Gee, it's a good thing the child does not look like her uncle" (Reference here to Walter is Walter Bierer, Lilli's first cousin).

He forwarded the gist of Lilli's recent letters to his friend in Washington and she will take up the matter with Reilly so that when the report of the Consul in Stuttgart reaches Washington the gentleman at the Department of State is properly cognizant of the facts of the case. "Gerard Reilly's favorable opinion of the case should help greatly because his office is the final authority on the matter. As soon as I hear anything from Washington I shall let you know, but I think that you may rest assured that everything will be straightened out satisfactorily. "

Things seem to be moving along here, quite satisfactorily, and no one sounds panicked.

August 23, 1938 — Lilli to Mr. H. J. L'Heureux. She reminded him that she visited his office on August 8 and apologized for bothering him again. She urged him, in very polite tones, to send the documents to Washington and to notify her when this has been done. "According to the great importance this case has for my husband, me and my child, I am sure you will understand I anxiously wait for the definite answer from Washington because I am not able to undertake any Fürther steps here unless this main question has not been decided in a favorable manner."

August 25, 1938 — Letter from H. J. L'Heureux to Lilli. A bombshell is dropped with this letter — and we have zerox copies of it in the files, indicating that copies were sent off, probably by Lilli to Max in Washington. I will reproduce it in its entirety here. It begins with Madam, rather than addressing her personally. It is written on Foreign Service of the United States of American stationary, complete with seal of the Department of State, with reference to File No. 811.11. Alfred Rahn. It was, incidentally, this file number that enabled me, in my research in writing this memoir, to obtain Alfred's file from the State Department files in Washington, DC.

Madam:

Reference is made to your letter of August 23, 1938 and your visit to the Consulate on August 8, on which occasion you left certified copies of the original and translations of the judgment of the court in the matter of the conviction of your husband of violations of paragraphs 34 and 43 of the German foreign exchange law of February 4, 1935, and of paragraph 156 of the German criminal code.

You were informed at that time that, in the event there appeared to be any doubt regarding the effect of your husband's conviction upon the status of his admissibility to the United States under the excluding provision of the American immigration laws, the case might be referred to the appropriate authorities at Washington for a ruling upon the points of law involved. If the conviction had pertained merely to a technical violation of the foreign exchange law and the offense had involved no false swearing the Consulate would have been pleased to refer the case, for appropriate instruction, to the authorities in Washington.

A careful examination of the court's judgment, however, reveals that your husband was definitely convicted of a violation of paragraph 156 of the criminal code reading as follows:

"Any person who gives evidence under oath before an appropriate authority and knowingly makes false statements, or who, with reference to such an oath, makes false statements, will be subject to a penalty of from one month to three years."

Section 3 of the American Immigration Act of February 5, 1917, provides than an alien, who has been convicted of a crime or misdemeanor involving moral turpitude, shall be mandatorily excludable from the United States. The American courts have consistently held that perjury — false swearing under oath — involves moral turpitude within the meaning of the law, and consular officers have been so instructed by the appropriate authorities in Washington. Furthermore, the American courts have held that if the alien has been convicted of a crime such as indicated, and the conviction is established, it is not the duty of an administrative officer, such as a consular officer, to go behind the judgment in order to determine purpose, motive and knowledge, as indicative of moral character.

In view of the foregoing facts, it is clear that the offense of which your husband has been convicted definitely excludes him from the United States. Hence, it is useless for the Consulate to refer the matter to the authorities in Washington. It is also probably that the solicitor of the Department of Labor, who you stated had expressed a favorable opinion regarding the admissibility of your husband, was not aware of his conviction of false swearing. The copies of the judgment of the court are returned herewith.

Respectfully yours, For the Consul General: H.J. L'Heureux American Consul

Enclosures: Copies of judgment of court with translation

August 31, 1938 — Lilli wrote to Max (in German) upon immediate receipt of the above letter. She numbered her letter No. 3. She is immediately ready to proceed with whatever the next steps must be — no feeling sorry for herself, despair, hopelessness, but one gets the feeling that she is confident it will turn out all right. Mr. L'Heureux was clearly tremendously sympathetic. Again, I'll copy this letter verbatim here.

Dear Max,

Thank you very much for your dear letter No. 19 of the 18th. In regard to the visa matter, much has changed here meanwhile. Unfortunately matters at this end, which is from Stuttgart Consulate, are not moving as smoothly as I had hoped after my visit there on the 8th of this month.

When I did not hear following my visit there on the 8th, about which I reported in my letter of the 9th in detail, until the 22nd, I wrote to them on the 23rd and by return mail received the enclosed letter, which I am sending you in the original. You can imagine that I was flabbergasted. I could not explain this matter at first but had the feeling immediately that from some third side some opposition must have arisen. I went to Stuttgart therefore to see the Consul again, who again received me in the most cordial manner and told me that he was already expecting my visit. The reason for his letter was the following: his legal advisor in the Consulate gave the opinion which was expressed in the letter. A presentation to Washington can only be made by his immediate superior, the General Consul, who usually does not concern himself with immigration questions; for these L'Heureux is generally responsible. But based on the reasoning of the legal advisor the General Consul has refused the forwarding for the reason given in the letter. L'Heureux said to me " I signed the letter with a bleeding heart and I thought of you all these days". He Fürther assured me that he would be only too happy to get the possibility of granting us a visa. That is, he wants a golden bridge built from there. I now consulted with him in a friendly fashion what was to be done next. He said that since you are now an American citizen it should not be difficult to put the pertinent documents on the way to the proper authorities so they could be submitted to Mr. Reilly "through the proper channel" so that he could make a corresponding decision. He thought you should make a petition to the responsible gentleman in the State Department; you have this right unquestionably. To what extent you want to refer to the letter by the Consul or not is up to you. Of course I must leave all the details of the tactics up to you. The direction now is that without the aid by way of the Stuttgart Consulate an official way has to be found in America to get the documents to the pertinent authorities in Washington, most of all to Mr. Reilly, so that these authorities can give the Consulate the appropriate directive, that it has to issue the visa. I hope that this way is possible. Mr. L'Heureux thinks it should be possible. It is true that it can probably not be avoided that you, dear Max, may have to appear in person in Washington. That, too, I must leave entirely to your judgment. But the matter is so important that any effort in time, money and energy is justified, and it is of utmost importance for Alfred to receive as soon as possible an official notification of the consulate here that he will receive a visa as soon as he shows up there. L'Heureux will give this notice immediately, of course, as soon as he has the word from Washington. He showed me an official cable from Washington which stated that people who had once received a visa which they could not use for reasons beyond their control would have a new visa immediately as soon as the person applies again. This is exactly our case and there is not doubt that Alfred will receive a visa in time when he needs it. Thus he can receive it immediately if the critical questions have been clarified. Concerning the legal opinion by the Consulate, L'Heureux thought that one could, of course, also defend a different opinion from the one expressed in his letter. It is a matter of opinion if the lawyer in question puts more emphasis on the "violation of foreign exchange laws" or the one of Sec. 156. His lawyer was of the latter opinion; he himself rather favored the former, and that corresponds to the opinion of

Reilly.

In any case I am sending you again the documents in triplicate, assuming you will need them. I am very glad that you are over there and I have the certainty that you take care of everything in the best possible manner. If you were not there I would really be completely helpless. I thank you with all my heart for your efforts that you take on our behalf. I hope that some day I can make it up to you. As soon as you have taken some measures and have some news, I ask you to notify me, since I am longing for the day when this matter is solved once and for all. For now my heartfelt greetings to both of you. Yours, Lilli

October 17, 1938 — This is the next letter in the file. In it Max wrote that he was happy Lilli received his news concerning his recent trip to Washington. He is writing this back in Puerto Rico. He said he can't give any Fürther news — but no reason for anxiety because a decision may be rendered tomorrow or it may take several weeks." I have been assured by competent people that I have done everything that can be done for the present." He said if he doesn't hear before he leaves for vacation in 2-3 weeks, "I'll go again to Washington and contact people in a position to push the matter along. I am quite certain that in the end I shall get a favorable decision. The problem of the immediate issuance of a visa after the decision on the principal question has been rendered is already satisfactorily settled. I won't sail before November 3rd." Whether Max felt anxiety or not, he was very careful not to communicate his possible concerns to Lilli in his letters.

November 18, 1938 — Lilli to Max, (in German) and her letter #15. It is actually easier to copy verbatim some of these letters than to try to paraphrase them. So I'll do that again with this letter.

Dear Max,

Because of your cable which reached Uncle Ernst yesterday, I was in Stuttgart today. But since they had nothing there, I could achieve nothing. Today I sent you two cables, one from Stuttgart and one from Nuremberg, after I heard by phone about your second cable from Uncle Ernst (I think this was Ernest Bierer, Lilli's Aunt Emma's husband,). The content of the two telegrams was as follows: Stuttgart: Cable State Department Stuttgart today not received. After its arrival, return for talks in Stuttgart. Consul will give visa only upon specific instruction Washington, or determination that there is no moral turpitude. Achieve words to that effect or at least direction from Consul to send all documents at once to Washington. Contact with Louis Kupfer of Kupfer Brothers, best friend of General Consul here. Cable directly to me in visa matters. Lilli

Nuremberg: Consul says that you must and can achieve that Washington gives positive determination based on official documents sent you by me, and that Stuttgart is advised accordingly."

The Consul [L'Heureux] was friendly as usual, although it gets harder and harder to get to see him with the incredible demand on him. But he explained to me again that he could not issue the visa unless the State Department declared specifically that there was no "moral turpitude". Since Mr. Reilly has expressed this opinion a long time ago, it should not be too difficult to have his official opinion sent to the State Department. This would be necessary. The mention in your letter at the time about Reilly's opinion is not sufficient for the Consul, he must have an official document from Washington in his hands. Will you be able to obtain that? Everything depends on that. You can imagine that the whole matter worries me very much; besides everything else it concerns our future. But I trust that you will succeed. Please write and cable in visa matters always to my address because that expedites things. I have not received a single letter from Mother if she has received my mail which I sent to the New York address of Mrs. Sammoje. Did she not receive it? Please let me know soon.

I found out by coincidence from a friend here, one of the owners of Kupfer Brothers, to wit Louis Kupfer, is a very good friend of the Stuttgart General Consul, Honaker. My cousin Heinz (Heinz Loeffler is Lilli's first cousin, the son of Lilli's aunt Carola, her father's sister) knew that and has also taken advantage of it for his parents. He knew this already in May, when he was here. He also knew about my difficulties with the consulate. That he did not drop a single word about this proves again his attitude. But also unfortunately that of his parents, whom I had considered hitherto as my good friends. If the knowledge of these facts, especially the friendship of Mr. H. with Honaker, could be of any use to you in our affairs (perhaps recommendation by K. To H.), please do everything in your power and have no consideration for Heinz. He does not deserve it.

On the same day I learned that I had a similar experience with my Uncle Ernst (Metzger). He emigrated yesterday with wife and child to Paris. He revealed to me in the morning at 7:30, half an hour before departure of his plane, and recommended the care of my lame 75-year-old grandmother warmly to me. I was rather put out. I am glad to do what I can for my grandmother, but I think I would have deserved enough trust that he could have discussed with me before-hand all necessary things. I have no power of attorney. I have no idea about her financial situation, nothing. I have demanded from him that he get a visa for France for her immediately so that she can go there to her children, since I have to refuse any responsibility. And this after Ernst has come to me for advice in all emigration matters for months, since I have unfortunately turned into an expert, but when I asked him once for advice, he refused. This, as well as many other things I am experiencing this year shall be a lesson to me. (Lilli's 75 year-old grandmother, Caroline Metzger, was never able to leave Germany and was taken to the concentration camp Thereisenstadt where she was gassed. Her death certificate, received many years later from the Red Cross, is in the appendix to this memoir).

I hope and pray that I will never have to ask anyone from this dear family, who have shown themselves from this ugly side, for anything, once we are over there. I have not the least fear that we shall make our way.

Forgive me if I bother you with these details that are of no interest to you, but sometimes one has to open up and I really have no one here with whom I could really talk. I sincerely hope that you will be successful in W. because that is the basis for all the rest. My warmest wishes for you and Maria and Mother, and especially thanks for all the trouble you take and which we hope will be able to make up to you some day. (By this time Johanna had already arrived in New York.)

November 21, 1938 — Max wrote to Lilli (in English) from the Willard Hotel in Washington, DC.

We have received your letter of November 4 and I have also read your various letters addressed to Mother. As you know, I am here since last Tuesday but yet nothing has been decided. I am ashamed to say that nothing at all had been done on the case during the last 8 weeks (since I left here in September) despite the promises of a few persons to watch that the case was not shelved.

Of course immediately upon my arrival I started things going again and the Dept. found it needed enlightenment on some legal points and they cabled to Berlin for the information required, asking for a cable answer. Until today, the answer has not been received but it should be here shortly. I am now in contact with the lawyer who is handling the case personally and while he is most sympathetic, he must of course guide himself by the law. I feel confident that we shall secure a favorable decision and you may rest assured that I shall not leave Washington again until the decision is rendered.

While Mother knows that I have come to Washington on Alfred's behalf, and some business matters, I did not stress the importance of my visit.

Do you know that Howard Charles Kunreuther was born last week? My love to you all, Max. P.S. I wrote Coules (?) and Co. today.

Maria adds her note — she said she was happy to be there with Max.

We have to remember that getting from San Juan to Washington, or NY was no small matter. It appears they went by ship, and always stayed in the Willard Hotel in Washington. Recently, when visiting Liz and family in Arlington, VA, we drove by the Willard Hotel in Washington. Liz stopped the car and I ran inside, just to see what it was like. The hotel was built in 1902 and the original reception desk — all wooden with small boxes for letters behind it — was still there on one side, though a much more modern one was being used on the other side.

I could picture Max standing in front of this old wooden reception desk, sending and receiving telegrams. In this letter Max promised to stay in Washington until the decision is rendered. Pretty amazing. The tone of his letters gives no indication of the anxiety and concern he must have felt. He recounts the birth of Howard Kunreuther, the son of his good friend, Richard Kunreuther, with whom he came to the United States in 1926.

November 26, 1938 — Letter from Attorney Rosenberg to Mr. Frederick Wirth, American Attorney, Berlin, Lutzowufer 17. Dr. Walter Berlin and Frita Josephsthal, Lawyers, Nuremberg were apparently also sent copies — their stamp appears in the upper left hand corner of the carbon copy of this letter, which they apparently sent to Lilli. (I don't know who these attorneys are, though Attorney Rosenberg was one of our family attorneys. He must have wanted to communicate with attorneys who either were American citizens working in Germany, or familiar with American law). He wrote:

> *Esteemed colleague: I refer to the visit of Frau Dr. Lilli Rahn, upon recommendation by the American Embassy, would like to seek your advice in matters concerning her husband, Alfred Rahn. Alfred Rahn was about to emigrate to the United States, all formalities had been fulfilled, especially the immigration for himself and his family, when he was arrested and convicted. His time will be completed on March 5, 1939. It is now a question if the conviction is an obstacle to his immigration to the USA. An authoritative source in the U.S. assured me that this is not the case.*

> *Frau Dr. Rahn would like to hear your opinion regarding the practical steps that must be taken and asks that you set up an interview with her. If at all possible, I shall be present at this conference (I had defended Alfred Rahn). In preparation, I am enclosing the verdict. I am looking forward to your earliest response and conference date. With greatest collegiate respect. (It has no signature, because it's the copy).*

(By this time, panic has set in — no wonder. Lilli is seriously considering sending me and Helen Lorz out separately, but that has its own complications. Lilli can get her visa and leave immediately, but Alfred needs one the moment he gets out, and she points out that even after a favorable opinion from Washington, there are still a number of hurdles to cross and it would take several months. She wouldn't consider leaving until she is sure he can get out. Time is fleeing. It appears that Walter is in Paris — she talks of joining him there and waiting for Alfred. I do wonder who G.B.M is, referred to in the letter below. He apparently is the lawyer that was recommended by Joint (Joint Distribution Committee). She again talks of Heinz's parents, her aunt Carola Loeffler, and her husband Julius. I also don't know who she is referring to as "my cousin from Geneva." This letter has quite a different tone.)

November 28, 1938 — Lilli to Max (her letter #17)

Dear Max,

I have just returned from Stuttgart where I visited the consulate again [Mr. L'Heureux]. From there I sent to the address of your firm in New York the following telegram: Cable Washington never arrived in Stuttgart stop Consul only needs official statement from Washington authorities or lawyer that no moral turpitude is included. Consul is sure you can get this. More such cases have already been positively arranged. Case is urgent do whatever you can.

I am worried because I have not had any letter from you since the last, unnumbered one of the 11th in which you mention the bad crossing to NY, with the exception of letter from Mother of 14th of this month, in which she reported lengthily about the visits she made with you, but which contained nothing else. Simply the two cables to Walter (Bierer) I have received. As I have cabled you already many times, the telegram from Washington never arrived in Stuttgart and could also not be found in Berlin. The whole matter has therefore disappeared from sight. I was at the consulate in Berlin and twice in Stuttgart and had a one hour talk with Consul L'Heureux today, who is always very friendly but definitely has to have the directive from Washington, that they are of the opinion that there is no "moral turpitude".

I personally cabled you on the 12th from Fuerth, on the 18th from Stuttgart and from Nuremberg (the latter telegram pre-paid response), on the 25th from Fuerth and today from Stuttgart. I also wrote you from here on the 18th and 22nd. You will understand that it upset me not to have any news from you, inasmuch as it is a question of the utmost importance for all of us. I have no idea what you have achieved in Washington and if I can still hope that the matter is going in the right direction. You know what depends on it for all of us. I MUST be able to show the immigration permit for Alfred, as soon as possible, because the yet outstanding formalities will take another few months. If the matter with Washington does not pan out I have no idea where else in the world we can go, and Alfred needs an immigration permit for another country by March.

I talked with L'Heureux today about the possible earlier immigration and emigration of the child. That is not so easy. If the child is to go with Mrs. Lorz for the time being by herself, her grandmother and you would have to send a declaration to this effect via Washington to the Consulate here, that you are willing under all circumstances to take care of the child. Fürther, the grandmother has to request the child specifically. We shall also need a new affidavit under any circumstances should the child and Mrs. L. precede us, so meanwhile we would need new ones for these two. Thus, it is not entirely uncomplicated. But it would be possible to send these two ahead for the time being. However, if this were to take longer because of the chain of command that needs to be followed, it would not make any sense. If I could receive the certainty that Alfred can emigrate there in March I would not set all this apparatus in motion, that is I would emigrate too right away, at least to go to Walter for the time being and wait until Alfred joins us, but already with this in hand, which I can receive any day. But until Alfred's affair with the consulate here has not been settled clearly I do not budge from here. If I were to apply for a visa together with the child from here, the above-mentioned difficulties would, of course, not arise.

The Consul told me again that the entrance permit could only be given from Washington. He cannot give it because the officials there could still make difficulties. He also said that it needs a judgment from an official lawyer; that it would have to be forwarded to him. Private opinions are useless. Because I thought to have an American lawyer in Berlin write an opinion, but I can understand that that carries no weight for an authority. As I wrote you already, the people at the Joint are definitely of the opinion that G.B.M. is the right man for an intervention. Fürthermore, turn to Dr. Mosbacher, my former physician — mother knows him well. He is in N.Y. of late. I do not have his address, but Ellen or Dr. Sahlmann, whose colleague he is, probably know it or can find it out. He has a relative in Washington and works in the Ministry of Justice and Dr. S. promised me to do all he can.

Heinz's parents (Carola and Julius Loeffler — Carola is Lilli's aunt, the sister of her father. They settled in California and I remember visiting them there when I was a child) got their visa today in Stuttgart and sail on the 16th with the Manhattan. I have already said good-bye to them.

I am asking you again to keep me informed under any circumstances, you can imagine that it worries me no end not to hear anything from you or how our affair is progressing. I also have no idea where you are, still in NY, or back in P.R. (Puerto Rico) and where I should write or telegraph. Since I am really in constant touch with the Consul it is best to send all correspondence and documents which don't go directly from one authority to him to me, because I take them personally to him. That does not only save weeks in time, but is better in all respects. Or, better yet, send one copy to him and one to me simultaneously. In any case, keep me constantly informed about everything, It would also be a good idea to inform one of your friends, Richard (Kunreuther) in NY, or a lawyer or anyone you consider suitable and instruct him carefully before you return to P.R. so that there is somebody who knows the score and put people who might come to NY into the picture. I hope you have meanwhile talked with my cousin from Geneva. No doubt he can do a lot and is suited to intervene in this matter. But he will have to know what you have already done. Thus I hope that you were still there when he arrived. He left Saturday on the Queen Mary.

Please forgive my somewhat dictatorial tone. But you understand it is a question of our existence, our future. Many many thanks for everything.

November 29, 1938 — Walter to Max (typed copy of telegram)

HIAs Jewish Palestine Organization
Walter's address was 108 Be. Excelmans, Paris

(This appears to be some information Walter sent to Max)

November 30, 1938 — Letter to "My dears" which appears to be addressed to Max, Maria and Johanna. She refers to an excerpt from Alfred's letter which arrived yesterday from prison. See the text in the section of this memoir entitled Prison Letters.

Enclosed is an excerpt from Alfred's letter which arrived yesterday. His optimism and the clarity of this thinking are truly remarkable. He is of course completely right and I really don't know what I should tell him my next visit, because all the arguments which I can bring against his opinion are not valid, with the exception of the one I cannot tell him about, namely the existing difficulties for the immigration visa for overseas. I fervently hope that you (Max) will succeed in bringing this matter to a good end, because it belongs to those things which simply have to be accomplished. How could I appear before Alfred if I had to reveal to him on March 5, '39 that all his hopes have to be dashed and he cannot now, as he had hoped, build up a new future for himself and us all.

Concerning the matter itself, I cannot understand why it has suddenly become so difficult, because in August it was simply a question of finding the proper way through channels. Now basic difficulties seem to have arisen. Unfortunately I can do nothing from here and have to wait and see what you can do. I am so sorry that we give you so much trouble, but you will understand that we can put our only hope only in you. If it is still impossible to receive the immigration permission soon, please write me what you think that I can still do. Because some immigration visa into some country has to be in my hands by March 5 or sooner to present to the officials.

My mother (Ida, living in Berlin) was here for a few days to work on the emigration of my grandmother (Caroline Metzger, Ida's mother. Caroline was living in Nuremberg and was taken from there to Theresienstadt where she was murdered). She is 75, lame. She goes to Paris to her children and grandchildren. But since none of them is still here, we have to take care of that too, since grandmother is of course unable to do so.

In answer to your cable yesterday from Washington, I sent you today the following cable, return pre-paid:

"Specific information about similar cases not available. Stop. Decision depends only on Washington's official lawyer's conception"

My Aunt Carola maintained that General Consul Honaker had told her that similar cases had already been decided positively, but when I asked her today for details she retracted and said he was only speaking generally. Yet she had read the telegram I had sent you and declared it good. What my opinion of my family is, I know. The second sentence always returns to the information of Consul L'Heureux, who said, when I saw him again Monday, quite despondently to his secretary, "Isn't it a shame we cannot help this woman"? He wants to, or has to have a golden bridge built, and God willing you will be able to build it.

I need not tell you how much I thank you for all your efforts. Best greetings to you and Mother.

This letter, and the others toward the end of November and December made me weep as I read them. What could she tell Alfred? She had done so much to keep his spirits up, and he himself had done that remarkably himself. The desperateness of the situation is closing in. Should she leave? Should she send Ruth and Helen Lorz out? Major anti-Jewish events were happening around her - Kristallnacht (the Night of Broken Glass) had occurred on November 9, 1938 — people were being arrested and deported, synagogues burned, Jewish store windows broken and looted. What exactly would happen to Alfred if he didn't have a visa on March 9? Would he stay in prison? Be arrested again? Be deported to a concentration camp? Should she apply for a visa to other countries? At age 27, I just can't imagine what she was going through and how she managed to keep her head about her.

A word about cables and telegrams at that time is necessary here. They had no punctuation, so the word "Stop" was used at the end of a sentence, and thus often appears in the middle of the message in these communications.

November, 1938 — Lilli's memo which is undated but from its contents appears to have been written toward the end of 1938. This seems to be a summary of events. It's not clear to me at this point for whom this was written — for Max, for the Consul, for American authorities, or for herself, but the typing is hers. Because it is in her words, and because it summarizes what had occurred up to that point, I will copy it in full.

At the start of 1938 Mr. R. was convicted for breaking a law against foreign exchange according to Par. 34, 43, #5 in conjunction with a false statement under oath to a year and two months in prison. The verbatim English translation, notarized, is as follows: "is being sentenced to one year and two months imprisonment and the costs of the proceedings because of continued transgression of the foreign exchange law according to paragraphs 34, 43, Nr. 5 of the foreign exchange law in connection with the continued misdemeanor of rendering a false affidavit".

Mr. R. and his family had already obtained an immigration visa to the US in 1937, whose validity ran out in March 1938 because the family did not emigrate by reason of Mr. R.'s conviction. Before the visa became invalid Mrs. R. inquired with the pertinent consul in Stuttgart, Consul L'Heureux, who opined at the time that one could simply let the visa lapse since they would issue new ones when the family was ready to travel. He also said that in principle there was no impediment to the emigration. The judicial verdict before him he had scanned briefly. Nevertheless he thought it would be good if the highest immigration office in Washington would give its assent that the penalty of Mr. R. would not be an obstacle to immigration; that this would be better than a simple statement from the consulate. He said that Mrs. R. should submit the verdict to him in German and English, with six copies each, and he would forward it to the Immigration Services in the U.S. The highest immigration office is the Department of Labor. The consulates, however, are under the State Department, so that the matter has to be directed to the Department of State first, which would then forward it to the Department of Labor, if it cannot or would not decide on its own. Mrs. R. however, did not send the desired documents to Stuttgart, but got in touch with her brother-in-law in America, the brother of her husband, Mr. M.R. who is an American citizen. He tried to establish a connection to the Immigration Department on his own hook, and notified Mrs. R. in August that Senator Reilly in Washington in the Department of Labor had made positive statements about the case and had declared that in his opinion this was not a case of "moral turpitude", therefore no impediment to Mr. R's immigration existed. Mr. Reilly had before him the documents that Mrs. R. had submitted to her brother-in-law, the notarized German and English texts of the judicial verdict. After receiving this information Mrs. R. went again to the consulate in Stuttgart, where the consul declared he would send the papers immediately to Washington. When Mrs. R. did not hear anything for a number of days she complained in Stuttgart. Thereupon she received a letter from the Consul in which he informed her that after a careful reading of the verdict he had concluded that the misdemeanor for which Mr. R. had been penalized included "moral turpitude" and that he had therefore lost once and for all the chances to emigrate to the United States. He returned the papers at the same time.

Mrs. R. went to Stuttgart again and asked the Consul what she should do now, since no other immigration country was possible. The Consul advised her to get in touch with her brother-in-law and to charge him with getting in touch directly with the responsible departments in Washington. He himself could not do any more, but would be very willing to issue the visa if he was advised to do so from there. Mr. M.R. in America has the unquestionable right to make appeals on his part of Washington for his brother. It is entirely possible, the consul said, that the departments in Washington could see the matter in a different light, but he could only go by his directives here and had to by the verbatim statement of the German judicial verdict. Based on that wording he was unable to issue a visa. If Washington, however, was of a different opinion he would be glad to do so but needed an official directive from there. Mrs. R. informed her brother-in-law of this. She does not know what Mr. M.R. in Washington undertook at this point, but he had indicated to her several times that he had done everything possible. On November 16 this year Mr. R. in America sent the following telegram to the uncles of Mrs. R. with the request to forward it to her:" Urgent you inform Lilli immediately that State Department is cabling today requesting their information and possible opinion of American Attorney resident there stop Lilli should contact consul and any other person on case to secure favorable report."

Upon receipt of this telegram Mrs. R. went immediately to Stuttgart, where, however the mentioned telegrams were not there. Fürthermore, the telegram of Mr. R. demanded exactly what Mrs. R. was unable to achieve, namely a "favorable report" by the consul in Stuttgart. The next day a second telegram from Mr. R. in Washington arrived, as follows: "Request of State Department was cabled only today to Berlin Consul General instead of to Stuttgart stop Believe information requested is whether violation committed concerned material or immaterial points stop After today's interview personal intervention in my opinion is a very delicate matter and should be attempted only if right approach available". After receipt of the first telegram and the failed interview in Stuttgart, Mrs. R. had already cabled her brother-in-law that the telegram was not there. After receiving the second telegram she cabled the consul again and he notified her again that it should be possible for Mr. R. in Washington to obtain favorable judgment and to achieve there what the officials there would direct to the Stuttgart consulate to issue a visa to Mr. R. An inquiry a few days later in Stuttgart found that the cable via Berlin had also not arrived.

Those are the facts up to this point. If Mr. R. in Washington has taken the right steps cannot be judged from here. What is clear is that IN THE SHORTEST TIME, that is at the latest by the end of this year, the permission to enter, that is the guarantee for it will have to be given, so that he can receive the visa the moment he leaves prison. A waiting period is out of the question for Mr. R. and his family because according to American immigration law anyone who has already received a visa which he could not use for reasons beyond his control will receive it right away again when he asks for it. Theoretically, therefore, Mr. R. can receive the visa immediately, if this principal question did not need to be clarified. This has to be cleared quickly and finally because otherwise Mr. R. would not receive a passport. This is therefore of greatest important for him and his future. The violation of Mr. R. consists of a combination of laws against foreign exchange with false affidavit. Since laws against foreign exchange do not exist in the USA this combination is there impossible and could be made formal — judicially from the American point of view against the refusal by the consul.

It cannot be stressed enough that release of Mr. R and his emigration are tied intrinsically to a positive solution of this immigration question and that therefore nothing must be left undone to enable the immigration for him. But since the petition for emigration, according to the information by local officials, has to be made at least two months before the intended emigration, the confirmation by the consulate that a visa will be issued immediately when he asks for it MUST be available at least before the end of the year, because Mr. R. will have absolved his penalty at the beginning of March. What steps will have to be taken in Washington is, of course, outside my ken, but presumably personal intervention with deciding departments by certain personalities is probably the way to achieve a positive and final ruling.

November 29, 1938 — Ely Goldsmith. An advertisement appeared in the NY State Paper and Herald, a German Publication on behalf of Mr. H. Ely Goldsmith, Immigration Consultant. Lilli, now reaching for any straw available, followed up on this ad and received from Mr. Goldsmith a more detailed description of his services, in both German and English. Through his office in New York City, as well as through his office in Havana, Cuba, he offered arrangements for immediate removal of persons from countries where aliens awaiting American Immigration Visas prefer to remove to some other country until their turn is reached in their respective quota. Specifically, he stated, "I obtain a distinct type of Entrance Permit into Cuba which authorizes immediate departure for Cuba and gives permission to stay in Cuba UNTIL AN AMERICAN IMMIGRATION VISA IS OBTAINED (capitals are his). He set forth certain conditions and stated that his fee was $300.00 and for children under 16, half price. He then described the procedure which basically involved getting a passport and steamship ticket, and Mr. Goldsmith would obtain a permit which would be sent to the American Consul abroad for issuance of a transit visa to travel through the United States, as the ticket would go via New York to Miami Florida and on to Havana. He stated that the Immigration Service generally permits the alien a stay of 30 days so that relatives may see their friends before departure for Cuba. Sometimes a surety bond has to be posted so that the alien will not stay in the U.S. illegally and will be supported by his relatives during his stay. He stated that arrangements have been made by the State Department to instruct American Consuls abroad to forward the files containing the visa application of the aliens to the American Consulate General in Havana for issuance THERE of the AMERICAN QUOTA VISA, when the time for issuance of same has been reached in Germany according to the waiting list established there. (Capitalization and underlining are in the original)

There are some handwritten notes at the bottom of this ad, which makes it appear that Lilli was considering, or did contact him. But doesn't this sound too good to be true? In fact, it was. Attached to the ad is a newspaper clipping, which appears to come from the New York Times and unfortunately is undated. I will quote it in full — it does provide some black humor in this otherwise suspenseful tale.

COUNSEL TO ALIENS GETS 7-YEAR TERM

Old Offender Used False Documents to Aid Immigrants

H. Ely Goldsmith, self-designated "immigration counsel" and a "sore spot to the Department of Labor for twenty years" was sentenced to seven years in prison yesterday by Federal Judge Henry W. Goddard. He was convicted a week ago of *using false documents in the operation of a scheme to make legal the status of several aliens who had entered this country illegally. Goldsmith, who had been convicted of similar offenses twice before, is 58 years old. The scheme he was convicted of operating involved the use of a legitimate rule of the Bureau of Immigration: an alien who is in this country illegally may go to some foreign port, apply for legal re-entry, and, if it is granted, return as a legitimate resident. Goldsmith however, assisted his "clients" to obtain false affidavits, where necessary, describing the clients as substantial and desirable residents. According to the government, he charged from $200 to $600 for his services. Opposing a plea that the defendant be put on probation, Sylvester Pindyck, Special Assistant Attorney General, told the court that Goldsmith had cost the government at least $100,000 in court costs and investigation expenses."*

(Fortunately, Lilli didn't have to resort to Mr. Goldsmith.).

November 30, 1938 — Telegram sent by Lilli to Max, who is now in New York since she sent it to him c/o General Cigar Company, 119 West 40th Street, New York

Specific information about similar cases not available stop Decision depends only on official lawyers conception.

December 4, 1938 — Letter from Max, on The Willard Hotel, Washington, DC stationery to Walter, who was still in Paris.

My dear Walter,

I should have written you a long time ago to keep you informed about my activities here. But the days go by and still I have not obtained the desired positive decision.

It will be three weeks tomorrow since I've been in Washington. I found that the files after my departure from here in September have been put aside. One must not rely on anyone in spite of the many promises which had been given me some time ago. I intend to stay in Washington this time until I have received the, let's hope, favorable decision. Shortly after my arrival I cabled you — Nov. 16 — that the State Department would send a cable with some explanations to Stuttgart. The following day I corrected my information since I found out that the State Department had cabled to Berlin, not to Stuttgart. When I cabled you I did not know exactly what information the State Department was looking for, but thought it would be good to confer with the consulate before the answer was written to Washington. The State Department was looking for the paragraph of the German Criminal Law book according to which Alfred had been convicted. The answer from Berlin did not harm Alfred, but it was not good enough to bring about an immediate favorable decision.

Alfred's case and the American laws are rather complicated: I shall simply explain to you that perjury is ipso facto considered as "moral turpitude", whereas "false statements under oath" is in certain cases a violation that is considered "moral turpitude", and in

other cases not. The American Law says — and the State Department must, of course, follow that — that the Consul, or in our case the State Department, can only consider the conviction and the paragraph of the foreign law. The Statement Department must not consider the reasons, etc. How often have I heard the sentence: "We are not allowed to go behind the judgment of the German court".

When a department cannot come to a decision about a legal point, it is obligated to submit such a matter to the Department of Justice. This has now happened with Alfred's case. The State Department has declared: this case is too complicated for us; here are the arguments pro and con, Mr. Justice, please, you decide.

The documents have finally been sent last Friday from the Department of State to the Department of Justice. I have hired a lawyer here who has worked many years for the Department of Justice, and has many connections there and is much esteemed. Fürthermore the Solicitor of Labor (chief of the legal department in the Department of Labor) will ask the Department of Justice for his opinion in the case. That is very good for our case — the Solicitor of Labor will send a favorable report. I believe it will take at least another two weeks before we receive the decision. We are hoping for the best.

After receiving your cable of Nov. 28 I immediately explained the case to Mr. Isadore Hershfield. The man was very nice but could suggest absolutely nothing to help our case.

Friday morning I talked with Mr. Goldman on the phone and his first advice was to get in touch with Hershfield. I told him I had done that already, and Mr. Goldman also had no Fürther suggestions. He offered to talk with Rabbi S. Wise, who is supposed to have very good political connections, but I have declined this help for the time being.

I have received your letter of Nov. 24. Many thanks for all your efforts. By the same mail I also had a letter from Ernst Metzger which is not quite clear to me. Since I do not know his travel plans I'm writing to you and ask you to discuss my letter with him. He writes "When I left Lilli was of the opinion to remain in Germany until the situation with Alfred is completely resolved, but she has seriously considered if she shouldn't send Mrs. Lorz and the child. She considers it absolutely necessary that you come to Germany in the spring in order to get Alfred out because she would no longer be in the country and somebody would have to be by Alfred's side.

I think Ruth Marion should be sent to me. Whatever Lilli may decide for herself, there is no sense in leaving the child in Germany and in my opinion she should send her out with Mrs. Lorz.

I am not clear how I could help Alfred if I came to Germany in the spring. I have been away from Germany for so many years. I wouldn't know where to begin. I don't think that my American citizenship would be of any help, especially now when the relations between Germany and the US are not very good.

Fürther I must not forget that I am not independent; I have a decent salary which we will need very much when Alfred and Lilli are here. Spring is our best season, and even if my boss would understand the reasons for my trip and would have no objections, the time might come when they might remember it unfavorably.

I would like to ask you discuss with your father, with Ernest Metzger and possibly also with Lilli what I have written in the two paragraphs above. It is difficult for me to judge from here how I could help Alfred. In spite of my reasons here not to go to Germany I would, of course be willing to change my thinking any time if you write and explain to me in detail how I can help Alfred.

Concerning Lilli, it is also very difficult for me to give advice. I think she should get out of Germany. Of course she has to make that decision, and Ernst Metzger's letter is not clear to me on that point. Please write me about that.

No more for today. My best wishes to all, yours, Max.

My wife sends her regards.

Max has begun to get discouraged. He feels strongly that I should be sent out. He feels, in this letter, he has done what he could and it's really out of his hands now that the matter has been turned over to the State Department.

Max here refers to two cables, which we have in our file. These were sent to Paris, to Walter. He is communicating here with Walter rather than directly to Lilli — perhaps to hide his increasing concern about the turn of events. He seems to be looking to Walter for Fürther advice and support. The first cable is dated **November 17, 1938** and reads as follows:

Urgent you inform Lilli immediately that State Department is cabling Stuttgart today requesting Fürther information and possibly opinion of American attorney residing there stop Lilli should contact consul and any other person on case to secure favorable report stop My address Hotel Willard Washington."

The next cable, which appears to be shortly after the one above, from Max to Walter reads:

Request of State Department was cabled only today to Berlin Consul General instead of to Stuttgart stop Believe information requested is whether violation committed concerned material or immaterial points stop After today's interview personal intervention in my opinion a very delicate matter and should be attempted only if right approach available.

November -- , 1938 (the exact date is punched through) Cable from Max to Lilli which reads as follows: "Have advised November 17 that Washington cabled Berlin and not Stuttgart stop Berlin reply received here week ago stop Specific information by cable about other cases already positively arranged might prove helpful stop Am using best efforts.

November 29, 1938 — Max cabled Walter in Paris: "Hershfield approves all steps taken by me and cannot suggest additional measures stop Final decision will require at least another ten days"

December 7, 1938 — Max cabled Lilli " Kupfer sailed for Europe Queen Mary last Friday" (I don't know what this means or who Kupfer is).

December 8, 1938 — Letter from Max to Lilli. Handwritten on Willard Hotel, Washington, DC stationery.

Dear Lilli,

It wasn't until the day before yesterday that I received your letters No. 15 (Nov. 18) and No. 16 (Nov. 22nd). Let me repeat again that we are doing our best to get a favorable decision as promptly as possible.

I cabled you 2 days ago that Louis Kupfer had sailed last Friday for Europe, although I don't know whether this information will be helpful in any way. I wanted you to know about his trip in case you felt you wanted to see him.

No more for today. Our thoughts are with you. Maria will write more. Love, Max.

Dearest Lilli,

Among all the thoughts that go through my mind these days, this one occurred to me and I want you to consider it. It might be helpful (and we would love to do it) to have us take care of Ruth Marion and the nurse in Puerto Rico until you and Alfred get settled after next spring. This offer and wish is also true any time you so desire. Should you find it convenient to part with the baby now, I want you to be sure that it will be a privilege for me to have her with us. My heart aches when I talk about this matter so bluntly to you, Lilli, because I know what your heart says to you. As to what decision to make in that regard no one but you can make it. I pray that you get strength and help to do the best you can. It will be a responsibility that you only can assume so successfully but I promise you that I shall do my best to take care of our little treasure.

What else can I tell you today, except to ask you again to take good care of yourself. Keep your chin up and hope for the best. We are doing all we can every day. My best love, Maria

This shows how strongly Max felt about having Lilli send me out now. He had Maria make the offer herself. This must have been utter torment for Lilli — the thought of sending her child out of the country, to Maria, whom she had never even met.

December 11, 1938 — Max sent cable to Lilli which reads as follows: Cable legal reasons for favorable opinion Berlin consular lawyer"

December 12, 1938 — Lilli wrote to Mr. Frederick Wirth, Leutzowufer 17, Berlin

Esteemed Mr. Attorney,

Following your advice I sent a telegram to my brother-in-law, Max Rahn, in Washington last Friday, 9th of this month, which reads as follows:

"Private opinion of American legal advisor to Consulate very favorable stop Decision according to experience 14 days after cable exchange Washington-Berlin stop Recommend to you today inquiry with State Department."

Today I received from my brother-in-law the enclosed telegram. As you can see from it that it seems to be very important for my brother-in-law to learn the legal reasons on which you base your opinion. Since it is very difficult for me to come to Berlin tomorrow in order to consult with you again, and since by good luck a close friend of our family, who knows the case happens to be in Berlin, I am asking you to receive Friedrich Landmann, who will call your office tomorrow morning, if possible in the AM, to give him the necessary information so that he can instruct my brother-in-law immediately by cable.

Although I know how busy you are, I'm asking you in view of the urgency of this matter to make it possible at all cost to see Mr. Landmann tomorrow morning.

I thank you for your troubles and sign, with exceptional esteem.

Inc.: l telegram. Text of telegram: "Cable legal reasons for favorable opinion Berlin consular lawyer".

December 12, 1938 - Letter from Lilli to Friedl (this is Friedl (Friedrich)Landmann, an old family friend.)

Dear Friedl,

You would do me a great favor by going on my stead tomorrow to Dr. Wirth. You will find his address in the enclosed copy of my letter to him by the same mail. Last Monday I gave him complete instructions and the case is known to him in all its details, as well as everything that has meanwhile been done by me and by Max. He still has a copy of the verdict.

You will now have to extract the following from him: LAW BOOKS AND EXACT PARAGRAPHS on which his opinion is based. In my presence he looked up several things, thus his opinion is not grasped out of the blue but based on legal documents in front of him. It would be best if you could get him to cable directly to Max, under his name. Costs of this telegram are immaterial. It should in any event be so detailed that Max can make use of it. He grasped immediately that the whole thing stands and falls with the question of "moral turpitude". That is, is it impossible; if it is not included, then there is no obstacle to emigration. Thus the telegram should read something like this: Moral turpitude not involved because according to Par. Par. ... and now follows reasoning. In any case, cable in English so that Max can present the original. Wirth puts special emphasis on the fact that, as is clearly and uncontestably evident from the judgment, the final sum given by Alfred is correct, that it was simply a matter of entering it in the wrong column. It seems to me that Alfred had not emphasized this point strong enough, although I kept reminding him. Furthermore, there is no question of tax evasion, etc. Also, the sum in question was neither withdrawn nor seized, which shows that there was no financial damage. This must be emphasized again.

If Wirth does not cable himself, you simply have to do it based on what Wirth had. I thank you so much for all your efforts and hope that you will be successful. Max's address is: Washington, Willard Hotel. Telegraph NLT. He will have it in any case Tuesday, and if possible with 15. —R.P. Warmly, your

Here Lilli is lawyering at her best — she often stated to me that she would have loved to be a lawyer — she would have been superb at it. She gets right to the point, and thinks so clearly about what is needed to resolve this issue, even going so far as to compose the telegram she wants Attorney Wirth to send to Washington.

December 12, 1938 — Lilli to Attorney Wirth in Berlin

Esteemed Mr. Attorney:

Mr. Landmann informed me about the telephone conversation he has had with you and I have informed my brother-in-law accordingly. Since I also gave him your address it is possible he will get in touch with you directly. Should you receive any news from my brother-in-law, Mr. Max Rahn, c/o Hotel Willard, Washington, or any other news in our case I ask you to inform me of it.

Most respectfully,

December 12, 1938 — Letter from Frederick Wirth, Jr. (from Berlin) to Lilli. His letterhead stated Law Offices of Frederick Wirth, Jr. of the New York Bar.

My dear Mrs. Rahn,

I duly received your letter of the 11th, instant, enclosing the original telegraph which you have received from Washington.

Mr. Friedrich Landmann also telephoned me this morning on your behalf and I explained to him over the telephone that in order to convince the American authorities that the charge against Mr. Alfred Rahn did not involve "moral turpitude", it would be best for him to see one of our Washington correspondents who is in a position to take the matter up with the immigration authorities. I gave him the name of Mr. Abbot P. Mills whose address is American Security Building, Washington, D.C.

My own reason for coming to the conclusion that the charges do not involve moral turpitude may be summed up in the statement that the figures given by Mr. Rahn with respect to his Davisen matter and which were also involved in the matter of the Affidavit executed by him in connection with such matters, were correct in substance if not in form. In other words, he gave the exact total figures of his capital and it was only a question of perhaps a mistake as to just how he set up the figures under the various items. A mistake of that kind cannot be said to involve moral turpitude as there was no intention when disclosing all he had by way of capital to conceal assets of any kind connected with the business in which he was interested.

If you feel that it would help matters to send a telegram giving the reasons for my opinion to Mr. Mills, please do so or have Mr. Landmann do it for you.

For my services in this matter, I request that you let me have the sum of Mk.60.

Very truly yours,

Enclosure (telegram).

December 13, 1938 — Letter from Lilli to Mr. J.H. L'Heureux, American Consul, Stuttgart

Dear Sir,

In order to get a new passport the passport office, Fürth i.B. wants me to prove that we have the serious intention to emmigrate (sic) to the US. Therefore would you kindly send me a few lines, if possible in German language, in which you will repeat what you already told me some weeks ago, that persons who once had obtained an American immigration visa and were not able to enter the U.S. before it expired, will get a new visa as soon as they are able to ask for it again.

I thank you very much and remain respectfully yours.

(This letter contains one of the extremely rare spelling errors — the English she has at her command is amazing throughout).

December 13, 1938 — Letter from Lilli to Max (her # 20)

Dear Max,

In the meantime I got the telegram Friedl did send you yesterday on my behalf after

his telephone conversation with Mr. Wirth. He cabled:

"Had another conference with Frederick Wirth, Lutzowufer 17, Berlin, consular attorney suggests consul Abbot Mills, high class Washington attorney stop Wirth's opinion moral turpitude not involved according to American legislation stop Most important is that the final sum was correctly stated by Alfred to currency authorities only rubricating of details was in question stop Wirth suggests if necessary for Mills to contact directly with him by cable. Lilli" This morning I got a letter from Mr. Wirth whose copy is enclosed. I hope all this will help you. You see we do what we can. For the money I spent this year only in connection with this visa affair for attorneys, railway, telegrams and so on I could have lived on another year!

My best wishes and all my love to you both. Yours.

(This is the first time she even talks about the costs of all this correspondence, cables, telegrams and travel. Fortunately for us all she was able to afford it).

**December 15, 1938 — Letter from Max to Lilli —
handwritten on Willard Hotel stationery**

Dear Lilli,

First of all, let me acknowledge receipt of your last 2 letters of November 28 (No. 17) and Nov. 30 (No. 18), both of which arrived here the day before yesterday. I also want to confirm our various cables; I sent you the last this morning and I hope to receive your reply tomorrow.

I cannot give you all the details of the status of the affair here because that would take too long. About 2 weeks ago the State Department decided it could not form an opinion and the case was submitted to the Department of Justice for decision. The case receives there the most sympathetic attention, but the people there resolved to study certain questions of principle involved — and therefore the delay. No stone has been left unmoved to call the officials' attention to the true problems adherent to the case.

I know and I don't forget for one moment what this delay means to you all. But please do not despair because of it. And even if the decision should be unfavorable, you must not lose courage. If it should come to that, I have no doubt that your immigration into Cuba can be arranged. Even though I expect a favorable decision for immigration into USA, I have asked Ben Wolfuer who left Monday for Havana to inform me about Cuban regulations. Therefore, you should make passport applications for you all at once. If it should be necessary when applying for passports that one has an immigration permit for some country, kindly cable me upon your receipt of this letter accordingly. Then — if I don't have at that time any assurances as to the USA visa, I will make arrangements for the Cuban permits. If the USA problems are solved satisfactorily subsequently, then you don't have to use the Cuban visa.

Concerning the last cable of today in which I inquired whether Mr. Wirth's name could be used by my attorney in talking to Government officials here, I want to explain that I don't know whether this will lead to anything constructive. But we have in mind that this man might possibly be well versed in German law and could therefore give the officials here a new angle on the situation. However, we wanted to be sure that such action was found proper by Mr. Wirth himself.

Regarding the child, we think she and the nurse should emigrate now — if for no other reason than to relieve you of that part of your work. In view of the complexity in connection with a child's immigration into USA — such as you describe — it might be preferable to send them for the time being to your relatives in France.

As I have already cabled you, I shall stay here as long as necessary. Next Friday we expect to go to N.Y. to spend Xmas with mother — but I'll return to Washington the following Monday or Tuesday. Love Max

Maria then adds the following: My heartiest wishes this Xmas and for 1939 you know what they are, Lilli dear. We hope that the coming weeks bring us the peace we need and seek. My best love, Ever. Maria

Max sounds pessimistic here — he's thinking of immediate alternatives and unlike previous correspondence, seems to doubt that a positive decision will be forthcoming. He again urges Lilli to send me out. I can only imagine the emotions of Max, Maria and Lilli at this point in mid-December. Significantly, he states that the State Department could not form an opinion and turned the case over to the Justice Department. In hindsight, this was the key to the ultimate favorable decision. The State Department was notoriously anti-Semitic and if they had rendered the final decision, it would, I believe, have resulted in denial of the visa.

December 15, 1938 — Handwritten letter from Max to Walter on Willard Hotel stationery. This letter was written the same day as the one above.

Dear Walter,

I confirm the receipt of your letter of December 4 and today I also received Friedl's letter of Nov. 28 which you no doubt have read. Tuesday I was in New York where I discussed Alfred's case with a Mr. Rifkin, to whom Mr. Goldmann had introduced me. Mr. Rifkin is a partner of the very well known Senator Wagner and Mr. Rifkin promised me the help and intervention of the Senator. We have to wait what success the Senator will have.

Concerning the situation itself, I have to tell you that absolutely nothing has changed. The Department of Justice has decided to treat Alfred's case as "test case" (how do you say that in German?) and the result may mean a complete change in attitude in regards to German convictions on the part of the American Government. As I wrote to you recently, American law does not allow the officials in the State Department to consider the reasons and circumstances which lead to a conviction by a foreign Court of Justice. Only the judgment has to be considered. But since German law is, according to American comprehension (or understanding) so "unlawful" all-in-all, the Department of Justice is studying now if it isn't time to forget the old-fashioned interpretation.

In spite of yours and Friedl's letter I have not changed my opinion with regard to a trip to Germany. I am of course turning the matter over in my head constantly. Meanwhile you must have received my letter in which I explained my reasons against trip to Germany. Please write me your opinion immediately.

We wrote to Lilli last week and again today, she should send Ruth Marion over. Cordially, Max.

Max has somehow found out that the Justice Department has decided to treat Alfred's case as a "test case", which in fact it turned out to be. It shows how closely he was watching the case. He also urged Lilli again to send me out.

December 15, 1938 — Telegram from Max (still in Washington) to Lilli

Argument of correct final sum has been stressed by my lawyer stop Consider it unwise to engage additional counsel or change counsel stop Intend to remain in Washington as long as necessary.

December 16, 1938 — Telegram from Max to Lilli:

"Cable whether my attorney William H. Ramsey Woodward Building may use Wirth's name in conferences with government officials and communicate with Wirth if necessary"

December 16, 1938 — Cable from Lilli to Max:

"Ramsey may use Wirth's name and communicate with him"

Here we have for the first time the name of the attorney Max hired to personally represent Alfred, William H. Ramsey.

December 16, 1938 — Letter from Lilli to Frederick Wirth, Attorney, Berlin.

Esteemed Mr. Attorney,

My brother-in-law cabled me as follows in answer to the telegram which you sent after the telephone conversation between you and Mr. Landmann: "Argument of correct final sum has been stressed by my lawyer stop Consider it unwise to engage additional counsel of change counsel step Intend to remain Washington as long as necessary".

Yesterday a second telegram arrived which reads: "Cable whether my attorney William H. Ramsey Woodward Building may use Wirth's name in conference with government officials and communicate with Wirth if necessary".

Before I answer my brother-in-law, I would have liked to talk to you by phone which was not possible for me in the course of today. But since I did not want to keep my brother-in-law waiting for an answer in the state in which matters are at the moment I have presupposed your agreement and have cabled him as follows: Ramsey may use Wirth's name and communicate with him." I did not wish to neglect to inform you immediately of this in case Mr. William H. Ramsey should get in touch with you directly.

Sincerely etc.

December 17, 1938 — Letter from Law Offices of Frederick Wirth, Jr to Lilli

To Dr. Lilli Rahn

Esteemed gracious lady, I confirm receipt of your message of the 16th of this month and thank you for the notification. I am entirely willing that Mr. Ramsey may use my name in the sense of your cable. With greatest esteem.

December 19, 1938 — Letter (in German) from H. J. L'Heureux on his official stationery with heading The Foreign Service of the United States of America — American Consulate. His file number is 811.11

In answer to your letter of 13 December, 1938, the consulate confirms, as you wished, that you and your family already had visa which had to become invalid, that you registered here legitimately on the waiting list and that you can apply legitimately for a new visa as soon as your husband and the rest of the family are able to do so. Sincerely, for the General Consul

H.J. L'Heureux, American consul

This must have provided enormous relief to Lilli, particularly since the waiting lists for visas were now very long. Again it seems Mr. L'Heureux was doing what ever he could and whatever was in his authority

December 24, 1938 — Letter from Max to Lilli. Handwritten on accounting paper in English from N.Y.

Dear Lilli,

You will pardon the stationery, but the only one we have here is very small and I don't like it. I believe I have acknowledged receipt of all your letters with the exception for the last one arrived this week; it is dated 12/11/38 (No. 19)

Maria had to come to NY last Monday night and I followed her Thursday because I

wanted to see some people on Friday and because of Xmas everything is closed from Saturday until Monday. Monday night I shall go back to Washington.

As you see, I have still been unable to secure a decision and I am sorry to say things do not look encouraging. I have done my best — you know that — but as matters stand today I hardly can hope for a reversal of the Stuttgart lawyer's opinion. Now mind you, no ruling has been issued and there is still a chance of a favorable decision. But at the same time we must seriously take into account the possibility of our unfavorable ruling and we must therefore look for other ways out.

I wrote you a week or two ago about the possibility of Cuba; please do not go and see any Cuban counsel until I advise you. Ben Wolfuer is making the necessary inquiries directly in Havana.

What I want you to do is to make inquiries yourself or have someone like Friedl (Landmann) do it, about the possibilities of entry into other countries. I shall do the same thing here. Even if there is at this time a visa available for a limited stay only, or a visa without a permission to work, you should of course take it.

I have written the above in a very matter-of-fact style, but you know that I feel otherwise.

As I told you above, I shall continue to work in Washington, trying to secure a favorable decision. As soon as anything is definitely decided, I shall cable.

I also enclose a letter with the information about mother's affairs.

I pray that the New Year will bring us all more happiness. Max.

Maria adds:

Dearest Lilli,

Again I say that I regret so much that letters are our only means of communication. Paper is cold and dry. Wish I could be near you Lilli to tell you how much we want and hope that things turn out for the better in 1939.

I also feel it my duty to tell you that as far as Washington is concerned I know that every possible resource has been tapped, every available help put to work and that Max has worked incessantly and desperately to get what we all want. We both gave this time with pleasure, Lilli, please do not apologize for it. We would gladly give so much more of ourselves if we could only be of assistance, you know that. I am planning to sail shortly after the first, but Max will stay on until we know the final outcome. And in every way and at all times my heart goes to you and I pray God that you keep healthy, strong, and hopeful. All my Love, Maria.

Max here is very pessimistic about a favorable outcome. It's really the first time he shared his lack of optimism with Lilli. And yet, he promised to go and remain in Washington, even while Maria returned to Puerto Rico, until a final decision was rendered.

December 24, 1938 — Max to Walter — a handwritten note.

Dear Walter,

Please tell Ernst Metzger that I have received his letter of Dec. 10 in which he confirmed the cable to meet Dr. Goldmann. Dr. Goldmann has obtained a very good introduction for me and the mediation may be able to bring about a favorable decision. But, honestly, the outlook is very bad. A decision has not yet been made either way, but I had almost given up hope that the officials here will come to another decision than the Stuttgart attorney. I have written Lilli the same thing, because she has to look for another country quickly. I am sure you and yours will help her. I have come to N.Y. for the weekend, but Monday night I go to Washington again, and as long as a possibility exists I shall stay there.

Mother has already talked with Loefflers. I shall see her tomorrow.

Let's hope that 1939 will be better than 1938.

Warmly, Max

Max is very discouraged — and painfully honest with Walter — "the outlook is very bad" he says on December 24. Lilli should look for another country...

December 29, 1938 — Letter from Lothar Weil (Lali) to Walter. He was an old friend of the family. It is typed, in German and written from Stockholm. His typed address is c/o H. Landmann & Söner A/B, Wahrendorffsgatan 1 , Stockholm

Dear Walter,

Our mutual friend Friedl is here for a short stay and I am writing at his request.

He reports about Lilli, so far good. My dear mother, however, could not stand this life any more and has left us last Sunday forever. If Ilse wants to write to Betty, her address is now: B.W. 77 Empire Court, Wembley Park, (Mdx.) England.

In matters re Alfred we had an exchange of cable with Max and I give you verbatim what regards Alfred.

Max to us: Washington may render decision next week, stop, Prospects not so good.

We to Max: Provided negative decision Washington urge you getting visas for Cuba for Alfred and Family immediately stop Possible through guarantee in Cuba

Friedl will inform Lilli himself about the difficulties, which, by the way, are already

known to Lilli. So, don't write to Lilli about it. But if the efforts concerning Cuba are without success, we ask you to do your utmost to obtain other visas. You will be informed in this matter either by Lilli — Friedl, or me.

Fürther, Friedl asks you to keep me regularly informed about the affair Canada. I reassure you that I shall not talk about this matter with anybody and will have the opportunity, on my part, to pass on news to Friedl within the framework of the correspondence.

Friedl asks to be excused once more for not writing himself to you, but you can imagine that there are oodles of things to take care of.

Receive for today most cordial greetings, also to Ilse, and please confirm the receipt of this letter. Yours, Lali

Handwritten at the bottom: Dear Walter, Please excuse the brevity but I am in terrible haste. Many thanks in advance. Have as happy and successful 1939 as possible. Yours, Friedl

December 30, 1938 — Letter from Roman Vishniac to Lilli (handwritten in German) This is the only letter from Roman in this batch of correspondence.

I would not, dear Lilly, write to you some mush about a new, for you happy new year, if I did not believe it myself. I have visited my cousin Walter and was really glad to see how neat and orderly the boy keeps his things. You will answer, what interest is that for me now! You do not see things entirely objectively. Traveling from here and the emigration to North America is much more complicated, difficult and unnecessarily more unpleasant than to Middle or South. You are interested in the Immediate-Program. Later comes afterwards. Also Max's trip would now be useless. You surely know that the thought had been approved very much by me earlier. It is not without reason that we are on such good terms with South America. I also consider, if it should be necessary later, a request from the Consul a possibility, since the emigrants are to become citizens some day. So, because it does not work now the way you thought is no great tragedy. Maybe it is just as well the other way. It suffices if Ruth-Marion takes the route of the old "Santa Maria". And the hearts of the Indians will shout with joy to her: "We are discovered". Because, in the first place things are different, and secondly, as one thinks (Erstens kommet es anders, und zweitens als man denkt — untranslatable witticism, says Eva, my translator. Literally, it means something like this: First comes something else, and second only as one thinks). That goes for the worst also. And now, on the last lap, to let the head hang? That goes beyond the line. Must we scan the coffee grounds in order to see the happy long trip, white caps on the waves, albatrosses on the masts and Alfred's face in the deck chair? I pray to God and wish you with all my might — unexpected joy! — Roman"

This letter is handwritten on plain white paper so I don't know where it was sent from. Was Roman in Paris, where Walter was? The reference to his cousin Walter — he isn't related to Walter Bierer, but perhaps because of their closeness he refers to him as family. Or is there another cousin Walter? By the time Lilli got this letter, she had the good news. The Indians could shout with joy to her.

Correspondence from December 31, 1938 to March 5, 1939, The Date of Alfred's Release from Prison

January 1, 1939 — Letter from Max to Walter (handwritten, in English)

Dear Walter,

I have made inquiries about the possibilities about admission to Cuba and although a strict application of the Cuban law would prohibit entry to Alfred because of his prison sentence, at times things can be overlooked in Cuba — especially since our lawyer in Havana has very good connections. But it is necessary that Alfred appear in Hamburg with a passport that does not show his conviction, and I am assured that the passport won't. As to the police report, this will of course show the conviction and must therefore never be shown to the consul. He will be instructed from Havana to overlook this; if he should ask, the reply should be: I can't get it from the German authorities.

I have not written the above to Lilli but I have written to her that the consul would have instructions to issue the visa on March 5 and that nobody should see the Cuban consul for the time being — until he has not been advised by his superiors in Havana.

Please tell Lilli also that she should engage an American or English attorney (living in Germany) to assist Alfred after March 5 in case she decided to leave Germany before that date.

I am still working in Washington for a favorable decision; but the prospects are not good. A decision may be rendered this week.

Let us hope 1939 will bring us all more happiness. Sincerely, Max"

January 1, 1939 — Letter from Walter to Lilli (handwritten, on Hotel Moderne des Dauphins Stationery in Grenoble, France):

My dear Lilli,

I have just read your very detailed letter to the parents and am always glad to hear good things. I wrote you last Tuesday in detail and suppose the answer is in the mail. If not, I ask you to think about the following and to call me if urgent (in the AM before 8:15 German time) AUT 85-73.

l. Assume the case that the USA visa will not be given, in that case I think we should get a visa for Cuba or the Dominican Republic or a South American state. I will be glad to pursue this here but need your consent.

2. In case it can be given, would you want to go directly or via here and stop here and there? In that case I would need to get a transit visa here.

3. What state would you prefer, Cuba or Peru? The latter is supposed to be easier. I'm expecting your prompt answer since one must count on some time for this to be done. Could you, if this is done, send personal papers (?) {or photo} of 3m or 4m. Would be good. Again my best wishes for 1939. Chin up. Your Walter

(So now it's Cuba, Dominican Republic or Peru!)

What both Max and Walter did not know when they wrote these letters was that on December 31, 1938, on his last day in office, the United States Attorney General Homer Cummings issued his final opinion as Attorney General, which was my father's case.

The entire history leading up to this decision as well as the decision itself are described in much more detail in the section of this memorandum entitled Homer Cummings. The last two paragraphs of Cummings' opinion are so significant that I will quote them here:

Indeed, it would appear that the acts here under consideration were performed under a compulsion as great as it was unjust. The alternatives open to the alien were to remain in Germany and be reduced to a state of penury and serfdom or to seek another life in another land. In selecting the latter alternative, he was confronted with the necessity of going forth with his dependent family stripped of all his possession or seeking to retain what was rightfully his own, in avoidance of a statute and a procedure which cannot be defended on the basis of morals or justice. It was a form of duress which in good conscience we would not be justified in ignoring.

I do not believe that the term "moral turpitude", as it is generally understood, can properly be ascribed to the conduct of this alien. I advise that you would be warranted in granting him a visa.

What is truly ironic is that Max, after all this correspondence and effort, read about the decision as it appeared on the front page of the New York Times on January 3, 1939. I can hardly imagine what he must have felt as he read this article. Although quoted in the section entitled Homer Cummings, I will quote it again here:

Headlined "Refugees aided by Last Cummings Opinion; Hiding of Funds was Held Not a Bar to Visa", the New York Times article of January 3, 1939 read as follows:

The last official opinion rendered by Homer S. Cummings as Attorney General, it was learned today, was in behalf of German refugees, and place a new construction on consular procedure in the granting of visas for the United States.

The case arose when a man, of whom it is known only that he has the initials "A.R.", stated in an application for a visa more than two years ago that he possessed only 1,500 Reich marks. Investigation showed he had neared 20,000, far more than the limit an individual was permitted to take from Germany. The man was convicted and sentenced to two years in prison. When he had served his term he again applied for a visa but, according to information obtainable here today, it was refused by American consular officials on the ground that he had been guilty of an offense constituting moral turpitude. Under the statute moral turpitude is a bar to the granting of a visa.

Mr. Cummings, in his opinion, which was rendered as his last formal official act, on the last day of the year, took a different view. He ruled, it was said, that the refugee had been guilty of false report, but under the circumstances, this was not moral turpitude and that ground for withholding a visa did not exist.

This was communicated to the State Department, which will have to revise visa procedure of years' standing in this important respect. The department must instruct that the visa should be granted the man unless it can find other reasons for withholding it.

No details of the opinion were forthcoming from the Department of Justice. The State Department would make no comment on the grounds that by law visa information is confidential."

Other newspaper articles also appeared in the New York Times, Time Magazine, and the Washington Post and are quoted or summarized in the section entitled Homer Cummings.

January 4, 1939 — Telegram from Max to Walter

Advise Lilli Washington decision favorable but will not be official for several days stop Should be kept strictly confidential especially at home stop Stuttgart should not be visited until Fürther notice from me. Max

[WOW — and yet caution is still merited because, as Max explains below, the Germans might still cause trouble]

January 4, 1939 — Letter from Max to Walter (handwritten on General Cigar Stationery, 119 West 40th Street, New York

Dear Walter,

I cabled you last night that the Department of Justice had decided Alfred's case favorably. The information is not to be spread under any circumstances; the decision is a radical departure from American jurisprudence here and unnecessary publicity — especially in Germany — might be harmful to Alfred. The official notification will be cabled to Stuttgart at the end of this or maybe only next week. Then I shall send Lilli a cable which only says "VISIT STUTTGART". I have thought about a trip to Germany long and hard and I shall not come to Europe. When I am in Washington again this week I shall discuss this question with a gentleman from the Department of State who might be able to give me good advice. If the gentleman has no advice Lilli should hire a foreign lawyer living in Germany. That's all for now. Warmly, Max"

Not quite clear what he means by "this question" here and why he recommended Lilli hire a foreign lawyer, at this point. He feared publicity — but the decision of the Justice Department was reported in the NY Times so apparently that had no effect on Alfred's release or anything else. But who could trust the Germans with respect to any question concerning a Jew at this point? Max was well aware that the decision was a radical departure from well established American jurisprudence.

January 4, 1939 — Letter from Walter to Lilli (typed, in German)

My dear Lilli,

I confirm our telephone call and was truly glad to be able to finally to give you good news. My heartiest congratulations in advance. I just got a telegram from Max which reads "Advise Lilli Washington decision favorable, but will not be official for several days. Should be kept strictly confidential. Stuttgart should not be visited until Fürther notification from me".

I am therefore waiting for a letter from Max and shall then call you again. In any case one must assume that everything is OK. Now, take a rest for 3 days, bring up a good drop from the parents' wine cellar and with your girlfriend drink to your future. Warmly, Walter

It is ironic, after all Max had done, that the final news was communicated to Lilli from Walter. For some reason, Max was reluctant to send any correspondence to Lilli at this point. Maybe he feared it would be intercepted, or that someone on the other end would block the decision. Walter's letter reminded me that we had been living in the Bierer house on Konigswarter Strasse (then called Adolph Hitler Strasse) since late 1937 after the Rahn house was sold and while Alfred was in prison. I hope she went to the cellar and drank that good bottle of wine he urged her to do, even without sharing it with her "girlfriend", which was undoubtedly a reference to me. What is even more amazing, and ironic, is that Walter himself lived in his old family home in 1946 when he was sent by the U.S. Army to be a translator for Streicher at the Nuremberg Trials. I wonder if those good bottles of wine were still there.

January 6, 1939 — Telegram from Max to Lilli;

Visit Stuttgart next Monday stop Cable acknowledgement receipt this message Willard Hotel.

January 7, 1939 — Telegram from Max to Lilli

Sailing Thursday for Puerto Rico stop Until then Gencigco, New York

Finally Max is able to go home. His job is accomplished, and he must have felt such relief. What he did was just phenomenal. I'm sorry I never knew this history in all its details, pains, anguish and ultimate success while Max was still living, so that I too could have thanked him and hugged him for saving my life. Like all of their life in Germany, and the saga of getting out, Lilli and Alfred never talked about this period of their lives. Whenever I come to this part of my memoir, I am emotionally exhausted, just from having read it.

January 19, 1939 — Letter from Max to Lilli — typed, in English, on General Cigar Co. stationery, Puerto Rico

Dear Lilli,

I have just received your letter or December 28 which you had sent to the Willard Hotel in Washington. Many of the questions which you bring up need no Fürther discussion.

I am happy to hear that you all are in good health.

Before leaving New York, or to be more exact, the day I left, Mother received a letter from Mrs. Lorz and after reading it and a letter of yours which you had sent to Mother, I told Mother that I would send an affidavit for Mrs. Lorz's young daughter. I could not do so immediately because we received that correspondence as we stepped into the taxi-cab which took me to the Puerto Rican steamer.

After arriving here I saw an attorney about the affidavit. On his recommendation, I shall not send you the affidavit. The reason is the following: Elsbeth is only 14 years old and because of that, many laws must be complied with that do not apply to adults. It is a most complicated procedure to get a visa for a minor under 16 years of age when such child will not travel nor live with the parents. I therefore recommend to let this matter rest for two or three months until the time when Mrs. Lorz will be in the United States. Then she can write an affidavit and apply as mother for a preferential status for the child, I shall be glad to supply her then with a supporting affidavit so that the Consul will convinced that the child will not become a public charge. I am sure you will understand my reasoning and explain it to Mrs. Lorz.

Maria is working hard and you will excuse her if she does not add her greetings to this letter; but I want this letter to catch the next airmail; you know that she also thinks of you all often.

We send you our very best wishes. Much love, Max.

Helen Lorz, my governess who came over with us, wanted now to bring her daughter to the United States as well. It is amazing to think that Max was again willing to supply the supporting affidavit and one can't blame him for wanting to wait a few months for this procedure to begin again.

Undated — Lilli appears to have drafted a telegram to Max at Gencigco, (short for General Cigar Company, his employer) New York. It is in her handwriting — block letters in ink, as if she prepared the minimum words for a telegram. It is written on the telegram form- Deutsche Reichspost. It has interlineations, so it wasn't sent. It reads:

Stuttgart got no information from Washington visit therefore was useless stop Return Fürth wait your Fürther instructions.

Undated — This is typed from Lilli in telegram form — her copy of the telegram she must have sent to Max. It reads: Cable Washington arrived Stuttgart stop Consul told me everything all right stop Thank you from all my heart

January 10, 1939 — Letter from Lilli to H. J. L'Heureux, American Consul in Stuttgart

Dear Sir,

I thank you very much for the information you gave me by telephone this afternoon. I am sorry to waste your time once more but the main question now being favorably decided there still remain some important questions and demands I want to ask you.

Would you kindly tell me if we need a new affidavit or any other documents or a statement of my brother-in-law — who gave us the affidavit — that his accounts did not diminish and that he is still willing to support his brother, Alfred Rahn, me, our child and our nurse Helen Lorz, nee Bergen, as long as we need his support in the U.S.

As I told you before it is of enormous personal importance for my husband not only to get his immigration visa for the U.S. as soon as he will be released but also to be able to prove this to the competent authorities before his release. You therefore could render me a very great service if you would ask us to come to the Consulate to make our applications for the new immigration visas on March 7, which is the earliest date my husband will be able to come. However, if — on account of technical reasons, passport, etc. — we should not be able to come to Stuttgart already on March 7th I would be enormously thankful if you would then now fix a new date some weeks later but allow us to come any day after March 7th as soon as we are able to come.

I thank you very much, dear Sir, for all you have done and you will do concerning this case and remain,

Respectfully Yours

The saga did not end with Homer Cummings' opinion ordering the consul in Stuttgart to issue the visa. The new problem was getting passports which were needed to emigrate. We uncovered this passport problem when we went to the Archives in Nuremberg. All this previous correspondence was about obtaining an American visa. Now Lilli had to obtain new German passports, which were nullified when Jews lost their citizenship. I will juxtapose the chronology of that correspondence with other letters during this period.

One hurdle, getting approval for the visa, had been overcome, and others were still on the horizon. Lilli mentioned here that Alfred had to prove to "competent authorities" that he has a visa before they will release him. This again is another wrinkle in the tale.

January 10, 1939 — Letter from Max to Lilli, typed on General Cigar Co. stationery from New York.

Dear Lilli,

Last week I finally received word that there is no objection against the issuance of a visa and after I had been assured that a cable advising the Consul in Stuttgart accordingly would be sent either Friday or Saturday of last week. I cabled you to go to Stuttgart on Monday, January 9. I thought, of course, that the Consul would by then have the advice and that you could attend to the remaining requirements.

You can imagine how sorry I was to learn when I came to the office this afternoon that Stuttgart had not received any information when you went there yesterday and that you had wasted your time completely. I called the respective gentlemen at the State Department in Washington at once on the telephone and he informed me that the cable had not gone out Friday or Saturday as I had been promised, but only yesterday at noon time. Therefore, I cabled you this afternoon as follows:

"AFTER RECEIPT YOUR CABLE HAVE TELEPHONED WASHINGTON AND AM INFORMED THAT CABLE TO STUTTGART LEFT WASHINGTON MONDAY NOON ONLY"

You know how sorry I am that this happened, but I sincerely trust that everything now will be straightened out. As I have cabled you already, I am leaving Thursday for Puerto Rico. Please keep me informed of everything.

Maria left last week already as she had to get back to her job and at that time we did not know that I was going to be finished here within another few days. If we had known, Maria would surely have waited another week and we would have sailed back together.

My very best wishes to all of you and all my love, Max.

Mother is well.

January 11, 1939 — Max to Lilli — the Telegram he refers to above (in caps)
January 11, 1939 — Max to Walter (handwritten in German)

Dear Walter,

Today only a few lines before my departure to Puerto Rico. The American visa question is now thank God resolved. . This morning I received a cable from Lilli that the visa from Washington had arrived in Stuttgart and that the consul told her that now "everything is all right". Let's hope the Germans make no Fürther difficulties. About the question of a trip to Germany we now seem to agree. If Lilli deems it right to hire a foreign attorney she should do it; if he wants to be paid not in marks but in $$ or another exchange, let me know.

Your letter of 24 December arrived two days ago, many thanks.

Cordial greetings to all, especially of course to you, and many good wishes, yours, Max

January 19, 1939 — Letter from Lilli to H. J. L'Heureux (this letter, written on January 19, apparently crossed with the one below written on January 18)

Dear Sir,

According to the advice you gave me by telephone on January 10th I wrote you at once, but as I did not get any answer from your office I fear that you did not receive the letter.

I wanted to know if we need a new affidavit or any other documents or statements from my brother-in-law who gave us the affidavit in fall 1937 — that his accounts did not diminish and that he is still willing to support our family (my husband, me, the child and the nurse, Mrs. Lorz, nee Bergen) as long as we need his support in the U.S.

As you know it is of extremely personal importance for my husband not only to get his immigration visa for the U.S. as soon as he will be able to ask for it but also to prove this to the competent authorities before his release. I therefore asked you in my last letter to give us the possibility to come to the Consulate on March 7th, which is the earliest date my husband will be able to come. And if — however — on account of technical reasons, we should not be able to come to Stuttgart on March 7th would you then kindly not fix a new date some weeks later, but allow us to come any day after March 7th as soon as we are able to come.

You would render me a very great service and I thank you, dear Sir, in advance for all you will do. As you know best the case is urgent because if I need new papers from my brother in law who resides in Puerto Rico that will take some time and everything must be settled till the beginning of March. I therefore would be very thankful if you soon would send me a few lines.

Respectfully yours,

(by hand) — P.S. If you think it helpful I always could come to the Consulate to see you and to discuss the matter.

January 18, 1939 — Letter from H. J. L'Heureux, American Consul to Lilli on his stationery. His file # is 811.11 WLK/EBS. Written on The Foreign Service of the United States of American stationary — Department of State (WLK are the initials of the Consul of the United States of America, William Lawrence Krieg — I found a small card with his name on it within the documents).

Madam,

With reference to your letter of January 10, 1939, the Consulate regrets to inform you that due to the long period of time which has elapsed since visas were granted to yourself, your husband, daughter and the children's nurse, new affidavits and up-to-date evidence of the income and resources of your sponsor, Mr. Max Rahn, will be required before Fürther visas can be issued.

It might be advisable you to cable the sponsor and request the new documents, which should be sent directly to you and not to the consulate. In view of the length of time that your case has been pending here, you may bring the papers personally to this office, and if they are found to be satisfactory, an invitation can be issued immediately for you and your household.

It is believed that by following the above procedure a minimum amount of time will be lost. As invitations are usually issued one month before the date set for a personal examination at the Consulate, there should be ample time to effect your husband's release and procure the necessary German documents.

Respectfully yours, For the General Consul, H.J. L'Heureux, American Consul

The procedure apparently involves an "invitation" (funny word) and then a personal examination. It doesn't end!!!

Undated — Cable from Lilli to Max (typed copy of Lilli)

Immediately need new affidavits for us and nurse and up-to-date evidence of your income and resources stop Send all documents to me directly stop Consul wants me to bring them to Stuttgart personally stop If you think it helpful let mother give an additional affidavit stop Cable acknowledge receipt this message

January 21, 1939 — Max to Lilli — cable

Message received stop will send documents earliest possible.

February 2, 1939 — Max to Lilli — cable

Mailing affidavit today

February 5, 1939 — Lilli to Lawyer Frederick Wirth, Jr. in Berlin (typed, in German)

Esteemed Mr. Attorney,

Assuming that you will be interested I do not want to fail to tell you that the highest authorities in Washington have decided beginning of January that there are no obstacles to my husband's immigration. The Stuttgart Consulate was notified by telegram from Washington, so that my husband can report there as soon as he is able and will receive his visa.

Sincerely,

February 8, 1939 — Letter from Law Office of Frederick Wirth, Jr. to Lilli

Esteemed gracious lady,

I received your letter from the 5th from which I was glad to gather that the officials in Washington have taken the same position which I had taken at the time in the case of your husband. I now hope that the issue of the visa will go smoothly and everything develops according to your wishes. Respectfully yours,

February 18, 1939 — Lilli to Max — copy of cable
Papers gratefully received
Undated — Lilli to Max — copy of cable
Papers all right received invitation March seventh.
(Again Mr L'Heureux accommodated Lilli as best he could by giving her the "invitation" to meet with him at the date she requested)

I want to add here some information regarding some documents I found in my files which show how the German government sought to strip the Jews of all of their possessions, whether they planned to emigrate or not. Even after Homer Cummings' opinion that the visa must be issued, there were still orders and decrees that must be obeyed before it was possible to leave Germany. On January 13, 1939 the German government issued an order that Jews report and assess all of their property prior to emigration. Every penny and every single item had to be accounted and the instructions are very detailed. Every single item had to be listed, giving the acquisition date, the purchase price and the current value. The list includes furniture, linens (bed and table), all kitchen utensils, children's toys and books, toiletries, clothing of all kinds, including nightgowns, (I didn't know my father had nightgowns!) undergarments, stockings, handkerchiefs, hats, luggage, appliances, skis and other sports equipment, rugs, etc. The total value was listed as 10,571 marks ($4228).

A 14 page, singled spaced typed response was prepared and submitted by Lilli to the designated attorney on January 16, 1939. All this was done by Lilli alone since Alfred was still in prison until March, 1939. The items of personal property which ended up in Denver had already been sent out of Germany to Antwerp in 1937, when we originally planned to leave. They remained in storage there until the request was made, once we were all in Denver, that they be sent there. I can only assume, therefore, that all these items on the list were left in Germany (after required taxes paid) and taken over by the Nazi Government.

Another step to strip Jews of all their valuables was a document entitled "Important Notification" issued to the Israel Cultural Community on March 2, 1939. It referred to a governmental ordinance dated February 21, 1939 according to which all Jews must surrender items in their possession which are made of gold, platinum or silver, as well as precious stones and pearls by Saturday, March 11, 1939, at the latest, in order to avoid a penalty, at a public location established by the Reich. The governmental ordinance stated that "After consultation with the office in Nuremberg which is responsible for the execution of this order, the following points are made:"

1. *Don't wait until the last minute.*

2. *The above mentioned articles are to be surrendered with the exception of a) personal wedding rings and rings of deceased partners, b)silver watches (wrist and pocket), c)silver tableware (4 pieces) per person: knife, fork, spoon, coffee spoon, d)silver items up to a weight of 4 grams per piece and a total weight of 200 grams per person, e)dental prostheses if in use by the person.*

3. *To be surrendered are in particular gold items regardless of weight, for instance, golden spectacles (without lenses), dentures not in use, watches have to contain their works.*

4. *In case of mixed marriages, the Jewish partner is exempted if there are children who are not classified as Jews. This is valid even if the marriage is no longer valid. In case of a childless marriage, the Jewish wife, if the husband is of German blood or Mischling 1st degree.*

5. *The items are to be delivered in packages with name and address (not in suitcases) and including typewritten lists in 5 copies, itemized. Do not forget name and address. These lists are to be delivered simultaneously but separated from the items. The enclosed form is to be signed. Persons who own no bank account have to establish one.*

6. *Office hours are AM 8-12, PM 14-17 and Saturdays 8-11 1/2.*

7. *Emigrants who have already received the written request from their foreign exchange office regarding surrender of jewelry, gold and silver items will have to submit the form issued by that office, filled out. This office is not involved in the surrender of tin objects, carpets, and other objects not subject to this order under RM 1000 ($400) in value. These objects may be sold on the open market.*

I don't know whether Lilli had to comply with this latest order, and assume that she had previously divested herself of almost all the items mentioned herein, including jewelry.

Given the dates of these orders, I inserted them here in this memoir.

Correspondence After March 5, 1939

March 8, 1939 — Postcard (handwritten) from Stuttgart from Alfred to Johanna, who is in New York. The address is Johanna Rahn, c/o Mrs. L(S)amoje, 905 Westend Avenue, 104th Street, Apt. 51, New York City, NY.

Dear Mother! I don't need to tell you how happy I am to be able to write to you again after a long time. It was a great relief to me to hear always that you were doing well.

Yesterday we received here the visas. Lilli went yesterday to Fürth while I will stay here a few more days with Miss L. (Helen Lorz) and Ruth, in order to move over to Ernst/ Emma (Bierer, who are living in Paris), from where I shall be able to write to you more in detail. Please excuse, therefore, the inadequacy of this card and be patient for another week. I just want to add that you have no idea what Lilli has accomplished and still does. She has outdone herself, she is fantastic — and Ruth Marion is a marvel, simply unbelievable, and fills me with an ineffable feeling of joy. I feel well, am looking, according to general judgment, better than ever. So, once again don't be angry if I do not write more today. I am looking forward to a reunion soon and wish you until then all the best and hug you warmly in my thoughts. Your Alfred

Alfred must have been overwhelmed with emotion and joy as he wrote this card to his mother — the first perhaps that he had written in 14 months. It was now written in freedom after this long ordeal. The reference to moving over to Ernst/Emma Bierer refers to the imminent move to Paris, where they are. A few days later he wrote the longer letter below describing his emotions and experiences over the past 14 months.

March 13, 1939 — Letter from Alfred (typed, in German) to Johanna and written from Paris.

My dear Mother! I am very happy to be able to write you directly again after a long pause. Ruth Marion and Mrs. L. have arrived here last night after many dangers, while Lilli still undertakes the last winding up affairs in Fürth and, I hope, arrives here soon. We are booked on the Washington for April 5.

Although I had no idea about the difficulties that existed in Stuttgart, the knowledge that Lilli and Maria/Max were doing everything possible gave me the strength to get through this year. Via Lilli I have received good reports about you, which pleased me, of course. Lilli was fabulous and outdid herself. You know only the least of what she has accomplished. She had the great worries about us, about our future, she took care of your affairs brilliantly, and I can tell you that by your departure much, very much has been spared you. Lilli managed, in her letters and when she visited me, to exert such an influence on me that I always remained calm — with a few exceptions — and if I find myself today in the best physical and mental condition, I owe this solely to her. Lilli experienced the terrible times in November; twice gangs invaded her house at night and only because of her circumspection was a disaster averted. In those days Lilli found the time to render services in the Jewish hospital until late into the night, where there were terrible scenes. Lilli is today an expert in matters of emigration and when I tell you that lawyers ask her advice (I am not exaggerating) you can imagine how much she is valued among strange people. She finds the time to be of help to all kinds of people. You simply cannot imagine what she has achieved and what she is still achieving.

Unfortunately she does not look well — but that is not surprising and one can only hope that she gets here soon and healthy. I am writing to Steinhardts and Richard Kunreuthers, to have them look for quarters for us. I think they'll do it right. Don't be angry when I close now, that is, continue this letter by sending you copies of the last two pages of a letter which I wrote to Max & Maria just now (unfortunately I have no copies of the first page).

Ruth Marion is terrific. I cannot describe the feelings which surged through me when I faced this child again after such a long pause. Ruth is not only a pretty, but also a well-brought up child; may God grant that she will continue to thrive. She was a blessing for Lilli; she was the only one who could still laugh, and it was she who made life bearable for Lilli. I shall never forget the large, beautiful eyes with which she looked at me, without saying anything, silently a week ago when I came into the house, until her eyes started to shine and she said with her sweet childish voice " Das is es Pappile" (that's Daddy). She is marvelous, and I am looking forward to introducing her to you.

So, I was released punctually on March 5, met by Lilli and Friedl, who has proved himself brilliantly, same as Luta-Roman, Bierers (especially Walter). Lilli had prepared everything fantastically. Exactly on March 6 I received my passport, same as Lilli, etc. and at the same time my good-conduct certificate. This certificate does not contain (by error or deliberately) any entry about my prison sentence. In my case an absolutely incredible circumstance. On the evening of March 6 we traveled to Stuttgart, where we arrived after midnight and spent the night in a small Jewish pension. On March 7 at quarter to six there is a loud ring. I woke up and say immediately: they are coming to get me again. Indeed — a knock — criminal police — "come along immediately for an interview." I got out of bed and can think of only one thing; now everything is lost. For the first time in my life I literally break down, without, however losing consciousness. After about two minutes I come to again. You have to imagine what that means for Lilli, who lay beside me in bed — and got dressed and ask why, pray tell, I am summoned. Answer: because of a statement given under oath. When I heard that I was, of course, somewhat reassured, because there had to be a mistake. The long and short of it, at quarter past 7 I was dismissed again from the police presidium with the comment that a radiogram of 1937 had erroneously not been expunged.

We then spent the entire day at the consulate where everything went smoothly. Lilli then went back to Nuremberg on March 8, Wednesday, where, after many wild goose chases and many inconveniences, she succeeded in getting the radiogram, mistakenly not yet expunged, withdrawn. I myself did not leave Stuttgart, because I would have been arrested again at any other place, or at the border. How people — not only I, were treated at the border, you cannot imagine. We missed — like all the other Jews, the train at the border, and thus arrived here only after 8 PM. But such chicanery is the rule.

I am very happy with Ruth, but this idyll is only diminished by the circumstance that Lilli is unwilling to leave her position in spite of all urging. What was still lacking was the permission to pack whatever was left to us to move, and Lilli expected this to come in ten to fourteen days. I am waiting for her here impatiently, because we plan to ship out on the "Washington" on April 5. After all, we do not have much movable property left. Jewelry, silver, paintings, rugs, tin (even the silverware) had to be handed over without any compensation. Of the other things, Lilli had to sell a great deal. For the remaining movable goods they demanded in Nuremberg the crazy sum of RM 32,800 ($13,000)— which we could not pay any more. Such demands are made only in Nuremberg — not in the rest of the Reich. The movable property had been estimated at RM 10,000 ($4000)— Lilli has now crossed off about DM 3000 ($1200) from the original list, and thereupon we received a new report, for "only DM 12,000 ($4800). It is annoying that Lilli has crossed off too much. But that could not have been foreseen — but, after all, that is now quite unimportant, the main thing is Lilli gets out well.

And now a few words about my "stay in the sanatorium" last year. Although the beginning was rough — it got better in time because one gets used to anything — I spent the year well, because I was really unbelievably lucky. I had — in contrast to all the other "patients" — a typewriter, pen and ink, pencils, paper galore — everything invaluable riches. My occupation as clerk was, of course, more pleasant than anything else. I did not overwork myself. Even if the food was not exactly great I managed quite well and have not suffered in this respect at all; have lost only 8 pounds — that is not much. I received quite good German books, after 4 or 5 months also English Books and (the following is written in Spanish and he says "don't bother to read it") (In Spanish, Alfred writes):" 8 months ago I started to learn Spanish. Since I have to learn it by myself, without any help, I can only read a little, very little. I cannot speak nor write, and I therefore ask you not to make fun of my foolishness. All my thoughts are with you and I can't tell you how happy I shall be when Lilli is here. Dear Maria, I am looking forward to meet you and shake your hand, all the more since everybody sings your praise and the good luck of Max to be married to you.

Everything I am today I owe to my dearest Lilli and to you. Thank you so much for everything you have done. Ruth Marion is marvelous — but you shall see her. Now I shall close this "letter" but I don't know how to do it — carambite — carambola — caramba."

He now says he has have to continue in English, and he does.

I have to continue in English fearing however that it will not be better, having forgotten a great deal of the little I knew before. The treatment in my sanatorium was very good. I was in an establishment where Jews and other people have the same rights. Where can you find that elsewhere in Germany? -- But now, the most important thing to do is to forget all that happened. As to myself I already have forgotten all. I feel very happy with Ruth Marion and I long for Lilli.

My dear ones, many, many thanks for all you have done. You are not only our nearest relatives, you are very good friends — and that is more.

All my love, Alfred

P.S.(this is in German again) Dear Mother, I thank you for your dear letter which I found at the Bierers and am looking forward to a reunion soon. Love, your Alfred.

In reading all this I was struck again by how little he knew of the difficulties Lilli had during the past 14 months. I was reminded again that he had never met Maria. His mother, Johanna was already in New York. I'm so impressed by his ability to write in 3 languages. He mentions how so much of their personal property had to be handed over without compensation, or "sold" at a sum much below its value. And all of this says nothing of the tremendous emotional impact of this letter — his own summary right after he was released from 14 months in prison. He talks about his willingness and ability, "to forget all that happened". This enabled him, I believe, to always look forward and not dwell on what they went through by not talking about it.

On **March 14, 1939** he wrote another letter from Paris which is addressed to "My Dears". It's not clear who this went to — other family or friends. Unlike the prison letters, this one was written on a piece of his own stationery, with his name printed on the top. It is typed and written in German. Because I am so moved by these letters, his first days of freedom, I will quote it in its entirety here:

I am happy to be able to write you again after a long pause. Two days ago, with all kinds of difficulties, chicaneries and annoyances, I crossed the border with Ruth Marion and the nursemaid, while Lilli takes care of the last formalities in loyal dutifulness and will follow here soon.

If I lived through the last year in the best condition imaginable — according to general judgment I look splendid, much better in any case than those who enjoyed so-called freedom — I owe this entirely to Lilli. You can't imagine what she has accomplished, how she managed to give me the strength to bear everything well, how she found the time, in those terrible November days, to care for those beaten to a pulp until late into the night, and how she was there during the last months for all kinds of people with all kinds of questions with advice and counsel. Only he who has experienced everything can fathom the real conditions in Germany. In any case you can count yourself lucky to have gotten out in time.

The treatment in jail was not only above reproach but very good — I was working at a typewriter, always had ink, paper, pen, pencil, etc — everything unheard-of riches. Also good German and English books, and also I started to learn Spanish. In my case, 12 months in jail are more pleasant than 1 month in Dachau.

Ruth Marion has developed marvelously. She is not only a pretty child, she is also smart and well brought up. (Also Lilli's work). I cannot describe what a feeling of happiness this child gives me; I shall never forget the moment when I was facing her for the first time and she looked at me for a long time with her large brown eyes, until they began to shine and she said with her sweet children's voice: "Das is es Pappile". In any case, I am a very proud "Pappi".

On 4.5 we plan to leave Le Havre on the "Washington". What I shall do over there I don't know yet. One needs to be an optimist these days and have a bit of luck, then we shall manage. If you would write to your friend Ullmann one of these days, like you promised, and also send me a recommendation for Ullman, I would be grateful. I am glad that you are doing well, would be even happier if we could see each other some day. How is it with the planned America trip?

If you want to write to me, write for the time being to the address of my mother, Johanna, c/o Mr. Samoje, 905 Westend Avenue, 104th Street, New York City. I would like to hear from you. In any case, all the best and best greetings from your, Alfred

Undated — This is another typed summary Alfred prepared. It's not clear to me exactly when this was written, or for what purpose. It appears to have had some official purpose since various documents were also enclosed for the recipient. The detail of quota numbers, etc. also indicates it has some official purpose. It seemed appropriate to include it here. We have two copies of this document, one which appears to be the "original" and the second a carbon copy. On the original, Lilli interlineated some corrections, deletions, etc. I have copied here the one without the corrections and deletions by Lilli. It is, however, a very succinct summary of all the correspondence which I have included above.

During the summer of 1937 my wife and I realized that there was no hope for an early end of the Nazi rule in Germany and we decided to leave for the US. My brother, Max Rahn, and his wife, both US citizens, residing in San Juan, Puerto Rico, furnished us with the necessary affidavits and on October 18, 1937 I applied for US immigration visas at the American Consulate at Stuttgart, Germany for myself, my wife, Lilli Rahn, nee Bechmann, my daughter Ruth Marion, then 2 years of age and her nurse, Mrs. Helen Lorz, nee Bergen, and furnished all required evidence and documents.

On November 18, 1937 we all appeared before the US Consul at Stuttgart and on the same day received US quote immigration visas (photocopies enclosed), Quota No. Alfred R. 8458, Lilli R. 8459, Ruth M.R. 8460, Helen Lorz 8461).

We purchased tickets for the S.S. Manhattan of the US Line which was due to sail from Le Havre during the last days of December. During October and November I sold our real estate and wholesale sheet metal business to a non-Jewish firm in Northern Germany which wished to establish a branch in Bavaria. These sales were subject to approval by the Nazi party and after the contracts were submitted, the approval was never given, however on December 25, 1937 I was arrested. In a fake trial, in January 1938, I was convicted to 14 months imprisonment.

The validity of our immigration visas expired on March 17, 1938. Mrs. Rahn therefore went to see the American Consul at Stuttgart before the expiration date to inquire what procedure had to be followed in order to get them renewed after Mr. Rahn's release. She submitted authorized translation of the sentence to the Consul, H.J. L'Heureux, and he said, after having read the document, that in his opinion there was nothing in it which would hinder Mr. Rahn from getting his visa renewed, but that he would rather have his opinion confirmed by the Washington authorities and he therefore asked Mrs. R. to supply sufficient German and English copies of the sentence which he would send to the proper authorities in Washington.

She was advised that whenever a prospective immigrant was unable for reasons beyond his control to use his U.S. quota immigration visa before its expiration date, the visa would be renewed and that she should not worry and come back as soon as they were able to leave and that their quota would be reserved for them.

During the spring and summer of 1938, however, due to the rapid enactment of anti-Jewish legislation in Germany the American Consulates were swamped with applications and Mrs. R. went again to see the Consul in order to make sure that their quota was still reserved for them. At this occasion she also furnished an authorized translation of the court sentence and Mr. H.J. L'Heureux, the American Consul at Stuttgart, after having read the document, again assured her, that in his opinion there was nothing in it which would hinder Mr. R. from getting his visa renewed, but Mr. L'Heureux said that he would rather have his opinion confirmed by the proper Washington authorities in order to eliminate once and forever any difficulties which he might have in renewing his visa or in entering the US. He asked Mrs. R. to supply 6 English and six German copies of the sentence which he would send to the proper authorities in Washington.

A few days later, however, to her greatest surprise, she received a letter from Mr. L'H (enclosed) in which he flatly denied to send the documents on to Washington and also refused to issue a visa, because the case, in his opinion, involved moral turpitude. The favorable opinion expressed by the solicitor of the Dept. of Labor, to which he refers in this letter was given to Mr. Max Rahn, who, on his own account, had inquired in Washington and had informed his sister-in-law that the general opinion he had received was a favorable one.

Upon receipt of this unfavorable opinion from Mr. L'H, Mrs. Rahn immediately went to see him and asked him for his advice because Mr. Rahn's very life was at stake. If he was not in possession of a valid U.S. visa the moment he was to be released, the

Nazis would keep him locked up indefinitely. During this visit Mr. L'H advised Mrs. R. to ask her brother-in-law, Mr. R. to contact the Washington authorities directly. He personally could not do anything, but he would, of course, issue the visas, if so advised by Washington. He declared that Mr. Max R. in the U.S. has the right to inquire directly and that it was entirely possible that the Washington authorities would judge the matter quite differently, but he had strict regulations and it was not his duty, as an administrative officer, to go behind the judgment in order to determine the real nature of the judgment.

Mrs. R. immediately contacted her brother-in-law, Mr. R. in Puerto Rico and advised him to take up the case in Washington. Mr. M. Rahn did so and on December 31, 1938 an opinion was given by the Attorney General, Mr. Homer Cummings which decided the question in favor of Mr. R. and once and forever established his innocence (Official Opinions of the Attorneys General, Vol. 39, P. 215-227). The State Department then immediately advised the US Consul at Stuttgart by cable to issue the visa. Upon the Consul's request (letter of January 18, 1939)) new affidavits and up-to-date evidence was submitted to him (enclosure) and new visas were issued for the entire family on March 7, 1939, two days after Mr. Rahn's release.

On April 15, 1939 all four of us entered the US at New York harbor on the S.S. Washington, U.S. Line (green card, issued at port of entry was submitted to the Naturalization Bureau with the application for the final papers). German Passport with original immigration visa, quota No. 12758 (Alf.R), and 12759 (Ruth M.R.) enclosed

I don't know what the reason was for this summary, but it is accurate. The voyage to the New York harbor on the S.S. Washington took ten days, from April 5 — 15, 1939. This summary leaves out, however, the enormous emotional toll on everyone involved. You might think that the story has its ending here. But not for the bureaucratic Germans!

October 14, 1939 — Letter from the Secret State Police (Gestapo) of Nuremberg to the Gestapo in Berlin. The letter has an identification number 3058/39 II B 3:

Concerning: Deprivation of German Citizenship of the Jew Alfred Hermann Israel Rahn, born 28.1.01 in Fürth, i.B. according to Par. 2 of the law of 14.7.1933 (RGB1 1 s 480 ff) and to execute the expatriation of the spouse, Dr. Lilly (sic) Sara nee Bechmann, born 10.2.1911 in Fürth, i.B. as well as the daughter, Ruth Marie (sic) Rahn, born 15.6.1936 in Fürth i.B. Alfred Rahn is the son of the Jewish couple Sidney Rahn and Hannschen, nee Goldmann. He, as well as his wife and daughter are racial and confessional Jews and have German Citizenship. Rahn has been living since birth in Fürth except for an interruption from 1921-1923 and has emigrated with his daughter to New York on 6.3.1939 where his wife followed him on 25.3.1939.

Criminally and politically Rahn has not shown up. But he was convicted by a judgment of Jury Court in Fürth on January 25, 1938 for a continuous breach of a foreign exchange law in conjunction with giving a false statement under oath to 1 year and 2 months prison. Further, there is presently a proceeding against Alfred and Lilly Rahn for attempted foreign exchange law transgressions (taking property out of the country without permit). The couple still have the following property values in the country, according to investigations:

a) property to be removed to new location, already packed in crates

b) an account with the Commerce-and-Private Bank branch Fürth, i.B of RM 12,28

There are no known debts in taxes or other public duties.

The basis of the conviction of January 25, 1938 is based on the following:

Rahn Alfred already intended to emigrate in the fall of 1937. At that time he had accumulated RM 30,000 — in his house with the obvious intent to get it abroad illegally. In the account of his assets prior to his emigration to the Department of Foreign Exchange he had kept this sum out, resp. only mentioned a value of 10% of the actual account.

Concerning the still pending procedure for attempted breaking of the foreign exchange laws it is clear that Rahn, who had already left Germany on April 5, 1939, via Hamburg, had begun that same day to pack his moving property in the apartment in Fürth. When this property was checked it was noted that a radio (Phillips-Super), still in its original packing, had not been approved either as moving property nor transport abroad by the Foreign Exchange Department in Nuremburg. Rahn Alfred and his wife have tried, with disregard of existing laws, to illicitly move property abroad without permission. They are therefore to be regarded as parasites of the German Volk. For this reason, the deprivation of German citizenship is indicated and justified. The extension of the expatriation to the spouse is necessary because, as legal executor, she prepared the emigration during her husband's incarceration and thus, premeditatively, tried to get the radio abroad without permission. The extension of the expatriation to daughter Ruth Rahn seems justified in view of the existing family bond.

The spouse Lilly Sara Rahn, nee Bechmann has received the Dr. phil. Title on February 2, 1934 from the University Erlangen.

Personal Information:

Rahn Alfred Hermann Israel, merchant, born January 29, 1901, in Fürth, i.B. racial and confessional Jew, German RA. Parents: Sidney Rahn and Hannchen nee Goldmann.

Rahn Lilly Sara nee Bechmann born February 2, 1911, in Fürth i.B. Racial and confessional Jew, German RA. Parents; Hugho Bechmann and Ida, nee Metzger

Rahn, Ruth Marie (sic) Sara, born June 15, 1936 in Fürth, i.B. Racial and confessional Jew, GermanRA. Parents, see above.

I.V. ges. Dr. Kiesel

Zu S-IV/II B nr. 10779/39

The phrase "racial and confessional Jew" appears here for the first time. So, we (all three of us) were called "parasites of the German Volk" and deprived again of German citizenship. The language, artfully justifying what they wanted to do anyway, is most interesting. Fortunately we were far beyond the reach of German authorities by then.

November 20, 1939 — Letter from the Offices of the Reichsfuehrer-SS (Eva Gordon. my translator says that's Himmler's office) and the Chief of the German Police to The Foreign Office in Berlin. Reference is made to the same number as above.

Concerning: Deprivation of German citizenship of the Jew Alfred Israel Hermann Rahn, born January 28, 1901 in Fürth, Bav. Proceedings: none; Enclosures: 2; Enclosed are two copies of a request for expatriation which has been prepared today to Department I of the Reichs Ministry of the Interior. Signed: Jagusch

Prison Letters

On January 25, 1938 Alfred was sentenced to 14 months in prison for violating currency laws. We have many, if not all of the letters he wrote from prison, and only a few Lilli wrote to him.

Initially, I will go through them here, with dates and summaries of what was discussed, as well as some quotes. I want to preserve as closely as possible the content of these letters. They are written in extremely small and almost illegible writing. Each consists of only one sheet of paper, as this is all that was allowed. Gerda Breit, our old family friend (of blessed memory), the person who translated them for us, had a lot of trouble reading them, but fortunately spent the time and did a magnificent job. The Breit family were also German refugees who had settled in Denver, and were among the first family my parents met when they arrived. They remained the closest of friends all their lives.

There are certain themes that go throughout — his food, exercise, request for "thick books" since he could only have so many books, his health, his self-flagellation at his stupidity and regret at what he is missing in being with Lilli and his child, his concerns about Lilli's health — that she worries too much, should relax, shouldn't lose more weight, shouldn't stay alone too much, and of course questions and pleasures in hearing about Ruth Marion, who is referred to at various times as Ruth, Ruth Marion, Madchen (little girl), Mauschen (little mouse), and then some thoughts of just using the name Marion. There is also a lot of concern about financial matters — receiving payments due, the status of various properties, contacting the lawyers about this or that matter, etc.

What struck me in reading these over again is how isolated he was from the outside world. He doesn't mention Kristallnacht at all, though perhaps he thought any mention would be censored. I believe he knew nothing about what was happening outside the prison. He apparently has no idea of the incredible difficulties Lilli was having in obtaining the visa, and in obtaining passports. She didn't communicate any of this to him, knowing he would worry incessantly, but what a burden this must have added to her concerns. Lilli and Alfred married in July 1933, so they had been married only 4 1/2 years when he was imprisoned in January 1938. He was almost of 37 (his birthday was January 28) and Lilli was just almost 27 (her birthday was February 10).

Initially he was taken briefly to Leipzig, which is halfway between Fürth and Berlin. Then he was taken for a short while to the court prison in Fürth, and finally to the prison in Nuremberg, which is very close to Fürth, where he served out most of his term. This prison is located and attached to the Palace of Justice in Nuremberg, where the famous Nuremberg trials were held. When Evy and I visited the Palace of Justice in February 1999, we saw the prison from a window, because it is now closed and no longer used. One of the reasons Nuremberg was selected as a site of the famous trials after the war is because of this large Palace of Justice with its attached prison. The prisoners could be brought to the courtroom through an underground tunnel, without having to go outside. The movie *Judgment at Nuremberg* was actually filmed in this courtroom.

In all, we have a total of 22 letters from Alfred to Lilli, and 11 letters from Lilli to Alfred. Initially, before Alfred was moved to the prison in Nuremberg, he could write every few days, but after he was moved to Nuremberg it appears that he could only write once a month. Six of his letters are written before the move to Nuremberg. As for Lilli's letters, all were written before the move to Nuremberg. Some are lengthy — four pages or so. We have none of her letters written while Alfred was there, i.e. the last one we have is dated 2/2/38. Were they taken away? For some reason they were not kept.

Alfred's letters from Nuremberg are all written on the official prison stationery, which has the following printed information on it:

At the top, the printed heading reads: Prison Nuremberg — Zellenstr.

Then there is a box where he has to write his name and prison number. He signs each letter Alfred Rahn, until the very end when he begins to add the required "Israel" to his name. All Jews had to identify themselves as Jewish on all documents and official correspondence. The men had to add "Israel" to their name, and the women had to add "Sara" to their name

Then are the specific instructions printed onto each sheet of stationery:

1. *For prisoners on step one, communication by letter, which is being censored, is permitted only, as a rule, with parents, grandparents, siblings, spouses and children.*

2. *Prisoners on step one may write and receive letters every 4 weeks, those on step 2 every 3 weeks, those on step 3 every 2 weeks. Letters, which may be written on important matters by relatives, may only be given to the prisoners if the discipline of the institution is not endangered.*

3. *Letters to prisoners must not be more than one sheet of paper, must be written clearly and in ink. Sender has to be identified on the envelope or in the letter by name and relationship to prisoner. No enclosures of money, stamps, stationery, free envelopes, printed matter, newspaper clippings or flowers are allowed.*

4. *Visiting hours for prisoners on step one are every 6 weeks, step 2 every 4 weeks, on Thursdays, on step 3 every 3 weeks on Saturday. Food, tobacco, soap, toothpaste, can neither be brought nor sent.*

5. *Be vigilant at visits of former prisoners!*

It appears that Alfred was on step one as it pertains to letters, but it also appears that Lilli was able to visit him once a month, which would make it step two for visits. I will precede each letter with the date on which it was written, and put into parenthesis my own comments.

December 28, 1937 — this is the first letter we have written from Leipzig at a detention center. Alfred mentions he had written one the day before also. He writes to Lilli in Berlin "again I address these lines to Berlin, hoping that they will reach you most quickly this way, while at the same time you, dear parents, get news from me". (Hugo and Ida, Lilli's parents were living in Berlin at that time — other letters to Berlin follow). He writes about books he is reading, and hopes to get to Nuremberg soon. "I ask all of you again, and firmly: keep your chins up and don't grieve about me. I have a clear conscience in the question at hand, so that everything will soon be well".

December 29, 1937 — Another letter from Leipzig included mention that his thoughts are constantly with you; getting some exercise; books, don't worry.

January 3, 1938 — Asks for sausage, cakes and some thick books. Following this is an enumerated list of financial and property items Lilli should attend to — money for herself and his mother; discontinue radio, banking matters, if rent payments have been made; transfer of funds, etc.

Thereafter there are four letters from Lilli to Alfred after he was moved briefly to a detention center in Fürth.

January 1, 1938 — She is so happy he is "here now. Now we are not so far apart at least in space. Sorry I couldn't bring sausage — against the rules." She asks whether he wants literature or world history books — "divide time so you don't finish too quickly because I don't know when I can bring you another book. Ruth Marion is teething, besides she is cheerful and jolly, anything but clean, which has something to do with the teething at least that's what we maintain in order not to make too bad an impression as pedagogues. Father wanted to come yesterday, talked him out of it because I know how busy he is. Ernst and Doris (Metzger) have been here quite a bit." (I was exactly 1 1/2 years old at the writing of this letter — clearly Lilli thought I should have been "clean", meaning toilet trained, by now. I had wondered, when I started writing this memoir, if my grandfather Hugo had ever seen me. He was living in Berlin when I was born and left for Sweden in 1938, so he did see me a few times, but not thereafter as he died in Sweden in 1942. Ernst and Doris refers to Ernst and Doris Metzger, Ida's brother and his wife.

Their daughter, Eva Metzger Brown, now lives in Amherst, MA. Ernst was 17 years younger than Ida. At that time Lilli and Ernst Metzger, her uncle, were still quite close, but incidents that occurred thereafter estranged their relationship.)

January 3, 1938 — Lilli to Alfred: Yesterday your mother and I had a meal at grandmothers. In the afternoon I had the child brought in and she was there from 2-5:30, very good and grandmother was pleased. Other family news. (Grandmother here is Caroline Metzger, Ida's mother, who was in a wheel chair at the time and later was taken to Thereisenstadt and murdered there).

January 5, 1938 — She asks for Ruth Marion's vaccination certificate and house keys. Johanna (Alfred's mother) added a few words to this letter.

January 7, 1938 — News of Ruth Marion; took and sent pictures. Mrs. Moehle is leaving (this evidently was the nursemaid, who was replaced by Helen Lorz).

January 8, 1938 — Alfred to Lilli: Thanks for pictures, apples and bananas. "One is happy with everything here and grateful for any little thing. I hope you can get me a thick book within the next few days. But my hunger for mental nourishment is very great and the satisfaction of this need very important." He says he wants to learn English and shorthand. He has the time here. A number of financial and business items are discussed. He asks her to take his dirty laundry. He asks her to ask Attorney Rosenberg if something can be done about the change of the ship tickets. Can you find a pair of comfortable shoes? (As we know, they already had ship tickets to the United States for December 1937).

More letters from Lilli to Alfred:

January 10, 1938 — Hope you have gotten the food-supply permission; if not, let them get you sausage, chocolate and anything else you are allowed to have. You are also allowed to have a glass of beer daily. Unfortunately I can't bring sausage or chocolate since that is not allowed. Discussions about sale of property. The Foreign Exchange Department has allowed us DM 500.00 ($200.00) for the household. Details of carpenter, paid for radio, cleaning matters, E has not yet paid the rent for the sports place (when we were in Germany in February, 1999, driving back from Nuremberg, Gisela Blume pointed out to us a property which she said was owned by my father; a sports center, or gym. It was pouring rain — I jumped out and took a photo, but it doesn't show much. I think this is the place he refers to in this and subsequent letters). She says he shouldn't worry about all these business affairs — she has gotten a good foothold already. "If something is not clear, I consulted with the two Ernsts and Dr. R. Ruth Marion had her hair cut today. We hope to encourage her sparse hair growth by trimming it a bit. She behaved in exemplary fashion there, and now she looks even more like a little boy. Do you need anything else — warm clothing etc? Yesterday, Aunt Emma, Uncle Ernst, Walter and Dora and I went for a two-hour walk in streaming rain and snow, as far as Weierhof." (The two Ernsts she refers to are Ernst Metzger, Ida's younger brother and thus her uncle, and Ernst Bierer, who was married to Emma, Ida's sister. Dora is Emma's daughter).

January 12, 1938 — She asks about books — "do you prefer entertainment, or history, or something thought provoking? In any case, I can only send you something every two weeks. Or would you like an English grammar? But then I cannot send anything else. Business matters;

don't worry. I have concluded a rental contract with Mr. Schulte. Notice to vacate the apartment can be given at the latest one month before the end of the quarter. Ship tickets are valid for two years." She plans to move to the first floor with the furniture.

January 16, 1938 — I hear you can supply your own food and are satisfied with that. Look forward to visit with you this week. Took 2-hour walk with Emma, Ernst, Walter and Dora (Emma and Ernst Bierer, her aunt and uncle, along with Walter and Dora, their children). Frau Lorz is now in the household. (Helen Lorz, whom I called Tante, joined the household in January, 1938, and lived with us for many years thereafter. She emigrated to the United States with us, lived with us for some time, and then got another governess job, returning to our household when Evy was born), "Mausle (this means "little mouse" and refers, of course, to me) is now developing some very typical characteristics. She must have gotten her love of tidiness from your mother. Yesterday her ball fell under her little bench. So she pushed the little bench forward, got the ball, put it in the middle of the room on the floor. Then she pushed the little bench again carefully against the wall, a little bit more to this side, because it was not quite in the middle. What can one say to this love of orderliness!"

January 21, 1938 — Happy to see you finally on Wednesday. Your mother departed yesterday afternoon, quietly and without any excitement. (She went first to Merin, Italy and then on to the United States.) Ernst was along in the same train albeit only as far as Karlsruhe whereas Max Lang, by coincidence, was in the same train, same compartment as far as Zurich. News of Lothar, Carola (Lothar Weil, an old family friend; Carola Loeffler was Lilli's aunt — she was her father's sister), etc.

January 27, 1938 — Lilli wished him Happy Birthday. She urged him to take this coming year as a year of contemplation and inner awareness, and "don't use the time of solitude and quiet, which will be around you so much now, for useless brooding, but think about yourself and try to find clarity about the many things for which there is so little time during one's daily life."

Maybe they can give you an Old Testament, or maybe I can bring you one. I think it would do you well to get absorbed in it from time to time." (I found this particularly interesting, as they seemed to be more religious then than I had thought.) She sends greetings from many and says how extraordinarily his mother has behaved during the last weeks. "I have gained the greatest respect for her. I will expect to hear from you when you are in Nuremberg."

January 26, 1938 — Alfred writes with the usual exhortations about don't worry, sleep well, eat well, don't get thinner, take care of your health and don't bury yourself in your four walls. "I just cleaned my cell with a bucket of water and a scrubber. Twice a week one is allowed to sweep one's cell with a wet broom. I wish I could do it more often because it needs it. Other days it is just swept." Lilli visited that afternoon. Need pajamas.

January 27, 1938 — Lilli to Alfred — "Your letters show me how calm you are. Just called your mother; cousin Alfred will look after her a bit. Uncle Ernst (Metzger) brought Mausle a big dog which she can ride. Lets herself be pulled up and plays her harmonica."

February 2, 1938 — Lilli to Alfred — "Last night I returned from Berlin. Father will travel for 2 months. At Luta and Roman's there is again fighting atmosphere. Roman, by the way, produces beautiful pictures and is putting together a series of articles. I helped him with the formulation of the articles and translated some into English, which I shall send directly to NY. He will go away in the near future to make a test film. The success here will determine Fürther orders. But up to now everybody is very enthusiastic about his work. Luta plans to come here as soon as the atmosphere at home has been cleared a bit. Big renovations in the house. Ernst and Emma are packing this week. Lothar wants me to go skiing with him a few days. Expect to hear from you soon that you are in Nuremberg."

Roman and Luta Vishniac, who were originally from Riga, Latvia, were living in Berlin, and met my parents in the late twenties. Luta had taken their daughter Mara skiing, and they met at one of the ski resorts. They became lifelong friends. The marriage was obviously on the rocks when this letter was written, and Roman was already involved with his future wife, Edith. However, Roman and Luta emigrated to the United States as a married couple and divorced thereafter. Luta never remarried; lived in New York ran a travel agency and was an extremely cultured woman. She remained very close to our family all her life. Karen and I visited her when she was well into her 90's and after we left her apartment I said to Karen that I hoped I would be that interesting when I was in my 90's. "Mom", said Karen, "you're not that interesting now!!!". I had to admit there was much truth in what she said because Luta was such an extraordinary woman. Roman Vishniac became a famous photographer with his photos of Polish Jews as well as marine life. His photos are in numerous books as well as in *The Family of Man*.

February 8, 1938 — Alfred to Lilli: "After a long pause I am finally able to write to you again today. This week I'm supposed to go to Nuremberg." He wrote about taxes, his mother's affairs, mortgage, a debt that was owed to him, inventory, etc. " I shall include a few lines for my mother, but tell her that this is an exception because I am only allowed to write to you. So keep in touch with Max, whom I cannot write either. Read with interest that MSF [MS Farrnbacher] has been renamed after all. I am afraid I won't be able to write you for many weeks."

March 19, 1938 — "Thanks for your letter of the 9th of this month. Surprised you have so much to do with Dr. R. " Wrote about business matters; confer with Max, insurance, mortgage, appeal on value added tax. "Important also is that the visa matter is kept in sight and is being taken care of as soon as possible. How are you getting along with Mrs. Lorz? Write everything down when you come so you don't forget anything in the hurry here. Who is moving into the second story? Except for Sundays I don't have a lot of free time. At quarter to six one gets up; 6:30 work begins until 9:30; outdoors until 10:30, except for Thursday when I go for physical exercise during that time; 10:30-11:45 work, then rest until 1:00, then work until 5:45; Saturdays until 4:45. You will have a lot of work with the moving and am sorry that such a load rests on your shoulders. Just watch out that nothing is left behind. (This refers to the move from 129 Konigstrasse, which had been 'sold", to the home of Emma and Ernst Bierer, who had already left for Paris). "We just have to be patient and will hope that we are looking toward a good future, which unfortunately today is so uncertain. When I think back today, I simply cannot understand that I could have caused such a misfortune, in which you have all been dragged. Had I not done everything with such haste lately, it would not have come to this. Just ask Mr. Eintler how scrupulous I have always been in the business when it comes to declarations under oath. Well — I have learned a lot, and such a thing will not happen a second time. (this is the only time he speaks of what he did, or didn't do, as the case may be. At least in the letters, there is almost no self-flagellation, feeling sorry for himself, anger, etc.)

March 2, 1938 — Mostly business matters — re contracts, a fence on the property; rental that's owed to him, a new rental contract, fees for town officials. The price cut of 20% for the merchandise has been specifically approved by the finance office, noted in the bookkeeping report of 1931. Discussions with Mr. Held (one of his attorneys).

April 14, 1938 — He writes again concerning some property — decided not to sell, instead rent; sports club; some bonds. "Held was here, but I can't talk about much in 15 minutes — he should see to it that he can come again and is granted sufficient time. Your idea to go to Berlin for a week with the child is very good in the interests of your parents. Nothing to report from me. I am living in memories and hopes and what keeps my spirits up is my love to you. I am not giving up. I want to stay intact, not only physically, but also mentally and spiritually. I have generally much work and I am working as much as I possibly can. It's been one year now since we took these beautiful tours in the Allgaeu. What will be a year from now?"

May 14, 1938 — He asks that she submit questions to Held in a particular order. Make him write down answers. Lilli had come to visit — he says " when I am talking with you I am always in heightened degree conscious of the disaster that I have caused. It is bitter that I have to be here. That I am separated from you is very bad. That I cannot witness the development of my adorable child doubles my punishment. But that full year of your young life has thus been destroyed is a fact that I cannot get over. How much easier it is for a bachelor to bear a punishment. But — enough of that. On 3.5 at 2:54 [sic] my time here is at an end — and until then we just have to be patient. Don't retreat into your four walls, stay in Berlin as long as possible because it will please your parents and is probably also very good for you. I just fortify myself with the usual Saturday night meal — an excellent marinated herring and potatoes. Later I shall read my newspaper, a weekly prison journal which is published in Berlin and which keeps one somewhat informed. As a constant book I have, besides the Prayerbook, the Holy Scripture, which is extraordinarily interesting once one has gotten into it a bit. (interesting that he asked for and is reading the Bible. Is this from religious motivations, or because it is so "meaty" and could keep him occupied for long periods with a shortage of books?)

June 11, 1938 — Happy about your dear letter of 2nd of this month. He asks about various financial matters and "what about Stuttgart?" (This is in reference to the visa problem, because that's where the American consulate was located). Another letter about finances; buy gifts for certain people. "Looking forward to seeing you in 12 days. I go to bed at 8:00 because we get up between 5:30–5:45. At that time and until 9:00 a.m. the sun reaches my cell and I appreciate every ray that reaches me. After all, one is exceedingly grateful for every small gift here. For instance, they recently gave us a small bunch of radishes, which I admired like a bouquet of roses for a while and they tasted good too! We are now frequently getting spinach and green lettuce; I manage with the food here; because of the many soups I even developed a little paunch, probably also caused by the unaccustomed sedentary lifestyle. Besides, I exercise as much as possible. We are now nearing the anniversaries of the most important dates in our life, June 15 and July 3 (Ruth's birthday and their anniversary). God willing we shall be able to celebrate these dates more cheerfully next year. Meanwhile we shall have to be patient and build a bridge until March 5, 1939. I send feelings of love and gratefulness. I am sorry that you are now all alone in your parent's house in Fürth — is that necessary? Did Ernst M.(Ernst Metzger) look after you a bit? The unborn child should not have prevented him. Buy gift for Ruth for June 15."

July 9, 1939 — Reproaches to Dr. Rosenberg of various business matters, lots of under linings, asking, "Can't something be done concerning Stuttgart, or has it been done? Correcting itemized inventory. Too bad the 15 minutes always flies by so fast only 15-minute visits; don't lose more weight. I get up daily shortly after 5:00 am (except Sundays) so I can work for myself very early for half an hour. Unfortunately there is very little free time, for, as you can imagine, I would prefer to work more for myself. Morning and noon from 12-1 I work on Spanish; in the evening I read English, and at 8 pm I am deadly tired. In July and August there is a swarm of birthdays — give all my best wishes." He talks about missing Ruth — "Just write me always what she does and she gets into! — because of my stupidity that I have torn one year not only out of my life but also out of yours — I just can't get over it!.

August 6, 1938 — " I enjoyed your visit so much again. Glad you have taken steps about Stuttgart." Again lots of details about properties; rental contract. He is getting fed up with Dr. Rosenberg, another attorney — "He who counts on strangers is lost". He now has gingivitis, which isn't getting any better; there is no remedy for this cultural disease. In this letter there are lines heavily crossed out by the censor. The main physical impairment Alfred suffered while in prison was his teeth. It wasn't long after he came to the United States that he had to have them pulled and got false teeth. He continues to study Spanish and read books in English. "I think one should give the child a decent name to call her by — I have no other choice for Marion. It shouldn't be too difficult to make the change in view of the alliteration."

August 13, 1938 — Received your letter of the 10th enclosing the power of attorney. He talked about James' (his brother, who was institutionalized) taxes and amounts to be paid annually to him.

September 3, 1938 — "Another month has passed and your letter of Aug. 25 pulls me out of monotony and makes me realize life outside continues. I notice here again and again how extraordinarily dependent one's physical well being is on one's mental state — but also, that one can achieve a lot by trying energetically to keep one's mental and physical well being in balance. I need not emphasize that the thought of you and little Marion is a tremendous help to me in that. (So here I am just Marion) Other business matters, and I will need a passport immediately, especially for Stuttgart the timely application for which you should see to. As of the first of the month I am in the so-called Leader class! I am allowed to order sausage, and artificial honey and I am thinking ahead whether I should order sausage or bacon instead of the honey in October because I feel a great need for fat. I look forward to squeeze your hand again on Sept. 15. It would be best if you could come at 9:30 since our walk in the yard is an hour earlier (8:30-9:30). It's been a year now that we clamored over the Blaums glacier and spent a few lovely days together. Let's now forget that we have also spent many beautiful hours together. At night I try to conjure up your image and little Marion (still Marion here). Send fondest wishes to my mother for her birthday; she must not worry and enjoy the days of her stay there fully". Wishes Lilli for the New Year (Jewish New Year was celebrated)

October 1, 1938 — Lots of business details discussed. Apparently MSF (M.S. Farrnbacher) was purchased, and moneys coming in were to be credited to the new firm only after October 23, 1939 — so discussion about the accounts receivable, debts, and proper crediting. He refers to the purchaser as "Sch". Discussions with someone he refers to as "Z" and talks of suing him personally. He refers to the known offer of Z during the negotiations in the presence of 3 Aryans. After the conclusion of the contract "Sch" was our dinner guest half a dozen times and repeatedly stated that he was always glad to respond to my invitation. In the midst of all this he asks — has confirmation from Stuttgart arrived? (He has no idea what is actually going on and the difficulties Lilli was encountering.) He talks about his reading — finished David Copperfield and Bleak House, but said they give him much trouble because of the rich vocabulary and the small print. He didn't work during the New Years — October 10,11,17 and 18. " According to a notification, we shall get our dinner on the 5th in order to be able to fast". (It is remarkable that even in prison they were allowed to celebrate the Jewish holidays and accommodations for meals and no work were made for Jewish prisoners so they could celebrate the High Holydays). "I work a lot now and have reached the top of the wage scale (very few people have). In order to compete with our daughter I have learned to do somersaults during my exercise program. That the Munich conference made a peaceful march into the Sudetenland possible gave me, as you may imagine, great peace of mind. Let us hope that peace will be preserved in the future!" (He is getting some news from the outside from the prison newspaper, but who knows how slanted it was). He asks about departure of various people —" happy your father is so content; what are your mother's plans; where is Alfred L. moving; when is Ernest M.(Ernst Metzger) going? A thousand questions. I wish my mother a good trip (she is about to go to NY from Italy). Please come at 9:00 because we exercise at 9:30 again."

October 29, 1938 — Received your letter of the 27th already yesterday. Again lots of business details re: the fence, sell property without the fence; sports club — the back fence was the original fence which existed already when my father bought the place (I learned here that the sports club is something he inherited from his father); Fürther discussion about the fence, abutting streets, the value, etc. (What strikes me in all these discussions is that he assumes, perhaps correctly or perhaps not, that everything is still being done exactly according to the law; that he has rights, that all details will be taken care of as if business matters are normally handled. I don't know if this is right or not; but he assumes he can make complaints, sue people, make demands, etc. etc.) He then goes into a discussion of the business — referring to the contract that has been checked and rechecked by Dr. H (Dr. Held, one of our family attorneys) and concluded with an unusually knowledgeable buyer of businesses, such a contract cannot be regarded as a worthless rag. "Sch" as well told me in December, after they had managed the firm for about 2 months, how surprised they were that the firm was running so well. Again and again they expressed their satisfaction. "Make it abundantly clear to him that he had declared at the time, in front of 5 witnesses, among them 3 Aryans, 'should you experience difficulties from any side, I assure you of my support in every case." (It appears here, and this was the case, that they were reneging on paying what had been agreed upon. There appears to be confusion about whether the house was included in the total price for the business.) He asks Lilli to make these points decisively and if that's in vain, Dr. R. should hand the matter over to another lawyer and the lawsuit should be advanced. " See that the mortgage is cancelled so there are no difficulties on sale. Concerning Stuttgart confirmation, I recommend to have it in the form of a specific day of loading." (There is some confusing talk about furniture, some of which is illegibile to read in the letter.) He is already thinking ahead for March and asks for certain purchases: a comb, a good hair brush, a soft toothbrush, a good pair of nail scissors and possibly ties that match the suits. (I found this quite touching — there was absolutely no concern he wouldn't be let out or that he was in any physical danger — life would resume with combs, nail clippers and ties that matched suits after March 5). He said that yesterday they pulled a tooth. He talks about what he read — learning Spanish, reading Shakespeare (Richard II and Merchant of Venice) and asks about various family members. Then, with respect to Marion — "Shouldn't one force right-handed activity a bit, so that later in school she won't have so much trouble? Ask about that!" (I was already showing that I would be left-handed).

November 25, 1938 — "More than ever I am with you these days to help you with your difficult decisions. First, the most important: in a way I am not (underlined in original) in favor to let the child leave ahead of us, and that not only because of the great sacrifice it would mean for you. On the other hand I am very much in favor and ask you urgently that you yourself with the child go most quickly to Emma/Ernst, which suggestion I would have made even without their invitation. What's the story with the visa for there? (This letter is written after Kristallnacht — he says absolutely nothing about it — does he know? Is he afraid anything he says might be censored? Or, is he completely in the dark, or at least primarily in the dark — which is what I think. He has absolutely no idea about the difficulties Lilli is having regarding the visa. Emma and Ernst are in the United States by this time, and evidently urged Lilli to emigrate there with me).

He also asks about the new Jewish tax — how high is it for me? It must not be paid for me under any circumstances; rather the Finance Office has to be reminded of my account. He also says in case James is affected, the guardian has to appeal to the Finance Office to ask for a waiver in this special case. The present income of James is just barely sufficient for his upkeep. "Did Stradrat S. tell you why the sale of the property is not recognized? It can't be because of the price because it is 1/3 less than the purchase price which was DM2 at the time (1912). Don't you agree to anything because you don't have power of attorney." (Although I do not know exactly what this "Jewish tax" was, it is clear that there were repeated additional taxes that had to be paid. I believe this was the reason Alfred kept cash at home, which was the origin of this whole situation).

He says again that he thought for days and days about his suggestion of Lilli's departure ahead of time. "In any case, I think it is right and you will come to the same conclusions when you follow my train of thought, particularly since you can continue to correspond with me, while maybe Friedl L.(Friedl Landmann, an old and dear family friend) can look after me a bit on March 5 and even visit me here. After Dec. 8 it is only a matter of 2 visits which would, however, require a special permit." He asks her to write down everything, all questions and get them to him before the visit because 15 minutes is so short; get insurance to apartment in NY; asks about his classmates. " I cannot tell you how happy I am that your father is successful. I also think it would be good if your mother follows soon." (Lilli's father, by this time, had left Germany and was living in Stockholm, Sweden. His wife, Ida, remained in Germany until she was sure Lilli and Alfred could get out safely). And then he says: "Dear Lillli, these past week have forged us together even tighter and I only regret that I cannot relieve you of the worries and loads that rest on your shoulders. My thoughts are really so much with you and I hope that the last few months will pass well, not only for me, but for you too. We shall keep our chin up and rejoice in the development of our child and keep our courage even if everything around us seems to break down. I say, " seems" because I look at the regulations regarding the Jews as a good fortune for the Jews and am convinced that God will guide everything for the best, even if we poor creatures cannot see the goal."

December 19, 1938 — Received your letter on Saturday. Again, business matters — asks Dr. R to transfer power of attorney to her. You should no longer bother about the property — if he needs a signature, let him get in touch with mother directly. I do not want to be the decision maker (after all the previous decisions, this comes as a remarkable statement. He sees the end now, and other things have become less important, I think) Please take tickets for all — 3 adults and one child as far as P.R. (Puerto Rico, where is brother Max lives) Again lots of financial data. He asks again about the furniture moving. Are we embarking in Hamburg or via France? He got a bridge made in prison for his lost teeth. (Still, at this point, he has no idea that we did not have visas, and that this decision was being considered at the U.S. State Department).

January 3, 1939 — a short letter, about taxes, and then a request "Please get the tickets to P.R. (Puerto Rico) under any circumstances."

January 21, 1939 — So happy to see you, even for only 15 minutes. He writes on about income tax corrections. "Did guardian of James apply for waiver of levy? You must get a ticket for a definite day from Stuttgart; has the matter of the affidavit been cleared? Concerning the French visa, please consider the possibility of getting that in Stuttgart - in that case we could travel on from Stuttgart without having to return once more to Nuremberg. But the most important thing is that you get me a small gift for Ruth. Don't forget to write Uncle Ernst's address to Max in time and to tell him from when on he should write there. Then follows some dreaming about being free when he writes about the boat tickets "The sooner you get the boat tickets the better is your choice. Too bad the sea voyage has now been shortened, seeing how much I like to travel by boat … but if possible, choose the port with the longer sea voyage". Consider my suggestion to let mother's DM 8000 ($3200) be impounded. When and how will your grandmother be able to travel? He writes again about his teeth — "I have a second bridge which cost DM120 ($48)— hope it works out because at that price it should be flawless. Unfortunately the doctor here is tremendously overworked. Meanwhile evening has come, the once weekly appearing newspaper has arrived and informs about the latest events. One can only hope that peace is kept in the world."

Alfred's Prison Letter, November 25, 1938

(One must wonder what paper he is getting; what the news is; but none of it seems to inspire fear of safety, or of being taken once he is out — in fact, I find this remarkable — that he has every reason to rely on the end of his prison term and no fears about what would happen to him after his release). He mentions his reading — "am now reading translated German and original English fairy tales —the moral in the latter is such that I cannot understand how one can give that to a child. I could use more books."

February 18, 1939 — This time he writes "from Israel Alfred Rahn" — (First time the word Israel appears on the official stationery.) This letter is full of questions, and his anxiety about all the details is most evident. He is unclear about all the details — passport office, Stuttgart, French visa, movers, worry that things are done in time. Bridge #2 is being completely rebuilt; the denture is useless (evidently he was without teeth for some time). He then talks about the future together — clearly a most optimistic tone which he acknowledges. He says, after discussing some of the books he has read, particularly Jewish related ones "I would like to occupy myself more with Jewish matters and regret that I did not do it more in earlier times. I also regret that we have not acquired the Judaica, which one might also get second hand. Glad that your mother will still be here in March. Maybe we can have a few pleasant hours together. What, by the way, is Luta doing, or what are their plans? If Ruth has grown so much, she won't be able to wear the pretty white winter coat of your father's any more. (I have photos of me in this beautiful white fur coat which came with us to the United States).

Here ends the Prison Letters. I have interjected throughout some of my thoughts as I read and re-read these letters.

Fortunately, he appears to have been largely ignorant of what was happening on the outside. Or, perhaps, the censors wouldn't allow any mention of those events, so he avoided discussing

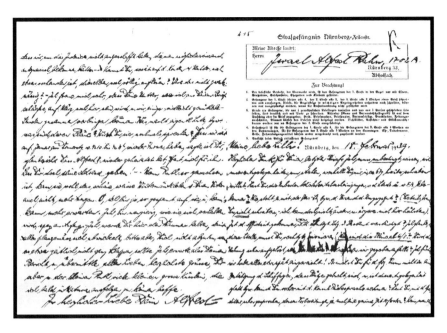

Alfred's Prison Letter, February 18, 1939

them. Lilli never discussed with him the enormous difficulties she was having regarding the visa, and then the passports. This would have driven him to distraction. She was remarkable in keeping his spirits up. He does not talk at all about any fellow prisoners or the conditions of his imprisonment. Perhaps this would have been censored. He was in solitary confinement, for which I believe he was very happy so that he could have some time to himself. He expressed no fears about being released, or about their plans to emigrate as soon as he was released.

There is constant exhortation for Lilli to gain weight — and urging her not to lose more weight. When she was dying in 1970 he did the same thing — did memories of this advice come to his mind and haunt him? Did it come to her mind?

In some letters he gives all kinds of instructions, details she must attend to, and then says, relax, take it easy, don't worry — actually kind of gallows humor from the distance.

I'm not a psychiatrist, but as I look back now at these letters, their lives and their deaths, I believe the prison term was a central experience for his life. He realized, and particularly learned later when he was released, how much Lilli had done to save his life, and he felt eternally indebted to her throughout his life. He simply could not imagine living on without her.

Lilli's Experiences While Alfred was in Prison

Among the many papers we have, we found some typewritten papers, as well as hand written notes, that Lilli wrote after our arrival in the United States. They are undated, and I do not know the purpose for which they were written. Apart from all the work and anxieties she experienced to obtain the visas and passports, these notes describe some of her personal thoughts and experiences during the time Alfred was in prison. The reference to SA is the abbreviation for Sturmabteilung, usually translated as "Stormtroopers. They functioned as a paramilitary organization of the German Nazi Party. SA men were often called "Brownshirts", for the color of their uniforms, and to distinguish them from the Schutzstaffel (SS) who wore black and brown uniforms. After Hitler took power in 1933, the SA became increasingly eager for power and saw themselves as the replacement for the German army. They were even more radical than the SS, and were particularly active in riots against Jews, destroying Jewish businesses and synagogues. The typewritten pages sound as if they may have been the basis of one of her talks, as she begins with an explanation of why we didn't leave earlier. I quote here first the typewritten pages:

Although my husband visited the U.S. in 1935, it took us until 1937 to make up our mind whether we should leave Germany forever and start our lives all over again in the New World. Years later, even our good friends here in this country, who by mere chance were lucky enough to make this start a few years before us, did not understand our "shortsightedness". But there are various reasons for it. First: the closer you are to a movement or event, the less likely are you to understand its complexity and all its implications. That's exactly what happened to all of us who got caught in the totalitarian countries. Second: my husband's business was founded 140 years ago by his great-grandfather and was ever since in the hands of the same family. During the postwar inflation its assets had been reduced to zero but thorough energy, work and loyalty he and his father had rebuilt the firm within the next ten years. Most of their employees worked in the 2nd generation, the loyalty of the father continued in the son. Most of the customers bought from them in the 2nd and 3rd generation and were loyal to the utmost even under the very difficult conditions. As long as actual laws did not prevent them from buying from their old Jewish supply house, not one percent of the customers wandered away of their own account.

You do not throw away such a thing without hesitation. Here, today, we know it was wrong to wait that long. But I do not feel that we are to blame for this reluctance. But in 1937 there was no doubt any more about the future possibilities for a Jew to make his living in Germany, and so we decided to leave. A large North-Germany concern offered to buy our firm in order to establish a Southern German branch. They were willing to pay an adequate price for both business and real estate that went with it. The contract was all agreed upon, the purchase price deposited with a local bank. But no deal between Aryans and Jews was legal until okayed by the party officials. Contract and details were submitted to the proper authorities. In the meantime we got things ready to leave. During the month of October we received our American visas and we procured steamboat tickets for the last day of December. From the party okay did not come. In the middle of December we realized that something was going on. Our home was searched several times by agents of the Secret Police for evidence. If we tried to inquire we got no answer at all or were subject to humiliating treatment. At last, on the 26th day of December, the blow came. My husband was arrested by the Secret Police. In the middle of January he was trialed (sic) and sentenced to 14 months imprisonment. The official report contains this statement."..." which reveals the atmosphere of the entire procedure. (Here she must have quoted from the judgment with its numerous anti-Semitic sentences.)

In the meantime the new owners had taken over the business, postponing payment indefinitely until the final ruling of the Party officials, which, of course, never came. Only a few days after my husband's trial the new owner informed me by registered letter that I had to leave my flat in the house which he now "owned". Fortunately my 18-month-old daughter and I found refuge in the home of a relative. The next 14 months were nothing but a chain of unpleasant memories. I was closely watched. All my money was blocked. I could not draw a penny from the bank account without permission from the Nazi authorities. I had to render accounts for each item I bought, for each pair of hose and each grocer's item. When my mother, who lived in another city came to visit me, she had to register with the police and could not stay an hour longer than the limited time which the local Chief of Police had granted her. Hours of humiliating waiting in front of closed office doors alternated with night long studies of new regulations affecting every phase of the personal life, and which changed so frequently that it was almost impossible to keep up with them. On the other hand, punishment for their neglect, voluntarily or involuntarily, was so severe that one could not take a chance.

The climax was reached in the pogrom days of November 1938. The child, the maid and myself lived all by ourselves in a couple of rooms of my uncle's big house. I woke up in the middle of the night by a noise which I could not identify. The noise of marching columns all night long was very familiar to me — the SA used to have many exercises of this kind. But this noise was a mixture of marching steps, of inarticulate sounds and the cries of women and children. I was still wondering when the doorbell rang. My clock showed two o'clock at night. It was November and a very cold night. I took a wrap and went downstairs. Our front garden was surrounded with an iron fence and we always locked it at night. Bare-feeted I went to the iron door in front of which six or seven Brownshirts demanded to be let in. They asked for my uncle whose address they had on their list, but who, fortunately had legally left for Paris some months ago. I explained that there wasn't any man in the house, just myself, the maid and the little baby. They wanted to look anyhow. So I opened the gate. Three Brownshirts and one official of the Secret Police searched the house from the top to bottom to the basement. The child woke up and cried. My maid, who happened to have a severe attack of rheumatism, could not get up from her bed. Finally they were convinced there wasn't any man. So they decided that I had to go with them since I was evidently the head of the family. I protested. The maid had had a severe attack of rheumatism the day before and was not able to get up. Who should care for the child? I asked. It was none of their business, they replied. But was it my firmness or the last evidence of some human feeling? — They told me to wait till they had received orders from their headquarters.

Then they left. I calmed the baby and waited. I heard them drag the neighbors in the street and saw them break into some other houses up the street where the inhabitants evidently did not hear them or were afraid to open. Ten minutes later they came back. This time only three Brownshirts in uniform. They told me that their superior had shown an exceptional understanding and since there was nobody to care for the baby they would allow me to stay in the house but the two Brownshirts had to stay with me. I was very relieved and the two boys, hardly over 20 years old, moved in. They put their guns in the dining room table and asked for an ashtray. They evidently did not feel at ease themselves. I asked them whether there was anything else I had to do. They told me no and I went upstairs to lie down in my bedroom. It was an odd situation. Two women and a child in a large house and two strangers, heavily armed to guard us. I was lying on my bed, wondering what the next move was going to be. I did not know what it was all about. I was not afraid, but very much alert. At six I got up, took a bath and dressed carefully. Somehow I had the feeling it might be the last bath for a long time. I went downstairs to prepare the breakfast for the nurse and the child. The two Brownshirts were still there. The man came who daily looked after the furnace. His face was ash gray. He was the first to tell me that they had rounded up the Jews in the city, brought them to the market place and had them stand there for hours and hours in the cold and the dark — even the women and little babies. That was also the noise I had heard - the crying of the women and babies. A little later I learned that I was one of the very few Jewish persons in the city who had not been compelled to the market place. Around 9 o'clock two SA officers came and told the two men in my living room to leave. I asked whether there were any others coming to replace these and whether I was supposed to leave the house or not. I was told I was perfectly free to move around and to leave the house.

I went to the grocer and the butcher to get something to eat for the family. Verstoerte (haggard, upset) faces wherever I went. I met a few Jews, women only. They told me in a whispering voice about their ordeal during the night. Always the same story: they stood in the market place for hours, subject to most humiliating treatment by Brownshirts. Later the women were released. The men were brought to a community house and, as we learned the next day, most of them brought to a concentration camp.

At noon I could not stand it any longer. I went to the Jewish hospital asking whether I could help them. I had heard rumors of hundreds of badly beaten and hurt people who had come there for help. What I actually found was worse than all my anticipation. Since the chief doctor was a very good friend of ours, he put me to work right away. The zustand (condition) of some of the people was beyond description. Every verwundung (wound, injury) which could be caused by beating, by nailed boots and clubs, was to be found in all possible variations. Very soon they started bringing in the victims of attempted or almost completed suicides. The enormous skill and unbelievable effort of the doctors saved some of the poor lives. But for what for? — we asked ourselves. It was their task to try everything within their power, but we felt that sometimes it would have been better to just let them pass away. They never could recover anyway from the physical and mental blows. I worked at the hospital for weeks. New patients came every minute. We had to put them on the floor — there weren't enough mattresses or blankets or even space. All these people showed a magnificent spirit of cooperation. There was not one who complained. There was a blind man who was badly hurt. He was lying on the floor for some days because he couldn't be provided with a bed. The ones who could walk helped the others. The nurses did not go to bed at all. I went home for a few hours of sleep every night.

I volunteered at the hospital for some weeks. Then they did not need me any more and got along with their regular help. What I have seen and heard there I will never forget. But I also will never forget how strong the will to live, to go on and to reconstruct can be in people under the most adverse circumstances. Each one of them was a hero, worthy of everlasting remembrance.

During the first days of March my husband was released. I had everything ready for him. He got his American visa right away and a few days later he and the child were in Paris. I had to stay some more weeks in Germany to settle some of our affairs. In fact, I still had some thousand marks and I had a hard time to get rid of them."

The hand-written notes are even more personal and explain to me, in large part, her hatred of the Germans and why she wanted nothing more to do with them after we had emigrated. Again, I do not know the purpose for which they were written besides recording an extraordinary experience:

Wednesday was a legal holiday. I was working in the hospital from early morning till I went home to get a few hours rest. I had hardly closed my eyes when the bell rang. I expected nobody — I knew at once that this was going to mean trouble. The maid came up, breathless and trembling: "Brownshirts — they want to talk to you". I was summoned to the City Hall and given half an hour of time. I knew at once this was my turn now to give up, voluntarily and legally all that had remained from our property. For days now one after another of our friends were summoned to the City Hall, preferably in the middle of the night, in order to sign their property away. The streets were quiet and empty since this was a holiday. But at the City Hall, Brownshirts and party officials were busily running around. I had to stand for several hours in the ice-cold entrance hall of the old fashioned building before I was admitted to the official's office. He sat behind a huge writing table in the middle of the newly elaborately decorated room. I knew this man very well. He was a little textile merchant who through his good connections with the Nazi party had twice been saved from severe punishment for bankruptcy. This utter failure in business life did not prevent his becoming a business expert after the Nazis had taken over the government. In his role as city councilman he, through threats and violence, forced himself in most of the director's boards of all the larger Jewish enterprises of the city, which not only provided him with an enormous income, but also gave him the opportunity to make things so unbearable for the Jewish executives and employees that they all, after a short while, voluntarily gave up their position. In this way he, for instance, became chief executive in my father's glass and mirror producing concern — a type of business of which he had not the slightest idea. Some years later, long after I had left Germany, I heard that he was sentenced to a long term in prison because of embezzling large sums from the Party funds. But in those dark November days of 1938 he was omnipotent, but evidently not without fear because when I entered his room he was surrounded by four or five heavily armed Brownshirts, who evidently had orders to watch closely every move of the victims summoned into the room. After I had entered the room I was left standing there for quite a while and nobody seemed to notice me. I was dreadfully tired and leaned against a table in one corner of the room. All of a sudden S. raised his eyes and yelled, "Get away from that table. This is not your living room, you dirty Jewish swine. You are not supposed to touch the furniture." I knew by my own and other people's experiences that any answer I would give him would only mean more abuse and even violence. I stepped some steps forward and remained standing in the middle of the room. He opened a dossier. "There is still some real estate in your name. This has to be transferred to the Party". "All our real estate has been sold through notarized contract". "What do you mean by sold", he said. "Did you get the money?" "No", I said, "You know that you have to okay it and did not do it yet." "It will never be done, you understand me. Your property is transferred to the Party". To one of his aides he said, "Make her sign this". The Brownshirt handed me an already notarized contract where only the signature was missing. "I have no power of attorney", I said. Now he became really angry. "How come?" "The real estate belongs to my mother-in-law and to my husband". "Where are they?" "My mother-in-law is in Italy and my husband is in jail". "Why is he in jail?" said he hypocritically, because he personally had brought about his sentence in order to get our business and property. "There is a new wind blowing now", he yelled all of a sudden, "we don't let you get away any more with your filthy tricks, you dirty Jews. You sign or else!" I knew from friends what that meant. Standing in pitch-dark basements with hands up and face to the wall, a score of Brownshirts behind you with knives and clubs to beat you and threats with guns to shoot you. They all had signed at the end. So I signed, and that was the voluntary and legal sale of our real property to the Nazi Party.

Documents from the Nuremberg Archives

In May 1996, when Evy and I were in Germany, Gisela Blume arranged for us to review documents concerning our parents in the Nuremberg Archives. We had been eager to see what was there, particularly about Alfred's case and imprisonment. These archives, as we understood it, are not open to the public in general, and we had to show all kinds of identification of who we were, our relationship to our parents, and proof that they had been dead for over 10 years. Fortunately Gisela's research had brought her to the National Archives many times so those in charge knew her and facilitated our entry. If our children or grandchildren go back to Germany in 60 years they will be able to see in the Archives in Nuremberg that on Wednesday, May 8, 1996, we took out these papers to look at the "official history" of Alfred and his mother. We spent the better part of a day there, and were able to make xerox copies of the documents we selected.

It was amazing, and moving and actually disconcerting, to see such "officialdom" at work. The mere volume of the files dealing primarily with Alfred, regarding every detail of his life, was overwhelming and so "Germanic". Nothing went undocumented, and everything was saved, which was the most amazing of all. In the midst of what was a very emotional pile of documents, there was also some humor, as evidenced by the folder, which included all of Alfred's traffic violations, going back to when he first obtained his license.

I will begin with the traffic violations, as they are the earliest documents chronologically, and also provide some levity to what follows.

These consist of letters (actually forms in which the blanks are filled in) from the Public Prosecutor's Office of Nuremberg to the Police Authority of Nuremberg and the Fürth Police Department. The earliest one, when Alfred was 27, dated February 8, 1928, is interesting because at that time, in contrast to the later Nazi time, Alfred was still referred to by his full name only, with no reference to his race or religion. The "charge" reads:

> *"The commercial/business employee Alfred Rahn of Fürth, Konigstrasse 129, born January 28, 1901 in Fürth, was sentenced for a violation of paragraph 21 of the vehicular law and fined 2 Reichsmarks. This sentence is final." Two Reichsmarks in 1928 amounted to less than $1.00.*

> *There was another violation on February 8, 1928 resulting in a fine of 5 Reichsmarks (just over $1.00). A third violation and sentence was meted on April 30, 1928, again for violation of paragraph 21. spelled out to include the following and the inapplicable ones were Alfred's only offense was "failure to use warning signal". Once again he was fined 5 marks and one-day detention." This must have been a "bad driving period" for Alfred (like a bad hair day) because on August 28 he was again sentenced for violating paragraph 21 of the law (don't know which offense he committed) and given a sentence of 20 Reichsmarks ($5.00) and 4 days of detention. This sentence also included the statement "The convicted has permission to operate motor vehicles".*

The violation that got us chuckling, however, was the one that occurred on April 1, 1929. The punishable offense was described as: Causing injury through negligence. Disregarding of proper caution, overly fast driving and failure to reduce speed so that the driver is able to meet his obligations, and failure to stop, thus endangering people". This sounded pretty serious until we read the report made by the Police Superintendent of what actually happened. This reads as follows:

"On Monday, April 1, 1929, at approximately 9:15 p.m., the accused Rahn, drove his car IIS-376 down Nuremberger Strasse into the city. At the same time the driver of the car IIN-4418 drove down Nuremberger Strasse out of the city (i.e. in the opposite direction). The latter, according to an eyewitness, had all four headlights of his vehicle on, creating a strong blinding effect. Rahn was blinded thereby to such an extent that he was unable to see anything, and hit a group of nine bikers near Nuremberger Strasse #61. The bikers were pushing their unlit bikes on the right side of the road heading into the city, and were walking in pairs behind one another. The bikers in the rear were thrown forward through the impact. Of the nine bikers, seven were somewhat hurt. Four of these were taken to their homes in ambulances. Most of the bikes were damaged. On the vehicle, the right headlight was bent towards the rear and the glass of the same was broken."

There is no indication of what the penalty was for this "crime".

What's interesting in this particular police report is that, like all the others, it lists only Alfred's full name, address at 129 Konigstrasse, date and place of birth (Fürth and January 28, 1901) and occupation. In this report, he is listed as "partner in business", as he had just become a partner of M.S. Farrnbacher.

We now skip to 1937, when Lilli and Alfred decided to emigrate to the United States. Now, every document lists the name, maiden name, date of birth, address and occupation, and "non-Aryan" or "Jewish by race and faith". In October 1937 they gave a Power of Attorney to Dr. Otto Rosenberg of Nuremberg for all matters concerning emigration and authorized him to act in their stead with all authorities. On October 12, 1937 Dr. Rosenberg wrote to the Police Headquarters and the Passport Office in Fürth on behalf of Lilli and Alfred and Helen Lorz, as follows:

As the authorized representative of the married couple Alfred and Dr. Lilli Rahn, as well as of Mrs. Helene Lorz, I request that they be issued documents certifying that they have no criminal record. The couple intends to emigrate to the United States of America with their daughter Ruth Marion and Mrs. Helene Lorz. The documents are required by the American consulate general, Stuttgart. Mr. Alfred Rahn was born on January 28, 1901. Dr. Lilli Rahn, nee Bechmann, on February 20 (sic), 1911, the child Ruth Marion on June 15, 1936. Mrs. Helen Lorz, nee Bergen, divorced, was born on January 16, 1900. Attached are powers of attorneys of the Rahns and of Mrs. Helen Lorz.

How simple a request! Yet the chain of events that followed becomes increasingly complex and far- reaching, on so many levels. The decision to emigrate must have been difficult; even though by this time in 1937 anti-semitism and laws against Jews had proliferated. Alfred was the partner in a business that had been in existence for almost 200 years. He was 36 years old, and the thought of starting over, in a new country with a new language (although he did speak some English) must have been daunting. He was responsible for his mother, as well as for his older brother James, who by this time was institutionalized. He really never had to begin a business, as he was able to step into M.S. Farrnbacher after an apprenticeship at another business and when it was still run by his father. For Lilli, I suspect the decision was somewhat easier. She was not employed, but must have felt confident, with her Ph.D. and her knowledge of English that she could be employed in the U.S. She certainly had a more adventuresome and courageous personality than Alfred, and with her knowledge of German history, was probably more fearful of what was yet to come in Germany. The decision to take Helen Lorz along must also have been difficult. Mrs. Lorz had been hired as a nanny (governess) for Ruth when she was born. She was 1/8 Jewish and thus was subject to the Nuremberg Laws just as much as fully Jewish Germans were. She was a year older than Alfred, was divorced, and had one daughter of her own. In the social circle in which they moved, it was very common to have a governess, and given that Mrs. Lorz wanted to emigrate, not uncommon to agree to take her along. She certainly had no criminal record, so there was nothing to fear.

The response to the October 12th letter was sent immediately on October 14, 1937 and the word "Sofort" (Immediately! note, followed by an exclamation point) is written in bold large letters at the top. The Secret State Police wrote to the office of taxes/revenue of Fürth regarding their preparations to move domicile abroad. The primary concern was to prevent tax evasion and flight of capital from the German Reich. As we discovered by going through the Archives, the State Secret Policed notified absolutely everyone with whom Alfred, Lilli or Helen Lorz had any contact as well as all the cities and towns in which each had ever lived. Copies were also sent to Finance Offices of any town in which any of them had lived; Mayors of all towns, numerous banks, Office of Currency Exchange, and Chief of the Regional Finance Authority in Berlin (central intelligence). Inquiries were also made for any exiting police files for Johanna's deceased husband, Sidney Rahn, who was born May 2, 1866 in London and had died in 1933. The letter outlined that Alfred Rahn, son of the commercially employed couple Sidney Rahn, died in Fürth, and Hannchen, nee Goldmann, resident of Fürth, partner/shareholder in the company of M.S. Farrnbacher, dealing in iron and metals, headquarters in Fürth, Konigstrasse 129, whose citizenship was: German Reich, and non-Aryan (first time this appears in a document as the word "Aryan" is crossed out), and his wife, Lilli Rahn, nee Bechmann and their child, intend to go abroad to North America (U.S.A.). Then it says — Cause of suspicion: Emigration.

The letter then states: If there are other relevant facts or reservations to be expressed, I ask that I be notified immediately (underlined) and no later than November 1, 1937. Should it be necessary, I leave it to your jurisdiction to take any measures to prevent tax evasion or capital flight. The departments listed below have received copies of this letter with the request for any relevant information they might have in this matter. The letter then states that they made note of the request in the Emigration Registry and "Emigration file started". Copies were sent to the following: (1) Chief of Finance in Nuremberg — office of customs investigations, (2) Mayor of the city of Fürth, city tax department, (3) National bank branch in Fürth, Moststrasse 21, (4) Chief of Finance in Nuremberg — office of currency exchange, (5) Chief of the Regional Finance Authority Berlin (central intelligence), and (6) Chamber of Industry and Commerce Nuremberg. It was easy to see that the taking of any money out of Germany was considered a serious offence and emigration was, ipso facto, a "cause of suspicion".

October 20, 1937 —What follows here in the Archives are the written replies of those who received this letter. A similar letter, with the same copies and replies was sent on behalf of Hannchen (Johanna). On October 20, 1937 the Mayor of the city of Fürth wrote to the Secret State Police "For my part, I have no objections to Alfred Rahn's, born January 28, 1901, and his wife's intentions to emigrate." The Seal of Bavaria, City of Fürth, was appended.

The legal advisor to the Chamber of Industry and Commerce Nuremberg wrote to the Secret State Police that "we inform you, that economic objections will not be raised against the emigration of the Jewish businessman Alfred Hermann Rahn and his family, partner in the company M.S. Farrnbacher, iron and metals business, Fürth in Bavaria, Konigstrasse 129. A disadvantage to the economic interests of Germany is not to be feared in the present case"

So, on **October 25, 1937** Dr. Otto Rosenberg wrote to the Police Headquarters Nuremberg-Fürth, Passport Office of Fürth, as the authorized representative of Mrs. Johanna Rahn, Alfred Rahn, Lilli Rahn and Helen Lorz (nee Bergmann), all then living at Konigstrasse 129, requesting the issuing of passports, as the above-named plan to emigrate. Mrs. Johanna Rahn will emigrate to Italy, all the others to the United States. I also ask that the child Ruth-Marion be listed in the passport of Mrs. Lilli Rahn. Passport pictures will be submitted later.

At this time there didn't appear to be any particular problems. It appears the plan was to send Alfred's mother to Italy, where it was easy to find a place for her to live (she lived at first in the Excelsior Hotel (!) in Milan) and left for the United States before we did.

Then we found one of the most interesting documents in the Nuremberg Archives. A postcard sent by a Mrs. Marie Hess. It is handwritten, undated but the postmark on the front says November 7, 1937. It's written on a pre-printed postcard, which has on the front the stamp of the eagle and the skyline of Nuremberg with the inscription "CITY OF THE NATIONAL PARTY CONFERENCE". The postcard is addressed to the "Office of the Residents of the City of Fürth in Bavaria, City Hall" and has the following message:

"Would you be so good and inform me soon whether Alfred Rahn, partner in the firm M.S. Farrnbacher, Fürth, is a Jew or is of Aryan descent. If he is a Jew, I have to begin a complaint against him as he has conned me. Please write me soon. I can't spend 40 M to drive myself there as I am unemployed and old. Thank you and Heil Hitler. Mrs. Marie Hess, Nuremberg, Waisenstrasse 163."

On **November 16, 1937** Dr. Rosenberg wrote to the Police Headquarters Fürth, Passport Office Fürth attaching the explanation of Mrs. Hess as well as a receipt. The statement which Mrs. Hess signed reads as follows: "I hereby rescind the claim that Mr. Alfred Rahn cheated me in the sale of a couch. Mr. Rahn has stated to me that he will grant me a discount of 20 Reichsmarks in consideration of his imminent emigration. I hereby explicitly state that I have no claims against Mr. Rahn and will assert no Fürther claims: /signature/ Marie Hess, Nuremberg, Waisenstrasse 163." Mrs. Hess also signed a separate receipt, handwritten by Alfred, indicating that she had received 20 Reichmarks ($8.00).

What to make of such a postcard? The amount of blackmail and extortion that went on as Jews were preparing to leave must have been enormous. Knowing that the machinery of the state, in all its forms, was on their side, individuals like Mrs. Hess could safely assert their "claims", fully aware of the leverage they had. I can only imagine the level of extortion that went on, not only between individuals, but at the corporate level as well. Alfred was never fully paid for his business or the real estate in which it was housed.

In the meantime, the official correspondence continues.

On **November 11, 1937** Dr. Rosenberg wrote to the Police headquarters Fürth and Passport Office on behalf of Mrs. Johanna Rahn, Alfred and Lilli Rahn and Mrs. Helen Lorz, stating, "I hereby request kindly to be informed by when the passports and documents certifying the lack of criminal records of the individuals named above can be expected to be issued. The documents are needed by the 16th of this month at the latest, as the above-named have an appointment on the 17th of this month with the American consulate general and must present these documents on that date."

I can only imagine the heightened sense of anxiety as the date approached to meet with the American consulate general in Stuttgart (which is 94 miles from Fürth).

On **November 12, 1937** The Revenue Office of Fürth wrote to the State Secret Police that there are no tax-related objections to the issuing of a travel passport for the businessman Alfred and Lilli Rahn and their child Ruth Marion. The national flight tax (Reichsfluchtsteuer) has been paid. (This appears to be yet another tax or fine levied on those wanting to emigrate from Germany.)

The document dated November 16, 1937 stated that Hannchen Rahn, Jew by race and confession, was to be issued and given a passport for domestic and foreign travel, valid for one year, for the purpose of emigration to Italy.

November 16, 1937 — the National Bank Branch Fürth writes to the Secret State Police that "there are no objections on our part to the emigration of Alfred, Lilli and their child Ruth Marien (sic) Rahn.

November 19, 1937 — The Military Service Registration Office of Fürth writes to the Police Station that on the part of the military service registration office of Fürth, there are no objections to the issuing of a passport to Alfred Rahn, allowing the holder access to the entire interior (i.e. Germany) and abroad, including Austria, and valid from November 16, 1937 to November 15, 1942.

Apparently the scheduled appointment with the American consulate in Stuttgart was cancelled or postponed.

Then, on **December 4, 1937** the bombshell dropped, in a letter from the Customs Investigation Office, Nuremberg to the Police Authority, and Fürth Passport Division. The subject of this letter was: Protective Order, and the letter read as follows:

"I request that the passports of Alfred Rahn and his wife Lilli, as well as of Johanna Rahn, all living in Fürth in Bavaria, Konigstrasse 129, held by your office, only be given to the holders thereof with the agreement of the foreign currency office Nuremberg, as criminal proceedings are currently pending against A. Rahn."

On **December 21, 1937** Hannchen Rahn wrote a Registered Letter to the City Residents Registry, Fürth, stating "I hereby submit to you my notification of my intention to move my residence as, on the 23rd of this month, I will be changing my permanent residency to Meran,

Italy. Yours faithfully, Hannchen Rahn."

January 5, 1938 — The State Secret Police responded to the December 4th letter as follows: "Per your request, the passports of the commercially employed couple Alfred Rahn, born January 28, 1901 in Fürth and Lilli Rahn, Nee Bechmann, born November (sic) 10, 1911 in Fürth, as well as the passport of the businessman's widow Hannchen Rahn, nee Goldman, born September 10, 1873 in Meiningen, all three Jewish by race and faith, living in Fürth, Konigstrasse 129, were retained. I obligingly request a statement regarding whether or not the criminal proceedings against Alfred Rahn are now closed and the passports might be given out."

A second page went on to say "Separate passports are to be issued for Alfred Rahn and his wife Lilli Rahn for use domestically and abroad for the duration of one year, and character references are to be given to them for the purpose of emigration to North America. Their child, Ruth Marion Rahn, is to be listed in the passport of Lilli Rahn.

January 13, 1938 — Letter from the Customs Investigation Office Nuremberg to the Secret State Police of Fürth, stating that the criminal proceedings against Alfred Rahn are currently still pending at the Senior Public Prosecutor Nuremberg-Fürth. It is therefore not yet possible to issue him his passport. We have no objections to issuing the passports for Lilli Rahn and Johanna Rahn. Below, handwritten is that notation: "Passport for Hannchen Rahn issued and given to her on January 19, 1938".

What was Lilli feeling at this point? Johanna could leave, and did. Lilli was left with me, able to leave but of course unwilling to do so.

On **January 26, 1938** the letter from the Police Superintendent to the Police Headquarters stated the following: Rahn left for Meran on Friday, January 21, 1938. Her son, who lived on the first floor (second floor by our standards)of the same residence as she, moved into her apartment. The new proprietor of the business moved into the son's apartment".

Now we got some understanding regarding the housing arrangements. Johanna had to leave — the home and business had been sold and the new owner wanted to move in.

Johanna had moved up to the third floor when Alfred and Lilli got married, and they moved to the second floor. Now, the second floor apartment was needed for the new owner. It was decided that Johanna would leave and going to Italy was probably the easiest place to get to — it was not far and apparently emigration from there would be easy. She lived in the Excelsior Hotel and they probably thought she would be readily available to leave with them when they finally got full permission to emigrate. However, she left for the U.S. from Italy in about September, 1938 and lived in New York City until we all arrived in April, 1939. Because the new owners moved into 129 Konigstrasse, Lilli, Ruth Marion and Helen Lorz moved to the Bierer residence on what was then called Adolf Hitlerstrasse, (formerly Konigswarterstrasse, which is its name again today). This was the home of Ernst and Emma Bierer (Ida's sister) who had left and were living in Paris. This house was only a few blocks away. Ruth was 1 1/2 years old when this move occurred. For the next 14 months we lived there, with Helen Lorz, until we emigrated. This also helped explain to me why I had no memories whatsoever of 129 Konigstrasse, the home we lived in when I was born.

January 31, 1938 — Letter from the State Secret Police of Nuremberg to the State Secret

Police of Berlin stating (I repeat here because this gives all the information).

We are notifying you that the businessman's widow, Hannchen Rahn, nee Goldmann, born September 20, 1873 in Meiningen in Thuringen, Jewish by race and faith, German citizen, formerly residing here in Fürth at Konigstrasse, 129, daughter of the commercially employed couple Abraham and Sara Goldmann nee Rosenau, both deceased, requested on October 25, 1937 the issuance of a passport for the purpose of emigration to Italy, and was issued and given this. Rahn was registered as moving to Italy on January 20, 1938 and did emigrate to there. (Every document, in true Germanic style, lists maiden name, date of birth, Jewish, address etc. etc.)

February 5, 1938 — Document entitled Notification of Penalty/Sentence

This is the official document of Alfred's sentence. "The above-mentioned individual has been found guilty on January 25, 1938 by sentence of the Schoffengericht (one judge and two lay judges) of one continued currency office to One year and two months in prison started after three weeks held on remand [i.e. in preparation for trial]. He was originally incarcerated in Fürth and then was to be moved to the Nuremberg-Zellenstrasse Prison. He is identified as German Reich (Jew by race) Other comments: Place of incarceration: Nuremberg-Zellenstrasse Prison. End of Sentence: March 5, 1939, 2:45 p.m.

I have commented elsewhere of how Germanic and official and efficient it was to list the exact time, to the minute, of the end of his sentence

On **February 24, 1938** Dr. Otto Rosenberg wrote to the Bavarian Mortgage and Exchange Bank, as Johanna's authorized representative, asking that she be issued documentation of her native citizenship and a character reference as these two documents were being requested by the Italian authorities. There were a number of letters back and forth, indicating that a complete background check had been done on Johanna, her deceased husband and her deceased parents, verifying that in the criminal registry there were no sentences.

The German Consulate General responded on June 14, 1938 to the Police Headquarters that they had no objections to the issuing of mentioned documents but asked that the validity of the documentation of native citizenship be limited to one year. This correspondence continues until finally there is notification from Dr. Rosenberg that Johanna Rahn had emigrated to the United States. They no longer needed documentation of native citizenship for submission to the American authorities, but needed two copies of character references.

All of the above is probably rather boring, but points out the enormous bureaucracy involved in every move, Whether Johanna ever got her character references, I do not know. By this time she was safely out of Germany so it really didn't matter. The long story of our obtaining visas is told elsewhere in this memoir.

The other batch of correspondence in the Archives refers to obtaining new passports, because, as Jews who had lost their citizenship by edict of the Reich in 1935, passports also became invalid. The Citizenship Law, enacted in September 1935, established the fundamental distinction between "citizens of the Reich" who were entitled to full political and civic rights, and "subjects" who were now deprived of those rights. Only those of German or related blood could become citizens. Thus, from that moment on, in terms of their civic rights, the Jews had in fact a status similar to that of foreigners. Fortunately, Alfred and his mother had gone to the

United States to "look around", as I previously discussed, earlier in 1935, before this law was enacted.

We have, in another section of this memoir, Alfred's personal prison letters. The correspondence here, which he wrote in prison, is in the Nuremberg archives, and relates to his request for passports.

January 3, 1939 — This is a typed letter, on plain white paper, from Alfred to the Police Station in Fürth. Since he was in prison at that time, it must have been prepared by Attorney Rosenberg and taken by him, or by Lilli, to the prison to have it personally signed by Alfred. There is no mention whatsoever that he is in prison, and the letter contains the address as Adolf Hitlerstrasse 26. Alfred here is simply requesting passports for himself, Lilli and Ruth. The letter reads as follows:

> *I ask the chief of Police of Fürth and Passport Agency Fürth, to issue all members of my family international passports and police certification documents, as well as citizenship certificates, as I plan to emigrate with my family to the United States in North America as soon as possible. Our personal particulars are:*
>
> *Israel Alfred Hermann Rahn, born in Fürth, Bavaria, January 28, 1901*
>
> *Dr. Lilli Sarah (looks like Alfred crossed out the "h) before signing) Rahn, nee Bechmann, born Fürth, Bavaria, February 10, 1911*
>
> *Ruth-Marion Sarah (h is crossed out again) Rahn, born in Fürth, Bavaria, June 15, 1936*
>
> *Three written confirmations from the Emigration Counseling Center Munich are attached. I request a separate passport for the child Ruth-Marion Sarah (h is crossed out) Rahn, so that she may possibly leave the country separately.*
>
> *I have also informed the mayor of the city of Fürth (city tax office), the chief of finance of Nuremberg (foreign exchange office), and the Fürth tax office of my intentions to emigrate.*
>
> *Signed: Israel Alfred Rahn*

The three attachments were Certifications from the Emigration Counseling Center in Munich for Alfred, Lilli and Ruth. They were forms, with blanks to be filled in by the passport agency. Each one stated that if the authorities are not notified of a long term (permanent) move within two months after issuing the passport, the passport would be revoked. Each certified that the applicant has demonstrated a serious intention to emigrate to the U.S.A. On Ruth's, it says that she has demonstrated, through her father, a serious intention to emigrate to the U.S.A. The fee for each certification was 2 Reichsmarks.

I was very struck and moved by the request by Alfred to obtain a separate passport for me so that I could possibly leave the country separately. Many questions present themselves out of this request. What did he actually know about what was happening outside the prison in January 1939? He wasn't aware of the difficulties and problems Lilli was having to get a new visa. Were they seriously thinking of sending me out separately? Where? With whom? Probably Helen Lorz had her passport already. Was there concern that he wouldn't be released when his sentence was over? Did they have friends who sent their children out separately? The Kindertransport sending children out alone, primarily to England, began in November 1938.

January 9, 1939 — This is a document, on a printed form, from the Police Headquarters Fürth and send to the Fürth Tax office, with copies to others. Again we get the beginning of official documents, with copies to banks, mayors, customs and tax officials, etc. It is just one of the many documents that has to be completed and filed before anyone could emigrate. The top of this document has Sofort (Immediately) written in bold print. The distribution list is:

a. Chief of Finance of Nuremberg — Customs investigations office

b. National Bank Branch Fürth

c. Chief of Finance (foreign exchange division) in Nuremberg

d. Mayor of the city of Fürth — tax office

e. Central customs investigations office in the department of the chief of finance in Berlin

The document stated that the businessman Alfred Hermann Israel Rahn, born January 28, 1901 in Fürth, Bavaria, citizenship: German; Jewish by race and religion, and his wife, Lilli Sara, nee Bechmann, born February 10, 1911 in Fürth, Bavaria, citizenship: German; Jewish by race and religion, as well as their daughter, Ruth Marion Sara born June 15, 1936 in Fürth, address: Adolph Hitler Strasse Number 26, plan, according to their own reports to move abroad to the USA. Reasons: Emigration.

The letter asks of each recipient to confirm that there are no liabilities regarding taxes. If there are objections to the issuing of such certification, they were asked to communicate any information for Fürther facts directly and immediately. The document Fürther requested a list of previous convictions for character references, and the State Police Nuremberg were contacted with a request for a statement and asked if there were any objections.

It was very interesting to notice that at the bottom of this form, actually printed right onto the document itself, were the laws by which Jews were defined. It states:

"In business dealings the following designations are to be used in the future: For a Jewish half-breed (Judische Mischling) (compare paragraph 2 section 2 of the First Publication to the Reich Citizens Law" of November 14, 1935 — RGB1,I, p. 1333 — with two Jewish grandparents; half breed of the first degree.

For a Jewish half-breed with one Jewish grandparent: half-breed of the second degree

Polizeipräsidium Nürnberg-Fürth
Polizeiamt Fürth
                                    Fürth, 9. Januar   1939.
(Dienststelle)   (Ort)   (Tag)

Geschäftszeichen: Nr. 61/VI.   Nürnberger Str. Nr. 18

Zimmer Nr. 52   Fernsprecher: 73 341

                                         Hausanschluß Nr.

                         Sofort!

Kanzlei: Schreibe mit 6 Durchschlägen:

                     An das
                 Finanzamt   F ü r t h /Bayern.

Gegenstand: Vorbereitende Maßnahmen zur Verlegung des Wohnsitzes ins Ausland.

Vorgänge: a) Erlaß des Geheimen Staatspolizeiamts vom 17. Dezember 1936 — II. 1 B 2 Allgem. Nr. 171 E —,
          b) Erlaß des Reichsministers der Finanzen vom 29. Dezember 1936 — O. 2011 A — 5 III/ O. 1729 — 1549 II —,
          c) Rundschreiben der Zentralen Steuerfahndungsstelle bei dem Oberfinanzpräsidenten Berlin vom:
             6. November 1935 — O. 2011 — I. 157/35 —, 7. Dezember 1935 — S. 1181 — I. 1/35 —.

Der   Kaufmann ( )
    Alfred Hermann Israel   R a h n ,
         (Vorname)   (Zuname)

geboren am   28. I.   1901 zu Fürth/Bayern,

Staatsangehörigkeit: Deutsches Reich,

                                    Rasse- u. Bekenntnisjude,

und seine Ehefrau   Lilli Sara,

geborene Bechmann,   , geboren am   10. II.   1911
zu Fürth/Bayern,

Staatsangehörigkeit: Deutsches Reich,

                                    Rasse- u. Bekenntnisjüdin,

sowie deren Tochter Ruth Marion Sara, geb. 15.6.1936 zu Fürth,

Anschrift: F ü r t h ,   Adolf Hitler Str. Nr. 26,

beabsichtigen —, nach eigener Angabe*) ins Ausland, und zwar

nach USA.

zu gehen.

Gründe: Auswanderung.

Oder*): Der Steuerpflichtige hat eine steuerliche Unbedenklichkeitsbescheinigung beantragt. Falls Bedenken gegen die Erteilung dieser Bescheinigung bestehen, bitte ich, sie mir innerhalb mitzuteilen.

Oder*): Falls von Ihnen noch weitere sachliche Angaben gemacht werden können, bitte ich, mir diese **sofort** mitzuteilen.

Die in dem umstehenden Verteiler angegebenen Dienststellen haben Abschrift von diesem Schreiben mit dem gleichen Ersuchen erhalten.

Anmerkungen ¹) bis *) auf der 2. Seite.

Vordruck A 107 f

Example of many decrees issued to impede emigration (page 1)

Zu 2: abgefandt
am .... 193.

2. Die gefertigten Reinschriften sind an die zu 1 und im Verteiler zu a bis g) genannten Behörden⁵) abzusenden.

Vermerk für die Kanzlei: Auf jedem Durchschlage ist ein anderer Empfänger **blau** zu unterstreichen. An den **blau** unterstrichenen Empfänger ist der Durchschlag abzusenden.

~~3. Zu den Akten~~

3.) Vorstrafenlisten f.Leumundszeugnisse erholen.

4.) U.A. 4 u. 5. Bestehen Bedenken?

5.) Stapo Nürnberg mit der Bitte um Äußerung.

6.) Wv. bei VI/2.

Im Auswandererverzeichnis
vorgemerkt:

....
(Unterschrift)

Verteiler:

a) ~~Geschäftsnummer~~ Oberfinanzpräsident in Nürnberg -Zollfahndungs-
stelle-

b) Reichsbank ~~XXXXXX~~ nebenstelle in Fürth

c) Oberfinanzpräsident (Devisenstelle)   in   Nürnberg

~~XXXXXXXXXXXX XXXXXXXXXX~~

d) ~~XXXXXXXXXX~~   Oberbürgermeister der Stadt Fürth -Steueramt-

~~XXXXXXXXXXXX~~

e) Zentrale Steuerfahndungstelle bei dem Oberfinanzpräsidenten Berlin, Berlin W15, Kurfürstendamm 193/194.

h) ....

i) ....

Anmerkungen:

¹) Im Geschäftsverkehr sind künftig in der Regel folgende Bezeichnungen zu verwenden:
für einen jüdischen Mischling (vgl. § 2 Abf. 2 der »Ersten Verordnung zum Reichsbürgergesetz« vom 14. November 1935 — RGBl. I, S. 1333 —) mit zwei volljüdischen Großeltern: Mischling ersten Grades,
für einen jüdischen Mischling mit einem volljüdischen Großelternteil: Mischling zweiten Grades,
für eine Person deutschen oder artverwandten Blutes: Deutschblütiger (Runderlaß des Reichs- und Preußischen Ministers des Innern vom 26. November 1935 — I B 3/324 II —, abgedruckt im Ministerialblatt für die Preußische innere Verwaltung 1935, Sp. 1429).

²) Über die Begriffsbestimmung »Jude« ergibt sich das Nähere aus § 5 der »Ersten Verordnung zum Reichsbürgergesetz« vom 14. November 1935 — RGBl. I, S. 1333 —

³) § 1 der »Dritten Bekanntmachung über den Kennkartenzwang« vom 23. Juli 1938 — RGBl. I, S. 922. —

⁴) Als »Verdachtsgründe« kommen beispielsweise in Betracht:
Antrag auf Erteilung eines Reisepasses, Auflösung des Geschäfts oder der Wohnung, Verkauf von Grundstücken, Beteiligungen usw.

⁵) Nichtzutreffendes ist zu streichen.

Example of many decrees issued to impede emigration (page 2)

For a person of German or related blood: German blood

2. *Details regarding the definition of the term "Jew" arise from paragraph 5 of the "First Publication to the Reich Citizens Law" of November 14, 1935 — RGBI, I P. 1333*

3. *Paragraph 1 of the "Third Publication regarding Mandatory Identity Cards" of July 23, 1938 — RGNI, I. P. 922*

4. *Reasons for suspicion include, for example: Application for the issuing of a passport, dissolution of business or domicile, sale of real estate, shares, etc."*

I find it remarkable that references to the laws concerning Jews were on the printed government forms and correspondence. Everyone should know exactly what the definition of 'Jew" was, and what the definition of "Mischling" was, and what "reasons for suspicion include". This was constantly to remind everyone of Jews in their midst, and how he or she was to deal with them.

Following this letter, responses were sent to the Fürth Police Headquarter by the recipients, uniformly indicating that there were no objections to the issuing of a passport for the purpose of emigration. The Fürth Tax Department Fürther noted that no taxes were owed, and that the Jewish capital levy, the Reichsfluchsteuer (a tax on those wishing to emigrate from Germany) and state flight tax had been paid.

Alfred's prison sentence was to end on March 5, 1939 at 2:45 p.m. — and yet the passports had not yet come.

On **February 23, 1939** Lilli, signing by proxy for Alfred, wrote to the Fürth Police Station as follows:

In a correspondence from January 6, 1939, Mr. Israel Alfred Rahn applied for the issuing of passports and police certifications (i.e. certifying lack of criminal record, etc) for himself and his family.

I now take the liberty to point out that the summons from the American consulate for the purpose of granting visas is now set for Tuesday, March 7, 1939 and I therefore ask that the passports and police certifications be prepared by March 6, 1939, at the latest. If there are still necessary certifications of unobjectionability outstanding, I will see that they are sent to you as soon as possible. She signed it Dr. Lilli Sara Rahn.

I can only wonder what was going through her mind as she wrote this letter. With so many offices having to sign off, would they really get their passports? Having just gone through the so much anxiety to finally obtain new visas, she had to maintain her courage and fortitude to request new passports. What would happen to Alfred when he was released on March 5, 1939, the date his sentence ended? What was it like anticipating the release of her husband, whom she had seen only behind bars for 14 months? What would she now tell him of all that had occurred during his isolation from these events? How did she feel having to add "Sara" to all her correspondence, or by this time was this just a minor nuisance in light of everything else. She is still living at Adolph Hitler Strasse, 26. What preparations had she made, or is she in the process of making, without the certainty that they would get their passports?

March 6, 1939 — a typewritten document with no letterhead, from the Police Headquarters Nuremberg Fürth, brought the good news. It reads as follows:

Subject: Emigration of Jews

"Alfred Hermann Israel Rahn and his wife Lilli Sara Rahn, both Jews by race and faith, are to be issued passports for emigration, valid for one year and character references in duplicate, and to be given these documents after they register their move. The daughter Ruth Marion Sara Rahn born June 15, 1936 is to be listed in the passport of her father. Alfred Israel Rahn was convicted on February 25, 1938 by the Fürth court [Schoffengericht — one presided over by one professional judge and two lay judges - of one continued currency offence and perjury, and sentenced to one year and two months jail. This penalty is not to be noted in the character reference."

Finally the passports were authorized, the day after Alfred's release from prison. This is a curious document. First, it doesn't have any official letterhead. And why is his penalty not to be noted in the character reference? This was certainly most fortunate. Alfred and Lilli then went to Stuttgart, got the necessary documentation from the American Consul there, and Alfred left with Ruth and Helen Lorz for Paris. Lilli remained in Fürth for another couple of weeks to oversee the last packing of furniture and other details. Ruth is listed on Alfred's passport, rather than on her mother's.

March 13, 1939 — the saga isn't over until it's over. This is a remarkable letter, and like the postcard of Mrs. Hess, shows the degree to which there were spies, undercover agents, informers, people willing to profit, extort and be bribed, knowing that the police would support them. In this case the informer was the moving company of Brasch & Rothenstein. As their letterhead indicates, they had offices in 24 German cities as well as their home office in Berlin. They also were an agent for England. They were an ideal informer. On March 13, Harry W. Hamacher, owner of the company, wrote to the Passport Agency of the Police Authority in Fürth as follows:

Subject: Dr. Lilli Rahn, Ph.D. Fürth, Adolph Hitler Strasse 26.

For the sake of order we are informing you that the above-named has charged us with the transportation of her property.

Should there be any objections on your part to the transportation thereof, please give us timely notification of these. Heil Hitler! Brasch & Rothenstein, Owner Harry W. Hamacher.

March 16, 1939 — The Police Headquarters Fürth-Fürth responded by stating there were no objections on the part of the police to the removal and transportation of the possessions of Dr. Lilli Sara Rahn, residing in Fürth, Adolph Hitler Strasse 26.

I wonder if Lilli ever knew of this letter. "For the sake of order" sounds like a code for "this is a Jew, planning to leave".

March 8, 1939 — the Fürth Police Station wrote to the Nuremberg Police Station what appears to be simply an information status letter, stating that Alfred Hermann Israel Rahn, German citizen, Jewish by race and faith, requested and was issued a passport and character references for himself and his daughter Ruth Marion Sara Rahn for the purpose of emigration to the U.S.A. His wife, Dr. Lilli Sara Rahn plans to emigrate to the U.S.A in the next few days. Rahn was sentenced to one year and two months in prison for perjury. The customs/tax investigation did not yield any complaints. Alfred Hermann Israel Rahn and his daughter, Ruth Marion Sara Rahn, gave notice of intention to go to the U.S.A. on March 6, 1939 and emigrated there. They then gave the passport number, issued by police headquarters, valid until March 5, 1940. His daughter is listed in her father's passport. This information was submitted as a report to the State Police Berlin, pursuant to a specified law.

March 25, 1939 — the Fürth Police Station wrote a comparable letter to the Nuremberg Police Station regarding Lilli. This letter stated that Dr. Lilli Sara Rahn gave notice of intention to go to New York on March 25, 1939, and emigrated there. Her husband Alfred Hermann Israel Rahn, as well as the child Ruth Marion Sara Rahn already emigrated to the U.S.A. on March 6, 1939. (These were the respective dates the passports were issued)

Thereafter, certain follow-up correspondence is in the Archives regarding revocation of German Citizenship.

On **May 20, 1940** —a letter was sent by the Police Headquarters Fürth to the following:

Mayor of City of Fürth

Mayor of city of the Reich party conventions Nuremberg

Mayor of the city of Munich

Mayor of the city of Karlsruhe

Mayor of the city of Hamburg

Mayor of the Reich capital city Berlin

Public Prosecutors Office for the Regional Court District Fürth-Fürth in Nuremberg

Note how the various cities are described — not just the city name, but also their place in the government of the Third Reich and the party. It is curious that Karlsruhe was included because Alfred did an internship there for about six months in 1921, when he was 20 years old. Karlsruhe in fact wrote back wondering why they were questioned and stated "Rahn is not listed in the Registries here." Similarly, Munich wondered why the correspondence was sent to them. Alfred had been a student there briefly for several months in 1919 and 1920. Apparently Karlsruhe and Munich weren't as efficient in their record-keeping.

Finally there is a letter was to inform the recipients that Alfred, Lilli and Ruth emigrated to the U.S.A on March 6, 1939 and were declared to have forfeited German citizenship according to the law (cited). This was sent for the purpose of correction of the Citizen's Registry and to the Passport Agency for correction of the Passport Registry.

I add here copies of Lilli and Alfred's birth certificates. dated December 13, 1938. They are copies which Lilli obviously needed as part of the many documents required or needed to have on hand. These are dated just weeks before Attorney General Cummings' opinion. They have the Fürth trefoil stamp as well as the Nazi stamp of the Third Reich, the eagle with the swastika. All four of their parents are clearly identified as "israelitich".

Lilli Bechmann's Birth Certificate

Geburtsurkunde E 1

(Standesamt **Fürth i. Bay.** Nr. 148)

Alfred Hermann R e h n ,

ift am 28. Januar 1901 in fürth geboren.

Vater: Sidney Rahn, Kaufmann, israelitisch,

Mutter: Hannchen, geborene Goldmann, israelitisch,

Änderungen der Eintragung:

Fürth i. Bay., den 13. Dezember 193 8.

Der Standesbeamte
J. V.

E.

Alfred Hermann Rahn's Birth Certificate

7
HOMER CUMMINGS' DECISION

Homer Cummings

Who was this man, who as U.S. Attorney General rendered an opinion that saved my life and that of my family? What was his background? What propelled him to render the strong opinion he did, in light of the times, and the clear opposition from other departments of the government, particularly the State Department? He, as head of the Justice Department received the request from the State Department for his opinion regarding Alfred's case the first week of December, 1938, and was already set to retire on December 31, 1938. He could have just "filed it away". What moved him to render his decision, which was contrary to established American law? I became extremely interested in finding out more about him and what prompted his decision.

First, some basic facts about the man.

Homer Cummings was born in 1870 in Chicago and received his undergraduate degree from Yale University in 1891 and his L.L.B. from Yale Law School in 1893. He then practiced law in Stamford, Conn. and in 1901 joined with Charles D. Lockwood to form the law firm of Cummings and Lockwood. He remained a partner until 1933 when President Roosevelt appointed him U.S. Attorney General. Cummings entered politics almost immediately after graduating from law school. In 1896 he supported William Jennings Bryan for President. The decision to support Bryan rested on his conviction that government, law and the Democratic Party were the instruments for the achievement of social justice in America. His progressive sensibility was reinforced by his gifts as an orator. He was an incisive, dramatic trial lawyer, and an astute, and loyal political manager.

In 1900, 1901 and 1904 he was elected mayor of Stamford, Connecticut where he instituted a progressive municipal program. He was nominated for congressman-at-large in 1902 and for U.S. Senator in 1910 and 1916, losing narrowly. During Cummings' last year as county prosecutor, a vagrant, Harold Israel, was indicted for the murder of a popular parish priest on a street corner in Bridgeport. The evidence, including a confession, appeared overwhelming, but Cummings, after scrupulous investigation, became convinced of Israel's innocence. In a gripping courtroom scene he asked for and secured dismissal of the charge. In 1931 the National Commission on Law Observance and Enforcement (the Wickersham Commission) praised this act, and a film, "BOOMERANG" (1947) dramatized the affair.

Cummings began his association with the national Democratic Party in 1900, when he was named committeeman from Connecticut, a post he held until 1925. He was delegate to many national conventions, and served as vice-chairman of the national committee from 1913-1919 and as chairman from 1919-1920. Cummings greatly admired Woodrow Wilson and delivered a passionate keynote address at the 1920 convention in praise of the stricken president.

Cummings married four times. His marriage to Helen W. Smith in 1897 ended in divorce in 1907. They had one son, Dickinson Schuyler Cummings. His 1909 marriage to Marguerite T. Owings was dissolved in 1928. The marriage to May Cecilia Waterbury in 1929 was happy; she died 10 years later. He published a memoir "The Tired Sea" (1939) as a tribute to Cecilia. In 1942 he married Julia Alter, who died in 1955.

With the coming of the Depression Cummings reentered politics. In 1932 he helped persuade 24 senators and numerous congressmen to announce their support for Franklin D. Roosevelt. At Chicago he planned strategy, operated as floor manager, and delivered a resounding seconding speech. Following the election, Roosevelt chose Cummings as Governor-General of the Philippines. However, when Senator Thomas Walsh, who had been designated Attorney General, died on March 2, 1933 on his way to Washington, Roosevelt named Cummings to lead the Justice Department on March 4th. He served almost 6 years as Attorney General; only one previous Attorney General had served longer.

Cummings transformed the Department of Justice. He established uniform rules of practice and procedure in federal courts. Appalled by the crime waves of the Prohibition era, he secured the passage of twelve laws that buttressed the "Lindbergh law" on kidnapping, made bank robbery a federal crime, cracked down on interstate transportation of stolen property, and extended federal regulations over firearms. He strengthened the FBI, called a national crime conference, supported the establishment of Alcatraz as a model prison for hardened offenders, and reorganized the internal administration of the department. In 1937 Cummings published "We can Prevent Crime" and, with Carl McFarland, an assistant Attorney General, "General Justice", a department history. "The Selected Papers of Homer Cummings (1939), edited by Carl B. Swisher, supplemented the history.

He and Roosevelt were rankled by the conservative Supreme Court majority who kept overturning New Deal programs. After Roosevelt took office, the judiciary was the only branch of government in Republican hands. During his first term Roosevelt had no opportunity to alter this at the highest level. After his overwhelming election of 1936 Roosevelt instructed Cummings to draft legislation for "court reform". He adopted the idea that Cummings had proposed earlier to add a judge for every judge who refused to retire at age 70 at full pay. Roosevelt launched the proposal, prepared secretly by Cummings, on February 5, 1937. The uproar that confronted the "court- packing plan" is well known. After 168 days the Senate killed the bill by returning it to committee.

It appears that Homer Cummings, as early as 1933, was sympathetic with the worsening plight of the 525,000 German Jews. The Nazis were boycotting Jewish businesses and had begun dismissing Jews from their jobs as doctors, academics and merchants. At a Cabinet meeting in April, 1933, most of the officials in attendance supported increasing immigration quotas and Frances Perkins, Secretary of Labor, as well as Cummings advocated it. However, State Department officials were opposed and insisted on adhering rigidly to the letter of the immigration laws. The U.S. consuls in Germany used whatever means they could to deny visas to desperate Germans fleeing the Nazis, according to Holocaust scholars.

Cummings retired on January 2, 1939. He entered private law practice in Washington as well as retaining his interest in the Connecticut Democratic party. He maintained a residence in Greenwich and served on the Greenwich Town Committee until 1951. He died in Washington, DC on September 10, 1956.

So what does all this have to do with me? Before I get into some observations that relate to my personal history, I want to tell this story.

Until a few years ago I really wasn't much interested in our family history. I did, however, know about Homer Cummings' opinion as Attorney General about our case. I had obtained a copy from the relevant volume of the Opinions of the Attorney General and researched the times this opinion had been cited in subsequent cases. As a Fellow of the American Academy of Matrimonial Lawyers, I attended each year their mid-year meeting, which was held in March at a resort location. In the spring of 1989 the meeting was held in Naples, Florida, and the law firm of Cummings and Lockwood, headquartered in Stamford, CT, had an office there. They invited the members to come to a cocktail party at their offices one evening. I knew and admired many of the lawyers from this Stamford, CT firm and I had made absolutely no connection with the name of this firm and Homer Cummings. I arrived at the building and took the elevator up to their office floor. As I exited the elevator, before me were two huge portraits — one of Mr. Cummings and the other of Mr. Lockwood. It was only at that moment, when I looked into that man's eyes through my teary ones, that I made the connection and said to myself, "I owe my life to you"

Shortly thereafter I wrote to the managing partner of the firm, whom I knew and who also was a Fellow of the Academy, about my connection and debt to Mr. Cummings. I thought he would be interested, not only because he knew me, but also because it put a more human face on one of the firm's founders. I never received a reply.

My story about Homer Cummings ends with his very last opinion as Attorney General, which is Alfred's case. Alfred is identified throughout the 16-page opinion by his initials, A.R. The last line of the opinion states " I advise that you would be warranted in granting him a visa" is gripping and suspenseful as one reads the file, which I obtained from the National Archives, which stores the files of the Visa Division of the State Department. If the long tradition of American law, and the precedent it sets for cases, had been followed, our visa would not have been granted. And if the visa had not been granted, Alfred would either not have been released from prison, or more probably, he would have been released and sent to a concentration camp where he wouldn't have survived, most probably along with his family. Or, perhaps Lilli would have left the country without him, and with Ruth in tow. Fortunately these scenarios didn't occur, but they were undoubtedly considered by Lilli who, being outside prison, was aware of the options available to her.

The decision rendered by Homer Cummings on December 31, 1938, in determining that Alfred's actions did not constitute moral turpitude, changed the course of American law. On January 3, 1939 the decision was reported on the front page of the New York Times which stated that the decision "was communicated to the State Department, which will have to revise visa procedures of years' standing in this important respect".

What follows is the story, chronologically, in what was acknowledged by the State Department as an extremely difficult and complex question. However, as will be seen, the prevailing opinion of the State Department was that Alfred's actions did constitute moral turpitude, thus barring him from obtaining a visa to enter the U.S. I refer here to the State Department, because this is where the case was researched, and where the several legal opinions were written. It was well known that the State Department during the 1930's was quite anti-Semitic. But because ultimately they felt they could not come up with a definitive answer, they decided to submit the question to the Attorney General, who heads the Justice Department.

The function of the Attorney General of the United States, as head of the Department of Justice and chief law enforcement officer of the Federal Government, is to represent the U.S. in legal matters generally, and give advice and opinions to the President and to the heads of executive departments of the government when so requested. In our case, the request was submitted by the State Department to the Attorney General, as head of the Justice Department, for an official opinion.

My very first job as an attorney, beginning in the summer of 1968, was with the Massachusetts Attorney General's office, then headed by Elliot Richardson. I worked in the Civil Division, and our job was to respond to inquiries and problems received from other state agencies by drafting an official opinion, signed by the Attorney General. These opinions of the United States Attorney General do not carry the same weight as judgments of courts, but they are published and bound in volumes entitled Opinions of the Attorney General and are often cited in appropriate cases.

This story begins back in November 1937 when Lilli and Alfred obtained visas to emigrate to the United States. They had reservations to sail in December, 1937. But after Alfred was in prison, the visa expired, which prompted Max to begin his unbelievably committed and arduous task, which resulted in Homer Cummings' opinion. Max contacted an attorney he knew, Sophie Nack, who was with the Puerto Rican Reconstruction Administration. She apparently knew Gerard D. Reilly, the Solicitor of the Department of Labor. Immigration issues were, at that time, handled by the Labor Department. Upon receipt of a letter from her, on January 4, 1938 Reilly wrote to John Farr Simmons, who was Chief of the Visa Division of the State Department. Simmons responded promptly and agreed to communicate by cable with the American Consul in Berlin asking him to submit a brief cabled report on Mr. Rahn's case. He promised to send copies to Attorney Reilly and to Attorney Nack, who would be charged with the cable charges. On January 14, Reilly wrote Ms. Nack stating that he received a cablegram from the American

Consul in Stuttgart indicating that Alfred Rahn, his wife and child were issued immigration visas at the Stuttgart office on November 18, 1937 and that the Consul General makes no mention that the visas were subsequently withdrawn. He goes on to say, however, that if Mr. Rahn and his family have encountered difficult in leaving Germany, neither the Department nor American Consular Office may properly intervene, since the question of their departure from Germany is one entirely between them and the competent German authorities.

On February 2, 1938 Alfred was convicted by the German court of violating paragraphs 34 and 43 of the German foreign exchange law of February 4, 1935, and of paragraph 156 of the German Criminal Code, and sentenced to 14 months in prison, the sentence ending on March 6, 1939 at 2:45 p.m. I cite the provisions under he was convicted here, because they loom so important later. Violation of the foreign exchange law alone would probably not have raised the issue of moral turpitude, but conviction under the German Criminal Code certainly raised that issue and was the subject of extensive legal memoranda later.

On March 11, 1938 Max wrote to the American Consul General in Stuttgart, Samuel D. Honaker, stating that Alfred, his wife and daughter cannot leave Germany before the spring of 1939 and asking the consul to expedite the issuance of visas to the Rahn family when they are in a position to emigrate. The Consul responded that he was unable to give definite assurance that the Rahn family will be able to qualify for immigration visas when they again make their applications, but "you are assured that prompt and sympathetic attention will be according to their applications." He suggested that prior to when they are ready to emigrate, Max provide new evidence of his willingness and ability to provide for them in the U.S. Max had previously had to provide all kinds of financial data and affidavits about his financial ability to provide for the family.

In July Mr. Reilly wrote his friend Ms. Nack again, informing her that Mr. Rahn was imprisoned and that the Consul is now doubtful as to his admissibility to the U.S. because of the provisions of the Immigration Act of 1917 which exclude persons who have been convicted of crimes involving moral turpitude. He informed her that the matter of issuing visas is entirely within the hands of the State Department and he really couldn't express an official opinion. His personal opinion, however was that this would not be a crime of moral turpitude because of the German government's policy of confiscating the property of Jewish émigrés.

The letter, which really got things moving, and was absolutely devastating to receive, was sent by H. J. L'Heureux to Lilli on August 25, 1938. Mr. L'Heureux was the American Consul in the Consulate in Stuttgart, the office with which Lilli had her numerous dealings. He acknowledged her visit, and receipt of her letters as well as the original and translations of the judgment of the court. Since this letter was such a bombshell, and since it sets out the legal issues which followed, as well as the long established principle of not looking behind the judgment for extraneous circumstances, it is quoted here:

> *You were informed at that time that, in the event there appeared to be any doubt regarding the effect of your husband's conviction upon the status of his admissibility to the United States under the excluding provisions of the American Immigration laws,*

the case might be referred to the appropriate authorities at Washington for a ruling upon the points of law involved. If the conviction had pertained merely to a technical violation of the foreign exchange law and the offense had involved no false swearing the Consulate would have been pleased to refer the case, for appropriate instruction, to the authorities in Washington.

A careful examination of the court's judgment, however, reveals that your husband was definitely convicted of a violation of paragraph 156 of the criminal code readings as follows:

"Any person who gives evidence under oath before an appropriate authority and knowingly makes false statements, or who, with reference to such an oath, makes false statements, will be subject to a penalty of from one month to three years."

Section 3 of the American Immigration Act of February 5, 1917, provides that an alien who has been convicted of a crime or misdemeanor involving moral turpitude, shall be mandatorily excluded from the United States. The American courts have consistently held that perjury — false swearing under oath — involves moral turpitude within the meaning of the law, and consular officers have been so instructed by the appropriate authorities in Washington. Furthermore, the American courts have held that if the alien has been convicted of a crime such as indicated, and the conviction is established, it is not the duty of the administrative officer, such as a consular officer, to go behind the judgment in order to determine the purpose, motive and knowledge, as indicative of moral character.

In view of the foregoing facts, it is clear that the offense of which your husband has been convicted definitely excludes him from the United States. Hence, it is useless for the Consulate to refer the matter to the authorities at Washington. It is also probable that the Solicitor of the Department of Labor, who you stated had expressed a favorable opinion regarding the admissibility of your husband, was not aware of his conviction of false swearing. The copies of the judgment of the court are returned herewith.

Max, however, does not give up. He contacted A. M. Warren, who evidently was in the Visa Division of the State Department. The memo is also initialed by RCA, evidently another attorney in the Visa Division of the State Department. I mention this here because of the extremely anti-Semitic memo RCA wrote at the end of this long saga, after Attorney General Cummins had rendered his opinion.

What follows here for some pages is a rather lengthy, detailed account of the issue concerning Alfred as his case moved throughout the State Department. It gets very legalistic, but I felt it important to be the historian here and recount the chronology. It is the only way I can preserve all the details of the case. I personally received Alfred's entire file in the State Department from the National Archives in Washington, DC after making a request for it.

Mr. Warren, on September 15, 1938, wrote an 8-page letter on Department of State stationery to Mr. Flournoy, requesting that he look over documents attached in the case of Alfred Rahn. Mr. Flournoy, as indicated by his stationary, was "The Legal Advisor" for the Department of State. He provided a history of the case as follows: "It appears that Alfred Rahn obtained an immigration visa at Stuttgart on November 18, 1937, but before he could dispose of his business and depart from Germany he became involved in difficulties with the German authorities in connection with the exchange restrictions. He withdrew the sum of 30,000 RM from his business and concealed it in a strong box in his home failing properly to report such cash on hand in an affidavit which he was required to submit concerning his property in order to obtain the permission of the German Government to depart from Germany." "He was convicted of a violation of the regulations concerning foreign exchange and also conviction of the commission of a crime under Paragraph 156 of the Criminal Code…" What followed was a lengthy legal discussion of the elements necessary to prove moral turpitude. He stated, quoting the provision of the German Criminal Code under which Alfred was convicted, that it did not appear to him that the provision of the German Criminal Code may be <u>invariably</u> (his underlining) considered crimes thereunder as crimes involving moral turpitude. The provision reads as follows:

"Any person who gives evidence under oath before an appropriate authority and knowingly makes false statements, or who, with reference to such an oath, makes false statements, will be subject to a penalty of from one month to three years".

The major distinction between being convicted under the Criminal Code and the German currency regulations is that punishment under the former results in imprisonment, while the latter results in only a monetary fine.

Warren stated that the offenses correspond somewhat to that of false swearing, as defined in Section 22 (c) of our Immigration Act of 1924. But he went on to say that they "fall short of a definition of the crime of perjury, in that the element of the materiality, which is necessary to perjury, is not included as a specific element of the crimes." He cited a previous Opinion of the Attorney General, in 1933, when Cummings occupied that post, which held that a violation of the immigration laws is to be considered an offense involving moral turpitude if such offense involves false swearing "<u>amounting to perjury</u>". False swearing not amounting to perjury, the Attorney General had indicated, does not involve moral turpitude. (The distinctions here became extraordinarily fine, intricate and legalistic to the utmost degree, which shows how easily the matter could have turned out differently). Mr. Warren stated that the facts in the present case of Alfred Rahn therefore seem to be that he was convicted of an offense amounting to false swearing under a provision of the German Criminal Code which does not specifically contain the elements of the crime of perjury. Mr. Warren's letter then went on to discuss the two legal questions which were 1) whether the false statements made by the alien actually were material and that the German court considered them material and 2) whether the fact that the statements were not made in connection with a judicial proceedings prevents the statements from being perjury under the law. He quickly dismissed the second issue by saying that courts in the United States have repeatedly held that perjury can be committed when a statute is violated, not just during a court proceeding.

Mr. Warren then referred to Mr. Reilly's opinion, stating "I do not think we need be concerned about his views" Yet, he said that although he understands his reasons, "None of us are in sympathy with the efforts of the German Government to confiscate the property of the Jewish emigrants, but we must not be carried away in our sympathy beyond the bounds of reason. If an alien has been convicted of an offense under a foreign law, and if the elements of the crime constitute an offense involving moral turpitude according to the standard of morals in the United States, which Congress had in mind when enacting the moral turpitude clause, we must hold the alien to be inadmissible into the United States, even though he be a German Jew whose property is being confiscated by his Government."

But then Mr. Warren stated that the German Penal Code in question does not completely define an offense involving moral turpitude. In short, does conviction under the German law require materiality as an essential element of the crime, or can the conviction be based on an immaterial matter? The memo stated "although the alien was not convicted on the element of materiality, it was nevertheless present. "As I see it, he was guilty of a crime involving moral turpitude, but I doubt whether we can hold that he was convicted of such a crime, in light of the Opinion of the Attorney General of October 13, 1933." (The legal hair-splitting here is incredible — it could have been so much easier simply to say that it was a crime of moral turpitude, and end it there. But somehow, despite the pervasive anti-Semitism in the State Department at the time, they did not do this). Warren then said they could withhold any decision in this case and look at German law to see whether any offense of false swearing includes materiality as an essential element of the crime, and which would therefore correspond to the crime of perjury under our laws. If they were to find that there is such a crime under German law, then they would be in a better position to hold that the alien was not convicted of an offense involving moral turpitude. In other words, he is saying that if other provisions of the Germany Criminal Law contain the requirement of materiality, the fact that this particular provision did not require materiality, must mean that it is not an essential element of the crime, and therefore, would not amount to perjury under American law. Is this hair-splitting, or what? Mr. Warren then asked Mr. Flournoy for his views.

On October 24, 1938, the Legal Advisor of the Department of State (initialed only by GSK — a Mr. Knight) submitted a 23 page legal opinion, which apparently went to Mr. Flournoy and perhaps others. The question in issue is stated as follows: "Does a conviction of the offense of false swearing under German Law exclude Alfred Rahn, under Section 3 of the Immigration Law of 1917, as a person having been convicted of a crime involving moral turpitude?" Knight reviewed the facts of the case as well as the translated documents. He referred to the memo of the Visa Division, dated September 15, 1938 and prepared by Mr. Alexander in which the conclusion was reached that Mr. Rahn "was guilty of a crime involving moral turpitude", but, it was added, that it was doubted whether it could be held that he had been underlined{convicted} of such a crime in view of the opinion of the Attorney General of October 13, 1933.

I cite these opinions in some detail, because the precise legal issue turned on such a narrow point and could have gone either way. Again I am astounded and amazed at how close we were to not getting out and that it all hinged on the intricate interpretation of statutes which were not all that clear, and open to interpretation either way. It was clearly a case of first impression, which means they had not specifically dealt with this issue before.

What followed in this legal opinion of the State Department was a lengthy legal review of crime of perjury — common law perjury, statutory perjury and false swearing which has not been designated as perjury by statute. Common law perjury traditionally was false swearing in a judicial proceeding, but had been enlarged and extended by statute to include false swearing in regard to any matter where an oath is required. He underlined a quote which reads "Some statutes eliminate both the requirement of materiality and that of a judicial proceeding, and courts construing such statutes have indicated that such is their effect." He then analyzed the 1933 Opinion of the Attorney General, previously cited, where the distinction was made between false swearing amounting to perjury, and other falsehoods such as concealment of a fact upon entering the country, using a foreign passport belonging to a friend to enter the country or evading peacetime military service. The basic difference is that the taking of a false oath is considered wrong independently of the statute, while the other offenses, though grave and properly penalized, cannot be said to possess the same inherent baseness in the concept of our people." But then Knight asked, "The question arises as to whether this last statement must be qualified by the earlier statement, namely, that false swearing must amount to perjury to constitute an offense involving moral turpitude". (If this sounds confusing and convoluted — it is to me too, even with the legal background I have). Another question raised by Knight was whether the false swearing must have been made on a material matter. Then follows 10 pages of legal discussion of how false swearing has been dealt with in insurance cases, disbarment proceedings, and cases of a general nature. He concluded by stating that "the ultimate question may be boiled down to this — are we to adopt in this and similar cases the maximum requirements of common law perjury in determining whether moral turpitude is involved or are we to adopt the minimum requirements of let us say the criminal statute of Vermont defining statutory perjury as follows: "A person of whom an oath is required by law, who willfully swears falsely in regard to any matter or thing respecting which such oath is required, shall be guilty of perjury". The main objection to adoption of the Vermont criminal statute is that it doesn't prevail in the United States as a whole."

 He concluded: "Under the authority of these cases, and considering that article 156 of the German Criminal Code, of which the alien was convicted, is situated within the chapter in the German Criminal Code headed "Perjury" and, Fürthermore, considering that the Attorney General's opinion of October 13, 1933 (supra) permits of doubt in construing the law, it is recommended that the questions raised by this memorandum be submitted to the Attorney General for an opinion."

But the submission of the matter to the Attorney General i.e. the Justice Department rather than the State Department didn't immediately occur. Mr. Flournoy had some second thoughts. On November 16, 1938, having received Mr. Warren's memo, he wrote a four page letter to Mr. Warren stating that when the case was first brought to his attention, he thought it would be desirable to submit the legal question involved in it to the Attorney General and that Mr. Knight's memorandum was prepared with a view to such submission. "However, after giving the matter Fürther consideration, it appears to me that it would be useless to submit the question to the Attorney General until we obtain information as to the scope of Article 156 of the German Criminal Code, that is, whether it relates only to false statements in regard to material matters or is also applicable to false statements in regard to immaterial matters." If the Consul General ascertains and informs the State Department that the statute in question relates only to false statements concerning material matters, it is believed that it will be necessary to hold that Alfred Rahn was guilty of an offense equivalent to the offense of perjury in the United States, which would make him subject to exclusion upon the ground that he was convicted of an offense involving moral turpitude. If, on the other hand, the Consul General informs that Department that Article 156 penalizes false statements concerning immaterial matters, as well as those concerning material matters, it may be necessary to present the question to the Attorney General for an opinion.

"As you know, the courts in this country have held that, in determining the question of whether an offense of which a person has been convicted involves moral turpitude, it is not permissible to examine into the peculiar facts and circumstances in which the offense was committed with a view to determining whether the person in question had an evil intent when he committed the offense. For example, in the case of a person who has been convicted of theft of food, it would not be permissible to consider evidence showing that he was in dire circumstances and in sore need of the food." It is important for me to reiterate here that the prevailing opinion of American law is, and was, that you cannot look behind the crime or the court judgment to the underlying circumstances.

He concluded by saying that this "whole problem is exceedingly involved and difficult. It may be presented in numerous other cases, especially cases arising in Germany in connection with the persecution of Jews. (Was he fearful of opening the flood gates?) "If we do not decide to submit the question formally to the Attorney General for an opinion, I think it would be desirable at least to discuss it with some of the legal officers in the Criminal Division of the Department of Justice. However, as indicated above, I think we should obtain more information in regard to the scope of the German law in question before going any Fürther. He ended by stating that it seemed desirable to obtain information concerning the scope and meaning of Article 156 of the German Criminal Code, and "I have drafted the attached telegram to the Consul General at Berlin accordingly"

So, on November 17, 1938 a telegram was sent to the American Consul in Berlin asking whether Article 156 of the German Criminal Code relates only to false statements concerning material matters or whether it is also applicable to false statements concerning immaterial matters. The Consul was requested to reply briefly by telegraph and fully in writing.

On November 18th Mr. Flournoy wrote another 4-page memo to a Mr. Hackworth who had apparently referred Mr. Max Rahn and his attorney, Mr. Ramsey, to him. Mr. Flournoy said he met with Mr. Rahn and Mr. Ramsey yesterday (November 17, 1938) and "I discussed the case of Alfred Rahn with them at considerable length. He outlines the nature of this discussion as follows:

Mr. Rahn's principal argument was that his brother is an honorable man with a good record and would not intentionally make false statements. In this connection he said that the affirmation made by his brother before the German authorities, which resulted in his brother's prosecution, conviction and imprisonment upon the ground that it contained false statements concerning the amount of his property in Germany, was in fact prepared by a so-called "trustee", upon whom Mr. Rahn felt he could rely. It appears that in the preparation of the statement in question Mr. Rahn and his trustee used the statement concerning his property which had been prepared at the end of the year 1936, whereas certain changes had occurred subsequent to its preparation, particularly with regard to the liquidation of certain property. Mr. Max Rahn argued that the changes in question were immaterial, since the total amount of the property at the time when the examination was made was practically the same as that which was set forth in the declaration made at the end of the year 1936. He said he had obtained this information from a letter from his brother's wife. I told him that if he cared to submit that letter it would be duly considered, although I was not prepared to say whether it would affect the Department's conclusion.

Mr. Max Rahn informed me that his brother had been imprisoned in February 1938 for a term of fourteen months, although he added that for some reason the term would normally expire, under the German law, in March 1939, that is, at the end of thirteen months from the time of the imprisonment. He also stated, however, that he had recently received a telegram from his brother's wife which he interpreted to mean that his brother would be released from imprisonment in the near future if the German authorities should receive information that he would be able to obtain an immigration visa, with which he could leave Germany and come to this country.

I told Mr. Max Rahn and his attorney that the Department was endeavoring to obtain more definite information through the Consulate General at Berlin concerning the scope and meaning of Article 156 of the German Criminal Code under which Alfred Rahn was convicted, in order that the Department might be in a position to decide whether the crime of which he was convicted was one involving moral turpitude, according to the standards recognized in the United States. I said that we hoped to obtain this information in a few days. I understand that the Department's telegram went out last night, and I assume that we will have a reply in the early part of next week.

This case is unusually difficult, and the decision in it will furnish an important precedent. [underlining mine]. On the one hand, it is hardly possible to ignore the extraordinary situation in which the Jews in Germany are now placed. The persecution which they are suffering naturally evokes sympathy, and from one point of view might be regarded as mitigation offenses which they commit with a view to circumventing to some extent the harsh measure imposed upon them by the German authorities. On the other hand, if the offense of which Mr. Rahn was convicted was clearly tantamount to perjury, it is difficult to see how the Department could properly authorize the issuance to him of an immigration visa.

Upon receipt of a reply from the Consul General at Berlin this case will be given Fürther consideration. It may be found necessary to refer the question to the Attorney General, although, in view of the apparent urgency it is to be hoped that this necessity will not arise."

It seems that the State Department wanted to decide this issue by themselves and not have to resort to transmitting it to the Justice Department. They also seemed to feel that submitting it to the Justice Department would cause Fürther delays. We know, however, that the delay did not occur.

The reply from Berlin came promptly. A telegram dated November 19, 1938 from Raymond H. Geist, American Consul, stated unequivocally "According to legal advice both article 153 and 156 of German Criminal Code make false declarations punishable offense even if such false declarations related only to immaterial matters. A condition for punishment is, however, that premeditation or negligence exists. An error generally precludes false declarations."

Mr. Geist, the American Consul in Berlin, followed up with a 3-page memorandum on November 21 1938 to the Secretary of State. He entitled the subject of his memorandum: False Statements Relation to Immaterial Matters Punishable under German Criminal Code.

Mr. Geist indicated he received his legal information from the Berlin law office of Mr. Frederick Wirth, Jr. He indicated that certain commentators make no distinction between material and immaterial matters. However, he concluded that "it is understood that persons are rarely prosecuted for the misdemeanor defined in Article 156 of the Criminal Code when the false statements made relate only to immaterial matters."

On November 23, 1938 Mr. Flournoy wrote what appears to be a memo to his file. It is written on his Department of State, The Legal Advisor, stationery, but isn't addressed to anyone. It is simply entitled Visa Application of Alfred Rahn.

Mr. Flournoy stated that he discussed the case with Mr. B.W. Butler of the Department of Justice with reference to the telegram received from the Consul General in Berlin, that is, that false declarations are punishable under Article 156 of the German Criminal Code regardless of whether they related to material matters. The memo continued:

I told Mr. Butler that we had been uncertain whether, in view of the information just mentioned, we should hold that Mr. Rahn had been convicted of an offense involving moral turpitude within the meaning of Section 3 of the Immigration Act of February 5, 1917. I mentioned the theory which has been advanced to the effect that, since false statements in formal declaration made before officials are punishable under Article 156 of the German Criminal Code, even though such statements related to immaterial matters, it is impossible to hold that convictions under this statutory provision are offenses involving moral turpitude. However, I also mentioned the fact that the opinion of the German judge explaining the judgment of the District Court at Fuerth, Bavaria, February 2, 1938, in which Alfed Rahn was convicted under Article 156 of the German Criminal Code, discussed at considerable length the false statement made by Mr. Rahn and showed that its object was to deceive the German officials and make it possible for him to take German marks out of the country surreptitiously, in violation of German law. I observed that it was thus entirely clear that the false statement in this case was not immaterial.

Mr. Butler expressed the view that it would be impossible to hold that the offense of which Mr. Rahn was convicted was not one involving moral turpitude. He observed that the offense of which he was convicted involved the element of fraud, which fact seems to necessitate holding that it was an offense involving moral turpitude. I remarked that the decision made in this case would be one of considerable importance, because of the likelihood that it would furnish a precedent for other similar cases. I said that we contemplated submitting the question formally in writing, and Mr. Butler said if we should do so it would receive careful attention.

This is the first time, in late November 1938, that the case was considered serious and complicated enough to be communicated to the Justice Department. Mr. Butler's views were unequivocal that it was moral turpitude. Mr. Flournoy could have stopped then and just let the matter drop. He was personally disturbed by this case, calling it "unusually difficult" and later called it "this is one of the most difficult cases I have ever had to deal with." He undoubtedly gained great sympathy for the matter by having met personally with Max. The anti-Semitism of his department or Mr. Butler's opinion fortunately didn't dissuade him. I know nothing about Mr. Flournoy, but he too was responsible for saving our lives!

Mr. Flournoy knew what he had to do, and therefore prepared, or had his department prepare, a 25-page legal memorandum for submission to Attorney General Cummings. The result was this lengthy legal memorandum prepared by the Legal Department of the State Department on November 25, 1938.

My copy has no letterhead and is not signed by anyone, but by initials it went to Knight and Flournoy and a couple of others. The question addressed by the memo was stated as follows: "Does the offense of knowingly making a false affirmation before an official, which is punishable under Article 156 of the German Criminal Code, involve moral turpitude within the meaning of the provision of Section 3 of the Immigration Act of February 5, 1917, when the record of the conviction shows that the false statement related to a material matter?" It is interesting to note here that the conviction by the very anti-Semitic German judge indicated it was a material matter, but the memo which they had by now received from the Consul General in Berlin indicated that convictions under Article 156 could be for material and immaterial matters.

The memorandum presented the legal arguments, with numerous case citations, on both sides of the issue. It concluded, however, with the following critical paragraph:

While, for the reasons indicated above, it is believed that the weight of opinion supports the view that the offense of which Mr. Rahn was convicted involved moral turpitude within the meaning of Section 2 of the Immigration Act of February 5, 1917, there are arguments on the other side of the question which merit consideration. It therefore seems desirable to obtain an opinion of the Attorney General in the matter.

On November 30, 1938 Mr. Flournoy sent a memo to Mr. Warren, which, because of the personal tone of the memo, I reproduce here:

As I have said before, I am convinced that the only satisfactory way to settle this case lies in the submission to the Attorney General of the legal question involved. This is one of the most difficult cases I have ever had to deal with. One the one hand, any person with natural human feelings must sympathize with Mr. Max Rahn, who has been visiting my office daily for some time. in his efforts to assist his brother Alfred Rahn in coming to this country from Germany. His brother was imprisoned in Germany February 2, 1938 because of conviction of making a false statement concerning his assets. The term of imprisonment was 14 months, but Mr. Max Rahn has received messages which convince him that his brother will be released from prison if he can obtain a visa for entrance into this country. On the other hand, it appears to me that the offense of which Alfred Rahn was convicted must be regarded, in view of the various decisions of our courts in cases somewhat similar, as one involving moral turpitude, so that he is subject to the exclusion under the provision of Section 3 of the Immigration Act of 1917.

In the attached memorandum to accompany the letter to the Attorney General I have endeavored to set forth the arguments on both sides of this question, although the arguments against the contentions made by Mr. Max Rahn in behalf of his brother seem greatly to outweigh those in support of it.

The strongest practical argument in behalf of Alfred Rahn lies in the fact that his false declaration was made under the stress of the persecution of Jews in Germany. However, I do not believe that this furnishes a legal argument in his behalf.

And so, on December 2, 1938, a letter was sent to "The Honorable Homer S. Cummings, Attorney General, from the State Department by Mr. Flournoy, as follows:

My dear Mr. Attorney General:

This Department desires to have the benefit of your opinion upon the following question:

Does the offense of knowingly making a false statement in an affirmation before an official, which is punishable under Article 156 of the German Criminal Code, involve moral turpitude, within the meaning of the provision of section 3 of the Immigration Act of February 5, 1917, when the record of the conviction shows that the false statement related to a material matter?

This problem has arisen in the case of one Alfred Rahn, a German citizen of the Jewish race, who made a false statement in a declaration concerning his property required by German law, who desires to obtain an immigration visa for use in coming to this country to reside, but who was convicted, under the statutory provision in question, by a court at Fuerth, Bavaria, February 2, 1938. An English translation of the judgment of the court is enclosed.

The problem presented in this case is regarded as one of considerable importance, especially in view of the precedent which it may furnish. In the enclosed memorandum an effort has been made to present arguments on both sides of the question. Sincerely yours, Acting Secretary.

Max had, as mentioned earlier, retained the legal services of William H. Ramsey, a Washington, DC attorney. On December 5, 1938 Attorney Ramsey submitted his eight page legal memorandum to the Secretary of State on behalf of Alfred's application for a visa. Ramsey prefaced his memorandum as follows: "As attorney for the applicant, I have the honor to present the following suggestions for such assistance as they may be to the Department of State in determining whether the visa shall be issued."

After reciting the basic facts and the law involved, Attorney Ramsey's memorandum focused briefly on the issue of moral turpitude, but the bulk of his memo focused on the provision of the 1917 Immigration Law which sets forth an exception: "Provided, that nothing in this act shall exclude, if otherwise admissible, persons convicted, or who admit the commission, or who teach or advocate the commission, of an offense purely political".

Attorney Ramsey focused on this exception, and argued that this case should be treated as a political offense. He argued that the term "political offense" isn't limited to affirmative acts or to deeds of violence, but may be committed by mere omissions or neglect. With the proper political environment, an offense committed in any of those ways becomes a "political offense". Because the approach he used is echoed in Cummings' opinion, and because he created an unusual argument, I will spell out most of his memorandum here.

He then stressed and outlined the political environment as follows:

For some years past, beginning with the rise of Adolph Hitler to power, the Government of Germany has been undergoing sweeping fundamental changes, resulting in the establishment of a dictatorship and the destruction of democracy in the Republic. One of the fixed and apparently fundamental policies of the new regime has been to reduce to a state of poverty resembling serfdom the great number of Jews heretofore living peacefully and prosperously in Germany, and they have been assailed as Jews - (his emphasis) and not as individuals. The gradual unfolding of this policy from week to week has resulted in excesses and brutality which have shocked the conscience of the whole civilized world. As the diabolical wickedness of this campaign of destruction increases from week to week, one wonders when and what the end will be.

As the march of conquest has gathered into the Reich first Austria and then a portion of Czechoslovakia, this hatred, humiliation, and subjugation of the Jews has spread coextensively with the Nazi supremacy.

If the Jews had banded together to resist these oppressions and overthrown the power of the present regime, and if this applicant had been a participant in such movement, any offense committed by him therein could properly have been classified as a "political" offense. But such is not the custom of the Jews. (My note: this transitional sentence says a good deal about Ramsey, but also provided a forceful way to argue his point). When the herdmen of Gerar strove with the herdmen of Isaac about the wells they had digged, Isaac twice removed to other places and dug other wells. Gen. 26:20-22. In the days of Queen Esther, they did indeed fight, but only as a last resort to save their lives.

I find these references to the Bible wonderful, maybe even a bit humorous, and certainly most unusual, in my experience, in a legal memorandum. Ramsey must have been a religious man — he knew his Bible — surely he didn't get these references from Max. In any case, I find this most interesting. He continued:

Their custom has been, not to rise up in revolution or insurrection, but to suffer in silence or to resort to flight. The offenses of which this applicant stands convicted were committed, if at all, in an effort to flee the despotic control of the Nazi regime (My note: brilliant and creative reasoning to make his point).

The outstanding feature of this persecution of the Jews is the very obvious purpose of the German government to restrain the flight of capital. As I understand, it is not difficult for a Jew to get a passport to leave Germany; but to remove therefrom and take his property with him is a wholly different matter. This, it would seem, is the purpose of the foreign exchange law, the law this applicant is convicted of violating — that is, that in taking his property out, a very generous slice, if not the lion's share, shall be left in the permanent possession of the Reich. See the following from an Associated Press article dated Berlin Nov. 24:

Driven from social life in Germany and ordered to get out of industry, Jews yesterday suffered a Fürther blow in an assessment of one-fifth of their fortunes above $2,000.

The money must be paid by August 15, 1939. For the some 60,000 Jews in concentration camps there was almost insurmountable difficulty in trying to arrange for the payments.

Few Jews have sufficient cash on hand to pay the fine, and their source of income is being curtailed rapidly by the taking over of Jewish stores by non-Jewish owners.

Nazis said today that the process of Aryanizing business at present was confined to the retail field, that it was proceeding 'exceptionally fast' and that the wholesale and export and shipping firms would be next.

The propaganda campaign continued, with the Deutsche Bergwerks-Zeitung, important industrial publication of Duesseldorf, editorializing that the anti-Semitic drive was justified because of the wealth of the Jews.

Attorney Ramsey placed tremendous emphasis on the current situation, quoting extensively from the newspaper and thereby creating a vivid picture of the entire context of the case and of his argument.

He continued and concluded, in summary, by stating:

The affidavit in this case, alleged to be false, was incidental to the enforcement of the foreign exchange law.

So, where a nation begins an unendurable persecution of a distinct class, not of a few individuals here and there but of a whole people, I respectfully submit that any unlawful act done by one or a group of those people in resistance of the one main purpose of the persecution should be considered and treated as a "political offense". If a shooting which occurred in New York City in a fight between Fascists and anti-Fascists is properly designed as a political offense (case is cited), then a fortiori, should the same term be applied to an effort to defeat pro tanto this colossal oppression of half a million Jews as such by the official action of the German Government?

If these were political offenses, it is immaterial whether they involved moral turpitude.

Here Attorney Ramsey artfully skirts the issue of whether the case rests on a determination of moral turpitude or not, feeling perhaps that focusing on that issue would be a losing matter. He then went into a brief history of the immigration law, pointing out that an earlier version had read: "Provided, that nothing in this Act shall exclude, if otherwise admissible, persons convicted of an offense purely political, not involving moral turpitude". The last phrase of four words was deleted from the existing law.

His conclusion stated: "This applicant, in committing, if he did, these alleged violations of the German foreign exchange law, and in making the alleged false affidavit, incidental to the other alleged offenses, was guilty of committing offenses "purely political." The visa should be granted.

Respectfully submitted, William H. Ramsey, Attorney for Petitioner.
Copy to the Attorney General."

Ramsey focused his entire memo around the violation of the German foreign exchange law rather than the Criminal Code, which had been the focus of the American Consul in Stuttgart and State Department memos.

There is a memo in the file from Mr. Flournoy confirming that:

The legal problem involved in the case of Alfred Rahn was submitted to the Attorney General last week. Before its submission I informed Mr. Rahn and his attorney, Mr. William H. Ramsey, that if the latter should submit to this Department a written argument in behalf of Mr. Rahn, I would see that a copy of it was sent to the Attorney General, for his consideration in connection with the memorandum submitted with this Department's letter. However, Mr. Ramsey, when he handed the attached letter to me yesterday, said that he had presented a copy of it to the Department of Justice. I therefore told him that it did not seem necessary for this Department to forward another copy to that Department.

It was interesting to note, as I reviewed these documents, how much of this communication was done by hand — speed was of the essence. They also must have known that Cummings would retire at the end of the year.

On December 8, 1938 Mr. Ramsey received written confirmation from the Acting Secretary of State, acknowledging his letter of December 5, and reiterating that since he told the State Department he had presented his letter to the Department of Justice, there was no necessity of the State Department to forward another copy.

On December 19th the Acting Secretary of State, who "presents his compliments to the Honorable Attorney General" enclosed the dispatch dated November 21, 1938 from the American Consulate General in Berlin, "which may be of some value in the consideration of this case".

And finally, on December 31, 1938, the last day of the year and the last day of Homer Cummings' tenure as Attorney General, a 16-page opinion is sent to the Secretary of State from the Office of the Attorney General. The opinion referred to Alfred Rahn by his initials, A.R. The Attorney General acknowledged the letter from the Secretary of State, dated December 2, 1938, requesting his opinion. This is incredibly fast turn-around time. Given how slow the law usually works, there must have been a reason that Homer Cummings reviewed this case promptly and wrote an opinion on his last day before leaving office. He could just as easily filed the matter away and left it for his successor. In his opinion, Cummings recited the basic facts, and the law in question, i.e. both the American immigration law and the German Law on Control of Foreign Exchange of February 4, 1935 as well as the German Criminal Code. At the risk of being redundant here, I'll deal expansively the contents of Cummings' lengthy opinion.

It appears from the translation of the judgment furnished by the Acting Secretary that the alien was sentenced by the court to one year and two months' imprisonment (with credit for three weeks of detention) for conviction of "continued transgression of the foreign exchange law according to paragraphs 34, 43, No. 5 of the foreign exchange law in connection with the simultaneous misdemeanor of rending a false affidavit" under paragraph 156 of the Criminal Code. It Fürther appears from such translation that the alien, shown by the judgment to be of Jewish extraction, was engaged with his mother in the wholesale ironware business; that on December 31, 1936, their interests in the business as shown by the balance sheet were respectively 38, 217.17 and 105,061.58 Reichsmarks; that since May or June, 1937, he had the intention of emigrating from Germany and withdrew a total of 30,000 R.M. from the business, which he kept in case, first at his place of business, later in his residence; that in October, 1937, in order to obtain the necessary certificate of emigration, he filled out two separate questionnaires give him by the foreign exchange office, one for himself and one for his mother, in each of which he put down as the amount of cash on hand the statement "about R.M. 1500"; that certain property standing in his mother's name, for which sale negotiations were pending, was entered on his mother's affidavit at the "last unitary value"; that he delivered his list to the authorities, together with an affidavit as to the complete and true statement of the various amounts of property possessed of by himself, his wife and minor children; that the declaration of his mother was also delivered to the foreign exchange office with an affidavit signed by her; that the alien's mother was "irrefutably lacking every vestige of survey of the financial and business situation" and that "the accused alone is responsible for the contents of [her] declaration of fortune.

The Opinion then quoted from the court decision, quoting the observation of the German court that "In meting out the measure of punishment there had to be considered at the expense of the accused the considerable public interest prevailing regards truthful information especially in the case of Jewish emigrants, since it must be avoided that non-registered capital is taken abroad and working there in Jewish hands against the German political economy and the German nation". I find it most interesting that Cummings chose to quote this dicta — the explanation for the court's judgment, which isn't based on law but on the atmosphere of the time.

The Opinion then continued to state that, although the question does not seem to have been presented to the Supreme Court," opinions of inferior Federal Courts and the Attorney General in the diverse cases submitted to them for decision have held for many years that the record of a foreign court showing conviction is to be taken as conclusive evidence of conviction of the crime disclosed by it, and that neither courts nor immigration officers may go outside such record to determine facts or whether in the particular instance the alien's conduct was immoral."

This repeats the long-standing and well established rule of American law, which recognizes the validity of foreign judgments and provides no authority or justification for going behind such judgment.

The Opinion continued by stating that the "question whether the crime involved moral turpitude, however, is to be determined according to its inherent nature and the standards prevailing in the United States generally — not by those of the foreign country in which the crime was committed and the conviction occurred." After citing relevant cases, the Opinion took its first significant turn. "It should be noted", stated Cummings, "however, that such of the opinions by which reference has been made above was rendered on the particular facts and circumstances presented, and that there was involved no question of conditions other than normal obtaining the foreign country where the crime was committed and the conviction had." Here he seems to set the foundation for what follows. After stating that moral turpitude is a vague term, he recites a number of cases, and then repeats the point by saying "I think it as clear that in determining whether or not moral turpitude necessarily is involved it is proper to look to any conditions other than normal obtaining in a foreign jurisdiction at the time of the commission of the crime and conviction by a foreign tribunal." Thereafter follows several pages of the Opinion in which cases involving moral turpitude are discussed in the traditional manner, as well as reference to the distinction between material and immaterial matters of the German Criminal Code.

The argument that the declaration of the alien was done under the advice of an economic trustee has no merit.

But then, beginning on page 12 of the Opinion, Cummings stated, "It has been urged on behalf of the alien, however, that the offense of which he was convicted was political. (Since Attorney Ramsey's memo was the only legal brief or document that used this argument and stressed this point, it obviously carried enormous weight). "The statute excludes from its provision an alien convicted of an "offense purely political" and extradition treaties, with few exceptions, contain a provision exempting in mandatory or permissive form political offenses from their operation. The term, however, is not defined in the Immigration Act, nor, apparently, in any of the treaties to which the United States is a party. It is generally agreed that no satisfactory and acceptable definition of the term has yet been found". This sentence was followed by two pages of numerous cites of cases and treatises whereby Cummings again is setting the stage for the basis of his decision.

Beginning on page 14, then comes the meat of the opinion, which I quote here:

Counsel for the alien suggests that the term "political offense" should apply "to any offense incidental to the resistance of, or flight from, great persecutions or oppressions by nations or ruling majorities against large racial religious, or political minorities.

While ordinarily it may not be proper to consider the motive or purpose of the offender in determining whether a crime of which he was convicted involves moral turpitude, I agree with your Legal Adviser that when the question is presented whether the offense was political it becomes necessary to take motive into account.

Attorney Flournoy, in his lengthy brief to the Attorney General had stated, "however, that it couldn't be considered political when the offense appears to have been deliberately committed for his own private gain. He said, remember, "In determining whether the crime is an '"offense purely political'" it seems necessary to take into account the motive of the person in question in committing the offense. If the motive relates solely to the advancement of a political measure, it would seem that the offense may be regarded as purely political, but this does not seem to be the case if the motive is personal gain." In other words, Flournoy sought to dismiss this "political offense" argument right away. Cummings, however, did not go along with this approach. Homer Cummings' opinion concludes with the quote below, which It is written in bold face because of how very significant it was, not only for our family, but because it was contrary to the long-standing tradition of American law which held that you do not look behind judgments of foreign courts but simply accept these judgments at face value.

> *It may be assumed, that, in ordinary circumstances, under the principles enunciated in the cases heretofore cited — most of which, it should be observed, presented instances of conditions not by foreign courts but by courts of this country — willful false swearing would involve moral turpitude. However, in view of the claim made in this case that the crime was political in nature or had political aspects, the question whether in its essence it is one debarring the alien from entry is a question which, if presented to a court in the United States, would, in my opinion, require consideration in the light of the present-day situation in Germany. I do not think that the case should be divorced from the realities of the world or that opinions rendered heretofore in this country dealing with the moral qualities of crimes of which persons had been convicted by foreign tribunals in tranquil times should be followed in the letter to conclusions antagonistic to the spirit of our immigration law and foreign to the intent of the Congress in passing it.*

> *There are in the United States no statutes comparable to the economic decrees of the Reich. It is well known indeed that the concepts of law presently existing in Germany are alien to those which prevail in this country (cite). It should be noted that the German court states in its judgment convicting the alien here involved that "the accused had the intention of emigrating from Germany since, being a Jew, he saw his commercial progress in Germany obstructed." It is common knowledge that decrees and orders have been issued in and are enforced by the German Reich designed to eliminate Jews from all phases of German life, and indeed from that country; and that judged by our standards, as well as by those of many other nations, the members of the Jewish race in Germany are under the severest kind of persecution. The State Department had occasion to observe during December, 1938, that the recent policy pursued in Germany shocked and confounded public opinion in the United States more profoundly than anything that had taken place in many decades, and that references here in public utterances to this state of public indignations represented the feeling of the overwhelming majority of the people of the United States.*

> *Under such conditions the terror and desperation extant among hundreds of thousands of Jews not living in Germany cannot be other than acute. It was apparently under*

such conditions and in connection with the enforcement of the decrees which brought them about that conviction was had of the crime here charged; I cannot bring myself to believe that in determining any moral or political attributes of that crime the courts of this country would close their eyes to those factors.

Indeed, it would appear that the acts here under consideration were performed under a compulsion as great as it was unjust. The alternatives open to the alien were to remain in Germany and be reduced to a state of penury and serfdom or to seek another life in another land. In selecting the latter alternative, he was confronted with the necessity of going forth with his dependent family stripped of all his possession or seeking to retain what was rightfully his own, in avoidance of a statute and a procedure which cannot be defended on the basis of morals or justice. It was a form of duress which in good conscience we would not be justified in ignoring.

I do not believe that the term "moral turpitude", as it is generally understood, can properly be ascribed to the conduct of this alien. I advise that you would be warranted in granting him a visa.

Respectfully,
/s/ Homer Cummings
Attorney General

On the same date, December 31, 1938, Cummings wrote to "The Honorable, the Secretary of State," asking whether he had any objection to the publication of, in accordance with the relevant statute, his opinion dated December 31, 1938 concerning the eligibility of a German alien for a visa. Sumner Welles, Acting Secretary of State, replied, acknowledging the receipt of the opinion concerning the admissibility of one Alfred Rahn into the United States, and said that the Department interposed no objection whatever to the publication of the Opinion. This letter, interestingly, went to The Honorable Frank Murphy, the new Attorney General since Cummings' last day in office was December 31. And so the opinion was published on January 3, 1939 on the front page of the New York Times.

Headlined "Refugees aided by Last Cummings Opinion; Hiding of Funds was Held Not a Bar to Visa", the New York Times article of January 3, 1939 read as follows:

The last official opinion rendered by Homer S. Cummings as Attorney General, it was learned today, was in behalf of German refugees, and place a new construction on consular procedure in the granting of visas for the United States.

The case arose when a man, of whom it is known only that he has the initials "A.R.", stated in an application for a visa more than two years ago that he possessed only 1,500 Reich marks. Investigation showed he had neared 20,000, far more than the limit an individual was permitted to take from Germany. The man was convicted and sentenced to two years in prison. When he had served his term he again applied for a visa but, according to information obtainable here today, it was refused by American consular officials on the ground that he had been guilty of an offense constituting moral turpitude. Under the statute moral turpitude is a bar to the granting of a visa.

Mr. Cummings, in his opinion, which was rendered as his last formal official act, on the last day of the year, took a different view. He ruled, it was said, that the refugee had been guilty of false report, but under the circumstances, this was not moral turpitude and that ground for withholding a visa did not exist.

This was communicated to the State Department, which will have to revise visa procedure of years' standing in this important respect. The department must instruct that the visa should be granted the man unless it can find other reasons for withholding it.

No details of the opinion were forthcoming from the Department of Justice. The State Department would make no comment on the grounds that by law visa information is confidential.

This was not the only newspaper article. Because this was such a significant case, not only as a matter of law, but also because it saved the life of my family, I will quote several other articles which appeared. Although lengthy and often repetitive, I quote them here in their entirety because part of my purpose in this memoir is to preserve the history of what actually happened.

On January 12, 1939 another longer article appeared in the New York Times headlined in large print: CUMMINGS'S RULING ON REGUGEE TOLD, and then subtitled; Letter to Welles Said in Reich Concealment of Wealth Was Not Moral Turpitude.

The last official opinion of former Attorney General Homer Cummings, ruling that a man convicted in Germany should not be barred from this country because of "moral turpitude" was made public by the Department of Justice today.

The story that Mr. Cummins had rendered such an opinion, which would materially affect consular visas, was exclusively announced in a Washington dispatch to The New York Times on Jan. 4, but the details were not then available.

In the finding, written on Dec. 31, Mr. Cummings held that "A.R.," otherwise unnamed, was not guilty of "moral turpitude" for stating in a visa application that he possessed only 1,500 reichsmarks, and being later convicted of making false statements in an effort to removed 30,000 reichsmarks, an amount much larger than he would be permitted to take out of Germany. "A.R." sought to enter the United States.

The Cummings opinion took into consideration "the present-day situation" in Germany, in the case of the man affected, a Jew.

"I do not think," said Mr. Cummings, "that the case should be divorced from the realities of the world or that opinions rendered heretofore in this country dealing with

the moral qualities of crimes of which persons had been convicted by foreign tribunals in tranquil times should be followed in the letter to conclusions antagonistic to the spirit of our immigration law and foreign to the intent of the Congress in passing it."

The former Attorney General asserted that concepts of law in Germany were alien to those of this country, and said that the members of the Jewish race in Germany were under the severest kind of persecution.

"Under such conditions," he added in his letter to Sumner Welles, Acting Secretary of State, "the terror and desperation extant among hundreds of thousands of Jews now living in Germany cannot be other than acute. It was apparently under such conditions and in connection with the enforcement of the decrees which brought them about that conviction was had of the crime here charged; I cannot bring myself to believe that in determining any moral or political attributes of that crime the courts of this country would close their eyes to those factors.

On January 13, 1939 the following article appeared in the Washington Post, and again, though lengthy, I quote it in its entirety. The heading of this article was "Cummings Clears Exile-Scores Nazis" and subtitled "Jewish Immigrant Absolved of "Moral Turpitude" in Farewell Legal Opinion":

A denunciation of the methods of Nazi Germany is contained in the last legal opinion of Homer S. Cummings before vacating the office of Attorney General, the Justice Department revealed yesterday.

The opinion, made public by Frank Murphy, his successor, absolves a Jew convicted by a German court for making a false statement concerning his property from "moral turpitude" as defined by United States Immigration laws.

The Jew, designated by the initials A.R. — one of the many subjected to Nazi terrorism — had applied for a visa to enter this country. His German "criminal" record had caused the United States consul to question whether this country would classify him as a felon.

ASKED OPINION. The State Department, on December 2nd, referred the case to Cummings for an opinion. The latter replied it would appear that the false statements for which the visa applicant was convicted "were performed under a compulsion as great as it was unjust." He added:

"The alternatives open to the alien were to remain in Germany and be reduced to a state of penury and serfdom or to seek another life in another land. In selecting the latter alternative, he was confronted with the necessity of going forth with his dependent family stripped of all his possessions or seeking to retain what was rightfully his own, in avoidance of a statute and a procedure which cannot be defended on the

basis of morals and justice. It was a form of duress which in good conscience we would not be justified in ignoring. I do not believe that the term "moral turpitude", as it is generally understood, can properly be ascribed to the conduct of this alien. I advise that you would be warranted in granting him a visa."

The opinion admittedly was highly unusual, although not without precedent. State Department officials pointed out that the Attorney General occasionally had been called upon to pass on questions of "moral turpitude" in connection with immigration visa applications.

HINGES ON TURPITUDE. No instance could be cited, however, where the Attorney General so forcefully had called attention to the differences in government in this country, and a foreign land. Cummings pointed out that "moral turpitude" would be used in classification of persons convicted by courts in this country of "false swearing".

"However," he said, "in view of the claim made in this case that the crime was political in nature or had political aspects, the question whether it is in its essence one debarring the alien from entry is a question which, if presented to a court in the United States, would, in my opinion, require consideration in the light of the present-day situation in Germany."

State Department officials explained that a person convicted of a felony in a foreign country is adjudged to be guilty of "moral turpitude" and, as a result would be barred under the immigration laws.

"A.R." was convicted by the Court of Assizes at the District Court, Fuerth, Bavaria, on February 2, 1938. He was sentenced to one year and two months imprisonment.

"It is well known indeed," Cummings declared, "that the economic concepts of law presently existing in Germany are alien to those which prevail in this country.... Under such conditions the terror and desperation among hundreds of thousands of Jews now living in Germany cannot be other than acute ... I cannot bring myself to believe ... the courts of this country would close their eyes to these factors."

According to a translation of the German court judgment, submitted to Cummings, A.R. was engaged with his mother in the wholesale ironware business. He had intended emigrating from Germany since June 1937, the judgment stated, and had withdrawn 30,000 reichsmarks or about one-fifth of the value of their business. In order to obtain a certificate for emigration, he had to fill out questionnaires listing the amount of cash which he and his mother held. In each case, he gave the amount as "about 1,500 reichsmarks".

Cummings said it had been stated in behalf of the alien that "when he submitted to the Germany authorities a false statement concerning his property, he did so under the advice of an economic trustee upon whom he considered he was justified in relying".

Cummings advised, however, against attempting to try the case over, pointing out that it had been the practice not to go behind the record of the foreign court.

In addition, the following short article appeared on January 23, 1939 in Time Magazine:

Perhaps not by sheer accident the last official opinion of outgoing Attorney General Homer Stille Cummings, published last week, tweaked the Jew-baiting nose of Nazi Germany. The State Department had asked the Attorney General to advise whether to deny, on grounds of moral turpitude, a visa to a German Jew who, in order to escape from Germany had lied about his money to Nazi officials.

Wrote New Dealer Cummings, whose department has prosecuted many a U.S. citizen for false income tax statements: "The alternatives open to the alien were to remain in Germany and be reduced to a state of penury and serfdom, or to seek another life in another land. ...I advise ... granting him a visa.

The next document in the file is a telephone message sheet of the Department of State, Visa Division. It shows that on January 4, 1939, the attorney with initials RCA received a personal call from Mr. William Ramsey, regarding the alien Alfred Rahn. Action requested: Cable Stuttgart regarding ruling of the Attorney General. Charge telegram to: Mr. Max Rahn, General Cigar Company, Caguas, Puerto Rico

Remarks: No letter necessary. Max Rahn knows about the Opinion of the Atty. Gen. He called Mr. Ramsey on the telephone from New York and stated that he had read the report of the Opinion in the New York Times. A note on this message sheet indicates that a cable was sent to Stuttgart on 1/6/39 by RCA.

I can only imagine what Max must have felt when he received this news by reading the article in the New York Times. After all he went through - his personal sacrifices, all the time he had spent and the trips back and forth between Puerto Rico and Washington, and particularly toward the end when he too was very discouraged and felt there was no hope or chance, to hear this news from the front page of the New York Times, is just unbelievable.

The next 3-page document in this State Department file is most interesting and revealing. It is on the letterhead of Department of State, Visa Division, dated January 8, 1939 and is entitled Memorandum for the Files. It's written by RCA, whose whole name I do not know.

I will copy it in its entirety here.

MEMORANDUM FOR THE FILES:

The attached Opinion of the Attorney General goes pretty far in exempting German Jews from the moral turpitude clause of our immigration law on account of their conviction under the Hitler regime of crimes which might ordinarily be regarding as excluding them from the United States. I believe there is likely to be some unfavorable repercussion in Congress and on the part of public opinion throughout the country as a result of this Opinion.

In the first place the provisions of the German Criminal Code, under which the alien in this case was convicted, were created long before Hitler, and they apply equally to Jews and non-Jews. Fürthermore, the German Law for the Control of Foreign Exchange, although promulgated under Hitler, is equally applicable to Jews and non-Jews. These are not law or decrees enacted for the sole purpose of oppressing the Jews. They apply to all Germans. Our own law prohibiting the concealment of assets in bankruptcy and the exportation of gold apply to all citizens alike. They are economic laws designed to prevent the perpetration of frauds upon creditors and to protect the nation from the drain of its resources in the form of money or capital.

The principle adopted in this Opinion, if followed in other cases — as it must be followed until overruled or until Congress changes the law — will result in setting up the Jews as an exalted people who, because of their oppression, may commit serious crimes which would exclude other aliens from the United States, but which will not operate to exclude the Jews under our laws.

I have every sympathy in the world for the Jews in Germany and in other countries, but I do not believe that Opinions such as this are likely to result in any appreciable improvement in their conditions either in this country or abroad. On the contrary, I am of the opinion that any special consideration shown to the Jews under the immigration laws is likely to engender a feeling of deep resentment among our people against all Jewish immigrants, a result which should be avoided it at all possible. One of the things most incompatible with the true freedom and abhorrent to every lover of a democratic form of government is a special privileged class which is above the law and which may commit crimes with impunity. If the doctrine of force majeure is extended to Jewish criminals they will bring all the pogroms of Europe with them to the United States.

This attorney, RCA, had been involved in the previous briefs which Flournoy had written and fortunately for us he was not the one in charge of the case. He never would have sent the matter to the Attorney General. It shows the rampant anti-Semitism in the State Department, which was, certainly later, so well known.

The final document has numerous stamps all over it. It is on a form entitled "Telegram Sent" on Department of State letterhead. It is charged to Mr. Max Rahn ($13.96). The telegram was sent to the American Consul in Stuttgart, Germany. The typing has a lot of marks on it, and there's a stamp stating "This cable was sent in confidential Code. It should be carefully paraphrased before being communicated to anyone". It was sent by RCA, and a couple of others whose initials appear thereon.

"Attorney General has held that the offenses of which Alfred Rahn was convicted on February 2, 1938 before the Court of Assizes in the District Court, Fuerth, Bavaria, under

Article 156 of the Germany Criminal Code, and under the German Law on the Control of Foreign Exchange of February 4, 1935, are not offenses involving moral turpitude. It is expected that Alfred Rahn will apply for another immigration visa upon his release from imprisonment."

The final document of the materials I received from the National Archives is simply a list of financial costs involved in this case — primarily telegrams to Stuttgart.

Going into this amount of detail of the legal efforts involved may be too much for the average reader. But what struck me when I first read all these materials, and continues to haunt me as I reread them, is how incredibly close we came to not getting out. The legal arguments focused on the most intricate interpretations of American law. In the end, however, it was Homer Cummings, assisted by the brief of Max's attorney, William Ramsey, who saw through all these intricacies and developed an opinion that was rooted in basic justice. What Max did was truly heroic. How I wish I had known about all of this while he was still alive. I do owe my life, and that of my family to these men.

These men did save my family's life and for this they are among the righteous Gentiles of our time. But it also makes me think that over everyone's life there are probably many who make an enormous difference and we never even know it. I hope that I and everyone who reads this comes to examine our own actions and inactions of thought and deed to know that we may affect, make a difference, and even save the lives of others if we are our best selves.

8
LIFE IN THE UNITED STATES

⁕

Despite the long history of the family in Germany, with all of the economic, social, and cultural ties, it must have been with enormous relief that Lilli and Alfred were finally able to get out of that country. Certainly for Lilli, who had so diligently pursued obtaining the American visa, and then German passports, the day of leaving must have seemed like a victory over the oppressors. But even at the last moment they could not leave together, because Lilli's passport had not arrived by the time Alfred was released from prison. And so, immediately upon his release, Alfred, Ruth, and Helen Lorz went to Paris in March 1939. It must have been approximately March 8 or 9, since they had to go to Stuttgart immediately upon Alfred's release from prison on March 6. Clearly they feared that if Alfred remained in Germany, even for a few days, as a Jewish man he might be taken away again, and the best plan was for him to get out of the country just as quickly as possible.

Ruth aboard the SS Washington — April 1939

The story is told that when I went onto the playground in Paris, I became furious with the other children because I couldn't understand them and they couldn't understand me. I apparently did the same thing once we were in New York. We spent several weeks in Paris before Lilli arrived, having received her passport and making final arrangements to have all the furniture and furnishings sent to Antwerp for storage. The moving company was instructed to await Fürther instructions as to where to ship the furniture once we had settled in the United States. On April 15, 1939, after a nine day boat trip aboard the SS. Washington which began on April 6, we arrived in New York. April 15th was always celebrated as the anniversary of our arrival, along with the payment of income taxes due that date.

Short Stay in New York City

Among the documents we have is a small black notebook which Alfred used to keep track of all the contacts, calls, and appointments he made while in New York. The first entry is on April 19, 1939, so no time was lost in attempting to get settled, and finding a job. It is amazing the number of contacts they had. Occasionally Lilli also wrote in the black notebook, but most of the entries are Alfred's. Lilli visited the office of Mrs. Stephen Wise, on the recommendation of Nahum Goldmann, and later with Dr. Stephen Wise, who wrote recommendations for Alfred to metal companies in Ohio. She also had appointments with a number of agencies, universities and theatre schools as well as such places as the American Friends Service Committee, Association of American Colleges, New Theatre League and Jewish Information Bureau. Meanwhile Alfred met with representatives of metal and steel products companies, as well as such places as Electrolux Corporation, American Smelting and Refining Company. The booklet identifies who recommended the particular individual, and in each case gives the address of the person with whom they met or spoke. Alfred's entries are frequently followed by the word "nichts", meaning "nothing". Each entry is dated, showing how very active, diligent and connected they were. It certainly appears that initially they were seriously considering staying in New York and if they had found meaningful employment, probably would have settled there.

At some point, however, they decided to leave and seek their future elsewhere. The last entry of an appointment in New York is on July 13th. I believe that by this time they felt confident they could make it anywhere, and that instead of going where there was an available job, they would go to where there were mountains and where they could enjoy the lifestyle they had so thoroughly enjoyed before their 14-month separation. They loved to hike and ski, and looked for a place with mountains where these activities could be resumed and where the life they had once lived and so enjoyed could be recaptured. They also both spoke English well, although Lilli's English was always superior to Alfred's. And so they bought an old Ford, and leaving me, my grandmother, Johanna Rahn, and Helen Lorz, the governess who came to the U.S. with us, in New York City, set out across the country to a place called Denver, Colorado. I was told later that they also had marked a place called Seattle, Washington on their map. I have often thought of the courage and determination it took to make this move. They knew absolutely no one in Denver and knew nothing about the city except that it was near mountains. Relatives and friends in the east told them they were crazy — New York was where other Jews and other immigrants were, they said, and where the money was to be had. But neither of these concerns was of importance to them. The story they told, and I believe it fully, is that when they arrived at the outskirts of Denver and the sun was setting over the mountains, they said "if we can make it here, this is where we want to stay". The story, as Evy recalls it, is that "they arrived in Denver in July of 1939 as the sun was setting over the Rockies and the mountains were silhouetted against the orange sky and that daddy turned to mother and said "Lilli, we will never leave here!". There is a small newspaper clipping in our files entitled How Denver has Grown which includes the census figures from 1870 when Denver had 4,759 inhabitants, to 1940, when the population was 318,415.

From the small black notebook, the first entry out of New York is on July 17, 1939 in Dayton, Ohio, where Alfred met with at least four steel and metal companies, and obtained the names of others to contact, including Continental Steel in Kokomo, Indiana, for whom he was later employed as the District Sales Manager. They also stopped in Cincinnati, where Alfred had a number of other appointments and Lilli visited the Ransohoff's. She stated that Martha was not at home and up to the time she wrote the letter she had not made her personal acquaintance, which she regretted. Martha's maiden name was Bechmann, and her grandfather, Henry Bechmann was the brother of Lilli's grandfather, Louis Bechmann. There are increasingly references to people to contact in Denver, so this is clearly where they were headed at this point. They stopped in Chicago and Evanston, Illinois, where Lilli had an appointment with someone at Northwestern University who gave her contact names at Denver University and Alfred met with several metal companies. They stopped in St. Louis and then drove on to Denver. It is unclear how I got to Denver after they arrived, but most likely I came on the train from New York with my grandmother, Johanna, and Helen Lorz.

On July 31, the first entry from Denver is inscribed. Here the entries are contacts to B'nai Brith, and to Denver rabbis. Again Alfred had appointments with employment agencies as well as various metal and alloy companies, such as Youngstown Steel, Mine and Smelter Supply Company, and Wright Engineering and Supply Company while Lilli met with the Western Teachers Exchange Agency, as well as the president of Colorado Women's College, Denver Public Library, and various departments at Denver University. On August 7 the entry says that the secretary of John S. Worthington Company, a company that dealt primarily with asphalt roofing, told Alfred he should stay in contact. When Alfred read about Mr. Worthington's death shortly thereafter he contacted his widow to ask if he could purchase the company name which he did. Although the company dealt primarily with roofing materials, it was under this auspices that he was eventually able to build his business as a district sales representative for some eastern steel companies. In August, Lilli also established numerous contacts with Jewish organizations, such as the presidents of the Council of Jewish Women, Temple Sisterhood, BMH Women's League, Hadassah, as well as the Denver Public Library, Colorado State Museum, Kent School for Girls, Dean of the School of Liberal Arts at the University of Colorado in Boulder, President of the State College of Education in Greeley, President of the School of Mines in Golden, Director of the Denver Art Museum, and various theatre groups. The last entry in the book is August 22, 1939.

It seems that by then Lilli was clear that Denver University was where she wanted to teach and be connected. As early as September 1939 she submitted an application to Denver University. This document also shows that our first address in Denver was 1565 Franklin Street, c/o Mr. Rasmussen. On September 5, 1939 she wrote to the Dean of the School of Liberal Arts of the University of Denver, informing him of our new address at 2655 Ash Street. We have, in our documents, an entire folder of correspondence with the University of Denver from 1939-1944.

On January 27, 1940, Alfred wrote a letter to Ida and Hugo, who were then living in Stockholm. Because it describes the house they purchased, I include much of it here:

> *Dear Parents. We are still living in our old apartment, but since the sale of the house was completed yesterday and we'll have to move in 10 days. I give you the new address. The house in question was completed in March 1939 — it is thus absolutely new. The price at the time for the building $5700 — the lots cost the owner a few years earlier $600. We bought the house including Frigidaire for $5300. Our down payment was exactly $417, or rather, including all arising costs, $460. The "loan" (mortgage), which we have, is more than 90% of the buying price. The interest is 4 1/2%, or to speak in numbers, we have to pay $48 or $49 per month, which sum does not only go toward the interest but toward the paying-off of the mortgage (20 years) and includes taxes. This house is located quite high with garden and garage AND view of the mountains, equipped with automatic, modern coal-heating system, a so-called stoker, whose motor transports the coal into the stove in a so-far incomprehensible way for me to fashion. Lilli can report better about the inside of the house, its furnishings.*
>
> *Our lift has arrived in Denver today. Because we were able to combine 12,000 lbs. with another lift (800 lbs.) from Texas, we were able to save a lot of freight. We think we shall undertake the unloading at the end of the week. Let's hope everything arrived in relatively good shape.*
>
> *And everything did arrive in good shape. Nothing was lost except one small item — the shamus on the beautiful silver menorah which I use every Chanukah. For me, it is another annual reminder of how lucky we were to get out of Germany and come to the United States.*

1195 Holly Street, Denver. Just built in 1939

Denver, Colorado

After a stay of about 6 months in a rented house in east Denver, my parents purchased our home at 1195 Holly Street, a two-bedroom, brick house where I lived until I left for college. The house was purchased in 1940 for $5300 (including the Frigidaire). It was new construction on what was then the outskirts of Denver with many houses being built around it at the same time. A big memory of my youth is playing in the vacant lots and in the houses as they were being built all around us. It was a small corner house with just two bedrooms but it had a full basement in which there were several rooms. When I later saw their homes in Fürth, I realized how small this Holly Street house must have seemed to them. Lilli certainly was no longer invested in acquiring material belongings. I never heard either of them ever complain about the size of the house, or even talk about the

homes in which they had grown up. In the pre-war years Lilli had been somewhat of a collector, as evidenced by such things as her pewter and ivory collections which Evy and I have, but the war experience changed all that as she saw how quickly and easily these physical possessions could be taken away. As a result, although our house was furnished nicely, and had beautiful rugs and other antiques from Germany, home decoration or emphasis on material possessions was not a high priority in our family.

In December 1958 Lilli, Alfred, and Evy moved into a larger home at 175 Forest Street. I had already been out of the house since 1954, when I left for college. This was a lovely corner house on a much larger lot than Holly Street, and across the street was a full block of park, called Robinson Park. It had previously been a brickyard, and I remember exploring it on my bike when we lived on Holly Street. They had a marvelous view of the mountains, which was, I think, a major reason they purchased this house. The corner lot had a low redwood fence around it on which roses grew. The prior owner (there had only been one) had installed a separate underground sprinkler system just for the roses, and Alfred took great pride in caring for them and his lawn. He actually won a prize one year for his lawn and beautiful roses. Karen skied for the first time on the small hill across the street in Robinson Park. When she was three we went to Denver in December and Alfred had bought her a small pair of skis. I had just given him a beautiful ski sweater, and when we decided to take Karen across the street for her first skiing lesson, he put on his new sweater, his Bogner ski pants, his ski boots and skis to take his granddaughter to the "slope". When I said to him that we were just going across the street and he didn't need to get so dressed up, he said, with righteous indignation "when I take my granddaughter skiing, I want to look my very best!"

Skiing and Hiking

From the first moments we arrived in Denver the mountains played a large part in our lives. Apart from the love of the mountains, and what they offered in all seasons, I think the mountains gave to Lilli and Alfred a way to recapture they joys they had early in their relationship and in the early years of their marriage, before the traumas of leaving Germany and their 14 month separation.

Alfred

In the summers we went to Estes Park (Rocky Mountain National Park), where we hiked, rode horseback and Lilli fished. She loved to go off by herself and fish for rainbow trout, and I think she enjoyed the opportunity to be by herself. We often took one or both of our grandmothers, and also went sometimes with the Breit family. Lilli, in one of her letters spoke about the wonderful weather and very nice accommodations "although as far as I am concerned, everything will do as long as I don't have to cook and make beds". We also did a lot of hiking and usually, five minutes after we left the parking lot, we were the only ones hiking on the trails. Occasionally, when we would meet other hikers, they were invariably European.

But the winters provided the biggest source of family activity as we skied almost every weekend. We skied before there were any lifts at all (hard to imagine) and there are a number of photos of me being dragged up Lookout Mountain, as we trekked to the top with skins on our skis and then skied down. The first ski tow was a rope tow at Berthoud Pass, installed around 1942 or so, at the Continental Divide. And then, slowly but surely skiing caught on and areas began to be developed. Lilli and Alfred went to Aspen the first year it opened in 1945. In 1946 I remember they returned saying they loved the town, and the Hotel Jerome, which was the only place to stay, because it had a Swiss chef and the food was delicious. Also, there were primarily Europeans there and they sat around in the evening and sang songs in German. But, they said it was SO difficult — the only "slopes" were

the areas under abandoned silver mines, and they were extremely steep. You can see those areas today from the lifts — they aren't even open for skiing any more! But then, over the summer, they read in the paper that some new slopes were cut, and thus began our annual trips to Aspen, where we went at least 2-3 times each season. They went to Alta (from where the letter to Ilse Sadler was written). I didn't go along on that trip because I had broken my arm falling from a horse. Skiing was the major activity we did together as a family. I became an avid competitive skier, won a number of races, and had a national ranking.

I have mentioned previously that they never talked about their time in Germany — it was truly a closed book for both of them. One might say that the memories were too painful, but certainly the times

Lilli and Alfred

Ruth and Alfred Skiing
Lookout Mountain

Ruth and Lilli Skiing
Lookout Mountain

they spent in the mountains, especially skiing, were among their happiest. But those memories were subsumed into the rest — never talked about. I never heard them exclaim, as we were atop the slopes at Winter Park, or Aspen, for example, that this reminded them of any of the many places they skied in the Alps. I know they were there, because we have the photos from Zermatt, St. Moritz, Davos, and many other beautiful skiing spots, but these experiences were also never talked about.

Lilli's Employment

As soon as we arrived in the Denver, Lilli made contact with Denver University. By the time detailed entries in the little black book cease Lilli was clear that Denver University was where she wanted to teach and be connected. She began in March 1941 substituting in the German Department. For 6 days of substitute teaching that month, she received a check for $30.00. In September 1941 she wrote to Denver University suggesting topics on which she was prepared to lecture, including German and French (grammar, reading, conversation and literature), History of the Theatre in Europe, broken down into various stages, European history, War and Art.

The Denver University Winter Quarter Schedule for January 5-March 20, 1942 indicates that Lilli taught a course on the History of the Theatre, 1500-1900. The course description was as follows: "Survey of the methods of acting and staging and the lives of the chief playwrights and actors, beginning with the Greeks and Romans. The theatre will be studied in relation to its civic and cultural environment through the ages." The course was taught again in the spring quarter (March 23-May 29, 1942). Then in the summer of 1942 she was hired to teach German during both terms of the summer quarter. Her remuneration was stated as $75.00 for each term, "provided at least 8 students enroll for the term, with Fürther adjustment of 90% of the tuition paid by students if fewer than 8 are enrolled during either term." Her acceptance letter indicated she was delighted with the appointment and opportunity to have a regular teaching assignment. She was, during the summer of 1942, in complete charge of all the German classes which the University of Denver offered in the Summer School (5 classes a day).

Some interesting aspects of Denver University during these wartime years emerge from the material we have. Denver University had an annual Week of Religious Emphasis in February 1942. In the notice from the President to all faculty, he states "In times such as these, it is my feeling that all of us must return more emphatically than ever to a consideration of the spiritual values which have given strength to the idea of Freedom." The speaker was the eminent religious leader Bishop Francis J. McConnell of New York. The faculty was asked to encourage all students to participate in these events.

A notice from the Office of the Chancellor to all members of the faculty asked that they be "as lenient as possible" with students of two organizations who missed classes because they petitioned for a bus line near the university. The notice stated that "Everyone recognizes the importance of this petition to the Tramway Company, in view of restrictions on the use of private automobiles" and also those who helped with registration under the Selective Service Act.

There were also memos to encourage economy in all the offices and departments of the University, including suggestions to save paper by avoiding the use of envelopes, half sheets of memo paper and utilizing messenger service wherever possible. "Avoid waste by not throwing away paper clips, and rubber bands. Rubber bands particularly are irreplaceable. Conserve on erasers, save typewriter spools, reuse file folders, return used carbon paper to the Business Office for renovating, do not send out unnecessary letters but use post cards wherever possible, shorten and eliminate long distance calls, and turn off lights whenever possible". Other memos to the faculty concerned procedures for petitions to draft boards recommending deferment or postponement of induction of students.

It is interesting to see how much the university was engaged in the war effort, and tried to integrate it into the curriculum and thinking of the faculty. In August of 1942, the Army issued a memorandum regarding the establishment of a voluntary instruction program for high school and college students of pre-induction age. They planned to use existing facilities of schools and colleges throughout the nation to meet the present and future critical needs for properly trained personnel in the armed forces. The purpose was to provide both basic and specialized knowledge prior to induction, thereby reducing the amount of training needed after induction. In October 1942 all faculty were asked to contribute to the Denver War Chest. Lilli responded by stating that she had only a very small class at the present time and prospects in her particular field are not too bright. "Nevertheless I hope that you will accept my small contribution and I certainly will make a greater one as soon as my circumstances will allow it." A check for $2.00 was enclosed. From time to time, Caleb F. Gates, Jr., the President of Denver University, distributed materials to the faculty he found interesting — for example, a talk by Wendell L. Wilkie on value of a liberal education.

By the fall of 1942 Lilli began to teach in the German department, and on October 6, 1942 she joined the Women's Faculty Club of the University of Denver. She taught two sections of Elementary German that academic year, and in April 1943 continued to teach Elementary and Intermediate German for the total salary of $300.00. She had 25 students in her Elementary German class and only 3 in the Intermediate German class. She also did some research and reading on linguistics for teachers of modern languages. She continued to teach German during the 1943-44 academic year.

In September 1942 she received a response from the Reference Department of the Denver Public Library to her inquiry regarding the colors of the academic costume of the philosophical faculty of Erlangen University. Evidently she wished to march in the academic procession and wanted to wear her doctoral colors. She was informed that "a hood with a white lining above Bavarian blue with a tri-chevron of black, white and red may be worn by scholars and professors in the United States who have received degrees from Erlangen University." I still have that academic hood.

She appeared to be a tough grader. The University distributed a grade distribution sheet for the autumn quarter, 1942-43. She gave 75% of her students B's and the remaining 25% C's. No A's were given.

On July 10, 1943 she offered to teach a four-week course on European History since 1914 and prepared a detailed outline of what she would cover. She taught the course that summer. In April 1943 the Aircorps of the United States Army instituted an Academic Instruction College Training Program at Denver University. She applied and was accepted to teach German in the Foreign Area and Language Division, ASTP (Army Specialized Training Program) Unit #4767 at the El Jebel Shrine, which apparently was taken over by Denver University for this purpose. The program was discontinued in the spring of 1944.

She stopped teaching in 1944 because, as she wrote to Ilse Sadler, Alfred was now earning enough to support them, and also she became pregnant with Evy, who was born on January 21, 1945.

Alfred's Employment

Alfred's first job in Denver was packing boxes in a warehouse. He continued to make calls, and after he saw the obituary of John S. Worthing in the newspaper, he contacted his widow to acquire his company which dealt with some metal works as well as asphalt roofing. He took over that company during the war years since working in the steel business was impossible during the war years. In addition, he sold plastic items. We had a small room in our basement at 1195 Holly Street which was the "sample room". In it he had samples of all the hard and soft plastic items he sold such as salt and pepper shakers, picture frames, corn cob holders, as well as garment bags, bowl covers, and other soft plastic items. At some point during the war and particularly after the war, when steel production once more could be sold commercially, he made contacts again with various steel mills, and became the District Sales Manager for several of them, including Contintental Steel in Kokomo, Indiana and Penn Metal Company in Parkersburg, West Virginia. He was always very indebted to Continental Steel for giving him a job, as an alien, during the war. After the war he learned they actually had conducted a thorough check on him to make sure he wasn't a "German spy" who would use his knowledge about U.S. metal products to help the enemy. Once they were satisfied that he was not, they offered him

April 15, 1959

Mr. Edmond P. Severns,
President
Continental Steel Corporation
Kokomo, Indiana

Dear Ed:

Today, 20 years have passed since I arrived with my family
from Germany, bewildered and confused and not knowing what
we would find here. Years of terror and of unspeakable
cruelties had left a mark, had caused us to lose faith in
man.

Today, I look back over those 20 years with a deep feeling
of gratitude towards this country which gave us the opportunity
to start our lives anew and to regain the faith and the
confidence which we had lost.

Today I would like to express a special "Thank You" to the
Continental Steel Corporation which has done more than anybody
else to make me feel "at home" in this country. Strange as it
may sound, I know today that corporations such as Continental
Steel are not the cold and money-hungry monsters, sometimes
pictured. I know today that even corporations can have a
soul and a heart - and it makes me feel good to think of my
Kokomo friends, the Howards and the S Arts, the Rabes and the
Bings, the Marvins and the Johns and all the others.

I look forward to many more years of pleasant association
and am with best personal regards

                                        Sincerely yours,

                                        ALFRED H. RAHN

Alfred's Letter to Continental Steel, April 15, 1959

the job. The letter he wrote to the President of Continental Steel on April 15, 1959, the twentieth anniversary of our arrival in the United States, truly shows his appreciation, his loyalty, and how grateful he was to the company. He was once again back in his old business, selling metal products to architects, civil engineers, contractors and the like. He worked alone in a one-room office in a building on 15th and Arapahoe (now near the Larimer Square area).

Among the documents we have is a relatively large folder of correspondence from about November 1945 until June, 1952 Alfred that had with Ernst Rosenbluth. Ernst, who was about Alfred's age, was an old family friend, and his parents had been friends with Alfred and Lilli and particularly with Alfred's parents. In March of 1996, out of the blue, Evy received a letter from him asking if she could identify some pictures he had, hoping she would know who they were (they were, in fact, our grandparents). When she called him in Jerusalem, where he lives, and he learned that we were soon to go to Germany on our "roots" trip, he recommended that we stay at the Park Hotel, in the middle of the town, and that we meet Gisela Blume. Both made our stay in Germany much fuller and richer experiences than had we done it all on our own. Evy and I then met him at the Nuremberg/Fürth reunion in the summer of 2002.

The folder of correspondence with Ernst, and his mother, says so much about Alfred, that I want to summarize some of its contents here.

Ernest's mother, Amelie Rosenbluth, had survived Auschwitz and was living in Malmo, Sweden and in London, with her son and daughter-in-law. She wanted Alfred to invest some money, around $4000, for her in the United States. The care with which he did this, accounting regularly for every penny, shows how conscientious and caring he was. In one letter, dated February 14, 1947, he wrote to her and Ernest that he and Lilli had just returned from a two week trip to New York City, and that it was the first time he had flown in an airplane (he was 46 years old). "We met quite a lot of old friends whom we had not seen for quite a while. However, it is good to be back in Denver which we really love for its climate as well as for the mountains which are pretty close". In February 1947 Ernest wrote to Alfred about his own career choices, asking specifically what he thinks his chances and prospects would be in America. He was, at that time, a salesman for a window display accessories firm in London, a job he didn't find altogether satisfying because of the travel involved. He was married and had a two year old son. He inquired about various lines of work. Alfred responded in March, 1947. saying he couldn't help him with the specifics, and then went on to talk about his own thoughts and experience:

"If you would be single without dependents, there would be not the slightest doubt in my mind that you should come over into this country which, in my opinion, still is full of opportunities whereas Europe, including England, is declining in every respect. It is my conviction that the USA will take — sooner or later — the place which Great Britain has occupied in the world over a long period of time I am sure you know that the general standard of living here is unbelievably high and I believe that this will remain so, at least in comparison with all other countries."

He advised that in Ernst's case, because he is not single, the situation is different. If Ernst did decide to come, he advised most urgently not to stay in New York City or in other thickly populated centers of the east. He pointed out that he couldn't make a living for a while, that it took at least a year to support his family, and then he wrote about his own experience:

"I arrived in NYC in April 1939, stayed 3 months in NYC and could not — most fortunately — find a job despite a pile of letters of introduction. So, we decided to leave NY and we picked Denver on the map because it was close to the mountains. This may sound ridiculous to you, but it is correct. We arrived in Denver without knowing a single soul, without having any recommendation, etc. etc. A week later, I had a job as common laborer in a wholesale steel warehouse, making $20/week. There I remained 1 1/2 years increasing my salary to $23/week. Then, I started for myself in 1941 as a manufacturers representative. The first year, I hardly made my expenses, and they were not big. Gradually, I worked myself up and — without wanting to brag - am living today better than I have ever lived in Fürth. But what I wanted to make clear to you, it takes time. And it might interest you that my wife Lilli worked too, first as a sales girl in a bookstore — after a few years she was head of the German Dept. at Denver University, but it took time. Later she devoted her time to the production of our second daughter, and the 2 girls keep her busy now."

Ernst apparently saw wisdom in Alfred's advice and became a chartered accountant. He moved first to Canada, and then to Israel, where he continues to reside.

Alfred worked very hard all his life, and although he never made more than $18,000 per year, we lived comfortably. Our family was always thrifty — lights had to be turned out, nothing was wasted, money was saved — all qualities that I inherited. And yet, when it came to things he loved or where quality was important, like ski boots or a watch or camera, he did not hesitate to spend the money.

Thanksgiving Talks at the Opportunity School

Among the documents I found in going through the various boxes, were copies of two Thanksgiving talks, one that Lilli and one that Alfred gave at the Opportunity School. Lilli's was given Thanksgiving, 1939, only a few months after arriving in Denver, and Alfred's was given the following year.

The Opportunity School in Denver was a school for new immigrants to teach them English and other skills they needed to pass the test to become U.S. citizens. It still exists. My parents probably did not enroll to learn English, or other skills, but perhaps to perfect their language, meet others, learn about American customs, and most likely, study to prepare for the citizenship exams, even though they could not become citizens for 5 years. They made friends there, and as is evident from the talks they gave at Thanksgiving, the experience of being part of this school was extremely moving and important to them.

I have the original version of Lilli's talk, double-spaced typed, and her command of English is truly impressive. There are almost no spelling or grammatical errors. Because these talks are so moving to me, I reproduce them here in their entirety.

Lilli's Talk — Thanksgiving Address — 1939

Ladies and Gentlemen,

It is a special pleasure for me, for several reasons, to have a chance to express my feelings of gratitude from this platform tonight. As refugees from Germany who only arrived in the USA a few months ago, my family and I are, as you may imagine, extremely thankful to have had the possibility to escape from a world full of horror, terror and mischief. But we are not less thankful to this country which has enabled us to find a haven and to the people of this country who have received us with open arms, who try every hour of the day to make us feel at home, to make us forget the hardship and horrors we had to pass through on the other side of the ocean. You may believe that nobody at this Thanksgiving eve can be more grateful to his fellowman in this country than we are, who have been exiled, homeless refugees only a few months ago, and who now not only found home and shelter in this community but also friends and kindhearted fellowmen.

Last but not least it has been due to this school that have been able to adjust ourselves so quickly, this school which in its entire setup is the most striking example of what real democratic spirit is able to accomplish. I know Europe pretty well and have traveled in many counties of the Old World, but I have never heard of anything equal to this institution. This school here has not only give us, during the few weeks of our attendance, the possibility to improve our knowledge of the language and the country, but it has also given us close contact with the inhabitants of this friendly city and there was not one among those whom we met in this school who didn't meet us with kindness and give us the feeling that people in this country haven't forgotten the brotherhood of mankind. And isn't that the last goal, the very meaning of every institution of learning and education? Let's give a big hand to all those who are in charge of this grand work!

But as I understand the message of this Thanksgiving day it is not enough to thank God, to thank our fellow man — but we should stop and think about the fate of the nation we live in and about the fate of other nations around us. Only this will give us the real appreciation of the country we are fortunate enough to live in, a country where the personal freedom of the individual is absolutely guaranteed.

Looking at the world around us we will not see but disorder, terror and horridness and the complete suppression of the individual. Men over there aren't but helpless pieces of wood, floating in a torrent, not knowing where the way goes and many of them are lost or perish somewhere on the way. You may think: Europe is far away. You may think what have we to do with their problems, with their rights and crimes they commit over there? I believe that injustice wherever it is committed should arouse the conscience of everybody, the conscience of the world. And isn't this the day on which every American should stop and think, why he should be thankful, what he should be thankful for? Certainly this is the day on which you should remember that there are vast parts of the earth where all the principles and ideas and ideals this democracy of yours stands for have entirely perished and that there are quite a number of other countries where these ideas are at stake at this very moment.

Americas are born free, are educated in freedom, how can they know what it means to live without freedom, without justice, to live in slavery? Do you realize what it means to have no right to say what you think, to have no free press and to have no possibility to get true information? Do you know what it means to be outlawed, to be taken away from your family without any explanation, to be sentenced and sent to prison without a trial, to be robbed in the name of the state, to be discriminated, helpless and hopeless?

If you realize that, if you use these hours of the Thanksgiving Day to think over these problems I am sure your heart will overflow with gratitude and the message of this wonderful holiday will be understood and beneficial for each of us.

Thank you.

Given that Lilli had been educated at some of the finest universities of Europe, and had her Ph.D., her admiration of the Denver Opportunity School is all the more impressive.

Alfred's Thanksgiving Talk — 1940 (a year later)

It is a real privilege for me to stand here tonight and to have an opportunity to express my feelings, my feelings of thankfulness and gratitude towards this country. Tonight we are here to celebrate the day of Thanksgiving and I ask: Why should everybody be thankful and why am I particularly thankful to live in this country?

This country rests on the pillars of free speech, free writing and free worship tolerance and equality before the law. On this day of the year we should stop and remember what we have got and achieved here in this country. We should stop and think and be thankful.

If we look around in the world we will find that not many places are left where people have an opportunity to express their ideas. Isn't this Opportunity School and especially this class a striking example for what this country has achieved. On this holiday of the year we should stop and think and be thankful.

Believe me that nobody can realize and appreciate better than myself what it means to live in a free country among free people. Two years ago I still was in a German prison; 1 1/2 years ago I came to this country as a refugee. Therefore, I know what it means to live in a country ruled by a dictator. I know what it means to live in a country the main doctrine of which is that the individual has no rights whatsoever and no purpose whatsoever save to serve the State. Our doctrine of life here is that the State exists to protect and serve the citizen. We here can enjoy the privileges of democracy and on this day of the year we should stop and think and be thankful.

However, to be thankful is not sufficient. Everyone in this country has to work and to do its best to preserve and to maintain these privileges. We must not forget that democracy is in danger and unless everybody, and this applies to every single individual, does his duty or democracy will perish. I have seen the development in Germany and I can tell you that every citizen is responsible for the dictatorship they have over there. We cannot prove our thankfulness toward this country better than to work, and I mean to work hard, for the preservation of democracy.

I am thankful with all my heart this country gave me an opportunity to live here. On this holiday let us stop and think and not forget that this country is and always has been a country of immigrants, a harbor for refugees, and let us be thankful that we, our parents or our grandparents could find here a place where to build up a new life.

I am thankful with all my heart that my little girl can grow up here in a free country and become a citizen with equal rights. And no doubt, she is on the best way to become a good citizen. The other day she came home from kindergarten and said to me "Daddy, do you know what I learned today?" "No", I said. "Tell me". And she with her sweet little voice started the first verse of the beautiful song: God Bless America.

On this holiday of the year let us stop and think and be thankful and let us pray every morning and every night: GOD BLESS AMERICA.

I have often read one of these letters at our Thanksgiving dinners.

Their admiration for what the Opportunity School did for them is, in an ironic way, exemplified by what became of the Rahn family home at 129 Konigstrasse in Fürth. This house is located on a major thoroughfare. Though not nearly as grand as the home on Honscuchpromenade where the Bechmann home was located, it is very large 4-story dwelling with a basement and a back terrace which used to lead down to the river. The façade of this building, along with others on Konigstrasse, is controlled by the city and considered a National Historical site so that the façade itself cannot be changed. When I first visited it in 1973, it had been converted to a rooming house for foreign laborers, mostly Turk and Yugoslav. There were over 20 mailboxes in the front hall. One could, however, still see some of the original molding that went from room to room, indicating its earlier function as a residence.

When I next retuned in 1996, it had been converted into a school for adult education, primarily for foreign immigrants. There were computers and other equipment, such as language labs, in all the classrooms. It was hard to tell it was once a residence, except that the outlines of the mezuzah could still be seen on the right side of the front entrance door. It has become, and is still, an Opportunity School in Fürth. I think Lilli and Alfred would be very pleased.

Lectures and Activism in the Early Years

It is remarkable to me that within months of their arrival in Denver, Lilli, and to a lesser extent Alfred, began giving lectures and speaking to a number of groups. I have already mentioned their "Thanksgiving Talks" at the Opportunity School, in November 1939 and 1940, as well as the talk entitled "Jewish Life in Germany, 1933-1939, which was given within the first year or so after arriving in Denver. We have, among the many documents in our possession, notebooks full of lectures and talks which they gave, as well as numerous letters to editors of newspapers and journals. The range of issues on which they spoke is amazing. For example, on November 5, 1939, just four months after arriving in Denver, Lilli gave a

Lilli Rahn

talk to members of the Broadway Baptist Church entitled National Socialism and Its Relation to Religion and Education. This talk was 5 single-spaced typed pages, and again, her English is almost impeccable. Other examples of talks during those early years include a talk on July 8, 1941 entitled German–Russian Relations 1918-1939 to an organization called Bundles for Britain. This talk consisted of ten single-spaced typed pages, and she had written at the bottom "38 minutes". In December 1939 she gave a talk on Immigration and Labor; in October 1941 a talk entitled Moral Defense in response to a Life magazine article. Another talk was entitled Back to Palestine in which she discussed the Zionist movement before Herzl. On October 8, 1939 (this is the earliest talk we have a copy of) she gave a lecture at the Denver Public Library on the trip she had taken to Tripoli, Libya. There also is a speech she gave on the Jews of Tripoli. It is unclear to me exactly when she took this trip, but the detailed report of it consisted of 8 single-spaced typed pages. She also wrote and spoke about National Socialist Youth Education. Our folders include copies of these talks and lectures, invitations to the event, newspaper clippings as well as numerous letters to editors.

Besides these talks and articles, and her employment as discussed above, she volunteered one day a week as a driver for the Motor Corps of the American Red Cross. I remember her well in the uniform she wore each Friday as she left for the Red Cross, doing whatever driving was necessary during her 8-hour days there. She made a number of friends from this activity, and I believe was probably the only Jew involved in this particular war effort. She commented in one of her letters that she was pleased to make friends with non-Jews, since this was the way they had socialized in Germany. Like with so many other activities, she received citations for her excellent work and contribution.

Alfred also was invited to speak and wrote numerous letters to the editors of the local papers. For example, he railed against the newspapers for being promoters of crime by printing such detailed stories of criminal activities on page one of the newspaper. He spoke on German

Life Before the War to Loyal Knights of Ye Round Table. This talk ended with the sentence "We have to become the arsenal of democracy not only by building ships and planes and guns, but primarily by cultivating and spreading the ideas and ideals of civilization". He wrote an article entitled Imperative to Extend Material Aid Short of Manpower to Great Britain in which he stressed, "We must not allow Britain to lose this war. At the present moment there is still a chance for England to win without our entering the war, provided that we make up our minds before it is too late". In all of these talks it is clear that he was an avid supporter of democracy and of the freedom that they experienced in America.

Lilli in Red Cross Uniform

They both became active and outspoken members of the community. They totally adopted America and the freedoms which it offered. At the risk of being redundant, I am including here a talk which one of them gave on March 20, 1942 at the Opportunity School in Denver. I think that Alfred gave this talk, as it appears to be typed on his typewriter and it sounds like him, but the date at the top is in Lilli's handwriting. It truly expresses their sentiments and seems so relevant today as we debate the value of opening our frontiers to immigrants.

I consider it a particular privilege to have been chosen to speak tonight for the foreign born, prospective citizens who four times a week gather in the citizenship classes of Opportunity School. Like all decent persons of foreign birth who came to the shores of America to escape racial or religious persecution, social or economical upheaval, national or personal catastrophe in the land of their origin and who found here not only a genuine welcome but a true home, the members of this class have the most ardent desire to becomes citizens of this nation as soon as legally possible in order to share not only the privileges which this democracy offers but to assume the duties which these privileges involve.

Tonight I will not speak about their loyalty and devotion towards their newly adopted homeland, but I will say a few words about America, the country of our adoption, and her attitude toward us, the newcomers, the foreign born.

Ever since the Mayflower days has this vast and rich continent been a haven for the oppressed and persecuted all over the world. And the fundamental right of any man from any land to come here and start life anew, as a free man in a free country has been made one of the cornerstones of this democracy. Generations have passed and millions have come and helped shaped this continent into one of the mightiest and richest on earth. All nations have contributed and many of them look proudly at the achievements of their sons and daughters in the New World.

But although many other countries called and call themselves democracies, none of them, except the United States, ever voluntarily opened their gates to any measurable degree to those unfortunate people who, for no fault of their own, have been driven from their native lands. And America not only took and takes them in, she welcomes them, she helps them adjust themselves, to feel at home, she encourages them to take part in her national life and thus enables them to become Americans, not only by law, but in spirit.

There is no other country in the world where citizenship classes are given as a free service to the newcomers. Oh yes, you may become a citizen in some of the other democracies too, but usually you have to live there for a long, long time, much longer than the 5 years required by the American law and even then you have to have some influential friends who pull the wires for you, and above all, you have to pay, either to the government or to your influential friend, or to both of them. The U.S. is the only country that admits the foreign born without any cost whatsoever, the only demands which she makes are character, knowledge of the history and institutions of the country and loyalty. Money means nothing, it may be lost overnight. But education, knowledge and character will never be lost. This is the principle on which the wonderful educational system of this democracy is built. But even in this country of free and liberal education, our Denver Opportunity School is an outstanding and unique manifestation, because of the variety and quality of its courses and its truly democratic spirit.

The citizenship classes this year are composed of 21 different nationalities. There is no hatred among them, no racial or religious or political antagonism. They are all united in one effort: to learn about the United States and what she stands for and they all strive for one common goal: to become citizens of this nation as soon as possible.
Due to war conditions the government has found it advisable to single out some groups among the foreign born. I speak about the so-called enemy aliens, the natives of the axis countries. I happen to be one of them, one of those who left Europe after 1933 to escape the very tyranny, oppression and persecution of the axis forces. Believe me, we who were in the frontline of defense against Nazism and fascism long before they became official enemies of the U.S.A, we, who lost our property, our homes, our businesses, our friends and relatives, we, who because of our fight against the axis ideology were officially deprived of our citizenship in our native country, we certainly appreciate the blessings of freedom and democracy as much, maybe even more, than any other foreign born. Although technically classified as enemy aliens, we, like all

other aliens, eager to become loyal citizens, have only one allegiance and that is to the U.S. America is our choice and we have inseparably linked our fate to her. And we therefore hope that one day in the future, when we foreign born will be legally eligible we also will be found worthy of the honor to be called a citizen of the United States of America.

Hadassah

It is clear that Lilli became involved with Hadassah shortly after we settled in Denver. It is one of the organizations mentioned in the little black book they had, and from newspaper clippings about speeches she gave later, it is obvious that by 1941 she already was very active in local and regional Hadassah affairs.

Hadassah describes itself today as follows:

Hadassah, the Women's Zionist Organization of America, is a volunteer women's organization whose members are motivated and inspired to strengthen their partnership with Israel, ensure Jewish continuity, and realize their potential as a dynamic force in American society. Founded in 1912, Hadassah retains the passion and timeless values of its founder, Henrietta Szold, Jewish scholar and activist, who was dedicated to Judaism, Zionism, and the American ideal. Committed to the centrality of Israel based on the renaissance of the Jewish people in its historic homeland, Hadassah promotes the unity of the Jewish people. In Israel, Hadassah initiates and supports pace-setting health care, education and youth institutions and land development to meet the country's changing needs. In the United States, Hadassah enhances the quality of American and Jewish life through its education and Zionist youth programs, promotes health awareness, and provides personal enrichment and growth for its members.

The Hadassah website, Hadassah.org, gives a very interesting brief chronology of all this organization has done since its founding in 1912. It is really very impressive.

All of these goals were ones Lilli could readily espouse. The passion for Israel, I believe, came from her own appreciation and gratitude for having been able to escape Germany with her family, and she wanted to support a country that would always have their doors open to Jews. After the difficulty they had in getting visas to the United States and knowing that there were many others who never got them, this became her passion. Her involvement with Hadassah and its Israel mission began before the state was declared in 1948. The issues of health care, education and youth institutions were ones she was committed to. She had volunteered at the local hospital during her last years in Fürth while waiting for Alfred's release from prison and for the visas, and she recognized the importance of providing health care to new immigrants. She volunteered to be a Red Cross driver soon after arriving in Denver. These areas also satisfied her intellectual curiosity and abilities as she so aptly proved. Finally, it propelled her into the company of intelligent and committed women with whom she made close, lifelong friendships.

We have a whole box of clippings and scrapbooks of her Hadassah years, but I will just summarize some of her experiences here.

She was President of the Mountain Plains Region, and a member of the National Service Committee, as well a National Vice –President. I was always led to believe that she would have been national president had we lived in New York. She was on the National Board since the early 1950's and in 1965 she became a National Associate of Hadassah, which means being a member for life of the National Board. In the 1960's she served as National Constitution Chairman and in the Central Pacific Coast Region as Zionist Affairs Chairman. In other words, she held every office there was to hold except National President.

Hadassah was her passion, her true vocation, and the love of her life. She worked at it as if it were a profession, though it was completely voluntary. I left for college in the fall of 1954, but even by then my memories of her are at the typewriter, writing whatever needed to be done. Hadassah, I believe, satisfied many of her yearnings and fulfilled her life in a way nothing else did. It was an organization with a purpose and a mission and provided an outlet for her many talents, including her role as poet, as she wrote many poems for the trips to Israel and the conventions she attended.

Between 1954 and 1968, representing Hadassah, Lilli went to Israel many times and to the Soviet Union once. She also went a number of times on her own, in a non-official capacity. Going to Israel was really a regular thing for her and she became an expert in certain aspects of Israeli life, especially what Hadassah was doing for the country. Her first trip to Israel was in March 1954 on a Hadassah Leadership Tour. She was one of 25 outstanding women of Hadassah from the United States picked out of the 300,000 members at that time. Two men also went along, one of whom was Alfred. Like all of her trips, she kept a detailed journal of the trip which she typed up after she came home. This one consisted of 26 typed pages, single-spaced. For this trip she also made a large scrapbook of articles, brochures, invitations, photos, and newspaper clippings. The group met with all the current Israel leaders, including Abba Eban, Ben Gurion, Mayor of Tel Aviv, Dr. Kalman Mann, Director of the Hadassah Medical Organization, Mrs. and Mr. Ben Zvi, President of the State of Israel, Roger Tyler, U.S. Consul in Jerusalem, and Mrs. Vera Weizman, wife of the first President of Israel. They also met with old friends, Ludwig and Lotte Heusinger and Hannah and Gabriel Kassiff. It was her first trip to Israel, and I think she soaked it up completely.

I have often asked myself why she didn't ask me to come along on that trip — I was in the last months of East High School and had already been accepted at Smith College. This question is one that is only hindsight — at the time I am sure I wasn't the least bit interested and probably would have needed urging to participate. Also, there were no other children on the trip and I think at that time is wasn't as common to take children along as we do today. What I do remember about that spring is the chance to have the car all to myself while they were gone. I have often wondered, however, how my relationship to my parents would have changed and how it would have affected my life if I had gone along.

Five years later, in 1959, she led the tour of Hadassah leaders to Israel and in 1963 she visited again on another Hadassah trip. In March of 1968 she led another Hadassah tour to

Israel with 29 participants, both women and men.

In October 1966 she went on a Hadassah leaders trip to the Soviet Union to study the condition of Soviet Jewry. They visited Leningrad (St. Petersburg), Moscow, Kiev and Odessa and were able to establish contact with hundreds of Jews from all walks of life. Again we have a very thorough and detailed journal of this trip, consisting of 29 single-spaced typed pages. The purpose of this trip was to visit the medical installations and schools and compare them to what was occurring in Israel and in the U.S. It was fascinating to read about this trip of 40 years ago. She commented on her previous visit to Russia in 1932 as a student to study the famous Russian theatre. She recounted that she remembered many of the sights. The Hadassah group began the trip in Copenhagen, where, as always, they met with the highest officials, including the Israeli Ambassador to Denmark. She mentioned in her journal that she had been in Copenhagen previously with her father in 1935. I found this fact interesting because it was the year between completion of her PhD and Ruth's birth, and she had already married Alfred. On her return from this Hadassah trip to the Soviet Union, she was a keynote speaker at a number of events throughout the country, describing her experience on this trip. She also was on the Steering Committee of the Committee for Soviet Jewry of the Allied Jewish Community Council of Denver.

I remember feeling on occasion while I was still living at home that my mother's commitment to Hadassah was more than her commitment for her family. These were rare instances, but I remember once when I said this to her, she became very angry and even cried, so I didn't do it again. I believe that she really wanted to move to Israel, but Alfred wasn't interested in doing that. If she had outlived him, I think she would have moved to Israel. She made Evy and me lifetime members of Hadassah, so we continue to receive their publications and notices. After Lilli and Alfred died in 1970, we gave funds, commemorated by a plaque, for a room in the nurse's quarters at the Hadassah Hospital in Jerusalem in their honor. When I first went to Israel in 1973 and visited the Hadassah Hospital, I went to the office and asked to see the room named in their honor. Everyone in the room remembered Lilli and expressed their sympathy about her death. When I next visited the hospital in 1983, 13 years after she had died, the exact same thing happened. She had not been forgotten.

It is Evy's and my intention to give this Hadassah material to the archivist of Hadassah, who has already expressed great interest in it.

Ida

If Lilli thought she was through with correspondence concerning emigration, she was wrong when it came time for her mother, Ida Bechmann, to come to the United States. A folder containing 78 items of correspondence, not including forms and copies of laws and regulations, is among the materials we have.

Ida Metzger was born on July 29, 1888 in Nuremberg and went to elementary and high school there. She moved to Hugo Bechmann's family home on Hornschuchpromenade in Fürth in 1910, the year of their marriage. They lived there until 1930 when Ida and Hugo moved to Berlin. In 1939, when she was sure that Lilli, Alfred and I could successfully emigrate, she moved to Stockholm, Sweden to join Hugo, who had moved there in 1937.

Hugo died in Stockholm on July 19, 1942 during a routine gall bladder operation. He apparently had been quite well and they had spent time together in the country in June. Ida immediately cabled Lilli, and we have in our files Lilli's two letters to Ida dated July 22, 1942. Lilli was obviously shocked and saddened by her father's death as I believe they were quite close. She asked Ida for all the details, and also where he was put to rest. "All our thoughts are now of course with you, dear Mother, and we shall try everything to

Ida Bechmann

bring you here quickly." In the second letter, which accompanied a letter from Johanna, Lilli said that based on new information, "apparently visas are issued only to people who are an "asset", that is, a useful addition to America and above all the American "war effort" — among women, for instance, those who are trained nurses, lab technicians, chemists, etc. One should consider, therefore, if you could learn something like that over there. I'm sure you understand this suggestion in the right way — it is a matter of being able to prove that you have knowledge in a field important for the war effort, such as nurse, x-ray technician, …" Lllli clearly was not asking her mother, who had never worked a day in her life, to think about supporting herself. In fact, the letters repeatedly asked Ida about her finances and how she is doing financially, telling her not to skimp, so they could do whatever is necessary. No one knew better than Lilli what it might take to get a visa application approved, and the suggestion to take a nursing course was done for that purpose. Ida followed up and did take some nursing course, so this could be added to her visa application.

On August 1, 1942 Lilli again wrote Ida, not having heard from her since being notified of Hugo's death. She talked about steps that needed to be taken to get Ida a visa, transportation possibilities, and about affidavits needed for the visa application to assure her support.

Two days later Ida cabled Lilli that she needed Lilli's certified authority to represent Lilli with respect to Hugo's estate. Hugo had died without a will and Lilli, as his only child, had some rights to his estate that she wished to surrender to her mother. This required completion of a lengthy form dealing with foreign exchanges issued by the U.S. Treasury Department, with copies going to the Federal Reserve Bank for the district. Where the form asked for citizenship, she responded:

> *My parents as well as my husband and myself are Jewish refugees from Germany, we were all born in Germany. Mr. Rahn and I were formally deprived of our German citizenship by the German government on March 20, 1940, while my parents come under the general expatriation decree of 1941. Mr. Rahn and I have received our First American Naturalization Papers on September 9, 1940 in Denver, Colorado and have*

lived in the USA since April 1939, while my father emigrated to Sweden in 1937 and my mother followed him in 1939.

The Treasury Department sent her copies of the regulations and Executive Orders and told her that to dispose of her interest in her father's estate she had to apply for a license from the Federal Reserve Bank in her district, which was in Kansas City, on the appropriate form. Once again Lilli is becoming truly a lawyer and expert with respect to immigration issues, interpreting the various regulations as well as a 43-page pamphlet entitled Laws and Regulations Affecting the Control of Persons Entering and Leaving the United States, dated February 1, 1942, in which she underlined a number of sections. Extensive correspondence with the Federal Reserve Bank in Kansas City followed and in October she received the appropriate license to enable Ida to complete the administration of Hugo's estate. In Lilli's October letter to Ida, she mentioned that she still had not had any news from her, and assured her that all papers for her immigration had been filed with the Department of State. "If it were not for the fact that we cannot communicate with you, which worries us quite a bit, we feel very happy here. Ruth Marion enjoys school very much and is always excited about it. We hope to hear from you soon. Amid all this correspondence regarding affidavits and finances is a letter written to the Director of Censorship in Washington, DC dated August 17, 1942. Apparently cables Lilli sent to Ida with respect to Hugo's estate never got there, and so Lilli contacted the Red Cross hoping they might be able to transmit a wire without delay. She was informed that normal commercial communication with Sweden was functioning again, but they could not cable for her, and advised her to contact the Director of Censorship to obtain a permit to send wires. A reply from the Office of Censorship, dated August 22, 1942 stated:

For your information, U.S. Censorship Regulations prohibit communications to enemy nationals and to enemy and enemy occupied territory. No permit is required to file a cable to friendly territory and hence none can be issued. All such messages are accepted for transmission at the sender's risk and may be stopped, delayed, or otherwise dealt with at the discretion of Censorship, without notice to the sender.

These forms were followed by the application and correspondence to obtain Ida's visa. This form requested biographical information about the applicant, and was sent to the Visa Division of the Department of State. Lilli had to provide information regarding close relatives living in the United States as well as in other countries. Those in the United States were Lilli, Alfred, Ida's only brother, Ernst Metzger, living in New York, Carola Loeffler, Hugo's only sister, and Emma Bierer, Ida's only sister. Among those in other countries was Caroline Metzger, Ida's mother for which Lilli stated that her address was unknown and "The last contact we had with Mrs. Metzger was in the early part of 1941. She was a woman of 76 years old and in ill health. We have had no word of her since the outbreak of the war, and do not know whether she is now alive". As we later learned, she was taken to the concentration camp at Thereisenstadt and murdered there on September 23, 1942. The application also required information about how the alien would be supported, so along with this application, Lilli had to submit, among other documents, certified copies of their latest Federal income tax return, affidavits from their banks giving a history and current balance of all income and accounts, official appraisals of all property, as well as certified affidavits regarding Lilli's character and standing in the community. The Affidavit of Support, prepared in 1942, listed their annual income as $2061.62 and assets totaling $11,580.05. Lilli's Affidavit, dated February 21, 1943, stated the following;

> *Because my mother is the last one of the family still in Europe, we all have the most ardent desire to have her join us here as soon as possible. My parents are Jewish and left Germany in 1938 because of the Nazi persecution and were deprived of their German citizenship. My mother enjoys excellent health. She informed me that she is taking a Red Cross Nursing Course at Sabbatsberg Hospital, Stockholm, under Surgeon Major Dr. Bauer, and she hopes to be able to utilize her knowledge and training after her arrival in the United States. My mother had a fine education and besides German, speaks very well English, Swedish and French. After her arrival, she will, of course, live with us in Denver, Colorado. I know that my Mother believes in the democratic form of government and I am convinced that she will become a good and loyal citizen of this country.*

I think it is remarkable that Ida, who did not have any education after high school and had never worked a day in her life, already knew several languages and, at age 55 was taking nursing courses. On March 31, 1943 the chief of the Visa Division for the Department of State informed Lilli that the Department had given approval for the issuance of an immigration visa and this was transmitted by telegraph to the American Legation at Stockholm. The visa had to be renewed four times again (September 31, 1943, March 31, 1944, September 28, 1944 and March 27, 1945) for six months each (more correspondence!) because the difficulty in finding transportation (it was during the war, after all) extended the time beyond the visa expiration date.

Then followed correspondence on how Ida was to actually travel to the United States. Lilli was aware that no ships ran any more between Sweden and the United States, and she wrote to the National Refugee Service in New York who informed her "that there is no transportation out of Sweden at this time. Boats, we were told, leaving Sweden, may not take former German Nationals and only the person herself in Sweden could arrange for the trip". When it became clear Ida had to go first to England, she needed Affidavits from residents there who would guarantee her maintenance during her stay in England until she could get passage on a ship. She asked Betty Ullman (Hugo's first cousin) and Fred Bentley (Fred Bierer, who had taken the name of Bentley), Ida's nephew, to provide these guarantees, and they both agreed. In March 1944 Alfred wrote Ida that he and Lilli did not feel the war would be over soon and "that it is definitely possible that the war, including the European war, will go on for quite a while. And that's why we don't know whether you should wait over there till war's end". He also urged Ida to sell everything because the costs of transportation and insurance are tremendous. "We realize that a lot of things may mean a lot to you, but on the other hand, we have long ago forgotten what we have lost over there and do have more things in our small home than we actually need". On June 1, 1944, the National Refugee Service informed Lilli "that travel to and from England is not permissible at the present time" so that Ida could not get a transit visa through the United Kingdom. Finally, on September 28, 1944 she obtained the necessary Transit Visa to go England and flew there in December 1944. Once there, Ida had to undergo yet another medical exam (she previously had one in Stockholm) and she waited for receipt of her visa so she could procure passage to the United States. The last letter in this file, dated April 5, 1945, informed the National Refugee Service that Ida had arrived in New York and was staying with her sister and brother-in-law, Emma and Ernst Bierer. She stayed there about a week before coming to Denver.

Ida's autobiography, which she wrote in 1972, with all its humor and modesty, is in the Appendix of this memoir. In it she describes the incredible voyage she took from Stockholm to New York, via Ireland, Portugal, French Morocco, Brazil, Trinidad, Puerto Rico, Bermuda and finally New York.

After Ida arrived in Denver, she lived with us briefly but she was determined not to become dependent on my parents. She was a woman who had grown up in considerable wealth with maids, chauffeurs, cooks, and governesses. She never had cooked for herself in her life and probably had never even boiled water. Nonetheless, despite the fact that she was in her late 50's and had never worked, she decided to get a job. Her first job was at the May Company in the stockings department. In her autobiography she describes with humor her experience. I quote it here because it shows her wonderful ability to deal with people and always come out ahead:

> *I went there and they took me immediately as saleslady in the stockings department. My English was not perfect. I never had sold anything in all my life, but the customers came all to me so I served. So came an older lady and she wanted brown stockings — not too light and not too dark, not too long and not too short, and at last she found what she was looking for. She said, "Do these stockings also last very long?" "Well", I said, "Lady, when these stockings would last for all your life, I would lose all my work here." She took a carton and a man came who was standing behind her and he said to me, "Lady, that was better than any show or theater I saw in the last time. Please give me three cartons." Then came the department chief and said, "Becky, you are our best sales lady. How did you do it?" Well, I did not tell her, but I looked for another job.*

That job was very short-lived and later she began to work in the dietary kitchen at the National Jewish Hospital where she prepared the trays for patients on special diets. She lived in the nurses' residence at the hospital and ate all her meals there.

She loved bridge and had a group of friends with whom she played. Evy remembers her bridge parties at our home. Getting ready she would fill all the glass lined silver candy dishes with M&Ms and other chocolates — Evy would sneak around to take some and would always end up with the "left-overs" after the party.

Ida continued to work in the dietary kitchen for many years. However, in 1965 when she was 77, new managers took over the kitchen services, and she was laid off. She was incensed that they would fire her, and initially she was perplexed about what she would do with her life and her energy. Lilli and Alfred arranged for her to take a cruise to the Mediterranean, as she had not been back to Europe since she emigrated. Since she always loved to have a glass of wine or two she made friends aboard the ship and was invited to accompany them on day trips off the boat. On her return she moved into Kentucky Circle, a retirement community where residents had their own apartments (with outside entrances and lawn) and could, if they wanted to, eat in a community hall. Once again, she had a place to eat dinner with others. She found new friends for bridge

Karen, Lilli and Ida — Estes Park

and she took daily walks to the supermarket, carrying groceries back not just for herself, but for her neighbors as well. And, she began to study art. She took up again what had clearly been a hobby in her early years, as evidenced by the charming book she had written and illustrated for me just before we left Germany. We encouraged Ida to cultivate her art. and so she did. She took classes, went to parks with her easel and she painted. She enjoyed copying pictures of landscapes from calendars of Colorado or Switzerland. I have some of her paintings in my home in Maine as does Evy in her Waltham home. Lilli and Alfred's deaths in 1970 left a hole in Ida's life. Her only child was gone. A year later she had a stroke and was somewhat paralyzed on one side. Evy and Bill moved to Denver in 1972 and Ida was the first person to see Leah, her great-granddaughter, when she was born. When Evy and Bill moved back to Boston in 1975, Ida moved with them. By then she needed to live in a nursing home, and she was visited frequently by all of the family. She died peacefully on January 2, 1978 at age 89.

Johanna

My grandmother, Johanna (Alfred's mother) lived in a basement bedroom room for much of my childhood. She had long white hair which she wore up in a loose bun every day. Her clothing consisted of black and white and she frequently wore her finest jewels, just for an afternoon coffee klatch with her friends. As I look back now, I think Alfred and Lilli never treated either of their mothers with the kind of respect I would have expected from my children, and there was considerable tension between Johanna and them. She was phenomenally neat, making sure that everything was always in its place. The story that Evy often tells is about

Johanna Rahn

her after-school experience. Evy would come home and immediately change into "play" clothes, throwing her school clothes on the bed. She then would go to the bathroom for a minute and by the time she got back into her bedroom her clothes were always neatly hung, folded and put away. Johanna could not tolerate disorder. She loved it when Max and Maria visited from Puerto Rico or Cuba and when I visited from college. On those occasions she spent days making butter cookies in all sizes and shapes for us. By the time Evy went to high school Johanna had moved to a very nice rooming house with other older residents where the proprietor cooked for all of them. It was located in a part of town were a number of other German-Jewish refugees lived, so she was much closer to her friends there. She lived her very last years in a nursing home. This was an era before there were assisted and or graduated living arrangements and I remember vividly Alfred's upset at having to visit her there and seeing how older people lived, even though she was well cared for. I think he made up his mind at that time that he never wanted to land in a nursing home with many other elderly residents.

Claims for Restitution

Among the many boxes of documents and correspondence which were brought over from Germany is a large box which contains the correspondence relating to claims for restitution which were made once Lilli and Alfred had moved to Denver. The entire claims correspondence with various lawyers in Germany spans a time period of 17 years, from 1946 to 1963. However, in another folder it is clear that correspondence with various banks began just as soon as we arrived in the United States. This correspondence goes back as early as June, 1939, when we were still living in New York (at 906 West End Avenue, 104th Street, Apt. 51.)

In addition to making claims for themselves, there is also a large folder dealing with Johanna's various holdings, real estate, claims against various people and banks which spans the period from May 1946 to June, 1961. The firms of Dech and Bing are mentioned. She apparently had an interest in not only the Farrnbacher firm, but in other assets as well, and received some compensation for these. All this correspondence with Attorneys Fuchs and Herbst is in German, and I did not translate most of it.

One of the vivid memories of my youth is recalling Lilli and Alfred sitting around the dining room table, surrounded by lots of papers, with evident stress and discomfort in what they were doing. It was clear that this was not a task they enjoyed; in fact, it probably was a source of dissension between them. I believe that Lilli did not care at all whether they got a penny from the Germans, believing that no amount of money could make up for what the Germans had done, not only to them, but also in murdering her grandmother and Alfred's brother — while Alfred was trying to recoup some of what was lost, not only so it could benefit the family, but perhaps also to assuage some of his own guilt in being a factor in the loss.

In the mid-1940's and during the time that these claims for restitution were made, the value of one German mark was about 40% of the dollar. In other words, 2.50 Reichsmarks (RM) (called Deutsche Marks after the war, or DM) equaled one dollar.

The bulk of the correspondence was largely between Alfred and Dr. Hans Fuchs, the attorney in Fürth. There were repeated requests, misunderstandings, clarifications, corrections, urgings by Alfred "what is taking so long", apologies or explanations by Fuchs, all in exquisitely stilted language, e.g. "your esteemed of (date)". The various proofs of assets taken by the Nazis were handed over to Fuchs, who kept them for 5 years before being allowed to destroy them. There was also extensive correspondence with Attorney Robert Herbst, whose letterhead indicated in English that he was "Attorney and Counselor at Law" and a Member of the German Bar. He had an office in Fürth, which was in the U.S. Zone after the war, and the correspondence is all in German.

One whole folder contains correspondence with the Dresdner Bank. Much of that correspondence was signed by Lilli during the time Alfred was in prison. Another folder contains correspondence and financial stipulations following Johanna's emigration to the United States. This correspondence was with the Commerz-und Privat-Bank in Fürth that also began while still in Germany and continued into the 1940's.

By letter dated June 10, 1947 from Alfred to the Department of Justice, Alien Property Custodian in Washington, DC, Alfred advised the department that he had claims against four German firms, namely: Brasch & Rothenstein, Deutsche Bank, Commerz und Privatbank and Bayerische Staatsbank. He inquired whether these firms had assets in the U.S., and pointed out that as an American citizen, he was entitled to file a claim with this department. He also asked for forms to be used for the claims of Johanna.

Uncle Max too had reason to file for reparations claims. His correspondence was with the Department of State, beginning in July 1945, as soon as the war was over. Max claimed an account at the Deutsche Bank in Fürth-Bavara amounting to, in the year 1941, 2234 DM ($894). In addition, Max made claims on behalf of himself and his mother for their inheritance from the estate of his brother, James Rahn, who was murdered by the Germans on January 21, 1941. This estate, according to the authorized agent, Mr. Georg Dimmler, consisted of a total of 46,456.18 DM ($18,582). Mr Dimmler had appropriated a substantial amount of this estate for himself. Max had tried to find out what happened to this property during the war years and was informed that the German Government confiscated the securities and bank balances in May 1944 and the balance was transferred to the Finanzamt Moabit-West in Berlin. He stated in his correspondence that "the confiscation took place despite the fact that the German authorities and the German bank officials knew that I was an American citizen. Most of the assets I owned in Germany represented my share of the estate of my late brother James Rahn. He was murdered in a German concentration camp in Poland and the official date of his death was January 21, 1941". Max became a naturalized U.S. citizen in New York on August 17, 1933 (Citizenship No. 3 748 465). In response Max received detailed instructions on how to verify his proof of claim, including a demand for original documents or certified copies of originals. Max wrote to Lilli and Alfred on February 14, 1946 acknowledging the difficulty of compliance and stating that "if you want to forget about the whole thing it is OK with me because after all you will have to do all the work, rounding up the evidence — if it can be done at all. Use your own best judgment — I don't care". Lilli and Alfred apparently didn't want to let the matter go, so the documentary evidence prepared by them and by Max was submitted in November, 1946 to the Secretary of State. The total amount requested was 24,430.00 RM, which Max calculated correctly based on the exchange rate at the time of confiscation, at $9772.40 in U.S. currency. On December 4, 1950, four years later, Max wrote the Secretary of State again, asking when he could expect any action. No response appears in the documents.

In the meantime, Alfred continued to pursue claims. When he had received no reply by April 1948, except for a postcard acknowledging receipt of the claims, he wrote again. On December 1, 1950, 3 years later, Alfred wrote the Office of Alien Property again, asking when his claims will be acted upon.

On August 2, 1951 Alfred wrote to Colorado Senator Edwin C. Johnson, on behalf of Max's claim for $9772.40, which was turned over by the Bank to the German Government which confiscated the account in 1941. "We are unable to understand why the State Department or the American Government are obviously not at all interested or willing to protect the foreign investments of an American citizen which were outright stolen from him by a country against which we just concluded a victorious war and which is now occupied by our troops." He then raised another complaint, which clearly had been bothering him tremendously, as follows:

We are even more at a loss to understand this attitude of the State Department since we know that hundreds of German students and Germany employees of the American Department of Information (America House) are flown over here as guests of the U.S. Government — which of course means at the expense of the U.S. taxpayers — for a three months sightseeing trip of the U.S. We have had the opportunity to meet a number of these guests of the State Department and assuming that the purpose of their trip is to give them a better understanding of American life and democracy, we were greatly disturbed by the lack of planning of their tours. They travel all over the country, in airplanes and sleeping cars, visiting the beauty spots, instead of being introduced to those features of American life which are really representative of our democracy, as for instance, a town Meeting, the swearing in of New Americans, school systems like our Denver Opportunity School, etc. You will surely understand that we are greatly puzzled by these actions of the State department which, on the one side, spends hundreds of thousands of dollars for travels of German citizens, and, on the other hand, does not move a finger to help an American citizen recover his property which had been stolen by these same Germans.

Alfred wrote the same letter to the Acting General Manager of the International Information and Educational Exchange Program of the Department of State. He also enclosed a copy of the letter to Drew Pearson, of the Washington-Merry-go-Round.

On December 20, 1950 the Department of State wrote to Alfred, in essence, that even though he had corresponded with the State Department, this doesn't obviate the necessity to comply with legislation affecting such assets. The law providing for indemnification required that the claimant must be a resident of Germany on January 1, 1947. "So it's not clear whether your case meets the residence requirements, and if you feel it does, you can write to the land office having jurisdiction, even though the deadline for filing claims based on this legislation has expired. And even if you are to be successful, payments are made in Deutsche Marks and not in dollars or foreign exchange and payments to non-residents must be deposited in blocked bank accounts. It is not expected that Germany will earn enough foreign exchange in the near future to permit the transfer of such funds out of Germany for an indefinite period."

On September 6, 1951 the Acting Assistant Secretary of State responded to Senator Johnson, acknowledging his letter of August 30, 1951 (With power and status, you can at least get prompt replies!) The gist of this letter was that the obligation for compensation of victims of Nazism rests with the German authorities. "Any recourse for claims, which do not come within the purview of legislation already enacted in Germany, will depend on future legislation and the terms of the German peace settlement."

On January 29, 1952 Alfred received a letter from George W. Baker, Officer in Charge of German Property Affairs in the State Department. He was informed that the Jewish Restitution Successor Organization (JRSO) filed claims to the Rahn properties. This organization filed claims to all properties against which no other claims had been filed. In short, if the Rahn claims were filed with the appropriate agency on or before June 30, 1950, they can be pursued under that law. If so, inform JRSO so they can withdraw their claim. If not properly or timely filed, arrange with JRSO to an assignment of its claims to the appropriate living heirs.

In addition, Alfred sought to recoup some of his other stolen assets. The following story of the moving company is just one small example of how private citizens also took advantage of the forced exodus of the Jews. On July 13,1947 Lilli and Alfred sent to the Office of Alien Property Custodian in Washington, DC a claim entitled Damages for Contract not Performed in the amount of $868.09. The specific allegation was that in 1939 Lilli and Alfred concluded a contract with the moving firm of Brasch & Rothenstein of Nuremberg to store and insure their personal belongings and household goods and to transport them to any port in the USA. They paid fully for storage, insurance and transportation costs in Reichsmark. They enclosed correspondence from the debtor acknowledging that he had been paid in full and that they would have to pay nothing in foreign currency except customs duties and delivery to their residence in the U.S. The debtor also acknowledged insuring the transport for $5000 against total loss in accordance with instructions. The claim stated that despite the confirmations that they had fully paid for transportation and insurance, the debtor refused to release the goods when they gave order to have them shipped to the USA on August 1, 1939. "The debtor again demanded full payment, this time in US dollars, and hereby took advantage of our status as Jewish refugees at that time. In order to avoid loss of all our belongings, we were forced to pay $758.05 for transportation and $90.04 for insurance." The claim was for the full amount of the second payment. There is no evidence they ever collected on this claim.

There are also folders of documents from 1937 containing questionnaires for those planning to emigrate, including various inventories of assets. They had to list every single item they owned, including silverware, furniture, linens, clothing, and even undergarments.

In addition to the tangible and intangible assets mentioned above, claims were made because of the circumstances under which both family homes - 7 Hornschuchpromenade, the Bechman family home and 129 Kongistrasse, site of the Rahn family home and business, were "sold".

Hugo Bechman, Lilli's father, was co-owner of 7 Hornschuchpromenade with his sister, Carola Loeffler. Hugo and Carola had grown up in this house, as did Lilli years later. Carola left the house years before, when she married. She and her husband, Julius emigrated to California. Hugo had moved to Berlin and then emigrated to Stockholm, Sweden where he died on July 19, 1942. His claim was acquired by his wife, Ida, who emigrated to the United States in April 1945, and immediately took out citizenship papers. On January 8, 1946, before a Notary Public and under oath, she assigned all her claims to her former home to Alfred and Lilli, who by that time were both American citizens.

One of the affidavits filed in the claim for restitution spells out the history of this property and the basis for making a claim. It reads as follows:

Carola Loeffler and Hugh Bechmann were joint tenants in common of the apartment house at 7 Hornschuchpromenade. As Jews living in Germany they were victims of Nazi persecution and forced to leave Germany in 1938. In order to prepare for their emigration, they sold, in August 1938, the above mentioned property to the Deutsche Tafelglas (plateglass) A.G. at a forced priced of RM 67,500 ($27,000)– while the true sale value of the property amounted to about RM 120,000 ($48,000). The purchasing corporation representing its directors took knowingly and willfully advantage of the then existing duress of the sellers, since the German officials who had to approve of the sale of Jewish property would not consent to a selling price higher than DM 67,500. The Deutsche Tafelglas A.L., is, therefore, liable for tort done to the sellers; the sellers claim from the buyers damages in the aggregate amount of $21,400 (DM 53,000) each claiming for her share half of the amount claimed = $10,700. The validity of our claim has been recognized by the debtor, the Deutsch Tafelglas Aktiongesellschaft, as evidenced by a letter which the company's president, Dr. Otto Seeling, wrote on October 17, 1946 to Mrs. Carola Loeffler, the co-claimant of this debt (residing at 447 North Doheny Drive, Beverly Hills, California) containing the following paragraph: "There does not exist the necessity of a trusteeship because I, hereby, in the name of my firm make the binding declaration to you and the heirs of your brother that my firm is willing either to return the house, upon request, to the former owners at the purchasing price plus costs of improvements occurred during the period of possession, or, to grant a supplementary payment on the basis of an authoritative appraisal in case it should be determined that the purchasing price did not correspond with the actual value of the property at the time of the sale."

Alfred, Lilli and Carola felt that this clearly substantiated their claims.

There is a large box of correspondence containing letters back and forth between Alfred and Carola Loeffler, Hugo's sister, and her son, Heinz, who lived in Chicago. This correspondence dealt with a number of issues regarding reparations for the "sale" of 7 Hornschuchpromenade and goes from December, 1946 until February 1951. Heinz stated throughout that he didn't know much about the situation, and left the handling of these matters to Alfred. Alfred kept stressing to Carola that any claims should be made jointly, together with her so as to avoid any duplication of effort. Letters went to German attorneys, as well as to the U.S. Department of Justice, Alien Property Custodian.

There were discussions back and forth about whether to make a claim for the house itself, or German marks, which might be difficult to take out of Germany. For a while Alfred felt that they should seek return of the house itself, and it is interesting to speculate what the outcome of this would have been. Alfred believed that Germany would be a major power shortly, and that real estate might be a very good investment. By 1948 it appears Alfred was getting a bit tired of these reparation claims (not surprisingly!), and asked Carola to take it over herself — anything she decided would be OK with him. In the end, it was the work of the private German attorneys that got the favorable result. Thereafter there is correspondence about which bank to use to bring the funds to the U.S. or alternatively, to invest in German Bonds and leave the funds there.

I am including below a description of the house that was sent along with the claim for reparations. Since this is a very full and complete description, I thought it was appropriate to include it here. This description, stating that the original cost of the house was DM 360,000 ($140,000) was as follows:

> *The house was built with top quality construction. The Deutsche Tafelglass Gesellshaft paid DM 67,500 ($27,000) in 1938. It was in perfect condition and was one of the most beautiful houses in Fürth. Aware of our inevitable forced emigration we agreed to that price. Jews, at that time, were forced to dispose of their property in order to be able to leave the country. We sold the house at the stated price although Mr. Loeffler was able to ascertain that the house was worth at least one-third of the original cost price at that time. These figures are the basis for the claim."*

> *The house is one of the biggest, if not the biggest in Fürth. It comprised a basement and four stories. To the house belongs a garden and a big garden house.*

> *The basement has a 3-room apartment for the janitor's family, room for central heating system, coal and coal storage room, and 5 cellars for storing belongings and supplies of apartment owners.*

> *First floor — 12 rooms, several very big*

> *Second floor — unlike first floor, divided in two 2 apartments. Again, a total of 12 rooms on this floor*

> *Third Floor — again 12 rooms*

> *Fourth floor — two smaller apartments, consisting of 4-5 rooms all together. Also storage space for each party, and a big space for drying the laundry.*

> *Not included in the number of rooms mentioned are bathrooms, kitchens, pantries and separate toilets, which are found on every floor. There are two staircases in the*

house, the main one made of marble and granite. The garden is surrounded by a wrought iron fence, and the entrance to the house is a wrought iron door. The total number of rooms was about 43-44.

Mr. Otto Seeling, Director of the Deutsche Tafelglass Fabriken lived with his family for many years on the third floor after our departure from Germany. Dr. Seeling built a special interior stairway from the third to the second floor, and by taking over part of the latter increased the size of his apartment.

It is still a magnificent mansion today, as I shall describe later. It appears that they finally received 20,287 DM ($8114) after the attorney deducted his costs.

The second major piece of real estate was 129 Konigstrasse, the site of the Rahn family home and business. In October 1937, as preparations were being made to emigrate, Alfred and his mother, Johanna, as the sole owners, transferred the property to Hans Terberger, a partner in the firm of Schulte-Wisserman. The sale price, which was agreed upon, was 70,000 RM ($28,000). The premises sold consisted of the residence, storerooms, storehouse, the connecting house, auto garage, yard and garden and garden house. The price also included the "good will" name of the firm. The sales contract listed the prior owners as:

Eugenie Farrnbacher — May 14, 1912

Sidney Rahn, husband of Johanna, born Goldmann — November 13, 1922

Hannchen (Johanna) Rahn, born Goldmann, sole owner — June 6, 1931

The records show that the sale occurred on October 25, 1937. This "sale" was in anticipation of their original plan to leave Germany in December, 1937. The buyer was to deposit this sum immediately into the Dresdner Bank in Fürth. The official printed announcement of the sale has two sides. On one side is a communication from Johanna and Alfred headed "To our Business Friends!

We politely inform you herewith that effective 25 October 1937 we have sold our family business which had been a family owned undertaking for over 100 years. The firm will be transformed into a company with limited liability and the personally liable associate will be Mr. Otto Schulte-Wisserman. The firm M.S. Farrnbacher led by us is without demands or debts, however the limited liability company is charged with calling in outstanding sums in order to secure normal business commerce. We thank you for your confidence which you have shown us for these many years and ask you to transfer it also to the new firm. Most respectfully yours, Johanna Rahn/ Alfred Rahn.

The other side of the document is from the new owners stating that they have taken over the business formerly owned by the family Rahn, and shall continue to carry on under the name of M.S. Farrnbacher, Ltd. Personally liable associate is Mr. Otto Schulte-Wisserman. "Co-workers of years' proven cooperation have been taken over by us. We shall always endeavor to gain your confidence by attentive service". It is signed: With German Greeting, M.S. Farrnbacher, Ltd.

The entry into the official Commerce Register of Fürth was done on October 28, 1937. A contract was prepared, but since the contract was never approved by the Nazi party, Alfred and Johanna never received the total due them. Because the house had a Jewish owner, a lien was placed on it by the German financial authorities. Public trustees were appointed of which Mr. Hochmockel, a long-time employee of the Rahn family and now an employee of Schulte-Wisserman, was one. Alfred had to acknowledge that the sale was absolutely in order and legal. We do know that the sum of at least 5621 RM ($2248) was never paid by the firm of Schulte-Wisserman or Mr. Terberger. All these matters arose again in 1948 as the subject of reparations in correspondence with Alfred's German attorney, Mr. Herbst.

By 1938 the firm was reorganized as Otto-Schulte-Wissermann, KG, with Otto Schulte-Wisserman personally liable for any debts. He died in 1945 and in 1949 Hans Terberger became the personally liable associate and the firm was headed by Mrs. Clara Schulte-Wisserman. In 1955 she resigned as chief, and Hilde Terberger became chief. In 1959 the corporation was dissolved and transformed into another entity. Mr. and Mrs. Terberger left the firm and Carl Spaeter G.M.B.H. of Duisburg took over. In 1964 the headquarters of the firm was moved from Fürth to Nuremberg. The purpose of the firm is now the production and sale of machines and machine installations, as well as commerce with mining, smelting and synthetic products.

However, when Evy and I visited 126 Konigstrasse in 1996 there still was a metal works business in the ground floor of the building and the operation looks, I believe, very similar to what it was in Alfred's time.

According to German law enacted in 1947, persons whose property was confiscated could seek to have it returned to them. Correspondence with Attorney Herbst indicates that he recommended this would not be successful, as Terberger paid most of the 70,000 RM in 1937. Terberger, Herbst advised, could probably easily prove that the sum paid at the time was truly a suitable price. Herbst therefore asked Alfred to consider the following proposition. Terberger had asked for a release from all liens on the property and business, and release from any past or future claims for restitution. Attorney Herbst advised "selling" this release as dearly as possible. Although he felt they didn't have much ground to stand on, being unable to either claim the return of the property or the amount of 5621 RM ($2248) Herbst felt they should milk this for what it was worth and even a partial amount could be used to defray the expenses of Alfred's other claims. He warned Alfred not to have any correspondence with Terberger as this could only interfere with his plans and intent. The correspondence between Herbst and Terberger continued and Alfred had given Herbst the green light to get whatever he could. Terberger wrote a "poor me" story: he lost his property in 1945 when the Russians marched into Dresden and his firm was dissolved with no compensation. His only son was killed in Hungary, according to reports of the SS, and his wife died as a result of the war in 1943. When he returned from the USA in 1945, having been a POW (prisoner of war) there, he worked hard on the reconstitution of the firm and charged Mr. Hochmockel with replacement of stock. For the benefit of the firm, he was very successful, mainly with iron and building materials. He himself focused on iron, sheet metal and other metals. He acknowledged this was made easier because of the firm's prior relationships. Now he had to decide whether to become independent or continue to work for the firm. He desperately needed this release. Herbst advised him that the decision was his, and he would consider whatever suggestions Terberger had. In short, after much additional correspondence, Attorney Herbst was able to get Terberger to agree to pay 15,000 RM ($6000). Alfred and Johanna signed the appropriate releases, and despite a currency reform, resulting in renewed negotiations about the price, Herbst was able to receive payment. Transfer of any moneys to the U.S. was not possible, but it was agreed that he would use the money to pay his fees, costs and expenses for this matter and other pending matters, including claims made by Max, Alfred's brother and Carola Loeffler, Lilli's aunt. He wrote Alfred that he was very happy to have created this money, so to speak, "from NOTHING".

As I reviewed all this correspondence, although I did not have it all translated, my guess is that after all this legalistic run-around, they never got a penny except the amounts mentioned below, which represent less than 10% of what they claimed. It appears that the only payments were that actually received were for the following:

1. *Payment for "emigration loss", i.e. the cost to emigrate. They got DM 5332.97 ($2133.00)*

2. *Payment for "fleeing the Reich" tax, i.e. forced payments demanded from Jews who planned to emigrate. This claim was made in 1947, approved in 1953 and paid in July 1959. They got DM 2211.97 ($885.00)*

3. *Payment for loss of professional income. Alfred's claim was harder to assess and trying to substantiate and flesh out this claim swallowed up a lot of correspondence. Ultimately he received DM 4607 ($1843). Lilli first received DM 5000 ($2500), but she later put in a claim following new laws and got another DM 10,000 ($4000). The justification for her claims was that in order to teach she would have had to complete some Fürther requirements that were denied her.*

4. *Payment from the loss of 7 Hornschuchpromenade — DM 20,287 ($8114)*

5) *Payment from Mr. Terberger relating to 129 Konigstrasse — DM15,000 ($6000)*

Therefore, as best I could figure, they received a total of $25,475.

In today's figures, that does not seem like much considering what was lost, and particularly the years of effort that went into obtaining it. I remember coming home once after I had graduated from college, and after my marriage, and seeing them still working on these reparation claims. Since Alfred went to his office every day, all of this had to be done on weekends or in the evening. But in the years after the war, this represented more than the annual income of Lilli and Alfred. When Alfred died in 1970, his records show that he never earned more than $18,000 a year. And I have never believed that the money was their primary motivation — they felt they were owed retribution from the Germans for all they had been through and for all that had been taken from them, and this was their way of pursing their sense of justice.

There is also a significant amount of correspondence claiming reparations for Johanna, Alfred's mother. I did not have this translated and therefore do not know whether she received any reparations, or if so, in what amount.

I have already recounted, in the section describing my other grandmother, Ida Bechman, her experience with receiving reparations, which she handled by herself, with assistance from a friend at the National Jewish Hospital. She received a payment of $499 every month, and it supported her until her death.

Correspondence with Ilse Sadler

One of the most interesting documents we have recounting this period of time is a letter Lilli wrote to Ilse Sadler, dated January 29, 1946, which details, in 3 single-spaced typed pages, what had happened to the family since 1933. It is written on stationery from the Alta Lodge, in Alta, Utah, where she and Alfred had gone skiing. As became clear at the end of the letter, they were snowed in and couldn't get out of the lodge, so she used the time to write. And of course using hotel stationery was something my family always did throughout their lives. I certainly never received a letter on "real" stationery.

Ilse Sadler and Lilli were related by common ancestors four generations back. The Sadler family had emigrated from Germany to Buenos Aires, Argentina. Lilli had apparently received an extensive letter from Ilse outlining what had happened to their family in the years since 1933, when they had last seen each other. Lilli's words, "Since we saw each other in 1933, much has changed" was certainly an understatement.

The best way, I believe, to relate Lilli's summary of these years is to quote at length from the letter Lilli sent to Ilse Sadler, in which she recounted her version of events.

Since we saw each other in 1933, much has changed. Alfred was with his mother in 1935 in U.S.A. and came back with confidence as he said at that time that he was sure he could always take care of his family in Germany. He visited with his brother who is here since 1926 but lives in Puerto Rico as a representative of the General Cigar Company. All the same, Alfred could not decide about his business in Fürth which existed for 5 generations in his family in 1937. Then he sold his business and our house and in October 1937 we all had the American visa. We wanted to travel in December and Christmas Alfred was arrested and was 14 months in jail in Nuremberg. As a result, we did not get a penny from the delivery of the house and the business. But the most important thing was that I could, in spite of all the difficulties, immediately obtain after his release the American visa and he traveled with our 3 year old daughter and our nurse to Paris in March, 1939. I had a number of things to wind up and followed month later and in April, 1939 we all arrived in New York. After spending there 3 months we had enough of this immense city, bought an old Ford and went westward. My mother-in-law, who arrived one year before in New York, and our nurse, together with our daughter, were left in New York. We visited the Ransohoff's when we were in Cincinnati. Martha was not home so that until now I have not made her personal acquaintance, which I regret.

When we arrived in Denver, it was love at first sight and before Alfred had any work, we wired to Antwerp where our furniture was in storage and had it sent to Denver. Everybody thought we were completely crazy — but it was right. A few days later, Alfred had his first job in the warehouse of the largest iron and metal wholesaler in Denver. He was attracted to his old trade, but this time at the other end.

A few days after the start of the war my small family came from New York. In January 1940 our furniture arrived, and we bought a pretty new house (small down payment — the balance was financed by the government) and this we also did not regret, particularly since then the land values increased 3 times and we bought at the lowest moment. Shortly after that the nurse left and my mother-in-law moved in with us. In the fall of 1940 I got a job in a Denver bookstore and as the owner opened his second shop, he made me the manager of the second shop. I was there until January 1942 when he sold the second store.

In the meantime, I tried all the time to make contact with Denver University and was called off and on to assist. In December 1941 I got my first job as instructor in the night school and taught theatre history. In the following spring the head of the German department went for a one-year vacation and I got the job. I would have preferred to teach something else rather than German, but I could not choose. In the meantime, Alfred had enough of his warehouse job and bought, in the spring of 1942 a manufacturer's agency whose owner, an old gentleman, had just died. The firm had good connections but due to the age of the owner had fallen pretty much asleep. Alfred has renewed since then many of the contacts and acquired new ones, and is very pleased. He represents the Continental Steel Corporation for the Rocky Mountain area and an asphalt concern in Chicago and several other firms and he has a lot of pleasure (satisfaction) with that. He is again in his old trade.

In July 1942 my father died in Stockholm (he emigrated there in 1938 and my mother followed him in 1939). We tried hard to have my mother come over but there were no means of transportation until the end of 1944. I had the American visa for her since March 1943. In December 1943 she flew to London and from there she arrived, in April 1944 by plane via Lisbon, Dakar, Natal, Trinidad, Puerto Rico and New York. Since then she is with us in Denver. After several months in which she did not acclimatize herself, she became nervous and before Christmas last year she took a job in a large Denver department store. We were very concerned how this experiment would turn out, since she is 56 years old and has never worked in her life. But she is very thrilled and finds it a big lark and it gives her a feeling of independence.

In summer 1943 the University of Denver was given an Army Specialized Training Program Unit and I became the leader of the German section. For this training the young soldier/students were trained for 9 months for the purpose of conquering and occupying Germany. They were taught language, geography, history, etc. I had 4 German teachers on my staff, all born in Germany. It was a very interesting but demanding job, and also very worthwhile. The students were all very nice — with many I still correspond. Most of them did actually go to Germany and a number of them are still there as occupation army. In March 1944 the program for the army was terminated and I was without a job.

In the meantime, Alfred was able to bring his business to a good level so it was not necessary any more that I earn money and I was able to dedicate myself to another subject. In January 1945 our little baby was born — a second girl and she is now one year old. She is, thank God, also a healthy and active child as Ruth Marion, who is now 9 years old, and is naturally extremely happy with her little sister. Since then I have given up working since the personnel problem is hopeless and I am most of the time without a cleaning woman or household help. Everything is very efficient in a modern American house so that without any help one can be more productive than in the old country. Since 1942 I am very active at the Red Cross Motor Corps and every week I give them an 8-hour day. One year after our arrival in Denver we became members of the Conservative Jewish Community. Because the religious service was not to our liking and within the community we didn't make any friends, we joined the Reform Temple this year. This is not exactly what we want because the service is not Jewish enough, although it means more to us. Alfred and Ruth Marion particularly like the religious school much better. Denver has many Jews — 18-20,000, though there is a deep separation between west and east side, meaning between Orthodox, and Conservative/Reform. Many of the Orthodox are first generation — they hardly speak English — mostly from eastern Europe. We were very amazed and shocked over the definite separation between Jews and non-Jews in the community in America. We did not expect that and we were not used to that in Bavaria. Through the Red Cross and various other community activities we made contacts with a mixed friendship group, but this is more the exception. We have some very good friends here who are also refugees and with many others the contact has more or less been lost. My own and Alfred's engaging activities did not allow us much time in the last years to cultivate social get-togethers.

Denver is a medium sized city of about 400,000 inhabitants. We are about 50 miles from big mountains in the Rockies, 11-12,000 feet. We drive 1 1/2 hours to go skiing and we are in 2 hours in the most beautiful mountainous area like Tegernsee (only the beautiful lake is missing). This is what attracted us so much to Denver when we first arrived and we are still very pleased that we landed there. It is a little far — 2000 miles from the east coast and 1000 miles from the west coast — but changes are not as great. One lives are more observant and less hectic and it is a very wonderful place for children. 360 days of sun and the children are always outside, which cannot be replaced. They are both, thank god, very healthy. My mother's closest relatives are mostly in the U.S.A. My poor grandmother was taken to Theresienstadt in 1944 and to Auschwitz to be gassed. She was 76 and was lame. I will never forgive the Germans for this. My mother's sister, Emma Bierer, with husband and daughter, live in New York. Dora, the daughter, just graduated from Smith College and goes now to Columbia University. The Bierer's younger son, Fritz, is since 1939 in the English army, at this time in Norway. The elder, Walter, who was with them in France, was for one year with the Foreign Legion, then returned to France and shortly after that his wife died. Then he went with his parents to Cuba where all were interned in Tiscornia for 8 months. From there they came to the U.S.A. Walter married a young lady who he met on the ship and since they did not like New York, upon our advice came to Denver and bought a small house not far from us. In October 1944 they had a baby; shortly after that he was drafted and is now in Nuremberg, a translator for Streicher in the war trials. (Julius Streicher, the publisher of Der Stürmer was known to be the most rabid anti-Semite in Germany). In the meantime, his wife had a second baby which he still has not seen. She lives in Denver and we try as best as we can to help as it is a lot to be alone with little children without help.

Ernest Metzger, the brother of my mother, is also in New York. His wife lost a leg in the bombardment of Paris in 1940. Everyone who is here is happy to be here and we can thank our god that we are outside. The reports which are slowly coming from over there are terrible and the worst is that here everything will be forgotten and that nothing will stay with people so that one helps the poor misguided Germans to get on their feet again because fear of the Russians has an overwhelming influence. With growing concern we are watching the developments in Argentina and we hope that the reports we get from there do not represent the truth and I am concerned that this is a ostrich policy. How does all this look from the inside?

We have here a very nice time, have tanned and rested very well. Alta is 30 miles from Salt Lake City and 500 from Denver. I am wondering when and how the car will be dug out and we can go home. I hope to hear from you and thank you again for your long letter. Best regards, also for your husband, for you and yours. Lilli Rahn.

I thought it important to quote this letter in full, because it says, in Lilli's words, what had happened to them in the intervening years. I am so impressed with the sophistication of her use of the English language. I might add that they purchased the home at 1195 Holly Street in Denver for $4500. It was a brand new home, and truly on the outskirts of Denver at that time.

As the city grew eastward, the streets to the east of Colorado Boulevard were alphabetical — two streets for each letter of the alphabet, with the second being a plant. The city had expanded only to Holly Street at that point, and gradually went to the letter Z, and beyond that was what became the suburb of Aurora. I remember this well, because I spent a lot of time playing in the large excavations where houses were to be built, and then in houses as they were being built. Our neighbor, Danny Buckley, and I collected slugs (small pieces of metal shaped like a coin which had been stamped out of metal sheets as houses were being built), and used them in the gum machines at the local drug store on Colfax Avenue. We also played in the empty lots, making small fires in gopher holes to smoke them out, and on rainy days, played a never-ending game of Monopoly on the basement floor.

In another letter to Ilse Sadler, dated April 9, 1946, she talks about her life as a Jew as compared to Argentina and her other activities.

> *Your comments about the situation in Argentina have interested us very much. We hope that your optimistic attitude is the right one. Here we notice not much open or obvious anti-Semitism. It is here in the west a little different than in the east where the Jews live in large numbers. In the schools in general there is no anti-Semitism — there are of course exceptions, but in most of the large schools it is a "numerus clausus". They don't admit it, but it is so. I have, and also Alfred, no difficulties here but the underlying feeling is always there. Otherwise we find the social anti-Semitism here much stronger than in Bavaria. Social life is sharply segregated. It appears to us that the Jews do not choose to leave their self-established ghetto. It could be that they are frightened because of it, or just not caring. Alfred and I, since we are here, have become active Zionists. I consider it very possible and worthwhile that Palestine becomes a Jewish commonwealth and I am convinced only Palestine and no other land is suitable. What I do not understand is that not all countries will help immediately with the burning Jewish question and facilitate immigration. But this has not happened and to make immigration easier has not happened and therefore Palestine is the only one. The Jewish communities are organized the same way as where you are, but it is getting more difficult. The humanitarian aid founded for that purpose is separate from the temples and poorly organized. Much energy and money is, in our opinion, wasted because of this. The religious community limits itself to religious service, religious school and social get-togethers and occasional benefit events. For several years they tried to put together a Jewish seminar, evening courses, which are led by rabbis and members of all the prominent congregations, but this year it already stopped. They could not get together — the water was too deep.*

> *You asked me with what family members are we in touch. Naturally with the Loefflers (you know probably that Heinz L. is divorced) and with Harold and Jean Beckman we are in contact by letter. Martha Ransohoff, who I do not know, -that is all from the Bechmann side. From mother's side, there are many more here. You asked me about*

our daily life — the personnel problem is practically unsolvable. Most people do all the work themselves. At this time I also have a woman twice a week. Everything is set up very practical — a lot of equipment in the home is very good but a lot remains to be done and I have very little free time. One whole day a week I go to the Red Cross Motor Corps for the past 4 years and since last year, an officer. Besides, I am a member of a number of organizations — Hadassah. I was for 2 years president of the local business and professional regional group and I am now a regional board member, and American University Women. All this takes a great deal of my free time — meetings, etc. I would love to write more but it is already late and my day starts early. Love Lilli

The themes of our lives during the early years in the United States are spelled out in Lilli's letters. I am also extremely impressed by her excellent English.

I add here a few words about how I obtained these letters. Over 25 years ago, as a practicing divorce attorney, I received a new client by the name of Jackie Sadler. She had an accent, and as she told me about her husband, Robert, who was in the wool business, something in my mind triggered familiarity with this name. I was not at all involved with my family history, but I did have the Bechmann Family History that my mother had written before I was born and which Evy updated in 1972.. When I came home that evening I looked into that history, and sure enough, Bob and I were related — the common ancestors were five generations back. In fact, the paintings of these common ancestors (husband and wife) hang in my front hall. I asked one of my partners if there was a conflict of interest, and was assured there was not. At one point during our negotiations, Bob submitted, through his attorney, a short list of things he wanted out of the marital home, including "pea soup". I had no idea what this meant, but since the list was short, we agreed. I had been eager to contact Bob, but of course could not do so while I represented his wife. I did not know whether he knew of our relationship or not. Then, at some point, Jackie became dissatisfied with me and went to another attorney. The very next morning I found on my desk a large can of "pea soup". Bob often traveled to The Netherlands in his business and loved the pea soup with sausage and apparently had brought back cases of this soup, located in the family home. He knew all along who I was, and we have since become good friends with him and his second wife. When his mother, Ilse, died, he found the letters, including the ones reproduced above, that my mother had written to his mother, and gave them to me. He also told me he fared much better in the divorce with Jackie's second attorney than he would have done had I continued to represent her. "I was tough", he said.

Lilli's Health and Lilli and Alfred's Deaths

The last eleven years of Lilli's life were marked by bouts of cancer, yet she never lived as if she were ill. She had her first radical mastectomy in 1959; five years later she had a hysterectomy to be followed in 1969 by her second radical mastectomy. In April 1970, on a skiing day at Winter Park, she was standing on the side of a slope waiting for Alfred when an out-of-control young skier plowed into her, crushing her leg. After surgery and a full leg cast she developed unrelenting and unbearable back pain. At first the medical community thought it was related to her fall and perhaps due to some internal injuries she might have incurred. They thought the pain would decrease when her cast was removed. However, when the cast was removed in July 1970 and her pain did not dissipate, we convinced her to come to Boston and be examined at Beth Israel Hospital. She and Alfred came to Boston over Labor Day weekend, 1970, and Max came also. When testing did not show anything, they decided to do exploratory surgery. Immediately following the surgery a team of 5 doctors met us in Evy's office (she was then a social worker at the Beth Israel Hospital) informing us that she had pancreatic cancer which had metastasized and that there was nothing that could be done for her. We sat there stunned, and I remember Alfred saying, "I'm not Guggenheim". He was referring to our family doctor, Albert Guggenheim, who was also a German-Jewish

Alfred and Max, September, 1970

refugee. Dr. Guggenheim's wife had died a few years earlier, and not only did he and Alfred often go skiing together on Wednesdays (doctors' day off) but he also was dating women and eventually remarried. We really didn't think anything about this remark at the time. It was the worst weekend of my life because Matt had told me, that same weekend that he would be leaving the marriage. I didn't know what to deal with first.

Lilli recovered from her surgery in Boston and then she and Alfred returned to Denver where either Evy or I visited every other weekend throughout the fall. Just before Christmas 1970 it was my turn to go and as I was preparing to leave on December 24th, Alfred called me to say that Lilli's kidneys had failed, her condition was deteriorating, and Evy should come also. We flew out on Christmas Eve and she died on the morning of December 27th. She was 59 years old — too young to die. My brother-in-law, Bill, and I accompanied Alfred to the funeral home the next morning where he made arrangements for two plots, side by side. I remember asking him why he was getting two, but he said he wanted to be buried next to her and it was cheaper to purchase the second plot now. It all seemed very consistent and in character for him. Uncle Max and Aunt Maria had already come to Denver and were staying in our house as well. That evening a number of people who had heard about Lilli's death came over, and Alfred warmly welcomed everyone. He made a warm toast to the lives and futures of the young people there, including Evy's friends who were in town visiting their families for the winter holidays. When they had left, we went into the study and he pulled out photographs of Lilli when she was younger and Alfred, Evy and I spent some time looking at these photographs, some of which had been taken by our old family friend, the noted photographer Roman Vishniac. We somehow felt this was appropriate as we all wanted to remember her as she used to look, and not how she looked during the last weeks of her illness. Evy, Bill and I then went downstairs to go to bed. The next morning Evy got up earlier and went upstairs, and I remember hearing her scream. Alfred had taken an overdose of sleeping pills and had died during the night. The funeral was held the next day, and since Lilli's death had been widely publicized in the newspapers, people came expecting to see only one coffin, but there were two.

Why did he do it? It's now 40 years later and I still don't have a satisfactory answer to that question and can only speculate. He truly felt he owed his life to her, and he decided that he couldn't live without her. She had given so much to get us all out of Germany and enabling him to live, and he was forever beholden to her, I think. Although between Labor Day, 1970, when she was diagnosed, and December, we had all talked about things he could do and how he could manage, he made up his mind shortly after she was diagnosed that he would not continue to live after her death. We know that because we have his suicide letter to which he added regularly during these months and in which he described her illness and his thoughts. It is clear that that his suicide was planned for months. He also never wanted to live in a nursing home, as his mother had. In retrospect, the phrase "I'm not Guggenheim" says so much — he couldn't see himself going on or being with another woman. He was 69 years old, but since he was always tanned from skiing or working outdoors in the yard, he looked, and acted, much younger.

They both would have enjoyed so much seeing the way Karen and Rachel grew up and meeting Leah and Adam who were born after their deaths, and learning what fine, competent and caring individuals they have all become. They missed so much of the joys and wonderment of being grandparents and, by their early and untimely deaths, our children missed some very special relationships. They would have loved seeing their great grandchildren, Addison, Gabriel, Emily, Nathaniel, Isaac and Omar. Certainly Lilli, who was born in 1911, could well have lived to see the next generation. I would have loved for them to have gotten to know our children and to meet our second husbands, and to really get to know our extended families.

Lilli and Alfred left a legacy that lives on in all of us; they had a profound influence on who we are as people and we often think of them — their lives, sense of justice, struggles, and their interests. I have so many questions now that I would love to ask them; so many conversations I would love to have. I regret that we were never able to share more of my life with them, yet I am grateful for the foundation they provided and for our families which have grown from their roots.

9
VISITS TO GERMANY

First Visit — 1973

As I was growing up, Germany was not a place I wanted to visit. My parents would not buy German products and this often led to a conflict because German cameras and watches, for example, were of the best quality. My mother refused to ride in a Volkswagen. My parents did, however, make one trip back to Germany in 1966. I think my mother was not keen on going, but my father was eager to see some of the "old places". I have no records of what their reactions were to this trip.

I have been back to Germany six times, which includes a visit to Berlin only, accompanying John who had a conference there. The five other visits were specifically to Fürth and neighboring Erlangen. All of these visits were after my parents' deaths, so I never had the opportunity to discuss my experiences with them.

My first visit was in the spring of 1973. In early 1973 Matt (my former husband) was changing jobs and I left the law firm where I was working. We decided to take several months off to travel in Europe and Israel with our children, Karen and Rachel, who were then ten and six resectively. We were gone for almost four months, and it was truly a memorable experience for all of us. Included in this trip was a visit to Fürth as I wanted to see the house where I was born and the city from which I had come.

So early in the spring of 1973, I wrote to Mr. Wilhelm Hofmockel, who had been the long-time bookkeeper of my

Mr. Hochmockel, Ruth, Karen, Rachel, Spring 1973
Notice discoloration left by mezuzah on right side of doorway.

father's firm. My uncle Max had been back to Fürth and had met with him, and recommended I write to him to tell him we were coming. Mr. Hofmockel, so the story goes, had been hired by Sidney and Alfred as the firm's bookkeeper. He said during his interview that he couldn't work on Saturdays. They thought they were getting a nice Jewish young man, but in fact he was a Seventh Day Adventist. As it turns out, he wasa very helpful to Alfred after the war as he had kept all the business documents so that Alfred had them when he applied for reparations in the late 40's and 50's.

Mr. Hofmockel wrote me back and agreed to meet us at 129 Konigstrasse, the Rahn family home where I was born. I will never forget our greeting. We arrived, and I had Karen (age 10) and Rachel (age 6) in tow. Tears welled into his eyes and his warm greeting, through his tremors due to Parkinson's disease, was overwhelming. Clearly it was extremely moving for him to see me since he remembered me as a baby and was fully aware of what had transpired, not only our exodus, but also my parents' deaths in 1970. He stayed with the firm until my parents left, and even thereafter when it had been taken over by the purchasers. He testified in favor of my father at my father's trial. The memories overwhelmed him.

The Rahn house at 129 Konigstrasse (King Street) is on the main street of Fürth. You can still see the mark left by the mezuzah on the right side of the doorway. The house had been declared to be in a historical district so the façade could not be changed. Mr. Hofmockel showed us all around the house. The house was basically a rooming house for foreign laborers, mostly Yugoslavian and Turkish from the looks of the names on the 20-25 mailboxes on the ground floor. The upper floors had been chopped up into very small rooms, but it was clear from the molding around the ceilings that they had once been larger, gracious rooms. From the rear one could see the sloping grass and fields down to the river. There still was a metal business on the first floor and adjacent to the house. One could see the large door for trucks to pass inside just to the right of the house. For me, going into the home of my birth was the most moving experience of this first trip to Germany and has been, in fact, the most moving experience each time we returned. I wept, as I always do when in that house — of what was and what might have been. How would my life have been different without the advent of the Nazi regime? I am, of course, not the only one to ask that question. But being in that house makes me appreciate so much the enormous change and dislocation Lilli and Alfred went through in uprooting themselves and coming to America. Our house in Denver was so small by comparison — two bedrooms, one bath, a living room and dining room, and a small kitchen that one couldn't eat in. Lilli did put up a retractable shelf that served as an eating area for one or two people, but we always ate in the dining room. We did have a full basement, where there was another bedroom and a play and project room for me and Evy and a toilet surrounded by a curtain. The only sink or running water was in the laundry room. When my grandmother Johanna lived with us, she lived in the basement. 129 Konigstrasse had three floors above the ground floor. When we lived there, the ground floor was the office of the firm, M.S. Farrnbacher. When Lilli married Alfred they moved into the second floor and Johanna, Alfred's mother, moved to the third floor. The maids lived on the top floor.

At the time, during this first visit to Germany when I knew little of the family history, I was a bit puzzled because I had many pictures of me on an outside balcony with a wrought iron fence around it and I could see nothing of this in the Konigstrasse home. I only learned later that when my parents decided to leave in 1937, they "sold" the home and business in preparation for their emigration. Then, after Alfred was imprisoned, buyers wanted to move in, so Lilli and Ruth moved into the home of Ernst and Emma Bierer, located at 26 Konigswasser Strasse, not far away. This home had the balcony with the ornate wrought iron fence and it is here that those many pictures of me were taken. I have a large folder of photos of me during this period, clearly taken so Lilli could show them to Alfred when she visited him in prison. This street was renamed Adolph Hitler Strasse during the war, so all the correspondence I have for this period came to this address. Today it has been renamed Konigswasser Strasse. The house, the former Bierer home, has looked the same from the outside on all my visits to Fürth. It appears to be the home and office of Galenika Dr. Hetterich. The many photos of Ruth as a child, on the balcony, in a hammock, on the potty, or cleaning the walls with the broom, are all taken in this house.

This visit in 1973 to the home of my birth was deeply moving, but not traumatic. We then went to Lilli's family home at 7 Hornschuchpromenade. This is a visit I will never forget. At that time there was still a glass business being operated out of the house as evidenced by the sign in front. I entered into the entrance hallway, with Karen and Rachel at my side. There was a glass partition with secretaries and other office personnel working behind it. To the side was a beautiful, wide marble staircase leading to the upper floors. An older man with a patch over his eye came out to greet us. I explained, in German, that this had once been the home of my grandfather and great-grandfather. I said we did not wish to disturb anything and asked if we might just go up the stairs to look around. He asked me what the name of my grandfather was. When I said the names Louis Bechmann and Hugo Bechmann, I could see his face visibly change, and then he said "You can't come in here". At first I did not understand, and assured him I did not want to intrude, but just wanted to look around. Again he said, "You can't come in here". Suddenly I got it — he knew the names, and in some way was responsible for taking control of this house and business after Hugo left. I grabbed the hands of my two children and we left immediately and drove immediately out of Germany. It was a most unsettling experience. It was 23 years before I returned to Germany.

Correspondence with Mr. Hofmockel

The documentations we have indicate that Alfred had, over the years, kept up his corresondence with Mr. Hofmockel, the Rahn family business bookkeeper. One such letter from Mr. Hofmockel is dated December 21, 1969, which was written, in part, to congratulate Alfred on Evy's wedding. He said he was:

> *...never idle and never bored as in the house and garden there is always work,*
> *summer and winter. To the wedding of your daughter Evelyn allow me to epress my*
> *most heartfelt wishes for happiness and blessings, also from my wife. From your letter*
> *I gather that you have again taken a nice trip to Europe. Again you have seen a lot,*
> *it will remain a pleasant memory. Especially Israel will have been interesting for you.*

Would you prefer to live in Israel? I think the USA is better and calmer, in spite of all the progress in Israel. Do you still remember the metal dealer Fleischmann - he is turning 75 today. I am emclosing a clipping, maybe you are interested. Many thanks for your New Year's wishes which I reciprocate, also in my wife's name. As an old ally I greet you. Yours, W. Hofmockel.

I was moved when I met him in 1973, and also 30+ years later when I read the following correspondence. He had always been loyal to our family, and their histories represented the history of much of the century.

I also acknowledged receipt of his letter to Alfred written on February 12, 1971, which, of course, Alfred never received since he died on December 28,1970. In that letter he expressed that Lilli's illness "has shaken us all up". It was a very moving and warm letter — I'll quote parts of it. The initial heading is to "Esteemed Mr. Rahn", but then in the middle of the letter he says:

Dear Mr. Rahn,

I would like to console you, please do not lose courage. All our lives are in the hand of God. It is no doubt a very heavy hat you have to bear now. Exactly 20 years ago I went through the same thing with my sister. I was very sad when the professor of the clinic who treated her told me at the time — we cannot heal your sister any more, we can only lengthen her life. Please think of your children. It will help you over many hard days. We wish and hope that you may keep your wife longer and that the illness improves. Think about how long your mother had to walk in her path in life alone. I wish you and your wife the best in the present situation and much strength and encourage to get through the difficult days. Many warm greetings also from my family and also for your dear wife, from your compassionate W. Hofmockel.

On March 27, 1971 I wrote to him about the death of my parents:

It is with overwhelming sadness and a heavy heart that I write you about the deaths of my parents, Alfred and Lilli Rahn. After a prolonged illness of cancer with much suffering my mother passed away on December 27, 1970. My father suffered right along with her and died that night from an over dose of sleeping pills. My sister and I now suffer a double loss, and as you may know, we are the only children. My mother's mother, Ida Beckman, is still living in Denver, and my sister and I both live just outside Boston. I know how happy daddy was to see you when they last went to Germany and he spoke often of you. They received your Christmas card this past year and this always meant so much to them.

I asked him to send me any documents concerning the firm and the business; as well as any pictures of records of the business and offered to pay for any expenses. On June 6, 1971 Mr.

Hockmockel wrote back to me, expressing his deep condolences. "The decision of your father to depart from life together with his wife, your mother, is tragic. I still cannot grasp it". He recalled meeting Ida and asked questions about our lives. He said he still had at hand my wedding announcement of 12/23/57. He also sent, along with this letter, some business documents and letters as well as photos. He said "I still have some pictures of your parents, yourself and your sister, as mementos. When you meet again with your uncle Max, please convey to him my heartfelt sympathy for the death of your parents and also my best regards. Should you come to Germany some day I would be glad to meet you personally."

In one of these letters he enclosed his professional card, which indicated that he was the authorized agent for the firm of Otto Schulte-Wissermann Kom.-Gee., and in smaller print, "formerly M.S. Farrnbacher — Gegr. Um 1800. Eisen-Bleche-Metalle" (translated means Established around 1800, Iron-Sheetmetal-Metal).

Second Visit — Ruth and Evy, Spring 1996
129 Konigstrasse Today

My second visit was in the spring of 1996, when Evy and I went together. I described in the Introduction to this memoir how John and I were planning to live in Lausanne, Switzerland for three months, and Karen suggested that Evy come over and that the two of us visit Fürth together which we did. We had planned to visit the sites we knew about — the Rahn house on Konigstrasse where I was born, the mansion on Hornschuchpromenade, where Lilli grew up, the hospital where I was born, and a few other places and addresses that we knew, and then we were going to spend some time in Switzerland before driving back to Lausanne. However, after meeting with Gisela Blume, whom I described in the Introduction, we ended up spending many more days in Fürth, visiting both the old and new cemeteries, the Nuremberg and Fürth archives, and various other sites in the area. We then went to the Dachau concentration camp, and Rottach and Tegernsee before driving directly back to Lausanne so Evy could catch her plane home again.

By the spring of 1996, 23 years after my only previous trip to Germany, the Konigstrasse house had been turned into a vocational school for adults, mostly foreign immigrants wishing to learn computer skills, as well as business and language skills so they could get jobs in Germany. It is now called PI, which stands for Private Institute. The complete name is Privatinstitut für KFM/Fort und Weiterbilding. (loosely translated it means Private Institute for Continuing and Advanced Training). It is an adult education school for business professional education and computer skills including tutoring, preparation for exams, homework help, language and computer training. The house had been split into many classrooms and was really unrecognizable as having been a private home. There were typewriters and computers in all the classrooms along with a kitchen and lounge area for the students. The ceilings had been lowered and plastered so all the old moldings were gone. The floors have been covered with linoleum so any internal charm was lost. Classes were in session and it appeared to be a busy place. When we looked out back of the house from the third floor, we could see the extension of the metal works premises that was my father's and grandfather's business. The house master/custodian showed us around

Helen Lorz and Ruth in doorway of   *Ruth in doorway of 129 Konigstrasse, 1996*
129 Konigstrasse, 1937   *59 years later*

with great pride and confirmed a distant memory of mine, that there was a park behind the house leading down to a river. We could now see the river only in the distance and he explained that the river had been rerouted. Formerly there was a park, and with the river below, it was quite a beautiful place to live. The Konigstrasse house has remained this way until today. Given how much the Opportunity School in Denver meant to Lilli and Alfred, I think they would be pleased to know that their former home is exactly this kind of school today — one which helps new immigrants and gives them skills so they can integrate into the society.

Adjacent to the house is a large doorway through which trucks can pass to the metal warehouse, which continues to be operated as such today. It looks like it hasn't changed since my father's time. The people who ran the metal business rented from the owner of the house and had been there for 20 years. A couple of men were there working, and they let Evy and me walk around and take pictures, much to their amusement and curiosity as to why two women from the United States wanted to walk around a dirty metal business warehouse.. They told us the building was now owned by the Saxe family, who also owned the house next door. They also owned the Scherer furniture store in town. We decided to see if we could locate a member of that family, but finding no one at home, we went to the furniture store. Mrs. Saxe-Scherer was there and gave us her time. Her father bought 129 Konigstrasse around 1958 and converted it into the rooming house I had seen in 1973. She explained that it was not profitable, since many tenants didn't pay, so after her father's death in 1980, when she inherited the building, she leased the building to the school. She remembered in some of her father's papers the name Farrnbacher, so it was not unfamiliar to her.

Going into this house, no matter how it looks today, is always the most moving experience for me. Each time I have gone there, I just wept. I had no personal memories of the house, since we had to move out of this house in 1937 when my father was in prison when I was not quite a year old. I spent the first year of my life here, and this is the house where I would have grown up but for Hitler. What is most interesting, is that after all this time, you can still see, to the right of the front entrance door, the small nail holes and the darker shadow of where the mezuzah had been attached. In fact, since Jews were spread out throughout Fürth rather than concentrated in one particular area, one can see the outlines and marks of where mezuzahs had been attached on many homes in the city.

Hornschuchpromenade Today

Lilli's magnificent former home on Hornschuchpromenade was, by 1996, no longer the offices of a glass company, but had become the Regional Headquarters of Quelle, one of the largest mail-order houses in Europe. During this visit, in contrast to my experience in 1973, everyone was most cordial and invited us to look around as we wished. We were able to roam throughout the house and see and photograph what we wanted. The house had been broken up into many rooms which served as offices. However, from room to room we could see the old moldings with very unusual carvings in the corners and on the ceilings. We could tell where chandeliers had once hung. One could certainly get the feeling of the elegance of this mansion. Entering the home is a large marble entranceway that goes up about 5 steps to a beautiful leaded glass door. In the entrance hall there are recessed niches where some sculpture or flowers must have been placed. The floor is a beautiful mosaic tile. There is a wide marble staircase leading to the second

Lilli's Home   *Ruth in Front Foyer*

floor, with a beautiful wrought-iron banister. A narrow back stairway serviced the maids. The rear side of the house looks out over what is today a parking lot, but from the wall around it and several large old trees in the parking lot, it appears that this was once a lovely garden. In my subsequent visits to Fürth, I saw that this home has now been converted into a large office building for lawyers, insurance companies and the like.

Bierer Home

This change in the attitude of Germans by 1996 was most evident as Evy, Gisela and I visited Meier Bechmann's former home next door at 8 Hornschuchpromenade. Meier was my great grandfather Louis' brother. This mansion had been divided into condominiums. It appeared there were 5-6 larger condominiums and about 15 smaller apartments. We only got to see the entranceway of this building, which also retained the original cherub-like frescos on the walls and mosaic flooring. While we were standing in the foyer, a young man was coming home and Gisela explained to him that we were the grandnieces of the former owners. He was quite cordial and open about what a wonderful place this was to live; how centrally located it was (it is right across the street from a very lovely parkway) and what a beautiful view he had from his top floor condominium. He explained there were five stories to the house, and how he benefited from the excellent taste of the Jews who built these beautiful homes and who no longer lived there. It was not said with hostility, anger or guilt — he was very matter-of-fact and friendly. He was a man who I think was not yet 40, so he probably never met a Jew since there were virtually none in Fürth in 1996.

During this visit to Fürth in 1996, Evy and I also walked to 24 and 26 Konigswarter Strasse, which during the war was called Adolph Hitler Strasse. Number 24 was the home of Walter Bierer's grandparents; Number 26 was the home of his parents, Emma and Ernest Bierer. Emma, my grandmother Ida's sister, married Ernst Bierer and Walter was her oldest son. This was the home where Lilli and Ruth stayed for fourteen months while Alfred was in prison. We have several albums of photographs of me before I was 2 1/2 because Lilli was able to take photos each time she visited Alfred in prison. A number of these photos show me on a small balcony with a wrought iron railing. I am often in the hammock or sitting on the potty. When I first went to Germany I looked for that small porch at my birth home at 129 Konigstrasse, and couldn't find it. On this trip I had brought some of those photos with me, and immediately recognized the porch grillwork in the Konigswarter Strasse home. It appears now to be the offices of a physician — the sign in front read "Galenika Dr. Hetterrich".

Gisela Blume cleaning James Rahn's gravestone

Cemeteries

Evy and I had not even planned to go to the cemeteries during this trip, but since Gisela seemed so keen on doing so, we agreed. We were so glad that she encouraged and guided us — it is certainly something we would have missed but for her enthusiasm.

We first visited the Old Jewish Cemetery in Fürth which was used for over 300 years. The first burial took place in 1607; the last in April 1936. During this period of over 300 years, there were approximately 20,000 burials. Today, approximately 6,300 tombstones still exist; the oldest legible stone dates from 1654. The tombstones of this old Jewish cemetery reflect the history of the important Jewish community of Fürth. The cemetery emanates an atmosphere of serenity and calm which is a hallmark of Jewish cemeteries and may not be disrupted by busy care for the graves. Gisela Blume took it upon herself as a long-term project to not only identify the gavestones, reconstruct the ones that were desecrated during the war and personally remove the moss from them with her own wire brush, but also to make a map of the cemetery for visitors seeking their ancestors. She did this for over 6000 graves. In 2008, she published a 400 page book entitled *The Old Jewish Cemetery in Fürth, 1607-2007*. It begins with introductory essays on the history of the cemetery, on the nature of Jewish burials, on the dead person-brotherhood (Chewra Kadischa) as well as on the Jewish calendar. In this section, a whole set of up to now publicly unknown plans are presented in pictorial respresentations and photo drawings for the first time. The second part of the book includes approximately 250 tombstones from the 17th to the 20th century with transcriptions and translations of the Hebrew inscriptions as well as biographical statements for the deceased. Her book has not yet been translated into English.

Originally a wooden wall surrounded the cemetery but this was replaced in 1653 with a brick and cement wall. The growing community in Fürth established this cemetery even before building the synagogue. The cemetery needed frequent extensions, because, unlike Christian cemeteries, a Jewish cemetery may not be used again after a certain period. According to the beliefs of orthodox Jews, the dead are supposed to rest in their graves until the coming of the Messiah when they will be resurrected. This is why a cemetery is called a "Good Place", or the "House of Life". The tombstones are huddled closely together. Most of them are facing East towards Jerusalem. The cemetery was defiled and largely destroyed by the Nazis. who obliterated and overturned many gravestones.

Caroline Rahn's Gravestone   *James Rahn's Gravestone*   *Sydney Rahn's Gravestone*

The Old Cemetery is completely walled in with an iron gate which is kept locked. Gisela had a key, which she said was available to Jews at the town hall. If non-Jews want to visit, they have to leave their passport and would not get it back until they returned the key. Gisela was a wealth of information as we walked into and through the old cemetery. To the right when we walked into the cemetery there is a grassy field now, but previously the Orthodox had a house there where they prepared the bodies for burial. As we walked past the various gravesites and tombstones, Gisela would see a name and immediately go into a long story about who this family was, what their history was, and what they had contributed to the Jewish community in Fürth. She has an astounding wealth of knowledge and we felt that these people had truly come back to life. Her vivid knowledge about family history and what went on, who was married to whom, and who did what for whom, made the people who were lying under those graves come alive.

As we walked down a path to the left, on the right hand side were gravestones — some standing and some toppled over, and on the left hand side there was a low wall with gravestones that were erect in perfect alignment. Gisela told us that the area between the low wall and the high outer wall of the cemetery was flooded by the Nazis and made into a pond which they used for firefighting, because water in that part of the city was in short supply and they could use this water to fight any fires occurring in the houses on the other side of the street. Later, the gravestones which had been flooded were resurrected by Gisela and put into very straight lines.

With Gisela's guidance we found gravestones of many family members and took photographs. In the family history my mother had written in 1935, which we had with us, she included photos of many gravestones. It was very moving when we actually found these gravestones, and Gisela pulled out her trusty wire brush and cleaned them off. The most meaningful grave we found was that of Caroline Farrnbacher Rahn, our paternal great grandmother. She was the daughter of Moses Farrnbacher, whose large portrait I have hanging in our hall. She married James Kahn and they moved to England, where he changed his name to Rahn. He died there when Sydney, was a baby and when Caroline was pregnant with her second son, James. After James was born, she moved back to Fürth and raised her two sons there. Sydney was our grandfather and his brother James, became a physician who treated his nephew and Alfred's brother, James, who was also named after his deceased grandfather. Both are buried in the old cemetery, having died on the same day.

Gisela told us some interesting vignettes about the cemetery. Near the entrance to the cemetery there was a place which had been cemented over, and you could tell it had been a low doorway. She told us that Orthodox Jews do not come into graveyards very often, and they would stand there, right outside the cemetery near the graves of their loved ones to say prayers. If they went into the cemetery, they could not go back to school or work that day, nor could they go into the synagogue. Another interesting story about the cemetery is that it slopes down from the entrance to a small river that is at the base of the slope. Wives who died in childbirth were buried at the bottom of the slope. According to Jewish tradition, after a woman gives birth she needs to go to the Mikveh. Because these women died before there was an opportunity to give them the ritual bath, they were buried there so they could be given their mikveh below ground.

Later we went to the New Jewish Cemetery, where we also found many of the graves of our ancestors. It is here, on a large wall inside the main building of the cemetery, that the names of those who were murdered in the Holocaust, including our uncle James Rahn, are inscribed.

Hospital

Evy and I also went to the Jewish Hospital where I was born. The Jewish Hospital, one of the oldest institutions in Fürth, was in bad disrepair and no longer serves as a hospital. It is now an apartment building, occupied primarily by Eastern European Jews and many from Russia who recently emigrated to Germany after the Berlin Wall came down. Mezuzahs could be seen on many of the doorways. The building itself was rather depressing with plaster falling off, electrical cords hanging, etc. We were assured, however, that repairs were planned and would occur shortly, and we learned thereafter that this was done.

Nuremberg and Fürth Archives

Gisela Blume also arranged for us to go to the State Archives in Fürth and where we were introduced to Dr. Helmut Lurfter who spent two hours with us going through all the Bechmann and Rahn documents they had. There are several Bechmanns and Rahns who are Protestant and Catholic and not part of our families. Religion is noted in all the documents. I saw, for the first time, my birth certificate, verifying that I was born in the Jewish Hospital in Fürth on June 15, 1936 at 2:00 p.m. I had never seen my birth certificate before and I have always used my U.S. Naturalization papers for identification purposes.

Gisela also arranged for us to go into the archives in Nuremberg, where official records, including criminal records, are kept. We had to sign many documents to obtain entry, including proof that our parents had been dead over 10 years. It was here that we found many of the documents described elsewhere in this memoir, including the record of Alfred's trial, the correspondence to obtain passports, and the enormous amount of correspondence by the German government to verify that, before our emigration, all taxes had been paid. Earlier documents used the regular names, but by 1936, the names "Israel" and "Sara" are inserted in every document, making it clear we were Jewish and not Aryan. Much of this record is discussed in the section of this memoir entitled Getting Out.

Alfred's School

Among the many interesting experiences Evy and I had during this May 1966 trip occurred on our last day in Fürth. It was a rainy day, yet we wanted to return to the Konigstrasse home, and in walking up the street we passed the Heinrich Schliemann School named after the man who discovered the city of Troy. Since it was on the same side of the street as our father's home and near to it, (it is at 105 Konigstrasse and the Rahn home was at 129 Konigstrasse) we thought this could have

Heinrich Schliemann School — Alfred's School

been his school. So, closing our umbrellas, we entered the school and went upstairs to the office where two women were working. We asked if they kept any records of students long ago. She asked for the names, and we gave her Alfred and Max Rahn, and although we didn't know the years they might have attended, we gave her their dates of birth. The woman reached behind her and pulled out a large book. We found entries for both our uncle Max and our father. This woman could not have been nicer to two bedraggled Americans who just walked in. We asked why these books of so long ago were so easily accessible to her, rather than in some storehouse. She explained that on June 22 they would be celebrating the school's one-hundredth anniversary and they were in the process of putting together lists of names of graduates who would be interested in this event. We walked through the halls of the school, thinking about the little boy who would now be in his 90's, taking his schoolbag and walking to and from school without having to cross any busy streets.

Following our time in Fürth, Evy and I drove south and visited the first concentration camp at Dachau, near Munich. There were many busloads of students there also, as the Holocaust is a required subject in German schools and all students must visit a concentration camp. A visit to any concentration camp is just unbelievable, literally. How could people do what they did to other people? Operation of these camps involved so many Germans so it was not just party members or the military that were intimately involved in the Final Solution. The sense of fear that kept everyone in line, both those in charge and the prisoners, must have been unbelievable. Alfred was in prison on Kristallnacht (November 9, 1938) and this clearly saved him from being deported to Dachau.

Dachau Crematorium

We ended our visit to Germany by going to Rottach, where Lilli summered with her family. A description of this magnificent spot is in the section of this memoir about Lilli.

Evy and Joe's Visit — July, 1997

In July 1997, Evy and Joe went to Fürth for a special memorial service, which Evy describes as follows:

In July 1996 when Ruthie and I went to Germany, Gisela Blume provided us with a window into our family's past that we would not have had without her insight and guidance. Having devoted herself to finding out about the Jews from Fürth who perished in the Shoah, Gisela's dream was to hold a memorial service in Fürth to honor them. This dream became a reality on July 29, 1997 and Joe and I were there.

Approximately 60 people came to this event. Thirty were "Fürthers" - people who had lived in Fürth and left as a result of the Nazis. The rest were descendents of "Fürthers" - like me. All stayed at the Park Hotel which is in the center of town and was the pre-eminent hotel before the war. With everyone staying at the same hotel there was an opportunity to talk and get to know each other. In many cases, our common language was German as people came from all over the world.

The weekend had three planned events.

Friday night the town and mayor hosted a dinner in a nearby hotel. The large unscreened windows on the second floor were open to the street so that we could enjoy the cool evening air. There was a cocktail hour, dinner, and speeches. Before dinner I met two people. Gisela introduced me to one woman, about Ruthie's age, who spoke with a British accent. Gisela said, "Talk to her — her story is like your sister's." So we talked and I learned that when she was about 3 she went to England but, her story wasn't at all like Ruthie's because when I asked her about her parents she asked, "Parents? I never saw my parents again." In fact, she had been part of the kinder-transport and had only recently learned of her German/Jewish roots. Her trip to Fürth for this event was her journey to reconnect with her past. The second was a young man wearing jeans and a brown t-shirt that said "BROWN" on it. Hesitantly I approached him, not even sure he spoke English. I asked about his shirt and he told me that he had just graduated from Brown University. When I told him my son, Adam Davis, had also just graduated from Brown he said that he had had many classes with Adam. This young man was at the memorial with his grandfather who had emigrated from Fürth. To me it felt like a small world since he, too, would have been part of Adam's Fürth community had both their grandfathers been able to continue their lives in Germany.

One of the attendees, a cantor from Israel, bellowed out the Shabbat songs before, during and after the meal. It was a moving experience to hear them sung in Germany and to realize the people passing on the streets below could hear them as well. A very different experience that what these Fürthers had felt in this same city 52 years earlier. Frank Harris was among the speakers. Frank has organized the Fürth-Nuremberg reunions in New York for the past 35 years. He is committed to continuing the legacy of the Fürth/Nuremberg community. Yet this was the first, and he said the only, visit he would make to his homeland and birth city. He had no interest in returning to German soil and only came this time to honor those who died at the hands of the Nazis.

During dinner I learned that one of the Fürthers was from Stockholm. Since our grandparents, Lilli's parents, had lived there during the war years, I thought she might have known them. In my best German, since that was our common language, I asked her if she knew them, "No," she responded, "the only Bechmann I ever knew was Lilli." Her eyes widened, her smile broadened, her face burst with pleasure when I told her that I was Lilli's daughter. She had been a schoolmate of Lilli's and knew her well as a young girl. She had read in the Aufbau, a German-Jewish newspaper to which Lilli and Alfred also subscribed, that Lilli had died at a young age and she was eager to hear more about their lives in America, about Ruthie and about me. For me, it was a very moving moment because we did not grow up in a community where we heard anything about our parents' childhoods.

The following day there was a memorial service at the New Jewish Cemetery. They unveiled a wall with the names of all the deceased, including our uncle, James Rahn. It was a solemn occasion, covered by the German press. Again, I was touched by the press, wearing yarmulkas and showing consideration for this awesome service in a country that had so violated its Jewish citizens only a generation before. From that service we have a book entitled, Zum Gedenken an die Von Den Nazis Ermodeten Fürther Juden 1933-1945 — To Remember the Fürther Jews who died under the Nazis, 1933-1945.

That evening there was one last event in a large community hall, again with speeches and a slide show honoring the lives of some of the deceased. One of the people highlighted was James Rahn, Alfred and Max's older brother. Neither Ruthie nor I knew about James when we were growing up — he was murdered in Germany in 1942 — and I felt that Joe's and my presence at these memorial events put to rest the secrecy and sadness of his death. It was at the community hall event that Joe and I met Professor Dr. H. Kugler and his graduate student, Markus Paul. Markus had contacted me earlier in the year — he was a student at Erlangen and had learned that the Jews' degrees had been revoked. He and Prof. Kugler were, at that time, trying to get the university to reinstate their degrees. Although this never happened, their department did establish the Lilli Bechmann-Rahn prize for outstanding scholarship in a dissertation and Ruthie went the following year when the first prize was awarded.

Attending the Memorial Service and its accompanying events brought closure and peace to a period of my life that was shrouded in secrecy and confusion. Through the work and efforts of Gisela Blume and through our efforts to better understand our family, we have been able to reconnect to the home of our parents and grandparents, learn about their past, and say good-bye to those we never had an opportunity to meet.

Erlangen Award

My next visit to Germany was three years later, in 1999, for a very special and unique occasion. I had retired from my law firm, Hemenway & Barnes, on the last day of 1998. Although I had been thinking of retirement for some years, the precipitating event was that John received a Fulbright Fellowship to teach in Lisbon, Portugal for 6 months in the spring of 1999. Although it was perhaps a couple of years earlier than I had planned to retire, a number of factors came together and I decided this was the right time so we could partake of this marvelous opportunity. On January 10, 1999, ten days after I left my law practice of over 30 years, we arrived in Lisbon and settled into an apartment there.

On February 3, 1999 John and I flew from Lisbon to Frankfurt, Germany and then took the train to Fürth. Karen joined us, having flown in from Boston. The purpose of our trip was to attend an award ceremony on February 5, 1999 at the Friedrich-Alexander University of Erlangen, which is very close to Fürth.

Again I want to give you some background. My mother studied at Freiberg (with Heidegger), Berlin, and Vienna, and received her Doctor of Philosophy (Ph.D.) from the University of Erlangen in 1934. One of the first of many anti-Semitic laws promulgated by the Nazi regime was the withdrawal of Jewish academic doctoral degrees. By October 15, 1935 this decree applied to all colleges and universities. At the University of Erlangen faculty meeting of December 6, 1935, the doctoral registry was amended to reflect this law. As a result, 163 doctoral degrees awarded by the University of Erlangen were revoked (this included law, medicine, political science) and 23 from the Arts Faculty, which included, among other areas, Government, Economics, Theology, Literature, Mathematics, Chemistry and Philosophy, the latter being the degree of my mother. Fifty years later, particularly in the 1980's and 1990's, Germany was taking a number of steps to assuage their guilt of what occurred during the Holocaust. Towns were inviting Jews back to visit, with all expenses paid. In fact, Evy and I were also invited by the Mayor of Fürth and went on such a trip to Fürth in the summer of 1999. Part of this effort of reconciliation and recompense was to reinstate doctoral degrees that had been revoked. The University of Erlangen, having been a center of the Nazi party with a particularly anti-Semitic student organization call the Brown Shirts, wanted to participate in these efforts but doing this was not without controversy within the university.

About a year before this trip, our friend Gisela Blume called Evy and me to let us know she had received a call from a graduate student, Markus Paul, at the University of Erlangen, informing her that the university was planning a ceremony to reinstate these degrees, and wondered if she knew Lilli Bechmann Rahn. Gisela, who "knows" all the dead Jews from Fürth, responded that of course she knew her, and really knew her (living) daughters well. We were informed that my mother's thesis had been selected as the best dissertation, and the university planned to establish a named prize in her honor.

The Arts Faculty of the University had established a committee which read all of the doctoral dissertations of the 23 whose degrees in their departments had been revoked. In an eight-page report, entitled, *Report on the Question of a Doctoral Prize "Lilli Rahn-Bechmann" of the Arts Faculty of the Friedrich-Alexander-University Erlangen-Nuremberg* the chairman of the committee discussed why they selected my mother's as the best dissertation stating "the graduation of Lilli Rahn-Bechmann was foregrounded for its suitability to the planned doctoral prize, based on the <u>quality of the dissertation</u> and the <u>dignity (worthiness) of the person</u>, (underlining in original). The first part of the report discussed the dissertation and referred to Professor Benno von Wiese who "was the stimulus and advisor of her dissertation". The University had established a personal chair for von Wiese stating, "He advises his doctoral students exceptionally well, so that the dissertations that emerge under his guidance are of the highest order." He gave Lilli's doctoral exam the grade "A", the highest grade possible. The discussion of her thesis ends with this Summary: "Lilli Rahn-Bechmann's dissertation belongs in the modern research context of an examination of sentimentality that begins to discover the emancipatory potential of art and the artist, and, at the same time, takes an important part in its exploration".

The second part of this Report by the Arts Faculty of the University of Erlangen begins with a biographical sketch and situates Lilli and the awarding of this prize to her into a historical, academic and political context which I find interesting. Although somewhat long, I have reproduced it here.

> The biography of the author attached to the printed dissertation and identical with the one in the graduation file is, in light of the political tension in the university and society of the time, unremarkable. Born in Fürth in 1911 as the only child of the businessman Hugo Bechmann, who lived in Berlin after 1930, and thereby of Bavarian nationality, she began to study German studies, History, and Art History as well as Philosophy in Freiburg in April 1930 after her Abitur (exam taken before finishing school and continuing to university), continued her studies in Berlin and Vienna, and finally, on October 25, 1932, registered at Erlangen University in her sixth semester with German Studies as her primary field. As far as can be discovered "Israelite" was listed on her registration as her religious community, not, however, in the doctoral application, which was, by the way, filled out according to regulations. The graduation regulations in effect asked, in paragraph 2, for proof of citizenship, not, however, for religious information; Fürthermore, university study of at least 6 semesters, of which at least 2 must have been spent at the University of Erlangen, had to be substantiated. In her third semester at Erlangen and her ninth semester in general, on February 17, 1934, Lilli Rahn-Bechmann, just 23 years old, passed the oral examinations with style and élan. In the same year she published

her dissertation. Of the 18 professors that particularly approved permission for the oral exams, 8 wanted a print copy of the treatise — beside B. von Wiese and F. Maurer the classical scholar and dean A. Klotz, the philosopher H. Leser, and the historian B. Schmeidler, among others. However seamless and sheltered this academic biography might seem — and to it is added the private happiness of her marriage to Alfred Rahn in Fürth on July 3, 1933 — this impression is false and misleading. Lilli Rahn-Bechmann begins a genealogical representation of the Bechmann family from 1935 with the following comment, among others: *In a time in which so many Jewish families are getting scattered over all parts of the civilized world, family-history and heritage gains a higher meaning as a unifying force.* Aside from being characterizable as a highly interesting variation of memorial-cultural activity, the sparse preliminary remark certainly captures a reflection of the contemporary political perception that, at the same time, had significance both on the level of the university and on that of the subject. This will be explicated below with a few paradigms from the list of university teachers who are mentioned, some with thanks, in the printed biography. For if one looks through this list it soon becomes clear that it literally represents the highly tense political mixture in the disciplines' history during the early thirties.

During studies in Berlin, attendance at the lectures of that scholar who was known nationally and internationally as "the first [foremost] German studies scholar in Germany" — Julius Petersen — was an unavoidable obligation; at the same time, however, his name and his work *are inseparably tied to that part of the subject's history which, as traditionally national-pedagogically oriented German studies, willingly were of service to national socialism.* Opposed to him was that other lecturer teaching at the same university — the Jew Max Herrmann — to whom the founding of the Institute of Theater Studies in 1923 in Berlin goes back, who protested against the "Explanation against the Un-German Spirit" circulated by the national-socialistically infiltrated German Students' Assembly in a letter to the Reich and Prussian Minister for Science, Art, and Education on May 1, 1933 and was forcibly retired (and in 1942, deported to the concentration camp Theresienstadt with his wife, on November 16 died at the age of 77, while his wife, in 1944, died in the gas chambers of Auschwitz).

When Lilli Bechmann continues her studies in Vienna and attends the lectures of Josef Nadler she comes into contact with a line of literary history that is shaped by "central themes" such as the following: *All European peoples have, as long as they were healthy and independent, considered living with Jews unwelcome and dangerous. All the young, ambitious Western European states of the Middle Ages eradicated the Jews among them down to the roots.*

And in Erlangen? Lilli Bechman stays true not only to the subjects of her primary concentration, but also to philosophy, which she began to study under Heidegger in Freiburg — a notorious "case" in his specialty. Herrigel, her local "teacher", reports about the course of a lecture trip to Holland in November 1934, during which he spoke out for the anti-Jewish policies of the NS regime — claiming a specifically German role, for example as follows: *Certainly — the Dutch, too, have difficult time understanding us. German life and fate has always been too unique to be put in simple terms. And then, especially in Holland, they have very scanty concepts about post-war Germany. Thus, for example, about the issue of the Jews ... For over an hour I tried to explain to him [the president of the Leiden Student Assembly, an extraordinarily wise student from an old Dutch family, who is extremely open-minded even towards strangers) that we in Germany truly have no other choice, that it was simply an act of self-defense to radically turn off the Jewish influence on politics, economics, the press, science, art, etc. if we were to keep Jewish spirit [intellect] from entirely growing over us.* Directly opposed to him was another lecturer of Lilli Bechmann's, one of the few university teachers who had to pay for their critical convictions, the historian for middle and modern history, Bernhard Schmeidler. The official gazette of the city of Erlangen from March 29, 1946 reports in its column "From the University:" *In the year 1946, the professor for middle and modern history, Dr. Bernhard Schmeidler, was let go with an extremely reduced pension because of disapproving statements about the 'Führer'... The university saw as its duty of honor to reemploy Professor Schmeidler in his office as professor.* However, Schmeidler was forced to ask to be relieved of the resumption of his duties because of health issues.

Summary: In light of the barbarity that has here been hinted at with a few examples, it is amazing that Jewish Lilli Rahn-Bechmann in 1934 still strove for graduation in the language and literature of the persecutors of her religious community and her world, particularly in view of the cultural assimilation of the Jews in Germany since the Enlightenment. Ruth Budd characterizes her parents as *quite assimilated Jews and well educated.*

When, at the end of 1935, Lilli and Alfred Rahn began to consider emigration because of the growing threat and went to the United States to find out the possibilities thereof, they returned early so that their first child (Ruth, born June 15, 1936) would be born in Germany — assuming that *the Nazi regime could not last — after all, Germany was the country of Goethe and Beethoven.* After a fourteen month prison term for Alfred Rahn because of a supposed currency offense (lasting until February 1939), after sensational reports of the U.S. Attorney General in the New York Times: *the members of the Jewish race in Germany are under the severest kind of persecution,* and the deportation of a grandmother of Lilli Rahn to Theresienstadt (where she died), the time was ripe for flight via Paris to the United States (April 1939). Lilli Rahn-Bechmann, who occasionally taught German at the University of Denver, died in 1970.

Recommendation: The Arts Faculty II would be well advised if it would alternate with the Arts Faculty I in awarding the "Lilli Rahn-Bechmann Prize" for the best doctoral work."

[signed] Prof. Dr. Theodor Verweyen

Despite the factual error that Lilli joined Alfred on his trip to the United States in 1935, and returned to Germany so that I could be born there, I thought this description of the circumstances and milieu at the time Lilli was completing her doctoral work was very illuminating. It really is amazing that she continued her studies in this atmosphere.

As a result of this Report and of the ensuing correspondence, I received a letter dated November 3, 1998 from the Dean of the Humanities Faculty I (they had divided the Humanities Faculty into two administrative departments) which I would like to quote here:

The two humanities faculties of the Friedrich-Alexander-University have unanimously decided to establish a doctoral prize. And they have also unanimously decided that this prize is to be named after your mother, Lilli Bechmann-Rahn. This choice of names is to be a reminder of the act of injustice that occurred during the National Socialist time, when the humanities faculty revoked the doctoral titles of its Jewish doctors, including Lilli-Bechmann-Rahn. The establishment of the Lilli-Bechmann-Rahn Prize is a symbolic act against that historic injustice, which comes too late and, regrettably, is of no use to those directly affected. But it is to encompass a plea for forgiveness, and the promise that, within the faculty, even now everything will be done to prevent such ideological and scientific disasters in the future.

In the humanities faculty, the titles of at least 23 doctors were revoked for ideological reasons during the Nazi Era. (At the university as a whole, there were far more than a hundred revoked). The name Lilli-Bechmann-Rahn stands in for all others. We chose the name for several reasons: Because your mother was the youngest and last of those to receive the doctoral degree in 1934, because she was a resident of Fürth and, thus, of our home, and, not lastly, because her dissertation is still recognized as a good scientific effort and is still cited in the field.

The prize is to be conferred for the first time at the next doctoral graduation ceremony, which is expected to be at the beginning of February. Once the exact dates are set, I will inform you of them, and would like to already sincerely invite you to participate.

For now, however, I would like to do the obvious and ask you for your consent in the choice of names.

With best wishes,
Professor Dr. H. Kugler

Of course I agreed to the choice of name, and looked forward to attending the ceremony in February 1999, particularly since we were already planning to be living for six months in Portugal in the spring of 1999.

What is remarkable to me is that the Professors and their assistants did an enormous amount of research, not only of my mother, but also of all the others who had their doctorate degrees revoked. It was clearly a project that involved many people at all levels of the university and one which was extremely important to them.

The graduation ceremony was scheduled for 5:00 p.m. on February 5, 1999, in the main administration building of the University, which was a former Imperial Palace. The University moved from another site in 1743 and thus recently celebrated its 250th anniversary at this site, though it was founded much earlier. John and Karen and I were seated in the front row, with my assigned seat right next to the Rector of the University. I was extremely impressed and pleased that he was there because I had heard there was controversy voiced by some over creating this award and dredging up the past, but his presence made it clear that this was supported by the University as a whole. And then, amazingly, the ceremony began with two young people singing Yiddish songs, accompanying themselves with a guitar and cello. Then, after some other greetings, the doctoral degrees were awarded to 39 candidates. After this part of the program, the two Yiddish singers again sang some songs. Then there was an introduction to the awarding of the Lilli-Bechmann-Rahn Prize. The Professors who had written to us spoke and generally relayed what I have summarized above. Then there was a most moving speech by another Professor who recounted the names of 23 people who had received Ph.D's from the University of Erlangen and whose degrees were revoked. In each case he read the names, date of birth, the title of their dissertation, and their date and place of death. For many, the place of death was Auschwitz, Thereisenstadt, or another concentration camp. Having them identified in this manner was extremely moving.

Then it was my turn to speak. I had previously asked the Professor with whom I corresponded if I could say a few words, so my greetings were part of the printed program. He had been rather surprised at this request, and reluctantly, I think, agreed that I could say a few words. He did not expect that I would speak in German. Although I speak German, I do not have the vocabulary to give a public speech. I had written out my remarks in English and decided that it was important to deliver my talk in German, so I faxed it to Gisela who helped translate it for me. We refined my remarks after I arrived. Rather than summarize what I said, I will reproduce it here:

Your Honorables, very Honorable Professors, very Honorable Doctorates, Friends and My Family

I hope you will excuse my poor German, but I thought I would try to address these brief remarks in German. I want to thank Professor Dr. Kugler very much for allowing me to say a few words here today. My friend Gisela Blume helped me to translate these words.

First, let me say it is a privilege and honor to be here, not just for my mother, but for all those whose degrees were revoked and who are honored today by what you have done.

I thought I would tell you a little about her life, and I had this photo produced. She was born and grew up in Fürth, at 7 Hornshuchpromenade — a very large and beautiful home which is now the European headquarters of Quelle. She came from a very old and established family. She had all the privileges imaginable, and yet, when she wanted to go to university, her parents felt it was not appropriate for a young woman of her station and sent her to Geneva to finishing school. However, she persisted and studied in Freiburg, Berlin, Vienna and received her doctoral degree here in February 1934 at the age of 23. By then she was also a published poet and had 3 poems in a book of promising young leading poets of the day. She also had married in 1933, and I was born, here in Fürth, in 1936. When she married my father, they moved to 129 Konigstrasse, his family home where the metal business which had been in his family for over 200 years was located. That house is now a private school. She also, during 1933-35, did research on her family history as it became increasingly evident that records would be destroyed. She was able to trace her family back to 1666. We have since brought it up to date. So my parents were very assimilated Germans and not religious.

My parents finally decided, in 1937, to leave Germany and getting out at that time was already extremely perilous and dangerous. It's a rather long story — my father was sent to prison for 14 months and their American visa expired. It took an opinion of the Attorney General of the US to the consulate in Stuttgart to issue the new visa which allowed my parents to leave — an extremely important opinion which allowed many people to emigrate. I am an attorney and I have researched this opinion, which has been cited many times. They left for Paris in March 1939 and arrived in New York in April 1939.

My parents loved the mountains — to ski and hike and they decided they did not want to stay in New York. So they looked at a map and saw a place called Denver, Colorado and decided to go there to make a new life. They arrived in Denver when the sun was setting over the mountains and said — if we can make it here, this is where we will stay.

My mother taught for a while at Denver University and also taught crash courses in German to American soldiers being sent over to Germany to fight. And then she became very involved with Hadassah, the women's Zionist Organization in America, where all her energies, intellect and passion were channeled. She led many trips to Israel and was very instrumental in establishing medical care, and the Hadassah Medical Center in Jerusalem where, after her death, a room was named in her honor.

For me it is interesting, and also sad, that the circumstances under which she left Germany totally changed her. She never talked about her experiences as a published poet, or a scholar, or her university work or her doctoral thesis, or the fact that it had been revoked or of the unbelievable stress she must have been under as she was torn away from her homeland. The Nazis killed this side of her life.

My mother led a good, fulfilling life and raised two daughters. Both my sister, who unfortunately could not be here today, and I have had professional careers, as have our children. My daughter, Karen, as well as my husband, are here today. We live outside Boston, Massachusetts. If we had stayed here, she might well have been a professor here at Erlangen. The awarding of this prize has enabled our family to see a side of her that we never knew, a side that stayed here as she was forced to emigrate. She never looked back and never complained about what might have been. Instead, she and my father committed themselves to building a new life in America. She died in 1970 from cancer at the age of 59 — too early and too young.

In closing I would like to sincerely congratulate the graduates here today. For establishing this prize in the name of my mother, and thereby to remember all of those whose degrees were taken away, I thank you from the bottom of my heart. It is a wonderful thing you have done.

Karen said you could have heard a pin drop throughout and after the entire talk. After a long pause, there was a resounding ovation with people clapping for a long time, and a few tried to make it a standing ovation, but apparently that isn't done in Germany. At the reception afterwards many people told me how moved they were. They had come for a graduation ceremony and had not expected what they had just heard. It was an extraordinary experience for me, and also for the University. I think I was able to help them accomplish exactly what they wanted to do, which was have this ceremony be a very human and personal event. Clearly they had worked very hard and done a tremendous amount of research for this occasion and the Professors were extremely pleased at my presentation. After the wine reception, we were invited out to dinner with the key Professors and also the student who was awarded the prize along with his mother and girlfriend. As we walked out of this former Imperial Palace toward the restaurant, we passed over a stone set into the cobblestone plaza in front of the University which read: "Here, in 1933, they burned the books." It struck me again how amazing it was that my mother could be finishing her doctoral work while, at exactly the same time, the Nazis were burning books in this courtyard.

The Lilli-Bechmann-Rahn Prize continues to be given each year, and I receive, annually, the invitation to the event, the name of the awardee, and a copy of their speech upon receiving the award. Frequently the recipient draws a connecting line between his or her dissertation and my mother. For example, one recipient, whose dissertation was entitled Tolerance in the Middle Ages, talked about the clash of cultures and their contingent prejudices, and referred to Lilli-Bechmann-Rahn as one who had to suffer from the worst consequences of such prejudices.

But it doesn't even end here. In February, 2010 I received a telephone call from Beate Gresser, a professor in charge of manuscripts at the Friedrich-Alexander University in Erlangen. She told me that Lilli's dissertation "remains still today a standard work in the area of the history of sentimentalism" and requested permission from me and Evy to publish the dissertation as well as put it on their web site. Of course we gave permission. When I wrote her that I was delighted that my mother's dissertation would soon go into print, I asked her again why it was being reprinted at this time, who would be interested in reading it or using it for study, and what the plans were for its distribution. Her response was:

> *The reason why your mother's dissertation is being reprinted follows:*
>
> *At the bestowal of the 2009 Lilli-Bechmann-Rahn Prize, Professor Köbele (Chair for Germanic and German Philology) indicated that the dissertation remains still today a standard work in the area of the history of sentimentalism. The university therefore seized the opportunity to reprint the dissertation as a facsimile. Along with the new parts (introduction, history of the award, Professor Verweyen's address at the launching ceremony of the prize) it will also be published as a full-text version on the university's document server.*
>
> *The book's bibliographical data will be registered in the German National Bibliography as well as the German Books in Print in order to make it generally available for purchase, and also get sent to library exchange partners. From now on it will be given as a commemorative present to the new doctors in the field of German language and literature.*
>
> *We are delighted to be able to send you your copies of the facsimile of your mother's dissertation with the additions made by the University. Finally your mother's work will be generally accessible to the scientific community to get its well merited reception.*
>
> *At the degree celebration of the Philological Faculty and the bestowal of this year's Lilli-Bechmann-Rahn Prize last Friday, the book was given to 43 PhD graduates as a commemorative gift, a gesture which was very favourably received.*
>
> *Many thanks to you and your sister for your friendly support and cooperation.*

It makes me extraordinarily proud that a thesis my mother wrote in 1933 is still considered an important "standard work" in her field.

Guest of the Town of Fürth — Ruth and Evy — Summer 1999

A number of German towns, in an effort to make restitution, have invited former occupants, or their descendants, back to the town for a visit, all expenses paid. Evy and I were invited on such a trip in the summer of 1999. Since we had both been in Fürth twice just a few years before, much of what we were shown and saw was already very familiar to us. We were wined and dined, and met other former Fürthers, so it was a very interesting and enjoyable trip, but not as personal as our previous trips had been.

One event that was unique during this trip was the opening of the Jewish Museum in Fürth which we attended. It is located on Konigstrasse, just down the street from the former Rahn home where Ruth was born. The museum is housed in a home that was once the home of an Orthodox family with a mikvah in the basement. What was troubling about the museum is that the "artifacts" were presented as if they were about a dead civilization and in no way would someone going through it recognize that there is still a strong, vibrant Jewish community throughout the world. We actually did some writing to the museum and city officials after we returned to the U.S. and over time, with a new curator, the museum has been updated to add more "life" to it. The director wanted Evy and me to contribute certain artifacts and other family items to the museum, but we both agreed that we did not want to send any memorabilia back to Germany.

Last Trip to Germany — Ruth and John — September, 2003

One interesting follow-up to this Erlangen story. In 2001 or 2002 I had begun correspondence with Gaby Franger, a Professor of Politics and History in what we would call Women's Studies at Coburg University in Germany. She was in the process of co-authoring two books entitled *Die Erlangishen Madschen sind recht schon und artig,* (The Girls from Erlangen are Quite Pretty and Well-Behaved), subtitled A History Book about the Women of Erlangen, and *History of Women in Mittelfranken* (Middle Franconia), subtitled Everyday Life, People and Places, published in 2002 and 2003 respectively. She had gotten my name from Gisela Blume, and had written to me requesting letters, photographs and other memorabilia which I could send her for the books. Ultimately each of these books had a chapter about Lilli, including photographs, and her photo appeared on the jacket cover center bottom of the first book.

Cover of Gaby Franger's Book
Lilli is in middle on bottom

For the first book the authors wanted to write a history of notable Erlangen women. They divided the history of these women into several epochs, beginning with the end of the 17th century. The stories of the women whose academic diplomas and credentials had been revoked by the Nazis is part of the section dealing with women in the 20th century. These women, she wrote, represented a new generation of women who wanted an academic career or were politically active and attempted to combine work, marriage and motherhood. Altogether the story of 25 women, including Lilli, was recounted, all of whom were women who stood up for their rights or were remarkable in one way or another. In the second book, *History of Women in Middle Franconia,* she wrote that the history of the Bechmann family, which can be documented going back to about 1700 in this area, was closely connected with the "landscape" of Middle Franconia. The chapter about Lilli is ten pages long, and also contains a number of photographs which I had sent her.

After publication, to promote the book and the work she had done, Gaby Franger was in the process of setting up an exhibit of the history of women from Middle Franconia, which would be shown at a number of museums throughout the Franconia section of Germany during 2003. I sent her a large packet of additional material, including some prison letters, Lillli's dissertation, copies of her courses and her diplomas, and additional photographs. These were all part of the traveling exhibit.

In the fall of 2003, John and I went to Germany and thus were able to actually see the exhibit ourselves. This trip to Germany followed a stay in Luxembourg, where John and I, along with the other Girl Scouts who had been Juliette Low awardees the summer of 1953, celebrated our 50th anniversary! I wrote about this experience at the Girl Scout center, Our Chalet in Adelboden, Switzerland, between my junior and senior year in high school, in another section of this memoir.

Gaby Franger picked us up at the airport. She is tall, and with her red flowing hair exudes an air of competence. She took us to her apartment in Nuremberg, where she had invited us to stay during this visit, to have a bite, before going to the Jewish Museum in Fürth. Her apartment, with it's high ceilings, is absolutely filled to the ceiling with books — I've never seen so many books in a private home.

The afternoon of our arrival Gaby drove us to the Jewish Museum in Fürth at 89 Konigstrasse, just a couple of blocks from my birth home at # 129 Konigstrasse. Evy and I had actually been to the opening of the museum when we visited Fürth as guests of the city in the summer of 1999. At that time we were rather critical of the exhibits because they seemed to portray the Jewish people as an extinct people with little relevance to current times.

At the Jewish Museum in Fürth we met up with Gisela Blume and Daniela Eisenstein, the new director who was committed to making changes in the exhibits. Daniela was born in the U.S. and moved to Germany when she was about 10 and is now in her mid-30's. She was the assistant curator at the Jewish Museum in Frankfurt before, and applied for this job, never thinking she would be accepted. She is very open, and said she wants to focus the museum on family stories. At the moment they don't have English translations next to the exhibits, but that's a project she wishes to complete. Her idea is to keep the exhibits simple and present an overview so as not to overwhelm the visitors, since most visitors are not Jewish. She is working on developing a library and outreach to schools. She stressed that she is trying to enliven the experience of the visitors and emphasize the place of the exhibits in history. She wondered if we might have some items to contribute to the museum, but Evy and I are clear that we do not wish to send anything back to Germany.

After this visit to the Jewish Museum, we went to Gisela's home for dinner, and she then drove us back to Gaby Franger's house in Nüremberg, passing en route the Palace of Justice where daddy was imprisoned. Gisela had recently converted to strict Orthodox Judiasm which presents a number of problems for her. For example, she has to drive to Strasbourg every few weeks, which is 180 miles away, to purchase her kosher food.

The next day Gaby drove us to the exhibit she had helped prepare with another colleague, in Abenberg, not far from Fürth and Nuremberg, and Gisela Blume met us there. Gaby Franger had arranged for the local press to be there, so they interviewed us and the article and photo appeared the next day in the newspaper. The exhibit is housed in an old castle which is now the Museum of Franconia. Germany has 15 divisions, of which Bavaria is one and Franconia is one of the departments of Bavaria. Fürth, Nüremberg and Erlangen are in Middle Franconia (there's also Upper and Lower). The exhibit was of women of Middle Franconia and began with some women in the 6th century. These were mostly nuns who wrote, transcribed and translated. The exhibit was divided into historical periods and Lilli is in the period called "after 1933". In this room there is a whole showcase of mother's work, documents, letters, notes, etc. plus a long poster with Lilli & Alfred's photo on top, explaining who she was. The showcase includes items which I had sent to Gaby — copy of doctoral certificate, notes from her studies at Erlangen, including von Wiese's class, passports, book of poems, copy of thesis, etc. Standing there I was truly overcome with emotion. "What would she have though of this?", I asked myself. Clearly she didn't need it for ego satisfaction. I think she would have thought — fine, you can do what you want and if this is what you want to do, OK, but my life has gone on.

Because Abenburg was very close to Bechhoven, where my original ancestors lived (the earliest was Rabbi Salomo who was born in 1666 and died in 1767, 101 years later) we went with Gisela to the cemetery in Bechhoven. Rabbi Salomo came from Kolin, Czechoslovakia, but around 1700 moved to Bechhoven. His first wife, Rebekka, died after having 3 children; the oldest, Jona, the mohel, is our ancestor. He circumcised all the male babies of the family, according to Lilli's family history. It is also interesting that the godfather of each male child is mentioned in the family history. This is clearly an important role which I hadn't realized before. Gisela had brought a copy of our family history with her, so we had that in front of us, including the copies of the gravestone photos. Gisela wanted to go the Bechhoven cemetery to look for the gravestones of Jona and Salomo's second wife, Edel. As Lilli writes in the Bechmann Family History, which is in the Appendix:

> After Rebekka, his first wife died, Salomo (our earliest known ancestor who lived from 1666-1767) married Edel., the daughter of Dajam Hess of Fürth. They had three sons, Abraham, Hirsh, and Mordechai, and all were circumcised by their much older brother, Jona. Edel died in 1748 (Yom Kippur 5509) and was buried in the Bechhofen cemetery.

I must admit that Gaby, John and I thought that looking for specific graves in this large cemetery was like looking for a needle in a haystack, but as usual, Gisela's enthusiasm was contagious. We found the cemetery — the stones are all erect because the town keeps it up. We began our search — the picture of Jona's gravestone was quite dark in the photocopy we had and it was hard to read. Edel's was a bit clearer — we could make out some markings and the overall shape of the stone was clearer and distinct. We wandered around the cemetery, and then John spotted one he thought might be it, but as we went near it I spotted the one next to it and said "what about this one"? Gisela pulled out her wire brush and began cleaning the writing and "Edel" appeared, as well as the dates. — we had found it! It was very exciting for all of us, and Gisela said it was one of the oldest gravestones she had identified.

Bechhofer was the name used in Fürth for people who came from Bechhoven and means "one who came from Bechhofen". In 1813 a new law was passed in Bavaria (Fürth had become part of the Bavarian Kingdom in 1806) which was meant to help integrate Jews, though this effect was questionable. Every Jewish family had to adopt a family name in order to be inscribed into lists which limited the number of Jews and what they could do. There were about 650 Jews who had such a number in Fürth at that time. Connected with this number was the right to get married, get a job, and to settle there and you couldn't get a number until someone moved away or died. You had to adopt a family name that would stay with the family so our family adopted the name Bechmann.

Gisela then left us and Gaby drove us to Fürth. We saw the Bierer houses on Konigswasser Street and went inside 7 Hornschuchpromenade. It is no longer the Quelle headquarters but has about 6 law offices, as well as a couple of other offices. The people inside were very nice — but not much is left of the original beyond the beautiful entranceway and marble stairs. A few rooms have the original moulding and one bath has what appears to be the original tiles. I had little emotion this time — it is past now.

In 2002 Gaby Franger had sent me a clipping from one of the Erlangen newspapers, dated January 22, 2002, indicating that a proposal had been made to change the name of one of the streets in Erlangen to the name of Lilli Bechmann Rahn. The article is entitled "Dispute of Agnes-Miegel Street — Renaming denied". The article read, in part:

> *The Agnes Miegel Street in Frauenrach will probably retain its name contrary to the petition of the Green List for renaming because the members of the Culture-and-Leisure Time Association have vetoed by majority vote in their judgment to the city council. The Greens had wanted to give the street a new name, because the renowned local poet had shown during the Third Reich great proximity to the thinking of National Socialism and had composed hymns to Adolph Hitler. The other parties and the administration, however, saw no necessity for it.*

> *Another reason for renouncing a renaming was the saving of a change of address for the inhabitants and saving the cost for the administration. The request by the Green List and the SPD for some indication on the street sign about the controversial role of the poet during National Socialism was rejected by 4 votes in order not to set a precedent.*

My reading of this newspaper article was that they clearly did not want to stir up old issues. It was interesting, though, that they considered naming a street in Erlangen after Lilli. In contrast to this vote by the town, the University of Erlangen had faced their history, acknowledged that there was no way to make true restitution, but did what they could to remember, document, honor, and move forward.

10
The Past Leads to the Future

꙳

For the most part, this memoir focuses on generations that are gone. Our family has inherited a rich legacy from Lilli and Alfred and, at the same time, we are creating our own legacy for the generations to come.

Ruth and Her Family

First, few words about my recollections of my early years in the United States. I arrived in Denver when I was three, and I started Elementary School at Park Hill and soon moved to Montclair Elementary School when we moved into 1195 Holly Street. This school was about 12 blocks away, and I recall riding my bike to school each day. I do not recall feeling different from other children, or feeling German in any sense of the word. In fact, I was somewhat embarrassed about my parent's Germanic ways and their accent, and recall asking them, when I had friends over, "Don't talk German". I don't recall ever having experienced anti-Semitism. I had skipped a half year of the second grade, so I was younger than most of my classmates. At Sunday School of our Reform Synagogue, they grouped us by age rather than by the grade we were at in public school with the result that I was with all the kids who were a year behind me in school. This was a terrible mistake, and had the effect of my totally disliking Sunday School and learning little. I was confirmed, but never had a Bat Mitzvah, which wasn't common for girls in that day anyway. Years later Evy started Sunday School at the same Temple and was also put one grade behind her class because she was born in January. She was very unhappy with this and when a new, Conservative synagogue was built two blocks from our house, she asked to go to Hebrew School there. Although our parents weren't observant, they made the change and Evy had a very positive experience at Beth Joseph where she both had her Bat Mitzvah and continued her studies through to confirmation. As far as religious observances were concerned, we never lit Friday night candles and for Seder we went, during the early years, to the Temple, and later to another family. We went to services for Rosh Hashanah and Yom Kippur and we fasted on Yom Kippur. My mother was not a creative cook, and although she did it well and efficiently, it was not something that she enjoyed or that gave her pleasure. Although she made a few German recipes like sauerbraten, wiener schnitzel and blau trout, I do not remember delicious home-cooked meals as part of my childhood. I was always very athletic, and loved horseback riding, going to Girl Scout Camp, tennis and skiing. I also felt a strong need to be accepted by others and beginning in junior high school, was always part of the student government or chairing various clubs.

On January 21, 1945 Evy was born. She was named Evelyn because that was evidently a name my parents liked, and Carol, after Lilli's grandmother Caroline, who was murdered in Thereisenstadt. I had been an only child for so long that I remember it being strange to have to share my room with anyone. We did, however, share the same bedroom until I left for college. It is the reason I was so keen, when we finally bought our first home in Lexington, to have separate bedrooms for my girls. Helen Lorz, who had emigrated with us and had found other employment, came back to live with us for a while to help care for Evy. Being 8 1/2 years apart made it difficult for us to really share a lot of things since by the time Evy was 8 1/2, I was ready to leave for college.

In December, 1946, when I was 10 years old, a "major tragedy", as Alfred called it in one of his letters, occurred. He drove to the post office to mail some letters and took Victor, our dog along. Victor was an adorable brown and white cocker spaniel whose name came from the white V on his brown forehead. Later in the afternoon the family realized the dog wasn't around, and Alfred remembered that he had taken him along in the morning, and he must have jumped out of the car when he went in to mail the letter, a fact he hadn't noticed. Ads were placed in the Denver Post — the editor even wrote a heartbreaking article on the second page with Ruth and Evy's full names; and the radio stations made spot announcements regarding the loss of this treasure. The post office was quite far from our home and in a neighborhood where Victor had never been. The week was cold, it snowed, and we gave up all hopes of ever seeing Victor again. Then, miraculously, about a week later, a scraggly, hungry and cold Victor came up our walk. We have absolutely no idea how he could have found his way home, especially since he had been dropped off in a car. But there he was — a true "Lassie Come Home" story.

Ever since Lilli and Alfred died I have had the painting done of me at age 9 by a talented German emigre artist hanging in my home. In going through the correspondence I found this paragraph in a letter Alfred wrote to Lilli's Aunt Carola (she was Lilli's father's sister).

"For my birthday, I got — it is worth mentioning — a just gorgeous painting of Ruth Marion which was done by an outstanding artist. I mention this not only because the painting is worthwhile mentioning, but in order to tell you a little story. Ruth Marion (being a Rahn) asked the artist in her frank way: Are you paid by the job or are you paid by the hour? And without waiting for a reply, she continued: Well, I am sure you are paid by the hour because you are going over the same spot again and again — and you are just stretching the job. And that was that." The painting hangs in my house.

I graduated from East High School in June, 1954. The summer of 1953, between my junior and senior year, I had been selected as one of four girls from the United States to attend a Girl Scout conference at Our Chalet in Adelboden, Switzerland, called the Juliette Low World Friendship Conference. We were 19 girls from 9 countries, and we spent a good part of the summer together. For over 50 years we have kept up with one another through an annual Newsletter, and, beginning about 30 years ago, started to have reunions about every five years.

We had our 50th reunion during the fall of 2003 in Luxembourg, and our 55th reunion in September 2008 back in Maine, where we had held our first reunion in 1984. It has been a wonderful international thread woven through my life.

In the fall of 1954 I entered Smith College, arriving on the train from Denver, and having never seen the college before. One of the main reasons I selected Smith was because they had a junior year abroad program, and I did, in fact, spend my junior year in Geneva, Switzerland. In December 1957, during my senior year at Smith College, I married Matthew Budd. We got married in December because his parents ran a children's camp on Cape Cod during the summer and it was impossible for them to take the time to come to Denver for a summer wedding. Matt was in his second year at Harvard Medical School and lived at his home in Newton that year. I commuted each weekend from Northampton to Newton until I graduated in June 1958. We then got our own apartment near the medical school and I enrolled in a year-long program at Harvard where I earned a Master of Arts in Teaching Degree in 1959. My career began as a high school social studies teacher in Lexington High School, and later at Needham High School, Byron Junior High School in Shaker Heights, Ohio and Concord-Carlisle High School in Concord, MA.

Karen was born on September 27, 1962 in Cleveland, Ohio, where we had gone for Matt's medical internship, and I stayed home with her the first year. "Is this it?" I asked myself, and I began to think of what to do next. I thought of returning to graduate school and getting a Ph.D. in history, my college major, but from friends who were doing that it all seemed so "irrelevant". "Relevancy" was a buzzword in the 60's. In the summer of 1963 we moved to Atlanta, Georgia for two years where Matt fulfilled his military service at the CDC (Center for Disease Control). Someone had suggested I think about law school, but I couldn't imagine beginning that with a one-year old. I visited Emory University Law School and talked to the dean, and learned they had a part-time evening program, taught by the same professors as the day program. I started that September, very tentatively, full of guilt, and often said that if Karen had been sick

Ruth — Law School
Graduation, June 1968

Ruth and Karen —
Law School Graduation, June 1968

those first few weeks I never would have continued. But I soon realized I loved the study of law, and knew this was what I wanted to continue. The Emory Law School dean was very supportive and eager to enroll women, even though all I had was my Smith College transcript. In fact, in October, a couple of months after I started, he came to me and said that it was a requirement for all students to take the LSAT (Law School Aptitude Test, which normally is taken as part of the admission process), which I had never taken. Could I take it, he asked me rather sheepishly, next Saturday? I did two years work at Emory, and then,

John and Ruth

after we moved back to Boston, I finished at Boston College Law School. I obtained my law degree in 1968, five years after I started and ten years after I graduated from college.

Rachel was born on July 16, 1966, while I was still in law school. There were only four women in my law school graduating class, and all four of us were at the top of our class. Having a pregnant woman in class was most unusual in those days.

I went to law school so I could do "good works" and serve in the public domain, so my first job, in the summer of 1968 was with the Massachusetts Attorney General's office when Elliott Richardson was our Attorney General. When Richard Nixon was elected U.S. president that fall, Mr. Richardson went to Washington and I then joined a small law firm for several years. As my marriage deteriorated, I realized I would have to think about supporting myself and then joined a very large law firm, Choate, Hall & Stewart, for five years, where I began to specialize in family law. In 1978 I joined Hemenway & Barnes where I spent the next 21 years. Hemenway & Barnes is now Boston's oldest law firm, having been founded in 1853, and I was their first woman partner. I chaired the Family Law Section of the Boston Bar Association, and then chaired the Family Law Section of the Massachusetts Bar Association. I became a Fellow of the American Academy of Matrimonial Lawyers and served as president of the Massachusetts chapter as well as on the National Board of Governors. For over 20 years I chaired an educational program for new lawyers entitled Divorce Law Basics, sponsored by the MCLE (Massachusetts Continuing Legal Education) and wrote Budd on Divorce Law Basics, a text which was revised annually. I also was co-editor of Massachusetts Divorce Law Practice Manual, a two-volume text for divorce attorneys. I gave many lectures and authored a number of articles, and was listed annually for over 10 years in The Best Lawyers in America. Some of the volunteer work I did was not only great fun, but also extremely meaningful, such as the case I had which de-sexified Little League in Massachusetts, allowing girls to play. I also wrote and testified before the Massachusetts legislature to get the law passed which allowed divorced spouses to continue to be covered on their ex-spouses' medical insurance after divorce, one of the first of such laws in the nation. I also had a number of high profile clients. I have now been retired for over 10 years, and look back with great satisfaction and pleasure at my legal career.

Matt and I separated at the end of 1976 and the divorce became final about a year later. I heard about John Ehrenfeld through mutual friends who said they knew someone who might call, either as a client or a date. When John called, in 1978 it was 100% as a client, and so I represented him in his divorce, which took several years. Never throughout the proceeding was there any hint of anything more. But when his divorce was over, we began to see each other in October 1980. I invited him to have Thanksgiving dinner with me, my girls, Evy and her family. Karen, who had left for Amherst College that fall, was home for the holiday. As Karen tells the story: "I came home for Thanksgiving and there was a man there — he had cooked the turkey, and sat at the head of the table and carved and served the turkey, and when I came home for Christmas vacation, he was living there". We married several years later, on August 7, 1983, and have "lived happily ever after!"

After graduating from Lexington High School, Karen (born September 27, 1962) went to Amherst College and graduated in 1984, majoring in anthropology. She spent part of her junior year studying in Nairobi, Kenya and the remainder of that year working in Israel. After college she obtained a Masters of Public Health from Harvard University. She recently described her life since college as follows:

> *The recent Amherst College alumnae magazine had an article called, "Lives of Consequence" the title of the college president's recent commencement speech. I noticed myself thinking about that phrase a lot, I suppose that with turning 50 now closer than passing the 40 milestone, it's a question that in one form or another I am asking myself, "am I living a life of consequence and what does the question really mean anyway?" It's been 25 years since I graduated from Amherst College and the past 25 years have taken many twists and unanticipated turns. While at Amherst, I completed the pre-med curriculum along with my Anthropology major. After leaving college, somewhat*

Tim and Karen

Tim and Karen, Emily, Nathaniel

Karen and Tim

Emily and Nathaniel

unsure as to the direction I wanted to take, I headed west and worked for 2 years at a non-profit based in San Francisco. It was a nice break from the east coast and it was in CA that I decided to pursue the field of Public Health. I headed back east to attend the Harvard School of Public Health where I received a Masters in Health Policy and Management in 89'.

I have spent the past 20 years working in the area of health care quality and improvement and have worked in New York, Boston and now in Maine. I am currently a Vice President at Health Dialog, a Boston-based patient self management education company that helps individuals become more informed health care consumers.

On the personal side, I have been married for the past 10 years to the wonderful Tim Swan who is a creative soul, a fantastic cook and fly-fisherman and without whom, I never would have ended up living on the beautiful coast of Maine. Tim and I are the parents of two high energy, very funny, and loving children Emily (born March 5, 2002) and Nathaniel (born February 23, 2004) (Emily's middle name is Lilli, after my grandmother.)

I think more and more about what it means to live a life of consequence and while I don't have any answers, I do know that the most important and consequential things in my life right now are my family and my work life.

Rachel and Curt

Rachel, born July 16, 1966, graduated from Lexington High School and thereafter from Harvard University, magna cum laude,

Rachel and Curt, Addison, Gabriel

Gabriel and Addison

in 1988. She began her career as Assistant to the Director of the Boston Redevelopment Authority where she completed a variety of projects relating to city planning and neighborhood development. After two years she moved on to serve as a Special Assistant and Research Fellow for a Commissioner of the U.S. Commission on Civil Rights. Concurrent to this work, she began consulting to a variety of entrepreneurial companies in Silicon Valley. She was hired by the executives of these firms to design and implement new business processes geared toward enhancing services, decreasing costs, and improving operations. In 2000, Rachel was hired to launch — design, staff and manage — a new California Customer Service Division for First Horizon National Bank, where she distinguished herself with the Senior Financial Associate award given only to the top 15 performers in the California Region. In 2004, she joined Opes Advisors, a financial services firm in Silicon Valley. As a Personal Finance Advisor, she continued her work advising homeowners on their mortgages, debts and assets, and provided financial education enabling clients to make prudent choices with regards to their financial future. More recently, she was Director of Annual Giving and External Relations for Harvard Hillel, Cambridge, MA.

Addison and Gabriel

Karen, Nathaniel, Gabriel, Curt, Tim, Addison, Rachel, Emily

On the personal side, Rachel married Curt Van Emon on May 18, 1997 and has two children — Addison Lillian Van Emon (born February 10, 1999 — same birthday as Lilli) and Gabriel Budd Van Emon (born January 26, 2001 — just two days before Alfred's 100th birthdate). I was hoping that both he and Addie would be born on Lilli and Alfred's birthdays, but Gabriel came two days too soon. In 2008 she and Curt moved their family from California back to Lexington, Massachusetts to be closer to grandparents and extended family.

My husband, John Ehrenfeld, was born in Chicago on May 16, 1931 and after living there, then in Milwaukee, he moved to Cincinnati, Ohio where he went to high school at Walnut Hills High School. He then went to MIT for his undergraduate and graduate degrees, obtaining his Ph.D. in Chemical Engineering in 1957. He had three children from his first marriage: Peter, born in 1957, Liz, born in 1959 and Tom, born in 1961. Tragically, Peter died of AIDS in 1992. Liz married Kenny Mendez in 1990, and they have three children: Nick, born in 1992, Will, born in 1994 and Theo, born in 1997, Tom married Hetchen and they have two children: Lucy, born in 1991 and Hayley, born in 1996. Together we now have 9 grandchildren.

John's career after obtaining his Ph.D. from M.I.T. has been full and varied and focused on environmental policy. He did research with a number of companies, started in 1967 one of the first few companies to engage in air pollution research, and was appointed by President Jimmy Carter to head the New England River Basins Commission from 1978-81. In 1986 he was asked to join the faculty at M.I.T. and became Director of the M.I.T. Program on Technology, Business and Environment. He retired from M.I.T. in 2000, but has continued to stay active in the fields of environment and sustainability. He served as the Executive Director of the International Society for Industrial Ecology from its founding to 2009. He was awarded their Society Prize in 2009. He has also served on the Council of the Society for Organizational Learning from 2003 to 2009. In October 1999 the World Resources Institute honored him with a lifetime achievement award for his academic accomplishments. He has written over 200 papers and reports, and in 2008 his first book was published by Yale University entitled *Sustainability by Design*. John and I spent three extended periods in Europe, living in Lausanne, Switzerland for 3 months in 1996, in Lisbon, Portugal for 6 months in 1999, and in The Hague, Netherlands for one year, where John was teaching and doing research at the Technical Univeristy in Delft.

Evy and Her Family

Evy arrived on January 21, 1945, the first person in our family born in this country. In many ways her birth symbolized the success of Lilli and Alfred in the U.S. and, as a young child she was often proudly introduced by them as "our native product". Evy started high school at East High, an old established Denver high school and transferred to George Washington High her junior year, one of 3 new high schools that opened in Denver that fall. In 1966 she received

Joe and Evy

her bachelor's degree in Anthropology from the University of California in Berkeley, a school that was on the forefront of the anti-war (Viet-nam war) and civil rights movements and she has often said that she learned more out of the classroom than in it. She then moved to Boston where she received her Master's Degree in Social Work from Simmons College School of Social Work in 1968. Her first job was as a social worker in a Beth Israel Hospital maternal and infant care program in Roxbury. In 1969 Evy married Bill Davis, then a physics Ph.D. candidate at M.I.T. and three years later (1972) they moved to Denver where Bill had a job at Ball Brothers Research and Evy worked in the pediatric out-patient department at the University of Colorado Medical Center. Their first child, Leah, was born in Denver on January 4, 1974. A year later, 5 months pregnant with her second child, Adam, who was born on May 21, 1975, they moved back to the Boston area as Bill landed a job at American Science and Engineering. They moved to Brookline where they began to raise their kids.

When Adam was a year old, Evy returned to work, part-time, as a social worker at Cambridge Family and Children's Services. And, then, in 1978, Evy was the first hire of a start-up company, Comprehensive Rehabilitation Associates, a rehabilitation/case management firm that assisted injured workers to stabilize medically and re-enter the labor market. Her career there spanned 20 years as Evy progressed from being a case manager to a supervisor to a manager of a district office to the Corporate Director of Staff Development to a Senior Vice President of a $600 million company that had 150 offices throughout the Unites States and Canada and 7700 employees. In 1998, after going public, mergers, and acquisitions, Evy, along with other senior management, was laid off. She then did some management and leadership consulting before becoming the Director of Human Resources for New England Organ Bank, a position she held from 2001 through 2007.

On the home front, Evy and Bill separated in 1983 and were divorced a year later. Evy subsequently met Joe Megerman whom she married in 1991. Joe is a Ph.D. biophysicist who headed the vascular research lab at Massachusetts General Hospital for 15 years before entering the private sector where he ran clinical trials for medical devices at Kendall Healthcare, Biolink, and Boston Scientific. Joe had two children from his first marriage, Josh (born in 1973) who is married to Rachel King and Rachel (born in 1977) who is married to Mark Krebs.

Leah and Jason Anderson, Isaac and Omar

Adam Davis

Evy's daughter Leah, who graduated from Brown University with her Bachelor's degree in Spanish and Stanford University with her Master's in Education, lives in San Francisco with her husband, Jason Anderson, who is a physician, and their two children, Isaac (born 2003) and Omar (born 2005).

Evy's son Adam also graduated from Brown University with a Bachelor's degree in psychology and then obtained his MD degree from the University of Massachusetts Medical School. He did his residency at Children's Memorial Hospital in Chicago and a fellowship at the University of California at San Francisco (UCSF). He now lives in San Francisco with his wife, Tricia, where he practices pediatric medicine.

EPILOGUE
11/21/09
By Evy Megerman

In December, 1970, nearly 39 years ago, our parents, Lilli and Alfred Rahn, died. In a 24 hour period the stable, predictable and seemingly forever lasting home in which we were raised was empty. Stunned by my father's suicide coming immediately after my mother's death from pancreatic cancer, Ruthie and I simply coped, day by day. We sat shiva in our parents' home where literally 100's of people visited us, uncomfortable and not knowing what to say to us, two young women whose lives had been so abruptly changed. We comforted them. We told them we'd be OK. But I, at age 25, kept wondering — where are the "grown ups"? A week after their deaths we returned to Boston, Ruthie to spend some time with her kids who had not come to Denver, and both of us to return to work and begin to resume some normalcy in our lives.

The third week of January, 1971 found us back in Denver where we dissolved the family home. We painstakingly went through all of our parents' belongings — clothes, silver, dishes, furniture and the like. We closed my father's office, located at 15th and Arapahoe. We moved my grandmother, Aami Ida, from a studio apartment to a two bedroom apartment — her intention was to have a place big enough for us to stay when we visited her in Denver. We solicited our dear family friend, Gerda Breit, to go through thousands of German books and help us determine what should be done with them — some were sent to her son, Peter, a political science professor at the University of Hartford — and most were donated to libraries, the majority to Denver University where Mother started her professional career in this country 30 years earlier. And, as we went through everything, room by room and drawer by drawer, we found boxes and trunks full of papers and documents — some written in the US but most from Germany. We carefully packed them and sent them to Boston where they sat for nearly 30 years, unopened, unexamined.

Unopened and unexamined, except one. Among the many documents was a family history which mother wrote in 1934 as she foresaw the end to Jewish life in Germany (Europe) as she had known it. She researched her own family history, recorded it and photographed the graves of ancestors. We found this history and I became fascinated by it. I was most interested in learning what happened to people mentioned in her history as a result of World War II. So, in 1971 Gerda Breit translated the document for me and in 1972, after quitting my job, I devoted my full time to updating the history by matching names in mother's history to names in her address book and writing to people all over the world to learn about what had happened to them and their families during and after the war. The result is an updated history, as of 1972. Thereafter, even that project remained dormant.

In 1999, after retiring from a demanding and successful law career, Ruthie decided to delve deeply into the many documents we had saved all these years to learn more about our family, to find a way to preserve the documents and to be able to record our roots and the story of our family for our children and grandchildren. She has done a monumental job, the result being this book which includes the fascinating story about our German Jewish heritage and our family's journey to a new life in the United States. This history has helped shape who we are today.

But, there is more to what Alfred and Lilli Rahn, our parents, left us than their European roots. As Ruthie and I reflect on our lives with our parents in the United States it is clear that Mother and Daddy left powerful legacies in the ways in which they lived, which have become central to us and to our children.

After a few months in New York, our parents drove across the country to start a new life in Denver. New home, new language, new culture, new friends, new customs and a war ravaging in Europe which was spreading family members, who for generations had lived near each other, all around the world — these were all part of the adjustments our parents made as they embraced this new chapter in their lives.

Let me start with Alfred's legacy. As you may recall, when he and Mother arrived, by car, in Denver, in July, 1939, the sun was setting over the mountains to the west. The sky was burnt orange, the mountains looked black and majestic, silhouetted against the blazing sky. Alfred turned to his wife, put aside the horrific two years they had just had in Germany, and, overcome by the beauty of it all, said, "Lilli, we'll never leave here." And, so began their new life in Denver, the city where both Ruth and I were raised.

My father's love of the mountains never waned. From October through April, conditions permitting, our family skied every weekend. And, in the summer, more weekends than not, we were again in the mountains, hiking. He was in awe and appreciation of nature's beauty and splendor; the sparkling, clean snow with the sun shining on it after a new snowfall; the golden sea of aspens changing color in the fall; the peaks layered on peaks of beauty seen from the summit of a ski slope; the colorful wild flowers along the trails that we hiked — all were enjoyed, discussed and worthy of our appreciation. He loved the outdoors — even taking care of his yard, nurturing his roses, and mowing his lawn (with, I might add, Texaco's broadcast of the Metropolitan Opera blaring from the house, loud enough so that he could hear it over the sound of the lawn mower). And, yes, he loved music (and with his Saturday afternoon concerts exposed our neighbors to classical music whether they liked it or not!!). It is a bit of a dichotomy, one with which Ruthie and I have had to live and struggle our entire adult lives, to say that a man who loved life ended it by committing suicide. But, he did love life. And his legacy to us which I believe both Ruthie and I have passed on to our children is his passion for the outdoors, for nature's beauty and for its grandeur.

My mother's legacy is also tied up in her passion and the commitment to act on it.

When mother was young, learning was her passion. She devoured books and languages and she traveled extensively. In an era and from a community that did not value young women's aspirations to higher education, mother forged ahead. Against her own parents' wishes she pursued an advanced degree and was, as it turns out, the last Jew to receive a Ph.D. from the University of Ehrlangen. The year was 1934.

When, three years later, she was in a hostile, dangerous world in Nazi Germany with a young child and a husband in prison, it was her tireless efforts against all odds, her endless correspondences with relatives and lawyers in the United States as well as with the Attorney

General's office, that ultimately made it possible for her to obtain visas for herself, her husband, and Ruthie to emigrate to America.

Despite being raised in a rather non-religious, certainly non-observant Jewish family, Mother became increasingly concerned and consumed by the plight of the Jewish people. Having been abruptly and viciously uprooted from her home in Germany, exiled for being a Jew, she became passionate about a Jewish homeland, and as Israel won its independence in 1948 Mother began a life-long commitment and dedication to the survival of the State of Israel. She taught seminars; she led educational tours to Israel; she became a leader in the largest women's organization in the world, Hadassah, where she was regional president, national vice president and a lifetime member of the national board. Day and night for years she relentlessly gave her time and her energy to researching and working on Middle-Eastern issues so that others would better understand and support the need for a Jewish homeland, a Jewish state. Nothing was too small for her attention. If a negative article was in the paper, my mother responded. When Arab students were holding a forum at the University of Colorado in Boulder, my mother went to make sure there was a balanced presentation. She acted on her commitment, on her passion — it was her love; it was her life.

Mother's passion was not limited to her Zionism. Just after she turned 40 a friend dared her to start playing golf saying that one couldn't really learn a new sport after 40. Mother, a life long skier and hiker, took up the challenge. Again, with passion and determination she became an avid golfer — eventually entering and placing in tournaments.

Illness intervened during the last 11 years of her life. After her first bout with breast cancer in 1959 she visited women who had breast cancer in the hospitals so that they would be more comfortable with their disfigurement and so that they could use her as a role model of someone who continued an active, involved life despite the disease. Years later, when she was wasting away from incurable, pancreatic cancer, Mother had a burning desire to organize one last educational seminar, scheduled for January, 1971. And, indeed, although she did not live to attend it, she was the driving force behind organizing it and from that seminar forward it was named the Dr. Lilli Rahn Hadassah Educational Seminar.

My mother was passionate about whatever she did; she lived for her causes and interests, she loved them, she acted on them, and she taught about them.

The Bechmann/Rahn heritage is a rich one, one that has survived the hatred of anti-Semitism, the emigration to a new country and an able adjustment to a new world and new cultures. And so, to those who read this book and learn about our history, take what you will from the documents and stories, but, above all else, remember the legacy left by Lilli and Alfred Rahn and live life passionately, follow your dreams and act on your passions.

Evy Rahn Megerman
Lilli and Alfred Rahn's daughter
11/21/09

EPILOGUE
By Ruth Rahn Budd

I have written at length about my parents, and want to close with some thoughts about them. I have missed them terribly over the years, and realize how young I was (34) when they died. I have been sometimes critical of them in this memoir, but at the same time I am deeply appreciative of what they did for me. I regret so much not having had the opportunity to talk to them about their lives, and to ask the many questions I have. I am sad about many things — that they didn't have the pleasure of knowing John, who I know they would have loved and admired, that they didn't have the joy of seeing my children grow up and become the wonderful women they have become; that they didn't have a chance to meet their husbands, and most importantly, their great grandchildren. Daddy particularly, who loved children, would have felt such joy in welcoming and playing with Addie, Gabe, Emily and Nathaniel, and often, as I play or ski with them, I think of the pleasure he and mother would have felt.

What saddens me to this day, as I recount my mother's broad and accomplished educational background, is that she never really shared her vast knowledge with me, or with Evy. I don't remember having intellectual discussion with her about what I was studying or learning. Even when I came home from college for Christmas vacation, armed with books to prepare for exams in January, I don't recall her ever asking what I studied, or discussing my courses with me Evy recalls the same, and regrets that she never took her to a museum. She was able to successfully teach others, and become their mentors, but didn't do the same for her children.

Nevertheless, they set an example and were truly role models for me. I felt I could accomplish anything I wanted to do, and my mother was very supportive when I decided to go to law school. In fact, I doubt that I would ever have gone to law school without her influence and encouragement. I thought that by going to law school I could do "good works" in the world — more than being a committed volunteer as my mother was for Hadassah. I wanted to become a lawyer (though I had no role model for that profession and didn't know any lawyers), not to earn money, but to work in the public domain and serve others. Upon graduation, I never applied to law firms, but worked in government for the Massachusetts Attorney General. Only when my first marriage began to fall apart did I have to shift my goals somewhat and think about supporting myself. The impetus to do public service and get involved in social action is a key legacy from my mother. And from daddy I imbided the love of nature, being outdoors, and being absolutely honest in my dealings with others.

I admire so much the courage it took for them to leave New York and venture to Colorado, where they knew no one, confident they could make a life for themselves near the mountains they so dearly loved. For me, it was a wonderful place to grow up and being out of doors, in nature and away from city life has been an important constant in my life.

Finally, I am grateful and thankful to be alive and healthy in my mid-70's. I am truly blessed in having such a wonderfully loving and supportive husband, and in being so close, including physically, with my children and grandchildren.

This memoir, though long and sometimes tedious reading, is a tribute to past generations and my parents and a way of commemorating their memory by passing on the rich heritage they have left to my children, grandchildren and future generations.

Appendix

Genealogy Charts

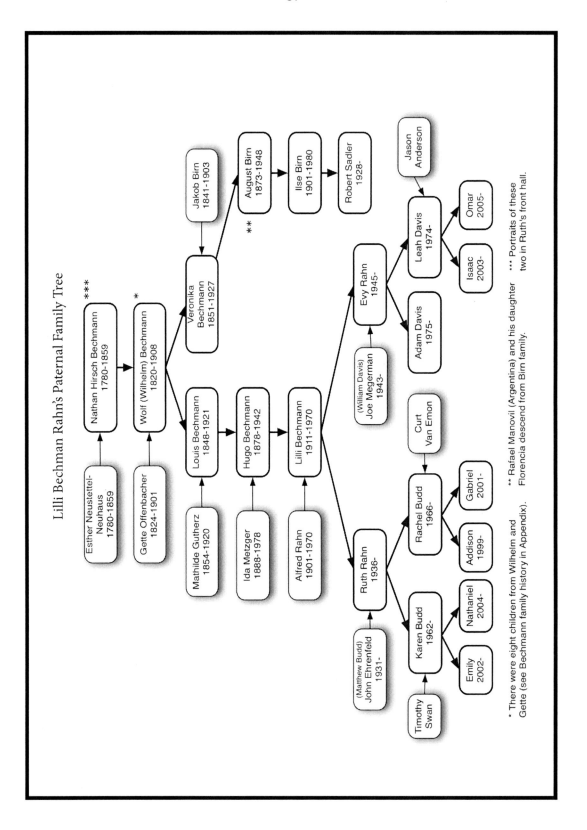

Lilli Bechman Rahn's Paternal Family Tree

Esther Neustettel-Neuhaus 1780-1859

Nathan Hirsch Bechmann 1780-1859 ***

Gette Offenbacher 1824-1901

Wolf (Wilhelm) Bechmann 1820-1908 *

Veronika Bechmann 1851-1927

Jakob Birn 1841-1903

August Birn 1873-1948 **

Ilse Birn 1901-1980

Robert Sadler 1928-

Mathilde Gutherz 1854-1920

Louis Bechmann 1848-1921

Ida Metzger 1888-1978

Hugo Bechmann 1878-1942

Alfred Rahn 1901-1970

Lilli Bechmann 1911-1970

Evy Rahn 1945-

Jason Anderson

Leah Davis 1974-

Omar 2005-

Isaac 2003-

Adam Davis 1975-

(William Davis) Joe Megerman 1943-

Curt Van Emon

(Matthew Budd) John Ehrenfeld 1931-

Ruth Rahn 1936-

Rachel Budd 1966-

Gabriel 2001-

Addison 1999-

Karen Budd 1962-

Nathaniel 2004-

Emily 2002-

Timothy Swan

* There were eight children from Wilhelm and Gette (see Bechmann family history in Appendix).

** Rafael Manovil (Argentina) and his daughter Florencia descend from Birn family.

*** Portraits of these two in Ruth's front hall.

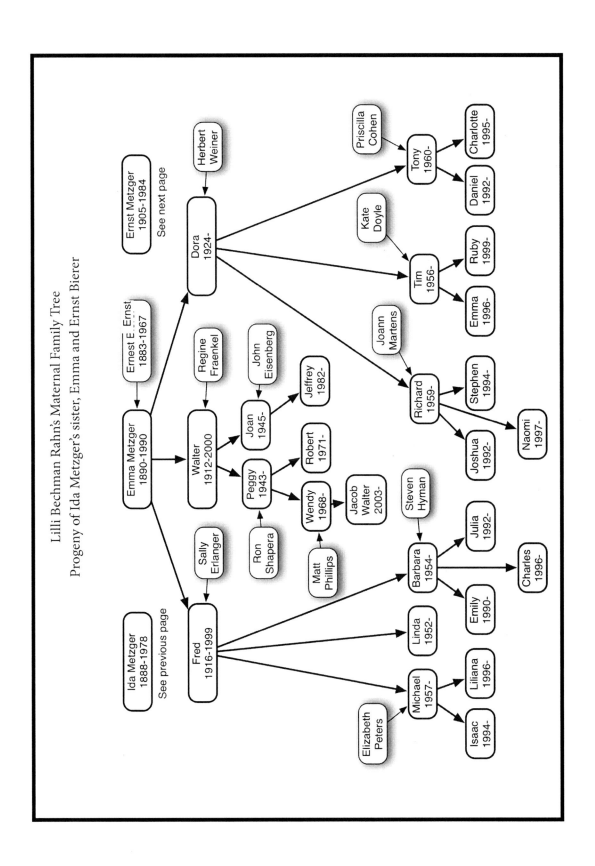

Lilli Bechman Rahn's Maternal Family Tree
Progeny of Ida Metzger's sister, Emma and Ernst Bierer

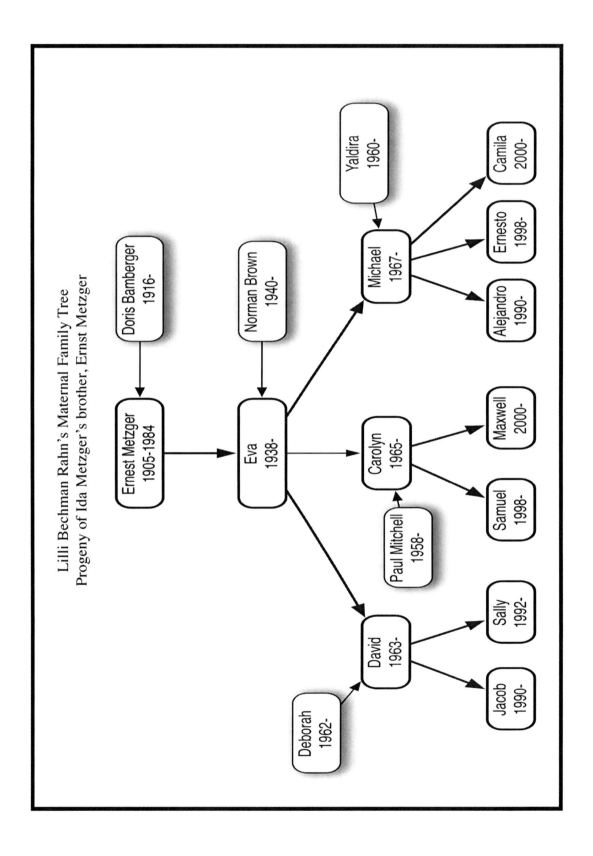

Lilli Bechman Rahn's Maternal Family Tree
Progeny of Ida Metzger's brother, Ernst Metzger

Ruth's Genealogy from Lilli's Tagebuch (Daybook)

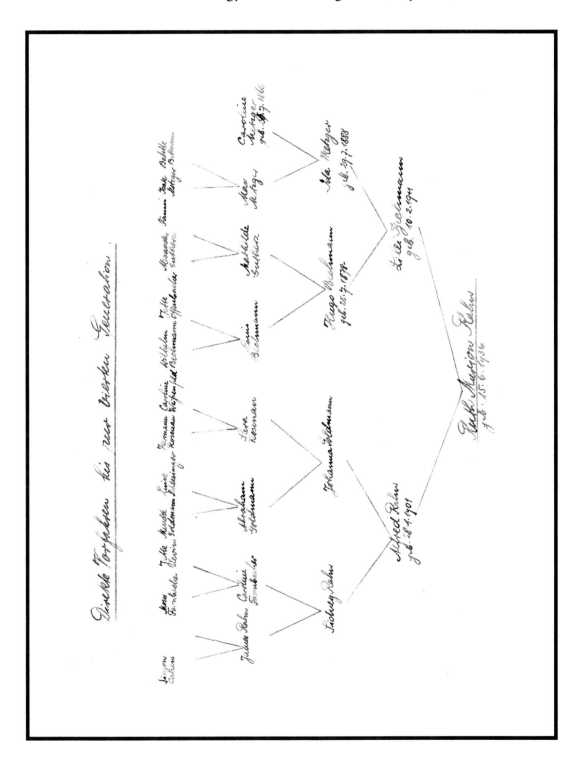

Karoline Metzger's Death Certificate

SERVICE INTERNATIONAL DE RECHERCHES
INTERNATIONAL TRACING SERVICE
INTERNATIONALER SUCHDIENST

D - 3548 AROLSEN

Tel. (05691) 637 — Telegr.-Adr. ITS Arolsen

EXTRAIT DE DOCUMENTS	EXCERPT FROM DOCUMENTS	DOKUMENTEN-AUSZUG

Votre Réf.
Your Ref.
Ihr Az. ------------------------------------

Notre Réf.
Our Ref.
Unser Az.   T/D - 544 273

Nom / Name / Name   **METZGER** ------------

Prénoms / First names / Vornamen   **Karoline** --------

Nationalité / Nationality / Staatsangehörigkeit   **nicht angeführt**

Date de naissance / Date of birth / Geburtsdatum   **26.7.1866** -----

Lieu de naissance / Place of birth / Geburtsort   **Brakel in Westf.**

Profession / Profession / Beruf   **nicht angeführt**

Noms des parents / Parents' names / Namen der Eltern   **nicht angeführt** -----------------

Religion   **nicht angeführt**

Dernière adresse connue / Last permanent residence / Zuletzt bekannter ständiger Wohnsitz   **nicht angeführt** -----

Arrêté le / Arrested on / Verhaftet am   **nicht angeführt** --

à / in / in   **nicht angeführt** ------

par / by / durch   **nicht angeführt**

Est entré au / Entered / Wurde eingeliefert in das   **Ghetto Theresienstadt** ---------

No. de détenu / Prisoner's No. / Häftlingsnummer   **nicht angeführt**

le / on / am   **11. September 1942** ----

venant de / coming from / von   **nicht angeführt** -

par / by / durch   **Geheime Staatspolizei München (Transport II/25-291)** -----------

Catégorie, ou raison donnée pour l'incarcération / Category, or reason given for incarceration / Kategorie, oder Grund für die Inhaftierung   **"Jüdin"** ------------

Transféré / Transferred / Überstellt   **nicht angeführt** ------------------------

Dernière mention dans la documentation des CC / Last entry in CC-records / Letzte Eintragung in KL-Unterlagen   **Ist am 23. September 1942 im Ghetto Theresienstadt verstorben.** --------------------

Remarques / Remarks / Bemerkungen   **keine** ------------------------

Documents consultés / Records consulted / Geprüfte Unterlagen   **Karteikarte des Ghettos Theresienstadt.** ------------

Expédié à / Dispatched to / Abgesandt an   **Mrs. Ida Bechmann**
3800 East Colfax Avenue
DENVER/COLORADO

Arolsen, **den 28. Juli 1975**

Ida Bechmann's Autobiography, 1972

AUTOBIOGRAPHY - IDA METZGER BECKMAN

I was born in Nürnberg July 29th, 1888. I was the first child
to my father, Max Metzger and my mother, Caroline (nee Salberg). My
sister, Emma (now Emma Bierer) is one year younger and my brother,
Ernest Metzger, is born 1905. My father died 1909 and I married Hugo
Bechmann May 16, 1910.

Lilli, my only child, was born February 11, 1911. Lilli was a
very good pupil and Hugo wanted always that she and I would be in
summertime in Rottach am Tegernsee, a wonderful place near München
in the Bavarian Alps. So, I took Lilli out of school in May til
September. We had rented a very nice cottage in Rottach and Hugo
came at the end of the week from Fürth to stay with us til Monday.

When Lilli was through with school, she wanted to go to a university but we did not allow it and I brought her to a school in
Geneva, Switzerland. But after a year in Geneva she insisted to
go to a university and she studied in Freiberg and Erlangen and
got her Doctor degree in philosophy in Erlangen.

She went with a group of students to Russia for a tour. I do
not know exactly which year it was, but it was already the Hitler
time and when she came back she was making a speech and I was scared.
Hugo was on business in Sweden and the Löfflers and all our friends
were happy that nothing happened.

The 3rd of July 1933 Lilli and Alfred Rahn married. We lived in
Berlin, Lilli and Alfred in Fürth.

My husband was in 1938 (October 15) in Sweden on a business trip
when the Gestapo in Berlin wanted to speak to him. I went to the Gestapo and they told me that my husband worked for Russia, that it was
espionage and they wanted to speak with him. So, Hugo could no more
come back to Germany. In September 1938 came two men of the Gestapo
and wanted to get my husband. Well, I was alone in Berlin and when
Lilli got Alfred out of prison in Fürth and left to USA, I left for
Stockholm.

In spring 1939 I came to Stockholm. Well, it had not been easy
to make the emigration. Hugo had lost his job of the "Deutsche
Glashandelsgesellschaft" in Berlin in April 1933 because he was a
Jew. He started a company in his own name and in 1936 he started as
director of the glass firm, Hultberg, in Stockholm. He could no more
come back to Germany.

I stayed in Berlin because I wanted to see Lilli to get Alfred
out of the prison in Fürth where he was taken by the Nazis. My mother,
Caroline Metzger, had a stroke and I had to get her out of her apartment. It was a terrible time in Germany. All our money was siezed
and I wanted once to go to Fürth to see Lilli. I had to go to the

-2-

"Finanzamt" in Berlin and the employee there said to me, "Oh, you have to go to the "Herr Oberfinanzrat" and he has not time today any more to speak to Jews." Well, I said to him I need the money to go to Nürnberg and Fürth and he sent a young man with me to the Oberfinanzrat. The young man said "Heil Hitler," Mrs. Bechmann wants to talk to you.

I told him that I needed some money from my account in the bank to see my daughter in Fürth. "Where is your husband?" he asked. Well, he is in Sweden. He said, "Are you separated?" Well, I said, we are separated as you are when one is in Sweden and one is in Germany. He threw a apaer with the ratification to get the money from the bank over his desk and said, "When you come next time you are divorced." (He thought I was the Christian wife of a Jewish man.)

Lilli could get out Alfred of the prison in spring 1939 and sent him immediately with Ruthie and a governess to Paris where Emma and Ernst Eierer lived. At the frontier the German officer took off Ruthie's clothes to see if there was money or jewels hidden. "Oh," said Ruthie, "They want to see a naked Fröschlein " (a German saying, "a naked frog). They laughed and let them go.

Lilli left Germany in spring 1939 and so I got my papers to go to Sweden in June 1939.

It was a terrible job to go to the German consulate, to give up your money in Germany, to get the permission to send your furniture to Stockholm. In Stockholm I had a very good time. Hugo was very well known there and I spoke Swedish good enough to get along. We had a very nice apartment in Nybrogatan.

But in spring 1941 came director Seeling (director of DEFAG, Frankfurt am Main in Germany) with a lawyer from Berlin to Sweden and Told Mr. Hultberg when the Jew, Hugo Bechmann, would not be fired immediately, the firm Hultberg would not get any glass from any firm in Germany any more. It was a terrible thing.

Hugo got sick and the 19th of July 1942 he died during a kidney operation in the hospital in Stockholm.

Well, I was alone. Lilli and Alfred wrote me, I should come to USA. I had difficulty to get the money the firm Hultberg still owed to Hugo. Well, I had a very nice, big apartment and Luta's sister (Luta is Luta Vishniac) told me that the Press Attache of the Netherlands, Dr. Williams, needed a place to live and to have his office. (It was difficult at that time to find a place in Stockholm because so many countries had their consulate in Stockholm.) So, I rented my apartment to Dr. Williams and went to a resort place at the wea shore.

In fall 1942 I came back and shared my apartment with Dr. Williams and the consulate of the Netherlands. In December 1944 Dr. Williams found a place to live and for his office.

-3-

Quite a lot of people came from Denmark because it was safer. Engineer Levy was one of them and he asked me to let him move in. He promised to take care of my furniture - sell it or send it to USA. Well, I lost everything. He died a short time after I left.

I tried hard to get visa to leave Stockholm and fly to England. At the end of December 1944 I got my certificate and had to leave immediately. The airplane took us from Stockholm to Prestwick (Scotland) and from Prestwick to London. My cousin Betty Ullmann took me to her apartment. She had warrented fro me. Lilli and Alfred had written and told her that they would take the guarantee.

But, it was impossible for me to get a ticket to USA. Only a war bride could get a flight to USA. Well, the war was on. I went to the bank where I had my money from Sweden and there was a nice employee and I told him I did not want to spend all my money in England. I wanted to go to USA. "Oh," he said, "my uncle is the head man at Cook's Travel Agency." I asked him to give me a letter of introduction to his uncle. I went immediately to Cook's and his uncle was very nice, went with me to the ticket office and said, "I do not know why Mrs. Bechmann could not get a ticket when she can pay for it."

So I went to the French Consulate and had my American visa. I went to the Spanish-Portuguese Consulate and the employee put his stamp on the papers before he saw my old German passport, "Ida Sara." (I was told Portugal does not give a visa to Jews.) So, I got my ticket for the flight.

We first flew to Shanon, Ireland. Here we got the Pan American airplane that took us to Lisbon, Portugal. All the passengers were very nice people, mostly diplomats and some girls who were engaged to American men.

From Lisbon we flew to Dakar, French Morocco. It seemed there was something to repair on the airplane. They took us to the military base, in the evening to a film and in the night we flew to Natal, Brasil. Ladies had to stay in a nun's cloister because it was too dangerous to let us in a hotel. Well, I looked out of the window of the cloister and I saw a bus driving by and I said to Martha, well, let us take a little sightseeing tour. So, we went down but I had no Brasil money. So I asked the driver if he would not tke for the fare American money. "Oh, yes," he said. I took out some bills. I do not know how much. It was out of my purse. There was an officer sitting next to us in the bus. He said, "Lady, take that money immediately back or it may be that you will not come out alive." He paid for two tickets - for me and Martha. Well, we got out at the next stop and went back to the cloister.

The next day we were flying to Trinidad and a guide showed the beautiful orange plantations.

_4_

The next day we came to Puerto Rico. Maria Rahn came to the airport. Max Rahn was on a business trip in Bermuda. I had never met her
before and she showed Puerto Rico and I had a very nice time. From
Puerto Rico we flew to Bermuda. There our passports were examined and
the next day we arrived in New York.

We went to the immigration office and there were some officers and
they said, "Oh, how are you today?" I thought they wanted to know how
I felt and so on because in England it is, "How do you do?" Immediately
I told them how the trip was, how I felt and so on. They laughed and I
got my papers.

My sister was at the airport. I stayed with her for a week. We
had not seen each other for years.

Then I came to Denver. I lived at Lilli's house and went to the
Opportunity School to learn American history to make the examination for
my citizenship.

I wanted to get a job and I spoke to a man of the Opportunity
School. I told him that I was good in short hand and typing, but, of
course, only in German, and I would like to work in a bank. He laughed
and said, "We do not need that in USA." But, after a short time he
called me and told me that I could work at the May Company.

I went there and they took me immedicately as sales lady in the
stockings department. My English was not perfect. I never had sold
anything in all my life, but the customers came all to me so I served.
So came an older lady and she wanted brown stockings - not too light and
not too dark, not too long and not too short, and at last she found
what she was looking for. She said, "Do these stockings also last
very long?" "Well," I said, "lady, when these stockings would last for
all your life, I would loose my work here. She tood a carton and a
man came who was standing behind her and he said to me, "Lady, that
was better than any show or theater I saw in the last time. Please
give me three cartons." Then came the department chief and said, "Becky,
you are our best sales lady. How did you do it?" Well, I did not tell
her, but I looked for another job.

I came to see a friend of mine. She worked at the National Jewish
Hospital in the diet department. She introduced me to Mrs. Foldi,
the department chief. Well, I went home and told Lilli I think I would
like to work there. It was a Friday and I went to Mrs. Foldi and said
to her, "I would like to work for the diet department." She said, "I
would like to take you but I have no opening." On Tuesday at 9 am
she called and said I could start immediately. So I moved to the nurses
home where I could have a room and work ed at the National Jewish Hospital from 1947 til 1966. In 1965 the Canteen Company took over the
diet department, the kitchen and so let all the older employees go.

-5-

I was very mad about it but Lilli and Alfred put me on a boat and I made a trip to Madrid, Milano, Naples, Venice, Madiera and back by boat to USA in 1967.

Lilli had been with her friend, Mrs. Betty Girsh, at the Kentucky Circle. It is a very nice place for Senior Citizens. You have your own apartment, can eat in the dining room. Betty wanted to see it because she wanted her mother to come here but you must be absolutely healthy or they would not take you. Betty's mother was not healthy enough to get in, but Lilli said that is a place for you and we made an application. It takes a time til you can get in here because they have quite a waiting list. After I returned from my trip I got the news that I could get an apartment at Kentucky Circle and I live here and like it very much.

Ida Beckman
February 1972

Kolin Torah Dedication by Rabbi Yales

RABBI YALES' DEDICATION SERMON FOR THE KOLIN TORAH
SEPTEMBER 27, 1972

The Kolin Torah

The letter began, "Scroll #330 will be sent to you within the next ten days by BOAC air freight. Scroll #330 came from the town of Kolin (Czechoslovakia) and was written in 1720."

So, after many months of correspondence, an old Torah scroll that had lost its way in the world, at a time when much of the world had lost its sanity, would now be making another long journey in search of just a little peace and love, and a Jewish home.

Tonight, Kol Nidre Eve, we dedicate this honored scroll. That our dedication may be worthy, it behooves us to know something of our Scroll's past, where it has been and how it has come to us.

Our Torah comes from Czechoslovakia. When one speaks of Czech Jewry, one speaks pre-eminently of Prague. Here in this once vital and populous center of Jewish life in Bohemia, is the Alt-Neu Schule, the oldest extant synagogue in Europe, built in the 13th century. This is the city of the famous Jewish Town Hall with its Hebrew clock. Here, too, is the Jewish cemetery known as the *City of the Dead*, where the Jews are buried on top of each other -- 200,000 of them, it is said, because Prague would not grant the Jews additional space for a new cemetery. Here is buried the Maharal, Rabbi Judah Loew, creator of the legendary "Golem."

If you visit Prague today and hear a Jew speaking about the wall, you must be careful not to assume that he is speaking about the "Western Wall" in Jerusalem. He might be speaking about the wall in the Pinkas Synagogue of Prague, the wall inscribed with 77,297 names of every man, woman and child in Prague known to have been murdered by the Nazis.

Our Torah Scroll has its beginnings some thirty miles east of Prague in the town of Kolin, one of the oldest Jewish communities in Czechoslovakia. A number of Jews lived there in the 14th century. A synagogue is mentioned as being old in 1512 and by 1618 the Jewish community of Kolin was second only in size to Prague. But, like our Torah Scroll, which I shall tell you about in just a minute, life as a Jew in Kolin was not an easy one -- certainly it was mercurial. Expelled in 1541, the Jews are invited to return in 1557, only to be expelled once more in 1561 and return again in 1564.

If you had been a Jew in Kolin in the 1600s, you would have been required to pay special taxes. You would have been permitted to own no other real estate except your own home. You might have difficulty finding work because you would not be allowed to engage in any trade in which Christian citizens were employed, nor could you have Christians in your employ.

Now, if I were a Jew in Kolin and I wanted to visit you, I would walk from my house on the Jews' street in Kolin to your house on the Jews' street. I could choose to visit you on a Sunday or a Christian holiday and know that you would be home or nearby, because on Sundays and Christian holidays, we Jews were not permitted to leave "our" street. The Christian community was certain that we Jews would poison their drinking water and, after all, what could be a more appropriate day for such a thing than a Sunday or a Christian Holy Day!

This was our life in Kolin. But it was not all so bitter. To be sure, there were always restrictions of one kind or another, at least until the middle of the 1900s; even as late as 1913, a young Roman Catholic priest in Kolin named Hrachovsky tried to implicate us in a blood libel charge following the death of a girl who had committed suicide because she was pregnant by him. So, you see, we could never quite let our guard down.

Still, it was not always bitter. We cannot forget the moments of joy we shared together.

Such a moment was the day in 1696 when we dedicated our new synagogue with its beautiful Aron Kodesh. Years later we would dedicate our new Sefer Torah, with its letters so brilliantly black and tall and noble on its clean, taut skin.

And, of course, we Jews knew the joy of a thousand simchas: the birth of our little ones, the Bar Mizvah of a son, the marriage of our children. And there was our Yeshiva! A Yeshiva of such distinction that the great Moses Montefiore himself endowed a foundation just for our students.

We Jews also knew the joy of mitzvah. During the harsh winters of 1846 and 1847, we contributed substantial sums for the relief of one hundred Christian families in our town.

Of course, there is more. More joy and more sorrow. Much more sorrow.

Jewish life in Kolin came to an abrupt halt on June 10, 1942. On that day the first of three transports deported 2,202 Jews, men, women and children, from Kolin to Theresienstadt. All but 104 of them died in Nazi extermination camps.

The second part of our story begins with the Kolin Scroll, the one that had seen all the vicissitudes of Jewish life in Kolin pass before it since the 1700s.

Our scroll was taken by the Nazis to the city of Prague, capital of the "protectorate" of Czechoslovakia. Adolph Hitler, history's diabolic monster, had decided that there should be visual reminders of testimony to the uncivilized, non-Aryan race he was determined to destroy.

He therefore ordered a museum created of Jewish artifacts, so that future generations could see for themselves how justified the Nazis were in exterminating the Jews. People would come from all the countries of a Judenrein world to inspect the memorabilia of a dead people.

A collection point was to be established for all ceremonial objects seized from the Jews and their synagogues. Preparations were made in 1940 to create this ghastly museum in the old Jewish section of Prague. Here, in lorries and trucks, were brought 1,564 Torah scrolls from central Europe. Here from synagogues throughout Czechoslovakia and other countries were brought Torah crowns, rimonim, breastplates of gold and silver, the curtains from the arks, menorahs, Passover plates of richly engraved silver, illuminated manuscripts and books, books by the carload. A thousand years of Jewish life in Central Europe were reflected in the ceremonial objects and ritual symbols dumped by the Nazis in synagogues, now used as warehouses, in the Jewish ghetto of Prague. Among these treasures was our Scroll from Kolin.

The task of arranging and cataloging this so-called "exhibition of an exterminated ethnic group" was assigned to talented Jews, who received a reprieve for their labor before being shipped off to their death.

When the "thousand-year Reich" came to an end, after a period infinitely less than the thousand years, but a thousand times too long, this great store of Jewish treasure remained in the synagogue-warehouses of Prague. The now decimated Jewish community was helpless, so the charge of these precious objects fell to the Czechoslovakian State which felt that it was important to maintain this Museum as a silent witness to what the Czech Jews endured and as an enduring appeal to the conscience of humanity.

Today, the museum is honorably maintained in the famous old Klausen Synagogue of Prague. Here are ceremonial objects, secular and religious records, and personal mementos -- in all, 200,000 catalogued remnants of 6,000,000 who once lived.

The problem the Jewish museum confronted was what to do with the most precious of these Jewish possessions; indeed, the synagogue's only essential ceremonial object --- hundreds upon hundreds of Torah Scrolls. Like the Holocaust victims, these Torah Scrolls had endured a sleep of death as they lay piled in a Prague synagogue for twenty years. Somewhere in this mass of Torah Scrolls was the one from Kolin. Unlike the Jews of Central Europe, these scrolls were to survive. Thus we unfold part three of our story.

A proper disposition of the scrolls was required. A few of them might be displayed but to keep all of them in store, rolled up and unused indefinitely, would be tantamount to passive vandalism, yet a proper disposition would require labor for which the Czechoslovakian authorities would not claim the competence. The original handling and transporting of the Scrolls by the Nazis caused damage, and more had been done by the long period of storage.

So, for nearly twenty years after the war, no alternative to the continued storage and deterioration of the Scrolls was found. The only authorities which would possess the means and the will to cope with the challenge which the Scrolls presented would be found on the other side of the iron curtain. And, although attempts from the West were made, they were unsuccessful, because, aside from the Czech authorities' general reluctance to do business with capitalist agents, they were conscious of a sacred trust and unwilling to consider an offer from a source which they thought might exploit the enterprise for profit.

Finally, a well-known London art dealer, who for some years has enjoyed enviable success in showing, in London, paintings and sculpture from communist countries was able to gain the confidence of Artia, the official agents of the Czechoslovakian Government for cultural properties. In 1963 this art dealer negotiated with them for the Sifre Torah.

On the seventh of February 1964, one thousand, five hundred and sixty-four Scrolls, the largest shipment of Sifre Torah in history, began to arrive at their destination in Westminster Synagogue in London. In the synagogue, in three rooms, shelves were erected and numbered one space for each of 1,564 Scrolls. Each of the Scrolls was given a number and placed in the space with the corresponding number, as if a naked corpse in shrouds had been put to sleep in a little bin. The Kolin Scroll slept in bin #330.

Then, the second stage, the work of examining and classifying the Scrolls began. Several skilled scribes were engaged in the task of inspecting each Scroll from beginning to end and making entries of their findings regarding the condition of parchment, writing, and of any noteworthy distinguishing features.

continued on page 10

The primary object of this undertaking was to separate the Scrolls into those in good condition, those beyond repair, and those which could be made right with greater or less effort.

At the same time, a Memorial Scrolls Committee was established to review the hundreds of requests for the Scrolls which have come from synagogues, universities, and museums throughout the world.

The concluding chapter of our story begins with a letter which I wrote to my colleague, Albert Friedlander, Rabbi of Westminster Synagogue, to inquire if our congregation might be considered as a home for one of the Torah Scrolls. I hastened to add in my letter to Rabbi Friedlander that we did not require a Kosher Scroll, one that had been restored. We have three such beautiful scrolls, generously and lovingly given by members of our congregation.

After many months of correspondence, the Memorial Scrolls Committee granted our request for a special Memorial Scroll, a scroll deemed "Pasul," beyond repair, and legally unfit for reading because of its many broken, erased, and otherwise illegible letters.

No doubt, after careful consideration, Scroll #330 was selected from the hundreds of scrolls, taken from its bin and packed with meticulous and loving care for shipment to Lexington. When I received the letter and I knew that the Scroll was on its way to begin a new life in a new home, I prayed that its trip would be an easy one, and its last one.

When Bonnie and I drove to the airport on that late day in June, we were both rather silent. I think we both knew that we were part of a drama, old and familiar to our people, but new to us. I thought of the many times in Jewish history that our people, in danger and in flight, were nonetheless preoccupied with the saving of their sacred Scrolls.

Remember the vignette in one of Chagall's paintings. There, in the corner of the painting, a little shtetl synagogue is burning, its scarlet flames leaping skyward. A pogrom is raging. Men are rampaging through the village, burning, looting, and killing. A frightened bearded Jew is running from the synagogue, a Sefer Torah in his arms. Four figures suspended in mid-air, tire, looking down incredulously, but the Jew runs, clutching his Torah, determined not to stop until he has found a resting place for his sacred burden, his tree of life.

At the airport, the box was placed on an office counter. After the accompanying shipping slips were read, a customs agent approached, looked at me, at the slips, and at the box. His question was altogether appropriate. I knew he had asked it a thousand times before, but under the circumstances, I knew also that I would never forget it. He asked, "What would you say is the value of it, sir?"

In your name, I answered, "Priceless."

Priceless because without it we would never have survived, even though six million of us are dead.

Priceless because it is the very breath and being of our people; because though we have seldom been able to live by it, neither have we been able to live without it.

Priceless because those strangely-shaped black letters form the words and concepts on which humanity is founded and on which it will always rest.

Priceless because anyone who wishes to understand us fully, must first understand our commitment to Torah.

Yes, and priceless, because a thousand voices have prayed over this scroll.

How many hands have touched this Torah? How many minds and hearts have been touched by it? How many young students became a Bar Mitzvah by it? How many gentle old men have studied from it? In its processions around the synagogue, how many lips have kissed it? How many? Lips of the old and the young. Lips lifeless now, that cried out to the executioners in fear and faith at Auschwitz and Dachau, "Sh'ma Yisrael Adonai Elohaynoo Adonai Echad."

"Priceless," I said, in your name, and in the name of every Kolin Jew, in the name of every Jew inscribed on the synagogue wall, in the name of every man, woman, and child, I say, we will not forget you, neither we, nor our children, nor our children's children.

Come, beloved Torah, your life has been long and hard. Come, enter into our lives that we may do you honor. We reverently rise.

Ribono Shel Olam, Master of the Universe, we humbly accept this Sefer Torah. We consecrate to Your holy purposes this sacred gift which honors the memory of Six Million.

Forgive its imperfections as we today are forgiven our own. Allow us every once and awhile to read its broken letters, O Lord, for this Torah has slept too long, and it yearns to be read and kissed as in days gone by.

As we dedicate this Torah in memory of the Jews of Kolin and the Six Million, help us, God, to rededicate our lives to all that it represents.

Amen.

Bechmann Family History

INTRODUCTION

In November 1935 my mother, Lilli Bechmann Rahn, then living in Fürth, Germany, wrote a history of the Bechmann family. In her introduction she said:

> "At a time when so many Jewish families are being scattered all over the world, the family history gains great importance as the last uniting link. And so it is with great pleasure that I am presenting just at this time the history and geneological table of the Bechmann family."

> "My researches concern mainly the male main-line Bechmann and their respective wives. Since in previous conturies it was a matter of course to have many children, it was of course, impossible for me to follow closely the descent of the respective siblings...I therefore limited myself in these cases to mentioning the respective following generation, namely the cousins (of both sexes) of the followed main line."

With the help of a family friend, Gerda Breit, this history has been translated from German into English. In addition, I have, to the best of my knowledge, brought it up to date.

While thirty-seven years ago my mother was concerned with the potential scattering of the Jews all over the world, I, today, have been interested to learn what happened to a family which was centrally located for over two centuries and then forced to disperse. Thus the descendants of Wilhelm and Gette Bechmann are followed in some detail.

To facilitate the understanding of the geneological table itself, let me explain the system whihh was used. The Bechmann family member whose descendants are traced on a particular page appears on the upper left hand side; the spouse on the upper right. Their children are listed numerically on the left side of the page with each descending generation appearing one step to the right, being set off with brackets. Spouses of these descending generations appear directly below the ii

Bechmanr descendant but receive no number for themselves.

In case any mistakes should have beenuunwillingly made in this presentation I would be grateful for corrections as well as additions of any kind.

I would like to extend my gratitude to all those family members who helped me up-date this history. Through lengthy correspondences and very prompt responses this work was made much easier. I hope some-day we will all be able to meet each other.

Evelyn R. Davis

Evelyn Rahn Davis

Cambridge, Massachusetts
July 1972

THE BECHMANN FAMILY HISTORY

The history of the Bechmann family was closely knit with the central Frankish landscape in Germany. For nearly 250 years members went from Schnaittach via Bechhofen to Fürth where they lived until the holocaust of the second world war dispersed them throughout the world.

The first direct ancestor about whom something is known is Rabbi Salomo (1666-1767), also Rabbi Salomo Schnaittach or Rabbi Salomo Eichberg or Salomo Kolin as mentioned in the book by Rabbi M. Weinberg, "History of the Jews in Upper Palestine" (III, page 119 ff).

It is not known whether Salomo himself came from Kolin (in Czechoslevakia) or whether his parents Nachman Löb and Gitel (or their ancestors) came from there to Franconia. It is possible that Salomo who was called Salomo Krakau in the book by Würfel about the Jews from Nürnberg (page 122) came to Franconia either with or at the request of the famous Rabbi Baruch Rappaport of Fürth. He might have come as early as 1711 when Rappaport began office. Favoring this assumption is the fact that Jona, Salomo's oldest known child was born in 1711, but since Salomo was already fifty-one years old by then Jona was probably not his first child, especially since he subsequently had more children, his last being born when he was seventy-seven. It might therefore be plausable that the younger children remained in the east. But, this is all only hypothesis. However, it is known that from 1723 to 1731 Salomo was vice-rabbi in Schnaittach under Rabbi Rappaport and Weinberg notes that in 1728 he took his oath of office as rabbi.

This activity stopped in 1732 and Würfel notes erroneously that he died at that time, but probably it was then that Salomo moved from Schnaitach to Bechhofen. The reasons for this move are not known.

-2-

Salomo's first wife, Rebekka, died in Schopflock where Salomo's
brother lived. She was buried there on the second of Schewat, 1719.
They had two children, Jona and Frumetle.

Their daughter, Frumetle, whose name and history are only mentioned
by Weinberg, was married to Simeon, born in 1715, the son of the teacher
Jaidel from the Bärmann School in Fürth. Simeon's mother who came from
a respected family, was the daughter of the director of the printer, Hirsh
Franfurter, in Fürth. Simeon, who had been circumcized by Baruch Rappaport, had himself and his son (born in Nürnberg in 1745) baptized in
Saint Sebald on September 21, 1748. During his baptism by deacon Konrad
Schönleben they received the family name of Matthaei. In 1751 Simeon Matthaei published a "Description of the Jewish Sabbath" with a preface by
hhe pastor of Sebal, Jakob Pfitzer, and a year later he published a second work, "The Depravities of Today's Judaism." In 1755 he became an
officer of the Dominican Church. This was certainly a great misfortune
and unhappiness for Salomo.

After Rebekka, hisffirst wife, died, Salomo married Edel, the daughter
of Dajan Hess of Fürth. They had three sons, Abraham, Hirsh, and Mordechai, and all were circumcized by their much older brother, Jona. Edel
died in October 1748 (Yom Kippur 5509) and was buried in the Bechhofen
cemetary.

Salomo survived her and reached the unusually old age of 101. "The
days which he lived on earth were 101 years and his vitality did not
fade, his eye did not dull so that he would have needed an eyeglass."
This is how his son, Jona, described his father in his Mohel book. According to another source he is supposed to have cracked nuts with his teeth
inhhis hundredth year.

-3-

Rabbi Salomo did not only assure himself to be remembered forever through his sons and grandsons, he was also active in the literary field. He composed a work, Sefer Jerioth Schelomo, that is described in his son's mohel book.

Jona Salomon Bechhofen's life corresponded rather closely to his father's pious and scholarly ideals. There are two sources of information about Jona. First, the community of Bechhofen in which he was active for many years as Mohel possesses a number of memorabilia from his hand, and secondly, Lilli Bechmann Rahn (1911-1970) found his perfectly kept and very detailed mohel book which she gave to the Jewish Museum in Munich in the 1930s. This book is part of the larger book, "Prayers Before and During the Circumcision" by Samuel ben Israel from Sobno, printed in Amsterdam in 1719 in the printing shop founded by Rabbi Josef Dajan. On the title page Jona wrote, "I bought it in honor of the creator, the little Jonas, son of the Rabbi Salomo Schnaittach from Bechhofen." In this book he not only made exact notations of the 157 circumcisions he undertook between his twenty-fifth and seventy-fourth years, but he also included a variety of events which took place during his life, such as the enormously cold winter of 1740 and the great famine of 1771. Furthermore, he discussed his profession as a Mohel and outlined prescriptions to stop bleeding during circumcision. These medical and folk opinions are described below.

> "Take three thimbles full of blood in three eggshells, boil, and apply."
>
> "Take a snail with its shell, burn it on the fire and whenever it wants to crawl out, push it back into the shell, pulverize the ashes, and put them on the wound."
>
> "In May take green frogs, boil them in a tightly covered

-4-

> pot and cement it with putty; add also strong wine, pul-
> verize everything and sprinkle the wound."

> "Take eggshells, burn them and sprinkle them on the wound.
> Also, as I heard, it is known to put dry grass which is
> called hay on glowing coals, then catch the rising smoke,
> and put it on the wound."

It is rather amazing that, despite these methods, the infant mortality
among the Jews, considered in comparison to the Gentile environment, was
still rather low.

As a youth Jona already showed great organizational and especially
graphical and calligraphical talents. In 1732 he drew a beautiful tab-
let with blessings for the Bechhofen community. On one side it contains
the blessings of the Haftorah, on the other blessings and prayers for
circumcision ceremonies.

His beautiful handwriting was hardly distinguishable from the printed
letter and can be recognized clearly from illustrations in his Mohel
book which he began to write at the age of twenty-one.

His apprenticeship was spent with the precentor and Mohel, Maier
in Ellingen. He performed his first circumcision when he was twenty-
five years old, on the 7th day of the Feast of Tabernacles in 1736. In
his Mohel book he described the extraordinary circumstances which led
him to do it.

> "With the heavenly help and the assistance of God!"

> "I will begin with God, who heard me on the day of my distress;
> I raise my spirit and sould to Him because He is the true
> Helper and I will always pour out my supplication to Him.
> Since my souldwas longing for the command, certainly since
> birth I was already destined to work as a mohel in my life.
> When I was still a student with my respected master, Mr.
> Maier Ellingen, I suddenly saw that very clearly. On the
> day of the half festival of the Feast of Tabernacles an
> excellent man came to me with the news of his son's birth
> and with the complimentary demand to take on the mohelship

-5-

and to lead his first born son under the wings of the divine splendor and to circumcize his foreskin. I said that I had already been a Mohel several times, but in reality I had not yet been privileged. But since all the other Mohels in the neighborhood did not want to leave their families on the feast day and said, 'You shall be happy in your house,' I said to myself, 'You could be a Mohel, too.'"

"Since I saw now that this was a divine providence, I blushed and my knees trembled in the thought that nobody could really assist me. But I remained strong like a hero with the help of God and so I came to Treuchtlingen on Friday afternoon, Erev Shabbath, Hoschanna Rabba. My heart stopped and I had to marvel at the moment. Nobody guessed my inner thoughts because I controlled myself in front of all the people. That night I did not sleep; then I prayed to my God in Heaven that he send me the angels of mercy since I carry out this command on the basis of a lie as is written in the Schulcan Aruch, Orach Vhain #331. In this case, however, our sages did not see a sin because the date of the circumcision must be kept on the eighth day of life. I performed the circumcision without any fear, anxiety, or dread - God was my helper!"

"So may the Eternal continue to strengthen my arms to perform the good and just in his eyes so that one does not hang empty ewers on me by claiming this man does not even possess the necessary knowledge for this office - there was, as mentioned, no other possibility. When they saw that the Eternal put good success in my hands, they said to me, 'At all times Jona shall be our Mohel.' As a matter of fact, I still came there many times and have always performed the circumcisions with speed as you will hear. Thus I bless all of you who love the Eternal, your God, may you all remain in life! Amen."

> The little Jona, son of the Rabbi Salomo from Bechhofen. In the year 5496 (1736).

Subsequently Jona performed other circumcisions in the Ellingen community. However, only a year later, in 1737, he returned to Bechhofen where on the 21st day of Elul he circumcized his brother, Abraham. Henceforth he remained in Bechhofen and married Jentel (probably in 1739), daughter of Salomon David in Bechhofen. This Salomon David belonged to one of the families that had been expelled from Herrieden in 1682 and had

-6-

been given permission to settle in Bechhofen.

On the tenth day of Teweth, 1740 Jona's first born, Nachum Löb, was born and named after his paternal grandfather. It is worth noting that Rabbi Salomo and Jona must have been held in high esteem because the most respected people in the community became god-fathers of their sons.

In Bechhofen Jona made himself immortal by founding and organizing the charity institution. It was a manifold activity which connected all the communities in the neighborhood because they brought their dead to Bechhofen for their funerals. Jona put down the statutes and resolutions in a special book which remained valid in the Bechhofen community at least until the 1930s.

Jona probably spend the last years of his life in Ansbach. He performed his last circumcision on Simchath Torah 1784 at the age of seventy-four "with surety, without glasses, with a quick hand, as if her were thirty-two years old," as his last entry reads. He died in 1786.

Jona's wife, Jentel, survived him by thirteen years, dying in 1799. The inscription on her grave reads, "Here rests Jentel, wife of Mr. Jona of Ansbach. A generally revered and respected woman who counts her praises. The loyal and good one, in the laws of womanhood she was conscientious and raised her children in the teachings. Mrs. Jentel, daughter of Mr. Salomo of blessed memory. She died and was buried on Thursday, the tenth of Siwan 5559 (1799). May her soul be bound up in the bod of life!"

Less is known about Nachman Löb Bechhofen-Berg (1740-1828) than about his father or grandfather. As stated, he was born in 1740 and was circumcised by his father. About 1766 he married Hanna, the daughter of Wolf Sulberg of Fürth. They lived in Fürth where they had a son on the

-7-

eleventh day of Ijar 1770 who was named after his paternal grandfather, Salomo.

Nachman Löb was a writing teacher and his activities may have consisted of nothing more than an intensive life-long occupation with the law as it corresponded to Jewish family traditions. Or, perhaps he actually taught writing. We do not know for sure.

In any case, he never gained much wealth. On the contrary, his name appeared in the testimonial books of Fürth in 1812 and 1825 as "quite poor" and later in his life as a sick man. These entries must be taken cautiously as testimonials of poverty were often exaggerated to allow a person to receive a donation or a charitable allowance. Nachman Löb died at the age of eighty-eight and was the first of the Bechmann ancestors to be buried in the old Jewish cemetary in Fürth.

Nachman Löb and Hanna had seven sons. The fifth, Jona Bär, born April 17, 1787, doubtlessly was given the name of his grandfather who died in 1786.

Around this time Jews began to take on family names which were frequently changed until the beginning of the 19th century when they were fixed by the state. The name giving of the Bechmann family came, as with many Jewish families, from their place of origin. Jona had already added Bechhofen, his actual place of residence, to his name. Nachman Löb appears as Bechhofen-Berg, the addition is not quite clear. Most of his sons called themselves Bechhöfer which means those coming from Bechhofen. The oldest son, Salomon, later omitted the second part of his name and appeared as Bech. The third son, Nathan Hirsch changed Bechhöfer into Bechmann and thereby became the creator of the Bechmann family name.

<u>Nathan Hirsch Bechmann</u>, (1780-1859) chose, the profession of his

-8-

father and became a writing teacher. Besides the exclusive occupation
with the Holy Scriptures, he carried out, at least in the later years of
his life, a kind of bookkeeper job. He went either by the hour or by
the day to some firms and there, with his exceedingly beautiful and
correct handwriting, he dept the books. For example, at least until the
1930s his personal entries still remained in the books of the MS Farrnbacher firm in Fürth.

One of Nathan Hirsch Bechmann's characteristics was his punctuality
and exactness. Thus it is said that he ended his writing work with the
stroke of the clock and also began in the same way, regardless whether or
not he stopped in the middle of the sentence. His work must not have
been very well paid because his wife, Esther, (1780-1859) daughter of
Jakob Löb Neustettel-Neuhauss in Fürth, was forced to contribute to the
support of the family by trading with all kinds of merchandise.

Even with this added income the Fürth testimonial book showed that
in 1821 Nathan Hirsch was the recipient of an annual salary of 90 guild-
ers from the Nehm Rindskopf Foundation and in 1823 he was exempted from
paying the school fee for his children since he could not afford it. In
1857, two years before he died, he applied to the Nehm Rindskppf Foundation to extend benefits to his wife after his death as she would feel the
loss of the stipend very severely.

In spite of his financial difficulties, Nathan Hirsch raised his
seven children to become competent, respectable, and useful citizens. As
is shown in the Last Will and Testament which he and his wife drew up
shortly before they both died (1859), his main interest and strivings
were not for material goods. The Will gives exact instructions as to
the division of certain family pictures and especially his bible and pro-

-9-

phet editions. He also chooses the prayers which are to be said at his grave and during his days of Jahrzeit. Only at the end does he give a brief instruction as to his estate. Nathan Hirsch died on June 19, 1859 and his wife followed him a few months later, on November 2, 1859.

With Nathan Hirsch's and Esther's children the Bechmann family began to enter the great emancipation movement of Judaism which took place in the middle to late 19th century. Whereas up to this time interests were directed primarily to the events and contents of Jewish life, the following generation began to turn its main attention to the world at large. This is shown outwardly both in the changes of first names and choices of professions. Names were no longer Jakob Löb, Wolf, and Jechiel, but rather Jaques Louis, Wilhelm, and Julius, an adaptation of names to residences. Work was no longer principally of Jewish content, but more secular. Jaques Louis went to Paris where he entered the mainstream of life and his sons became engineers, members of the Board of Trade, and Knights of the Legion of Honor.

Wilhelm Bechmann (1820-1908), Nathan and Esther's sixth child, was a strong and energetic man. The time was ripe for enterprising people and he was a hard worker who found a great deal of success. He began the fabrication of mirror and mirror glass. The firm developed into one of the first in Fürth. Through his success the family gained great respect from the last third of the 19th century until the National Socialist Revolution.

On October 21, 1847 Wilhelm married Gette (1824-1901), daughter of Mayer Offenbacher-Oppenheim in Fürth. Gette came from a very respected family. Her grandfather, Juna Offenbacher-Oppenheim, was Dajan in Fürth, later a country rabbi. Her father was a dealer in mirror glass

-10-

in Fürth and he probably provided the incentive for his son-in-law to get involved in the fabrication of mirror glass.

Gette was a pious woman and carefully executed all religious laws in her house. However, Wilhelm took on these obligations more out of piety towards his parents and respect for Gette than out of personal conviction. Therefore, as he grew older he allowed himself small deviations, especially from the Kosher laws.

At the end of the 19th century, already in his late seventies, Wilhelm withdrew gradually from all honorary offices, e.g. from active congregation administration as well as from business life. He left the management of his firm to his sons, Louis and Maier. On May 24, 1905 the firm merged with W. Kupfer and Sons and was changed into a joint stock company with the name Bavarian Mirror and Mirror Glass Factories, A. G., formerly W. Bechmann, formerly W. Kupfer and Sons.

Gette died on March 25, 1901 and Wilhelm died eight years later at the age of eighty-eight on November 14, 1908.

Wilhelm and Gette had ten children, two of whom died in infancy, all of whom were born in Fürth. All of their descendants who lived beyond the 1930s left Germany under Naziism. Thus, the family with its roots in one area for generations and even centuries dispersed such that there is no one living in Germany and, in fact, no one living on mainland Europe. It was possible to trace the descendants of Wilhelm and Gette through their grandchildren and great-grandchildren.

Several trends have emerged. Interestingly, a number of people whom emigrated were able to re-establish themselves in their new country in a similar business to that which they had in Germany. In fact, most of Wilhelm's and Gette's children and grandchildren were in business while

-11-

later generations became educated for professions. No one remained involved with anoobservant Jewish, religious life style. On the contrary,
there emerged considerable intermarriage and conversion so today there
are family members who are both Catholics and Protestants. However,
there have been several members who have involved themselves with Jewish affairs and have been active in Hadassah, United Jewish Appeal, American Jewish Committee, etc. Also in their new countries there have
been slight changes in sur-names as with William Beechman, Alfred Beecham, and Ida Beckman.

There will be some attempt to describe what has happened to various
descendants. The geneology in the back shows the full line of descendants.

Veronika Bechmann (1851-1927) moved from Fürth to Munich where she
married the art dealer, Jakob Birn (1841-1903). They had one child,
August (1873-1948), who went to Buenos Aires, Argentina with his wife,
Marie Wortsmann (1877-1965) in the 1930s. There they both died. Their
older daughter, Ilse (1901-   ), married Emil Sadler (1893-1956), also
of Munich and in the corn business there. When they emigrated to Buenos
Aires in 1934 he was able to work in the same field, exporting to Bo-
livia. They had three sons; Alfred (1924-   ) who is a chemist in Sao
Paulo, Brasil; Teo (1926-   ) who is a physician in Buenos Aires, Argentina; and Robert (1928-   ), a wool merchant in Boston, Massachusetts. All
three are married with children. Hilde (1903-   ), Veronika's younger
daughter, married Edwin Grünstein (1901-   ) of Ansbach and they emigrated
to Argentina in 1937. After several moves he became a merchant in Bar-
iloche, situated in one of Argentina's national parks. There they have
been quite successful. Their oldest child, Ester (1938-   ) studied
mathematics and works for IBM. Their son, Jorge (1941-   ) is married,

-12-

has two children, and works with his father.

The offspring of Berta Bechmann (1853-1948) and Benno Dünkelsbühler (1847-1923) spent their lives in England. Their oldest daughter,
Selma (1874-1965) was married for a short time to Hermann Kahn. They
had one son, Ludwig (1897-1966) who became a banker in New York, was
married twice, but had no children. Emma and Betty were twins, both
lived in England. While Betty (1877-1962) who married Bruno Ullmann
was childless, Emma (1877-1966) married Sam Wimmel and they had one
daughter, Ada (1903-). She and her husband, Harry Lindeck (1898-),
who was a businessman and now is retired but volunteers five days a week
for the senior citizens, had two children. Their older son, Peter (1931-)
is a clergyman and John (1933-) is an accountant, married with three
children.

Maier Bechmann (1856-1947), as previously mentioned, became a manager
of the Bavarian Glass Factory along with his brother, Louis. He married
Emma Gutherz (1871-1938) who died in Fürth. But Maier and his two
children moved to England. His daughter, Else (1883-1957) married the
lawyer, Leopold Honig. Anna Sahlman (1906-) and Robert Holmes (1911-),
their children, have both gone into business for themselves. Maier's
son, Paul (1888-), is in the export business with his son, William
Beechman (1921-). They both became members of the Church of England
in 1940.

Henry Beckman (1860-1940) is the only descendant who left Germany
prior to the 1930s. As a young man he came to Cincinnati, Ohio where
he married Ida Frohmann (1863-1934) and became a successful businessman.
His son, Harold (1891-1964) was trained as a metallurgic engineer and
was active in Jewish civic affairs along with his wife, Jean Jacoby (1895-).

-13-

Their son, James (1924-), studied forestry. He is married and has
two children. Henry's daughter, Martha Ransohoff (1894-), and her
children live in Cincinnati, but little is known about them.

Erna Heymann(1895-), the daughter of Simon Bechmann (1862-1914)
and Frida Weil (1873-1962) lives in New Jersey where her husband, Sidney, died in 1943 at the age of fifty-two. In Fürth Sidney manufactured
elastic ribbons used in items such as belts and suspenders. In New York
he worked in a knitting mill. Erna lives next door to her daughter,
Lisa (1922-), married to Eric Silbermann (1921-) who works for the
Presto Lock Company. Their older son, Steven (1950-), is an engineer.
Erna's other daughter, Greta (1927-), lives in New York with her
husband, Peter Jacob (1920-) and their three children. Peter is an
accountant. Erna's brother, Alfred Beecham (1902-) married Marie
Frohmann of Nürnberg in 1930. In 1933 they migrated to Belgium and in
1935 to South Africa. They were divorced in 1937 and a year later he
married Esther Shapiro of Johannesburg who died of a heart attack in
1950. On December 2, 1954 he married Sophie Kaplan, a pediatrician,
and in 1959 they moved to Melbourne, Australia. He worked in a government office until he had to retire at the age of sixty-five and now
he is with a brokerage firm.

Emilie and Nathan Klugmann had three children, the oldest of whom
died very young. The other two, Marta and Walter, married, but were
childless.

Mathilde Bechmann (1865-1960) married Carl Ullmann (1867-1939) and
had two sons, both became physicians. Hans (1893-1964) emigrated from
Germany to England in 1939 where he married Hilde Dresel (1896-).
In 1940 he came to the United States and was a doctor in New York until

-14-

his death. His brother, Robert (1889-1964) came to the United States
four years earlier, practiced medicine in upper-state New York and had
one daughter, Lynn, about whom little is known except that she and her
family are Catholics.

The descendants of <u>Louis Bechmann</u> (1848-1921) are my direct descendants. On April 24, 1876 Louis married Mathilde Gutherz (1854-1920),
daughter of Alexander and Fanni Gutherz from Lichtenfels. Alexander was
the only one of his six siblings who had remained in Germany, all the
others had emigrated to America. (Maier's wife, Emma, is Mathilde's
youngest sister.)

Louis and Maier co-managed the Bavarian Glass Factory. Their sons,
Hugo and Paul, were also active in the firm. A few years after World War I
they merged with the fanzy goods firm, Max Offenbacher, in Fürth.

Louis and Mathilde died within a year of each other and were both
cremated. Their urns rest in the Jewish Cemetary in Nürnberg.

From their marriage came two children. Karola (1881-1960) married
Julius Löffler, (1873-1946), a judge in civil court and later a Councillor
of the Superior Provincial Court in Nürnberg. Both of them emigrated to
the United States and died in Los Angeles, California. Their daughter,
Lisel (1905-1936), married Alfred Loewi, who had two children from a previous marriage. Lisel and Alfred had one child, Frank Loy (1928-   ),
and Lisel died in Jena, Germany in 1936. After Alfred died in Los Angeles
four years later, Frank was raised by a housekeeper and his grandmother,
Karola, until he went to college. Frank is married to Dale Haven. They
have two children and he is a Senior Vice-President of Pan American.
Heinz (1910-   ), Karola's son, lives in Chicago, Illinois where he came
as a young man, initially to learn English. He never left and today is in

-15-

the paper industry. He has had extensive military involvement with the navy. Married to Jean Campbell, they have two children.

Louis and Mathilde's second child was my grandfather, Hugo Bechmann (1878-1942) who married Ida Metzger (daughter of Karoline and Max) on May 16, 1910.

Until 1928 Hugo was active as director of the Bavarian Glass Factory in Fürth. In that year he resigned from the firm. In 1930 he moved to Berlin where he again became active in the glass business until he was forced to leave by the Nazis. He then moved to Stockholm, Sweden where he became a director of the glass firm, Hultberg.

Hugo's wife, Ida, stayed in Germany until thier daughter, Lilli, could leave with her family. Therefore, in 1939 Ida joined her husband in Sweden. Two years later (spring of 1941) a director of a German company told Mr. Hultberg that if "the Jew", Hugo Bechmann, was not fired Germany would sell not more glass to Hultberg. Hugo lost his job and a year later died during an operation. Since there were no male descendants from this marriage, Hugo Bechmann was the last male bearer of the name from the branch of Louis Bechmann.

My grandmother, Ida (1888-   ), stayed in Stockholm three more years and then moved to Denver in 1945 where she still resides. Not wanting to become financially dependent on her daughter she worked for a short time in the foundations department of the May Company. Thereafter, for nearly nineteen years she worked in the diet department of the National Jewish Hospital until they forced her to retire at the age of seventy-eight. She then moved into a senior citizens community where she is today.

My mother, <u>Lilli</u> <u>Bechmann</u> (1911-1970) was born into what was by then a rather wealthy family. The household was run by maids, cooks,

-16-

chaffeurs, and she was raised by a governess. Every summer, with her parents, she went to Rottach im Tegernsee, in the mountains. She was a bright, energetic, and rebellious child.

When she finished school she wanted to go to the university, but her parents would not allow it and instead sent her toaa "finishing" school in Geneva, Switzerland. After a year she insisted on the university and went both to Freiberg and Erlangen, receiving her PhD from the latter in 1934.

In addition to her academic pursuits she wrote a great deal of poetry, some of which was published.

On July 3, 1933, Lilli married Alfred H. Rahn (1901-1970), son of Johannah and Sidney Rahn, also of Fürth. He was a co-owner of the firm, M.S. Farrnbacher, which dealthwith metals. (His older brother, James, was later killed by the Nazisaand his younger brother, Max, came totthe United States as a young man in 1926.)

Although tensions were increasing for Jews, the Rahns made no plans to leave Germany until 1937, a year after their first daughter, Ruth, was born (1936). They were prepared to immigrate when Alfred was arrested for possessing much more money than he declared; an amount far above the limit a Jew was allowed to take from Germany. He had a trial and after being found guilty was sentenced to fourteen months in prison whichhhe served.

While in prison Alfred's visa expired and a new visa was refused by American consular officials on the ground that he had been guilty of an offence constituting moral turpitude. In the last official opinion rendered by Homer S. Cummings as Attorney General of the United States (1937) he ruled that under the circumstances, ie the persecution of the

-17-

Jews by Germans, keeping one's own money was <u>not</u> moral turpitude and there were no grounds for withholding a visa. The visa was renewed. Therefore, when Alfred was released from prison in March, 1939, he and his family went immediately to Paris and from there to New York where they arrived on April 15, 1939. After a few months they moved to Denver, Colorado (and the Rocky Mountains).

In Denver, my mother, Lilli, worked in a book store and taught German at Denver University. During the war she also volunteered extensively for the American Red Cross. My father became a salesman for various concerns, finally getting back into the steel business which he knew from Germany. After the war my mother's life became deeply involved with Jewish affairs and predominantly Zionist affairs. For Hadassah she was Chapter, and Regional President, National Vice-President, and a life member of the National Board. Her life became a cause for Israel and she became an expert on the subject, speaking throughout the country and leading tours to Israel.

Our family led a very "out-door" life, especially taking advantage of the mountains with such activities as hiking and skiing.

For the most part my father enjoyed good health all his life. But my mother suffered a great many illnesses, her first bout with cancer in 1959. She died of the same disease eleven years later, in December 1970. My father's death followed hers by a day.

My sister, Ruth (1936-), is an energentic and successful woman. She graduated from Smith College (1958) and received her Masters at Teaching from Harvard University (1959). Married to Dr. Matthew A. Budd (1935-) on December 23, 1957, she taught school for several years before they had their first daughter, Karen (1962-). When

-18-

Karen was a year old, Ruth began law school and graduated five years later (1968) from Boston College. She is now a practicing lawyer in Boston, her husband a physician in the same city. And, they have had one more child, Rachel (1966-).

I, Evy Rahn Davis (1945-), graduated from the University of California, Berkeley campus (1966) and received my Master's Degree in Social Work from Simmons School of Social Work in 1968. I subsequently worked in a community health program in Boston. I married William B. Davis (1943-), a physicist, on June 15, 1969.

And, thus it is that the Bechmann family has dispersed all over the world into all walks of life.

-19-

MAINLINE OF THE BECHMANN FAMILY

I.   Nachmann Löb   Gitel
        d. before 1740   d. before 1756

II.   Rabbi Salomo Schnaittach   Rebekka
        b. 1666   d. Schewat 2, 1719
        d. fall 1767

III.   Mohel Jona Bechhofen   Jendel
        b. 1711   d. Siwan 10, 1799
        d. Siwan 3, 1786

IV.   Nachman Löb Bechhofen-Berg   Hanna Sulzberg
        b. Teweth 10, 1740   b. 1744
        d. 11-16-1828   d. 7-29-1836

V.   Nathan Hirsch Bechmann   Esther Neustettel-Neuhaus
        b. 10-11-1780   b. 1780
        d. 7-19-1859   d. 11-2-1859

VI.   Wolf, known as Wilhelm Bechmann   Gette Offenbacher-Oppenheim
        b. 6-25-1820   b. 4-17-1824
        d. 11-14-1908   d. 3-25-1901

VII.   Louis Bechmann   Mathilde Gutherz
        b. 9-4-1848   b. 10-24-1854
        d. 5-23-1921   d. 6-9-1920

VIII.   Hugo Bechmann   Ida Metzger
        b. 7-25-1878   b. 7-29-1888
        d. 7-20-1942

IX.   Lilli Bechmann   Alfred H. Rahn
        b. 2-11-1911   b. 1-28-1902
        d. 12-27-1970   d. 12-28-1970

-20-

Joseph
d. before 1742

Nachman ISS   Gitel
d. before 1740   d. before 1756

1. Rabbi Salomo Schnaittach (see page 21)
   b. 1666
   d. fall 1767

2. Josua Schälein
   in Schopfloch   { 1. Joseph

3. David

4. A daughter who was married to Mosesiin Heidenheim.

-21-

Rabbi Salomo Schnaittach   Rebekka
b. 1666   d. Schewat 2, 1719
d. fall 1767   Schopfloch, Germ.

1. Mohel Jona Bechhofen (see page 22)
   b. 1711
   d. Siwan 3, 1786

2. Frumetle
                          ⎱ 1. A son
   Simeon   ⎰   b. 1745
   b. 1715   baptized with his father

3. Wolf

Rabbi Salomo Schnaittach   Edel
b. 1666   d. October 1748
d. fall 1767   Bechhofen, Germ.

1. Abraham
   b. Elul 17, 1737
      Bechhofen, Germany

2. Hirsch
   b. Schewat 13, 1740
      Bechhofen, ?Germany

3. Mordechai
   b. Jjar 23, 1743
      Bechhofen, Germany

SIMEON'S TREE

Jaidel   Hendle
b. 1665
d. 7-27-1746
teacher at Yeshiva

1. Simeon
   b. 1715 in Fürth
   teacher
   baptized, 9-21-1748
   surname-Matthaei

-22-

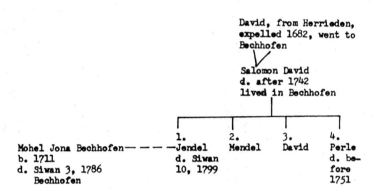

David, from Herrieden,
expelled 1682, went to
Bechhofen

Salomon David
d. after 1742
lived in Bechhofen

Mohel Jona Bechhofen— — — —Jendel	2. Mendel	3. David	4. Perle
b. 1711	1. Jendel		

Mohel Jona Bechhofen— — — —
b. 1711
d. Siwan 3, 1786
Bechhofen

1.
Jendel
d. Siwan
10, 1799

2.
Mendel

3.
David

4.
Perle
d. be-
fore
1751

1. <u>Nachman Löb Bechhofen-Berg</u> (see page 23)
   b. Teweth 10, 1740
   d. 11-16-1828

2. David
   b. Siwan 9, 1742 in Bechhofen

3. Joseph
   b. Nissan, 13, 1744 in Bechhofen

4. Rebekka
   b. Adar 24, 1746   ⎰ 1. Samson
      in Bechhofen   ⎱   b. Siwan 14, 1767

   Moses Edernheim

5. Menachem Mendel
   b. Kislev 19, 1748 in Bechhofen

6. Abraham
   b. Elul 14, 1749 in Bechhofen

7. Perle
   b. Siwan 24, 1751 in Bechhofen

8. Samuel
   b. Jjar 21, 1753 in Bechhofen

9. Gitel
   b. Av 10, 1756 in Bechhofen

10. Nendele
    b. Elul 11, 1759 in Bechhofen

11. Elias
    b. Jjar 18, 1762 in Bechhofen

12. Elchanan Bär
    b. Teweth 12, 1764 in Bechhofen

-23-

Nachman Löb Bechhofen-Berg
b. Teweth 10, 1740
    Bechhofen, Germany
d. 11-16-1828
    Fürth, Germany
writing teacher

Hanna Sulsberg
b. 1744
d. 7-29-1836
    Fürth, Germany

1. Nathan Salomon Löb
   Bechhofen-Bech
   b. 4-29-1770
   d. 3-19-1852
     Fürth, Germany

   Esther Koblenz
   b. 1793
   d. 6-14-1821
     Fürth, Germany

   1. Seligman Jonas
     Löb Bech
     b. 10-21-1813
     went to American

   2. Jette Bech
     b. 3-4-1818
     d. 5-23-1826
      Fürth, Germany

   3. Herz Bech
     b. 10-27-1819
     d. 10-28-1819
     one day old

2. Josua, known as
   Gehita Bechhöfer
   b. 8-15-1776
   d. 6-13-1856
     Fürth, Germany
   pewter and brass
   dealer

   Hanna
   b. 1776
   d. 11-12-1837

   1. Babette Hesslein
     Arnstein, Germany

   2. Jette Hermann
     Fürth, Germany

   3. Zerta, known as
     Zilli Nordmann
     d. before 1856, all
     three children were
     still minors

         1. Emanuel Nordmann

         2. Jakob Nordmann

         3. Zilli Nordmann

3. **Nathan Hirsch Bechhöfer-Bechmann** (see page 24)
   b. 10-11-1780
   d. 7-19-1859
     Fürth, Germany

4. David Bechhöfer
   b. 4-20-1783 in Fürth

5. Jona Bär Bechhöfer
   b. 4-16-1787 in Fürth

6. Baruch Bechhöfer
   b. 4-24-1788 in Fürth

7. Salman Bechhöfer
   b. 5-12-1793 in Fürth

-24-

Nathan Hirsch Bechmann
b. 10-11-1780
d. 7-19-1859
   Fürth, Germany
writing teacher

Esther Neustettel-Neuhaus
b. 1780
d. 2-11-1859
   Fürth, Germany

1. Jette Bechmann
   b. 2-18-1810
   d. 6-19-1876

   Eisig Birn
   b. Urspringen, Germ.

1. Leopold Birn
   b. 6-30-1839

2. Jakob Birn
   b. 10-27-1841
   d. 11-2-1903

3. Sophie Klein, née Birn
   b. 6-20-1843

4. Hannchen Schlosstein, née Birn
   b. 2-25-1845

5. Babette Silber, née Birn
   b. 7-4-1847

6. Jette, known as Julie Birn
   b. 6-17-1852
   d. 2-2-1911

   Julius Bechmann (her uncle)
   b. 6-18-1822
   d. 7-20-1907

7. Moritz Birn
   b. 1-21-1854

2. Edel Bechmann
   b. 10-31-1812
   d. young

3. Jeanette Bechmann
   b. 11-27-1814

   Wolf Goldstein
   b. 4-12-1811

1. Samuel Goldstein
   b. 4-20-1844

2. Leopold Goldstein
   b. 4-11-1847

3. Jakob Goldstein
   b. 9-14-1850

4. Jonas Goldstein
   b. 3-20-1857

5. Sophie Wangersheim, née Goldstein

-25-

Nathan Hirsch Bechmann   Esther Neustettel-Neuhaus (cont'd)

4. Lea, known as
   Luise Bechmann
   b. 9-9-1816
   d. 7-1-1893

   David Lenkersheimer

   1. Emil Bechmann
      b. 1-31-1847
      d. 2-7-1847

5. Jakob Löb, known as   2. Georges Bechmann in Paris, France
   Jaques Louis Bechmann   b. 1-1-1848
   b. 8-30-1818
   d. 12-31-1895   3. Alfred Bechmann in Paris, France
      Paris, France   12-26-1855, b.

   Jeanne Constantine Hesse 4. Edmond Bechmann in Nancy, France
   b. 11-21-1820   b. 8-3-1851
   d. 1-18-1901
                             5. Anna Cohen, née Bechmann
                                b. 12-15-1858

6. Wolf, known as
   Wilhelm Bechmann (see page 27)
   b. 6-25-1820 in Fürth, Germ.
   d. 11-14-1908 in Fürth, Germ.

7. Jechiel, known as
   Julius Bechmann
   b. 6-18-1822
   d. 4-20-1907

   Therese Offenstadt

   Julie Birn (his niece)
   b. 6-17-1852
   d. 2-2-1911

-26-

Nathan Hirsch Bechmann3   Esther Neustettel-Neuhaus (cont'd)

8. J

1. Ludwig Bechmann
   b. 8-4-1852
   d. 10-27-1918

2.
21 Heinrich Bechmann
   b. 7-16-1853

8. Jonas Bechmann
   b. 3-11-1824
   d. 11-10-1888

3. Jakob Bechmann
   b. 2-1-1855

Friederike Ellern
b. 8-22-1827
d. 8-3-1892

4. Nathan Bechmann in London, England
   b. 8-10-1860

5. Joseph Bechmann
   b. 5-13-1863

-27-

Wolf, known as
<u>Wilhelm Bechmann</u>
b. 6-25-1820
Fürth, Germany
d. 11-14-1908
Fürth, Germany
mirror glass factory
owner

Gette Offenbacher
b. 4-17-1824
Fürth, Germany
d. 3-25-1901
Fürth, Germany

1. Louis Bechmann....................see page 28
   b. 4-9-1848
   d. 5-23-1921

2. a boy, died after 11 hours
   b. 1-30-1850
   Fürth, Germany
   d. 1-30-1850
   Fürth, Germany

3. Veronika Birn, nee Bechmann............see page 29
   b. 7-14-1851
   d. 5-29-1927

4. Berta Dünkelsbühler, nee Bechmann......see page 30
   b. 4-21-1853
   d. 1-21-1948

5. Rosa Bechmann
   b. 7-22-1854
   Fürth, Germany
   d. 12-12-1854
   Fürth, Germany

6. Maier Bechmann.........................see page 31
   b. 1-26-1856
   d. 3-7-1947

7. Nathan Hirsch, known as Henry Bechmann.see page 32
   b. 1-10-1860
   d. 8-30-1940

8. Simon Bechmann.........................see page 33
   b. 4-26-1862
   d. 9-15-1914

9. Emilie Klugmann, nee Bechmann..........see page 34
   b. 3-3-1864
   d. 10-18-1940

10. Mathilde Ullmann, nee Bechmann........see page 35
    b. 8-7-1865
    d. 7-11-1960

-28-

Louis Bechmann
b. 4-9-1848
   Fürth, Germ.
d. 5-23-1921
   Fürth, Germ.
factory owner

Mathilde Gutherz
b. 10-24-1854
   Fürth, Germ.
d. 9-6-1920
   Fürth, Germ.

1. an un-named boy
   b. 2-24-1877
   d. 2-24-1877
      Fürth, Germany

2.

2. Hugo Bechmann
   b. 7-25-1878
      Fürth, Germ.
   d. 7-19-1942
      Stockholm, Swdn.
   factory owner

Ida Metzger
b. 7-29-1888
   Fürth, Germ.

1. Lilli Bechmann
   b. 2-11-1911
      Fürth, Germ.
   d. 12-27-1970
      Denver, Colo.
   Ph.D. Erlangen U.

Alfred. H. Rahn
b. 1-28-1901
   Fürth, Germ.
d. 12-28-1970
   Denver, Colo.
steel repres.

1. Ruth Rahn
   b. 6-15-1936
      Fürth, Germ.
   lawyer

Matthew A. Budd
b. 5-26-1935
   Boston, Mass.
physician

22. Evelyn Rahn
   b. 1-21-1945
      Denver, Colo.
   social worker

William B. Davis
b. 11-11-1943
   Richmond, Va.
physicist

1. Karen Budd
   b. 9-26-1962
      Cleveland,
      Ohio

2. Rachel Budd
   b. 7-16-1966
      Boston,
      Mass.

3. Karola Bechmann
   b. 9-17-1881
      Fürth, Germ.
   d. 9-13-1960
      L.A., Calif.

Julius Löffler
b. 2-15-1873
   Fürth, Germ.
d. 10-1946
   L. A., Calif.
councilor of
supperior pro-
vincial court

1. Lisel Löffler
   b. 6-30-1905
      Fürth, Germ.
   d. 9-13-1936
      Jena, Germ.

Alfred Loewi
d. 9-1940
   L.A., Calif.

2. Heinz Loeffler
   b. 7-9-1910
      Fürth, Germ.
   businessman

Jean Campbell
b. 2-4-1922

1. Frank Loy
   b. 12-25-1928
      Nürnberg, Germ.
   businessman

Dale Haven
b. 3-1-1935

1. Susan Campbell
   Loeffler
   b. 7-28-1948
      Chicago, Ill.

2. PatricianLynn
   Loeffler
   b. 4-24-1953
      Chicago, Ill.

1. Lisel Loy
   b. 5-19-1966
      Wash. DC

2. Eric Anthony
      Loy
   b. 4-28-1968
      Wash. DC

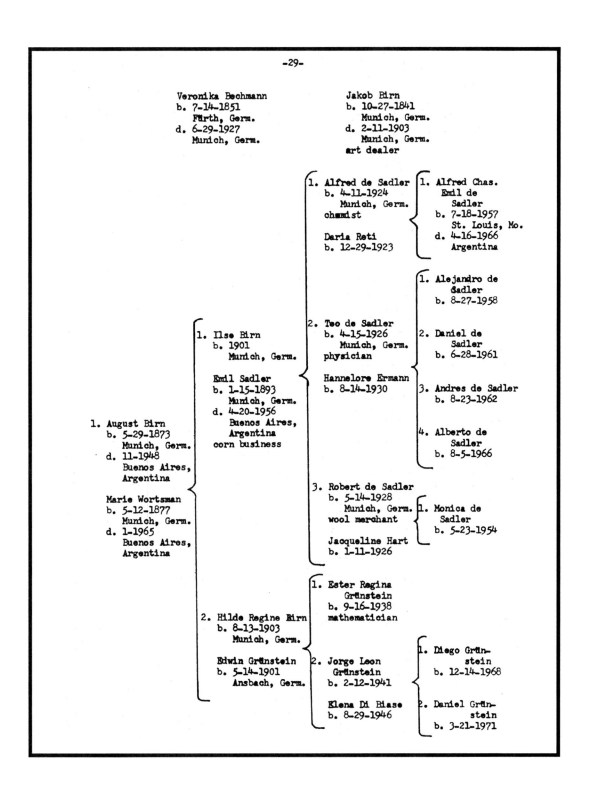

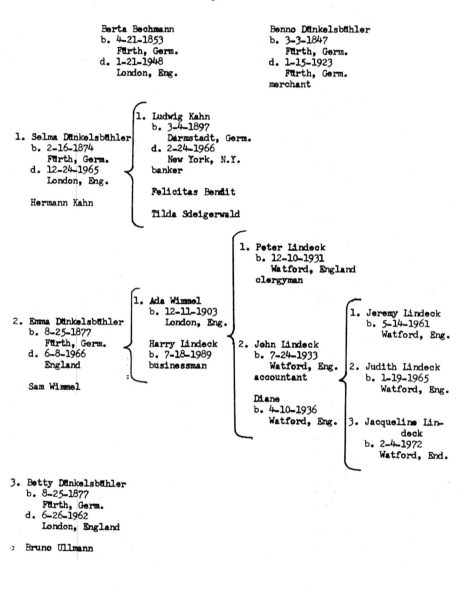

-30-

Berta Bechmann
b. 4-21-1853
Fürth, Germ.
d. 1-21-1948
London, Eng.

Benno Dünkelsbühler
b. 3-3-1847
Fürth, Germ.
d. 1-15-1923
Fürth, Germ.
merchant

1. Selma Dünkelsbühler
b. 2-16-1874
Fürth, Germ.
d. 12-24-1965
London, Eng.

Hermann Kahn

1. Ludwig Kahn
b. 3-4-1897
Darmstadt, Germ.
d. 2-24-1966
New York, N.Y.
banker

Felicitas Bendit

Tilda Sdeigerwald

2. Emma Dünkelsbühler
b. 8-25-1877
Fürth, Germ.
d. 6-8-1966
England

Sam Wimmel

1. Ada Wimmel
b. 12-11-1903
London, Eng.

Harry Lindeck
b. 7-18-1989
businessman

1. Peter Lindeck
b. 12-10-1931
Watford, England
clergyman

2. John Lindeck
b. 7-24-1933
Watford, Eng.
accountant

Diane
b. 4-10-1936
Watford, Eng.

1. Jeremy Lindeck
b. 5-14-1961
Watford, Eng.

2. Judith Lindeck
b. 1-19-1965
Watford, Eng.

3. Jacqueline Lindeck
b. 2-4-1972
Watford, End.

3. Betty Dünkelsbühler
b. 8-25-1877
Fürth, Germ.
d. 6-26-1962
London, England

⊃ Bruno Ullmann

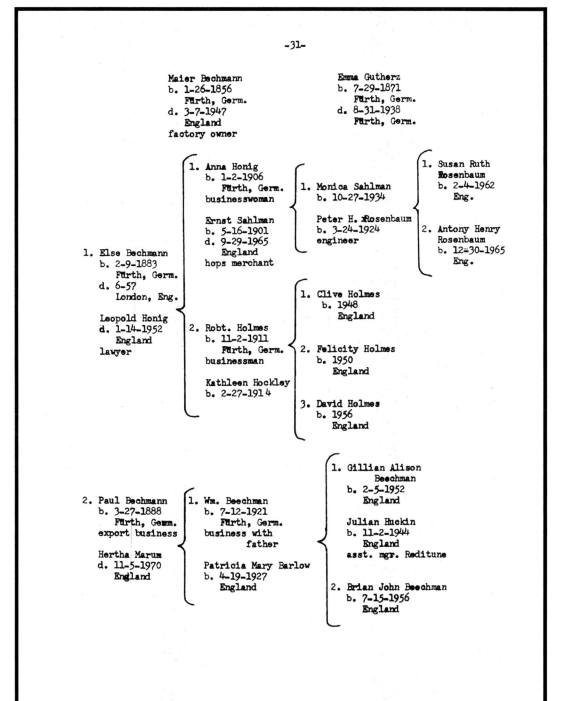

-31-

Maier Bechmann
b. 1-26-1856
  Fürth, Germ.
d. 3-7-1947
  England
factory owner

Emma Gutherz
b. 7-29-1871
  Fürth, Germ.
d. 8-31-1938
  Fürth, Germ.

1. Else Bechmann
b. 2-9-1883
  Fürth, Germ.
d. 6-57
  London, Eng.

Leopold Honig
d. 1-14-1952
  England
lawyer

1. Anna Honig
b. 1-2-1906
  Fürth, Germ.
businesswoman

Ernst Sahlman
b. 5-16-1901
d. 9-29-1965
  England
hops merchant

1. Monica Sahlman
b. 10-27-1934

Peter H. Rosenbaum
b. 3-24-1924
engineer

1. Susan Ruth
   Rosenbaum
b. 2-4-1962
  Eng.

2. Antony Henry
   Rosenbaum
b. 12-30-1965
  Eng.

2. Robt. Holmes
b. 11-2-1911
  Fürth, Germ.
businessman

Kathleen Hockley
b. 2-27-1914

1. Clive Holmes
b. 1948
  England

2. Felicity Holmes
b. 1950
  England

3. David Holmes
b. 1956
  England

2. Paul Bechmann
b. 3-27-1888
  Fürth, Germ.
export business

Hertha Marum
d. 11-5-1970
  England

1. Wm. Beechman
b. 7-12-1921
  Fürth, Germ.
business with
        father

Patricia Mary Barlow
b. 4-19-1927
  England

1. Gillian Alison
   Beechman
b. 2-5-1952
  England

Julian Huckin
b. 11-2-1944
  England
asst. mgr. Reditune

2. Brian John Beechman
b. 7-15-1956
  England

-32-

Henry Bechmann
b. 10-1-1860
   Fürth, Germany
d. 8-30-1940
   Cincinnati, Ohio
merchant

Ida Frohmann
b. 12-30-1863
d. 3-9-1934
   Cincinnati, Ohio

1. Harold Beckman
  b. 3-14-1891
    Cincinnati, Ohio
  d. 2-21-1964
    New York, N.Y.
  foundry supply
  business

  Jean Jacoby
  b. 3-23-1895

1. James Beckman
  b. 8-13-1924

  Lucille Sendach

1. John Harold
  Beckman
  b. 9-11-1961

2. James David
  Beckman
  b. 8-14-1963

2. Martha Beckman
  b. 6-23-1894
    Cincinnati, Ohio

  Nathan Ransohoff

1. William Ransohoff
  physician
  married with four children

2. a boy, married with four children

3. Daniel Ransohoff
  civil servant

-33-

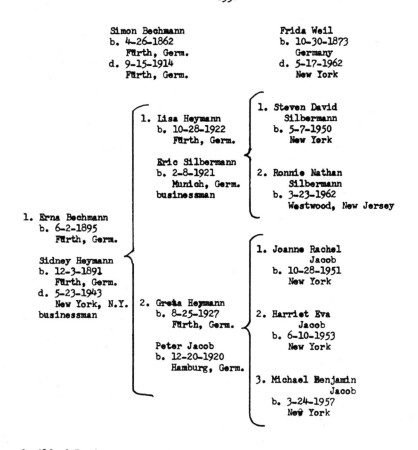

Simon Bechmann
b. 4-26-1862
   Fürth, Germ.
d. 9-15-1914
   Fürth, Germ.

Frida Weil
b. 10-30-1873
   Germany
d. 5-17-1962
   New York

1. Erna Bechmann
   b. 6-2-1895
      Fürth, Germ.

   Sidney Heymann
   b. 12-3-1891
      Fürth, Germ.
   d. 5-23-1943
      New York, N.Y.
   businessman

   1. Lisa Heymann
      b. 10-28-1922
         Fürth, Germ.

      Eric Silbermann
      b. 2-8-1921
         Munich, Germ.
      businessman

      1. Steven David
            Silbermann
         b. 5-7-1950
            New York

      2. Ronnie Nathan
            Silbermann
         b. 3-23-1962
            Westwood, New Jersey

   2. Greta Heymann
      b. 8-25-1927
         Fürth, Germ.

      Peter Jacob
      b. 12-20-1920
         Hamburg, Germ.

      1. Joanne Rachel
            Jacob
         b. 10-28-1951
            New York

      2. Harriet Eva
            Jacob
         b. 6-10-1953
            New York

      3. Michael Benjamin
            Jacob
         b. 3-24-1957
            New York

2. Alfred Beecham
   b. 11-4-1902
      Fürth, Germ.
   businessman

   Marie Frohmann (div'd)

   Esther Shapiro
   d. 1-20-1950
      South Africa

   Sophie Kaplan
   b. 11-25-1904
      pediatrician

-34-

Emilie Bechmann	Nathan Klugmann
b. 3-3-1864	b. 8-13-1856
Fürth, Germany	Fürth, Germany
d. 10-18-1940	d. 12-29-1929
London, England	Fürth, Germany
	businessman

1. Fritz Klugmann
   b. 5-1-1884
      Fürth, Germany
   d. 9-8-1895
      Fürth, Germany

2. Marta Klugmann
   b. 9-8-1886
      Fürth, Germany
   d. 11-26-1970
      Newark, New Jersey

   Soloman Fellheim
   b. 7-26-1875
      Burgkundstadt, Germany
   d. 10-1939
      England

3. Walter David Klugmann
   b. 2-26-1897
      Fürth, Germany

   Jennie Sniderman
   b. 12-25-1897
      Pittsburgh, Pennsylvania

-35-

Mathilde Bechmann
b. 7-8-1865
   Fürth, Germany
d. 7-11-1960
   New York, New York

Carl Ullmann
b. 2-9-1857
   Fürth, Germany
d. 12-8-1939
   Fürth, Germany
dealer in hops

1. Hans Ullmann
   b. 9-15-1893
      Fürth, Germany
   d. 11-24-1964
     New York, NY, physician

   Hilde Dresel
   b. 6-25-1896
      Berline, Germany

2. Robert Ullmann
   b. 1-2-1889
      Fürth, Germany   1. Lynn Willett
   d. 2-22-1964   b. about 1937
     New York, New York   married and has
   physician   children

   Mary Ullmann

-36-

APPENDIX

TREE OF HANNA SULZGERG, wife of Nachman Löb Bechhofen-Berg (1740-1828)

1. **Lase Sulzberg**
   b. 1-6-1741
   d. young
      Fürth, Germany

2. **Hanna Sulzberg**
   b. 1744
   d. 7-29-1836
      Fürth, Germany
   married Nathan Löb Bechhofen-Berg

3. **Abraham Sulzberg**
   b. 12-18-1749
   d. 3-4-1750
      Fürth, Germany

4. **Sechagjah Sulzgerg**
   b. 1-17-1752
      Fürth, Germany

Wolf Sulzberg
d. before 1801

5. **LaseSulzberg**
   b. 2-17-1753
      Fürth, Germany

6. **Lase Sulzberg**
   b. 8-11-1761
   d. 1-14-1816
      Fürth, Germany

7. **Mardechai Sulzberg**
   b. 3-15-1763
      Fürth, Germany

8. **Schöndel Sulzberg**
   b. 6-25-1765
      Fürth, Germany

-37-

TREE OF ESTHER NEUSTETTEL-NEUHAUS, wife of Nathan Hirsch Bechmann (1780-1859)

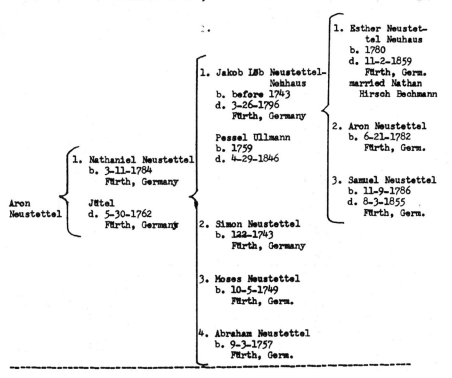

Aron
Neustettel

1. Nathaniel Neustettel
b. 3-11-1784
Fürth, Germany

Jütel
d. 5-30-1762
Fürth, Germany

1. Jakob Löb Neustettel-
Nehhaus
b. before 1743
d. 3-26-1796
Fürth, Germany

Pessel Ullmann
b. 1759
d. 4-29-1846

2. Simon Neustettel
b. 122-1743
Fürth, Germany

3. Moses Neustettel
b. 10-5-1749
Fürth, Germ.

4. Abraham Neustettel
b. 9-3-1757
Fürth, Germ.

1. Esther Neustet-
tel Neuhaus
b. 1780
d. 11-2-1859
Fürth, Germ.
married Nathan
Hirsch Bechmann

2. Aron Neustettel
b. 6-21-1782
Fürth, Germ.

3. Samuel Neustettel
b. 11-9-1786
d. 8-3-1855
Fürth, Germ.

TREE OF ESTHER NEUSTETTEL-NEUHAUS'S Mother's side of the family

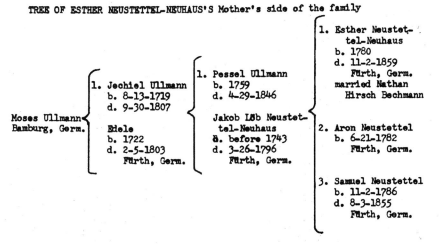

Moses Ullmann
Bamburg, Germ.

1. Jechiel Ullmann
b. 8-13-1719
d. 9-30-1807

Edele
b. 1722
d. 2-5-1803
Fürth, Germ.

1. Pessel Ullmann
b. 1759
d. 4-29-1846

Jakob Löb Neustet-
tel-Neuhaus
b. before 1743
d. 3-26-1796
Fürth, Germ.

1. Esther Neustet-
tel-Neuhaus
b. 1780
d. 11-2-1859
Fürth, Germ.
married Nathan
Hirsch Bechmann

2. Aron Neustettel
b. 6-21-1782
Fürth, Germ.

3. Samuel Neustettel
b. 11-2-1786
d. 8-3-1855
Fürth, Germ.

-38-

TREE OF GETTE OFFENBACHER, wife of Wolf, known as Wilhelm Behhmann (1820-1908)

Mayer Offenbacher
b. 6-21-1765
    Fürth, Germ.
d. 11-15-1851   1. still born twins
    Fürth, Germ.   b. 2-4-1796
mirror glass dealer

Jütel Schnaittacher
d. 4-16-1896

                           1. Feilche Offenbacher-Offenstadt
                               b. 2-28-1798
                               d. 7-2-1855

                           2. Juda Offenbacher
                               b. 6-30-1800
                               rabbi in Prmasens

                           3. Joseph Offenbacher
                               b. 5-28-1802
                               d. 1-28-1861

                           4. Abraham Offenbacher
                               b. 1-17-1804
                               d. 1-21-1806

Mayer Offenbacher   5. Henriette Ellern, nee Offenbacher
                               b. 10-2-1805
Maile Schnaittacher   d. 7-13-1881
b. 2-8-1782
    Fürth, Germ.   6. Isak Offenbacher
d. 2-14-1860   b. 1-31-1808
    Fürth, Germ.   d. 10-15-1810
Jütel's younger
    sister   7. Seckel Löb Offenbacher
                               b. 9-10-1809
                               d. 11-2-1866

                         8. Rebekka Bamberger-Feuchtwanger, nee Offenbacher
                               b. 5-25-1811
                               d. 9-27-1851

                         9. Jette Adelsdorfer, nee Offenbacher
                               b. 7-23-1815
                               d. 2-27-1851

                      10. Therese Offenbacher
                               b. 10-19-1816
                               d. 12-5-1888

                      11. Gette Bechmann, nee Offenbacher
                               b. 4-17-1824
                               d. 3-25-1901
                               married Wilhelm Bechmann

-39-

CURRENT RESIDENCES OF FAMILY MEMBERS (1972)

Barlow, Patricia Mary (Mrs. William Beechman)	England
Bechmann, Erna (Mrs. Sidney Heymann)	Westwood, New Jersey
Bechmann, Martha (Mrs. Nathan Ransohoff)	Cincinnati, Ohio
Bechmann, Paul	England
Beckman, James	New York
Beckman, James Harold	New York
Beckman, John	New York
Beecham, Alfred	Melbourne, Australia
Beechman, Brian John	England
Beechman, Gillian Alison (Mrs. Julian Huckin)	England
Beechamn, William	England
Di Biase, Elena (Mrs. Jorge Grünstein)	Bariloche, Argentina
Birn, Hilde (Mrs. Edwin Grünstein)	Bariloche, Argentina
Budd, Karen	Lexington, Mass.
Budd, Matthew A.	Lexington, Mass.
Budd, Rachel	Lexington, Mass.
Campbell, Jean (Mrs. Heinz Loeffler)	Chicago, Illinois
Davis, William B.	Cambridge, Mass.
Dresel, Hilde (Mrs. Hans Ullmann)	Taunus, West Germany
Ermann, Hannelore (Mrs. Teo de Sadler)	Buenos Aires, Argentina
Grünstein, Daniel	Bariloche, Argentina
Grünstein, Diego	Bariloche, Argentina
Grünstein, Edwin	Bariloche, Argentina
Grünstein, Ester	Bariloche, Argentina
Grünstein, Jorge	Bariloche, Argentina
Hart, Jacqueline (Mrs. Robt. de Sadler)	Boston, Mass.
Haven, Dale (Mrs. Frank Loy)	Washington D.C.
Heymann, Greta (Mrs. Peter Jacob)	Plainview, L.I., N.Y.
Heymann, Lisa (Mrs. Eric Silbermann)	Westwood, New Jersey
Hockley, Kathleen (Mrs. Robt. Holmes)	England
Holmes, Clive	England
Holmes, David	England
Holmes, Felicity	England
Holmes, Robert	England
Honig, Anna (Mrs. Ernst Sahlmann)	England
Huckin, Julian	England
Jacob, Harriet	Plainview, L.I., N.Y.
Jacob, Joanne	Plainview, L.I., N.Y.
Jacob, Michael	Plainview, L.I., N.Y.
Jacob, Peter	Plainview, L.I., N.Y.
Jacoby, Jeanne (Mrs. Harold Beckman)	White Plains, N.Y.
Kaplan, Sophie (Mrs. Alfred Beecham)	Melbourne, Australia
Klugmann, Walter	Forest Hills, N.Y.

-40-

CURRENT RESIDENCES (cont'd)

Lindeck, Diane (Mrs. John Lindeck)	Watford, England
Lindeck, Harry	London, England
Lindeck, Jacqueline	Watford, England
Lindeck, Jeremy	Watford, England
Lindeck, John	Watford, England
Lindeck, Judith	Watford, England
Lindeck, Peter	Watford, England
Loeffler, Heinz	Chicago, Illinois
Loeffler, Patricia Lynn	Chicago, Illinois
Loeffler, Susan Campbell	Chicago, Illinois
Loy, Eric Anthony	Washington.D.C.
Loy, Frank	Washington D.C.
Loy, Lisel	Washington D.C.
Metzger, Ida (Mrs. Hugo Bechmann)	Denver, Colorado
Rahn, Evelyn (Mrs. William B. Davis)	Cambridge, Mass.
Rahn, Ruth (Mrs. Matthew A. Budd)	Lexington, Mass.
Ransohoff, Daniel	Cincinnati, Ohio
Ransohoff, William	Cincinnati, Ohio
Reti, Daria (Mrs. Alfred de Sadler)	San Paolo, Brasil
Rosenbaum, Anthony Henry	London, England
Rosenbaum, Peter	London, England
Rosenbaum, Susan Ruth	London, England
de Sadler, Alberto	Buenos Aires, Argentina
de Sadler, Alejandro	Buenos Aires, Argentina
de Sadler, Alfred	San Paolo, Brasil
de Sadler, Andres	Buenos Aires, Argentina
de Sadler, Daniel	Buenos Aires, Argentina
de Sadler, Monica	Boston, Mass.
de Sadler, Robert	Boston, Mass.
de Sadler, Teo	Buenos Aires, Argentina
Sahlmann, Monica (Mrs. Peter Rosenbaum)	London, England
Sendach, Lucille (Mrs. James Beckman)	New York,
Silbermann, Eric	Westwood, New Jersey
Silbermann, Ronnie	Westwood, New Jersey
Silbermann, Steven	Westwood, New Jersey
Sniderman, Jennie (Mrs. Walter Klugmann)	Forest Hills, N.Y.
Ullmann, Lynn (Mrs. Lynn Willett)	Springfielf, Va.
Wimmel, Ada (Mrs. Harry Lindeck)	London, England

CPSIA information can be obtained at www.ICGtesting.com
Printed in the USA
BVOW021121220413

318070BV00005B/4/P